DESCENDENTS OF KAṆĀDA

LIFE SKETCHES OF SOME INDIAN SCIENTISTS

EDITORS

Prof. Shri Praksah Mani Tripathi
Prof. Naveen K. Sharma
Dr. Vijay Paramanik
Dr. Vikram Pratap Singh

Indira Gandhi National Tribal University
Amarkantak (M.P., India)

Published by:

Jodhpur
5 A, New Pali Road, P.O. Box 91
Jodhpur - 342 001 Rajasthan (India)
E-mail: info@scientificpub.com
Website: www.scientificpubonline.com

New Delhi
4806/24, Ansari Road, Daryaganj,
New Delhi - 110 002 (India)

ISBN: 978-81-962465-1-8 (H/B)

Printed in India

ABOUT THE BOOK

India is celebrating 75 years of its Independence (Azadi Ka Amrit Mahotsav). The book '***Descendents of Kaṇāda***', is an attempt to celebrate the lives of scientists who paved the way for our intellectual and scientific growth. Many of them have been well-recognized for their contributions while some remained unsung. An important facet of their lives is that besides being extraordinary in their research, they have been excellent students and teachers. Our choice of scientists was simple; those who devoted their lives to promoting the culture of science, not just publishing scores of scientific articles in journals of repute. It has been a common observation that ineffective communication with society and a lack of interest in historical accounts among young scientists are major hurdles to the popularization of science in India, which is uncalled for, history allows us to put things in perspective. The book is a compilation of biosketches of some of those who worked with immense dedication and practiced science as *Dharma*.

TABLE OF CONTENTS

DEDICATED
to

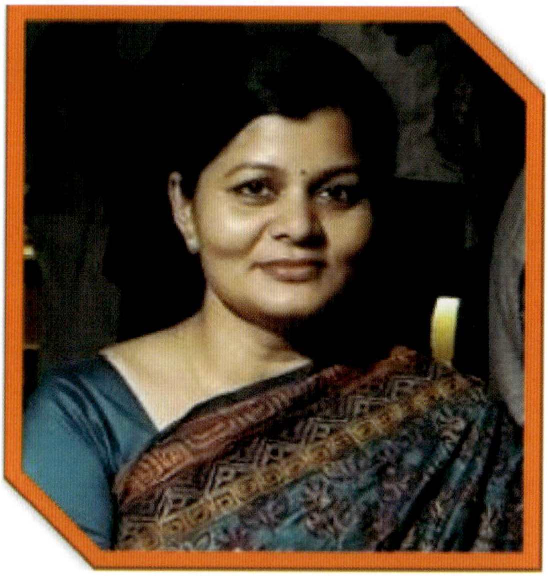

Prof. (dr.) Sandhya Gihar
Ex. Dean, Faculty of Education
Indira Gandhi National Tribal University,
Amarkantak (M.P., India)
(05/10/1974 to 07/05/2021)

INTRODUCTION

Science is an attempt to understand, explain and predict the physical and natural world (we live in) through observations and experiments. Science is not just a certain subject (physics, chemistry, biology, etc.,) nor limited to technological advancements or innovation, but rather a worldview. If so, then religion also is a worldview. Then the obvious question is – what it is that makes something a science?[1] It is a particular way to investigate or think about the physical world around us through experimentation (say a distinctive methodology of understanding) and theory construction. It inherently encompasses social commitments resulting in a just and egalitarian society.

Every generation has its own knowledge systems. Modern science started and diversified in between 1500 – 1750 AD in Europe (i.e., The Scientific Revolution). However, it will be naïve to say that this revolution occurred from nowhere! The ancient and medieval times too had their scientific traditions[1]. Bharata (a part of which is now known as India) is an ancient civilization, a land known for its rich and often esoteric wisdom, and its philosophers (sages). Science and mathematics were highly developed in ancient India. The great sages (Rishi - *Mantra-drashtas* or "the seers of thought") of ancient times made some extraordinary discoveries and developed ideas and concepts that are incredibly accurate to what we know today. For example, as per the Rigveda (probably the oldest written treaty), the speed of light is approximately 198177 miles per second, which is close to the values assigned by modern science (186000 miles per second approximately) (**Box 1**). Our ancient text contains many such examples. Other praiseworthy contributions include the idea of cosmos with many solar systems, Zero, the number system, the decimal system, the value of pi, the ten-digit counting system, physical law and variance, Panini's computer-friendly grammar, invisible germs causing diseases, the importance of immunization to prevent certain diseases, the notion of health and harmony, and idea of interrelatedness in nature[2]. Disciplines such as geometry, algebra, trigonometry, calculus, and Ayurveda were all born in India. Implements of brass, bronze, and copper were made almost 2000 years ago. Vegetable dyes were used as coloring materials[3].

The above descriptions make it clear that before the Middle Ages, India was the world's leading nation in science. Noted Muslim historian and philosopher of science, Said Al-Andalusi, who wrote about the sciences of different nations in his book Ṭabaqāt al-Umam (Categories of Nations), posited that the sciences, particularly mathematics and astronomy, are most advanced in India, and categorized the country as the first nation[2,4]. Frequent foreign invasions and lack of interest by the then rulers could be the possible reasons for the decline of science in that period.

The limited focus of the British in India, during the East India Company (1785-1858) and the British period (1858 -1947), when modern science was flourishing in the backyards of Europe, particularly science education, took a nose dive in India. In 1920, India's scientific services had a total of 213 scientists of whom 195 were British! Nonetheless, adversity always comes with certain opportunities. During that period also some extraordinary minds such as Srinivasa Ramanujan, Jagadish Chandra Bose, Chandrasekhara Venkata Raman, and Satyendra Nath Bose, to name a few, heralded the journey of science in India in a very exemplary way. These scientists provided great patronage and support to science and built major institutions in Independent India[3].

Long-term progress demands exclusivity, not selectively. Indeed, we must remember our glorious scientific traditions and impressive accomplishments of the yesteryears; we should also analyze major bottlenecks bringing constraints to our present achievements. Notably, the lack of appropriate infrastructure, skilled manpower, funds, publication heterogeneity, and diversity[5,6,7,8]. It will be rather myopic to denounce the great achievements of modern science in relieving human beings from once unfathomable miseries. In the last three centuries or so, modern science has unbelievable impact on society[9].

If we look at the lives of great people, including scientists, some common traits that define their lives are – supreme optimism, indomitable spirit, utmost dedication and honesty to their work, and dedication to make the world a better place. Better life always needs strong philosophies. Unfortunately, our present education system mainly focuses on technical aspects of science only. Its philosophy and worldview are given only a cursory treatment. We need to equip our coming generations with love for humanity, respect for the land, scientific temper, rational and logical thinking, and a shift from an anthropocentric to a biocentric worldview. We often find a disconnect between society and science, which is non-negotiable and dangerous for both. Furthermore, we need better tools to take science to common people, as the lack of social support for science is quite alarming. Therefore, promoting quality research in social sciences is a need of the hour.

Apart from teaching science as a kind of subject, we need to teach our graduates about the history and philosophy of science. Limited institutions in our country have included these all-important aspects of science in their curricula. Superficial teaching of science as a subject has no long-term relevance. For a long, there has been a debate over the correct method of seeking the truth about nature. The correct path of doing science has become a rarity. A researcher/student of science must be taught about the basic characteristics of science such as - objectivity, falsifiability, reproducibility, causality, etc. The western attempts of distancing Science from Religion have little significance to India. Though they follow an entirely different approach to reach a conclusion, in the Indian concept of Dharma, they meet, interact, and are part of a continuum. Selective choice of the worldly aspects of religion for criticism, while ignoring its core philosophies is objectionable, and only breeds alienation. Certainly, there is no logic in getting blindfolded and defending irrational beliefs and superstitions in the name of religion. In hindsight, if one talks to a layman, s/he may have plenty of examples to criticize Science (atom bomb to spread of diseases). Does it mean that Science *per se* is dangerous for society? Obviously no! science has its defined role, and the use and misuse of technologies is a moral subject, dependent upon our value systems (familial, social, and cultural thought processes). To tackle these emerging aspects, we need to teach students about values and ethics. Only the promotion of healthy family and social ideas can prevent such misuses. However, these debates are rather esoteric in nature and hard to comprehend by a common man. We need to discuss both *True Dharma* and Science with young minds.

Our quest to succeed at all costs has led to serious misconduct. The recent Theron scandal wherein Ms. Elizabeth Holmes and her colleagues promised that with a few drops of blood, they could detect many diseases without the hassle of needles, is a glaring example of such quests. Likewise, cases of scientific misconduct are on the rise today. To gain the trust of people, the scientific communities need to address such issues firmly. In recent times, the peer pressure of publishing has badly affected the credibility and probity of scientific findings. Issues such as fabrication, distortion, and plagiarism have rooted deeply in our pursuit to publish at any cost. All these issues require significant reform in science education.

Presently, we are celebrating 75 years of our Independence (Azadi Ka Amrit Mahotsav). A generation where the masses often have no benevolent dream to follow is a fertile ground for negativity to creep in, further accentuated by politically motivated and biased media, run with financial ambitions, not social responsibilities. Society needs hope, and examples from the past. The post-independent India started its scientific emergence with the 1948 Indian Policy Resolution and subsequent Second Five-Year Plan. Since then, the country has made significant growth in Science and Technology. However, this is not up to our potential and expectations. **Kaṇāda** (also known as Ulūka, Kashyapa, Kaṇabhaksha, Kaṇabhuj) was an ancient natural scientist and philosopher (lived sometime between the 6th to 2nd century BCE) who founded the *Vaisheshika s*chool of Indian Philosophy. He is probably the earliest known Indian Physicist, who propounded the concept of *Paramanu* (atom) thousands of years (approx. 2500 years) before Jon Dalton. The book ***'Descendents of Kaṇāda'***, is an attempt to celebrate the lives of our scientists who paved the way for our intellectual and scientific growth. Many of them have been well-recognized for their contributions while some remained unsung. An important facet of their lives is that besides being extraordinary in their research, they have been excellent students and teachers. Our choice of scientists was simple; those who devoted their lives to promoting the culture of science, not just publishing scores of scientific articles in journals of repute. In recent times, it has been observed that ineffective communication with society and a lack of interest in historical accounts among young scientists have been major hurdles to the popularization of science in India, which is uncalled for, history allows us to put things in perspective. Many shy away from taking science history writing as a project.

Apart from avoiding hagiographic writing, we tried to edit minimally and maintain the style of the individual author. Consequently, readers may find variations in the style and content of the individual chapters. Another deviation is that the references given at the end may or may not be cited in the text and vice-versa. This is a common problem faced in biography writing as often authentic sources are missing. To balance this anomaly, we have used the apt term 'bibliography' rather than 'reference'. Further, we arranged the chapters based on the date of birth of the scientists; not the magnitude of their contributions. We are grateful to all the contributors because of their cooperation it was not possible to accomplish this work. Finally, let us celebrate and cherish the lives of some of those who worked with immense dedication and practiced science as Dharma. This is a small piece, but we would definitely like to bring out further volumes of the book on the lives of many who deserve remembrance.

Box 1. Speed of light according to the Rigveda (open-source information).

Sukta 50, Couplet 4 of the Rigveda says -

तरणिर्विश्वदर्शतो ज्योतिष्कृदसिसूर्य। विश्वमा भासिरोचनम्॥ (ऋग्वेद १. ५० .४)

(*Swift and all beautiful art thou, O Surya (Sun), maker of the light, illuming the entire radiant realm*)

Accordingly, Sage Sayana (14th AD), a great commentator on Vedas calculated the speed of light as-

तथा च स्मर्यते योजनानां सहस्त्रं द्वे द्वे शते द्वे च योजने एकेन निमिषार्धेन क्रममाण नमोऽस्तुते॥ (सायण ऋग्वेद भाष्य १. ५० .४)

(*O light, bow to you, you who traverse 2,202 Yojanas in half a Nimesha*)

Here, Yojana and Nimesha are the ancient units of distance and time, respectively.

As per Manusmriti 1/64, in 24 hours there are 486000 Nimishas. Hence, 1/2 Nimisha is equal to approx 0.08889 seconds.

निमेषे दश चाष्टौ च काष्ठा त्रिशित्तु ताः कलाः | त्रिशित्कला मुहूर्तः स्यात् अहोरात्रं तु तावतः ||
(मनुस्मृति १. ६४)

As per Shrimadbhagwata one Yojana is approximately 8 miles.

Thus, in 0.08889 seconds light travels 2,202 Yojana (17616 miles)

In 1 sec it will travel 17616/0.08889 = 198177 miles.

Bibliography

1. Okasha, S. (2002) Philosophy of Science: A very short Introduction, Oxford University Press, New York. p. 144.
2. Kak, S. (2021) A Brief History of Indian Science. Academia.edu, 1-14.
3. Rao, C.N.R., Rao, I. (2021) Founders of Modern Science in India, India Academy of Sciences, Bengaluru. p. 103.

4. Salem, S.I., Kumar, A. (1991) History of Science Series, No. 5, University of Texas Press, Austin, p. 118, translated the book of Ṣāid al-Andalusī's, Science in the Medieval World: "Book of the Categories of Nations."
5. Tewari, R., Bhardwaj, M. (2018) Mapping patents and research publications of higher education institutes and national R & D laboratories in India. DST-Centre for Policy Research, Punjab University, Chandigarh. P. 231.
6. Kanaujia, A., Singh, P., Nandy, A., Singh, V.K. (2022) Research contribution of major centrally funded institution systems of India. Current Science 123, 1082-1088.
7. Pratap, G. (2022) Mapping academic recognition to research area performance. Current Science 123, 1422.
8. Paliwal, A. (2023) India's scientific diversity: Caste barriers. Nature 613, 230-234.
9. Chaturvedi, S., Srinivas, K.R. (2015) Science & technology for socio-economic development and quest for inclusive growth: Emerging evidence from India. In: Ladikas M., et al. (eds.) Science & Technology Governance & ethics, Springer Cham. P. 83-97.

Prof. Shri Prakash Mani Tripathi
Prof. Naveen Kumar Sharma
Dr. Vijay Paramanik
Dr. Vikram Pratap Singh

Brahmagupta

(c. 598 – c. 668 CE)

BRAHMAGUPTA: LIFE AND CONTRIBUTIONS

Raghav Prasad Parouha

The contributions of Ancient Mathematicians are either overlooked or disputed by Western and Westernophile historians. Here, I recount the contributions of Brahmagupta, a well-known Indian mathematician and astronomer. He holds an inimitable place in the history of Ancient Indian Mathematics. A descendant of the Ujjain school of mathematics after Varahamihira. He taught astronomy to the Arabs before they come to know Ptolemy's work (refer to Al-Biruni's India). The Arabic text *Sinshind* and *Al-Arkhand* are the translation of Brahmagupta's *Brahamasphutasiddanta* and *Khandakhadyaka*[1].

Life and Contributions

Brahmagupta (c. 589 – c. 668 CE) was born in 598 CE in Bhillamala of Gujardesa (present-day Bhinmal in Rajasthan), situated on the north border of Gujarat in South Marwar. The area was then ruled by Vyagrahamukha of the Chavda dynasty. His father was Jishnugupta. Not much is known about his early life. He (also known as Bhillamacharya) was an astronomer of the *Brahmapaksha* school, one of the four major schools of Indian Astronomy during this period. Later on, he moved to Avanti (modern Ujjain), a noted center of mathematics in Ancient India, where mathematicians like Varahamihira had worked and established a strong school of mathematical astronomy. Brahmagupta wrote his books in elliptic verses in Sanskrit. At the age of 30, he composed *Brahamasphutasiddanta* (628 CE, the Opening of the Universe), largely a theoretical treaty. The book contains 1008 verses (slokas) distributed over 25 chapters. Of which, two chapters were on Mathematics: Chapter 12 on Arithmetic and Geometry consisting of 56 verses, while chapter 18 deals with Algebra containing 102 verses. At the age of 67 (665 CE), in Ujjain, he wrote his second book *Khandakhadyaka* (meaning edible bite or preparation of sweets from sugar), a practical manual for students, containing 9 chapters and 194 verses. It covers the topic of astronomical calculations[2]. It is used in many countries including India as a practical handbook for astronomical calculations. He calculated the length of a year as 365 days 15 gatika and 30 pale (365 days, 6 hours, 5 minutes, and 19 seconds). His third book *Uttar-Khanda Khadyaka* was a supplementary to *Khandakhadyaka* and contains four chapters. In the book, he corrected some of the values described in the *Khandakhadyaka*, and also put up some mathematical methods. The book has been studied by many Indian mathematicians and also translated into Arabic by Al-Fazari (Muslim astronomer) in the 8th century and by Al-Biruni in the 11th century[3]. He also wrote *Grahaṇārkajñāna.* Bhaskar II was greatly influenced by the work of Brahmagupta and referred to him as "Ganaka Chakra Chudamani", which means 'The gem of the circle of mathematicians'. Brahmagupta died probably in Ujjain between 660 and 670 CE.

His incredible contributions to mathematics led to the development of many basic mathematical rules that helped in finding the solutions to real-life problems. Some of the major contributions of Brahmagupta are listed hereunder, and some are elaborated on in the next section.

(i). Noted discrepancies in the Āryabhatīya, a treaty of Āryabhata. And, also criticized the two Suns and two Moons assumptions of *Jainas*.

(ii). Defined quantities having properties of modern zero and defined some properties of modern zero.

(iii). Presented a general formula for Baudhāyana tripls as $(2mn, m^2 - n^2, m^2 + n^2)$.

(iv). Suppose a side a (other than hypotenuse) is given then for any rational number m the sides of a right-angled triangle are given by a, $\frac{1}{2}\left[\frac{a^2}{m} - m\right]$ and $\frac{1}{2}\left[\frac{a^2}{m} + m\right]$, It is useful if one side of a right-angled triangle is known.

(v). The sides of a right-angled triangle having hypotenuse c, are specified as c, $\frac{2mnc}{m^2+n^2}$ and $\frac{m^2-n^2}{m^2+n^2}$, where m and n are integers. It gives a rational right-angled triangle.

(vi). A method of construction of a triangle when two sides and altitude through their point of intersection rational using result (iii).

(vii). The formula for the length of segments of the base of a triangle by the perpendicular through the vertex and length of perpendicular.

(viii). He stated that 'The product of any 2 sides of a triangle is = to the product of its circum-diameter and altitude tired on the 3rd side'.

(ix). He stated the formula for the area of the cyclic quadrilateral whose sides are known, and the formula for the diagonals of a cyclic quadrilateral.

(x). A simple method of construction of cyclic quadrilateral whose sides are integers. He obtained this result from two different or non-similar right-angled triangles.

(xi). He provided a solution (infinitely many) to the equation $Nx^2 + 1 = y^2$.

(xii). He found out sine ratios using second-order interpolation formula. The second-order interpolation formula is one of his greatest contributions.

(xiii). Formula for sum of the square of first n natural numbers and sum of cube of first n natural numbers. He also obtained the general solution of a quadratic equation.

The concept of zero and negative numbers[5,6]

Once zero ('0') came into the present notational form. The obvious question was Who discovered zero? Āryabhata was aware of the place value system. He gave the methods of finding square, cube, square root, and cube root in Āryabhatīya. However, it is impossible to find cube, square, cube roots, and square root without knowing the concept of zero and place value system. In 'Brahamasphutasiddanta' Brahmagupta defined some quantities as having the properties of modern zero. He described the following properties of zero.

- When '0' is subtracted or added from a number, the number remains unchanged.
- When '0' is multiplied by a number, the result is '0'.

In terms of a positive number (fortunes) and a negative numbers (debts), he defined the following arithmetical rule.

- '0' minus '0' is '0'
- A debt minus '0' is a debt
- A fortune minus '0' is fortune
- A debt minus '0' is fortune
- A fortune minus '0' is debt
- '0' multiplied by debt or fortune is zero
- '0' multiplied by '0' is '0'
- Quotient or product of 2 debts is 1 fortune
- Quotient or product of 2 fortunes is 1 fortune
- Quotient or product of a debt and a fortune is a debt

Though, he committed a mistake in a division by '0'. He wrongly stated that '0' divided by '0'is '0'.

Right-angled triangle[7,8]

The property of a right-angled triangle $a^2 + b^2 = c^2$ where c is hypotenuse and a and b are the two sides, is well known to Indian Mathematician from the period of Śulbasūtras. The concept is illustrated in Figure 1.

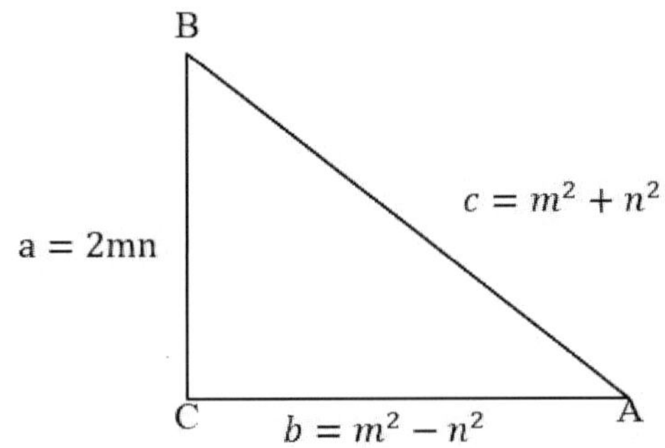

Figure 1: Sides of a right-angled triangle.

Brahmagupta gave a general formula for Baudhāyana triplets (the text Śulbasūtras in 800 BCE). He gave a general solution of right-angled triangle ABC as $a = 2mn$, $b = m^2 - n^2$ and $c = m^2 + n^2$, where m and n are unequal non-zero rational numbers and $m > n$. He modified the above results for construction of the right- angled triangle. Two constructions are given below.

a. Side other than the hypotenuse

Suppose a side 'a' (other than hypotenuse) is given then for any rational number 'm', the sides of a right-angled triangle are given as -

$$a, \frac{1}{2}\left[\frac{a^2}{m} - m\right] \text{ and } \frac{1}{2}\left[\frac{a^2}{m} + m\right]$$

For example, suppose a = 6. Take m = 2 we obtain the sides 6, 8, 10.

b. Specified the hypotenuse

The sides of a right-angled triangle having hypotenuse 'c', are specified as-

$$c, \frac{2mnc}{m^2+n^2} \text{ and } \frac{m^2-n^2}{m^2+n^2}\, c$$

While, Bhaskara II provided the formula

$$c, \frac{2pc}{p^2+1} \text{ and } \frac{p^2-1}{p^2+1}c \text{ (if we put } \frac{m}{n} = p \text{ we get above result)}$$

c. Application

This is the application of above result. Suppose a rational number is given. Then we can construct right-angled triangles having side X. The two triangles are placed side by side. Then the triangle obtained by placing these two triangles is a required triangle of which two sides and latitude to third are rational (Fig. 2).

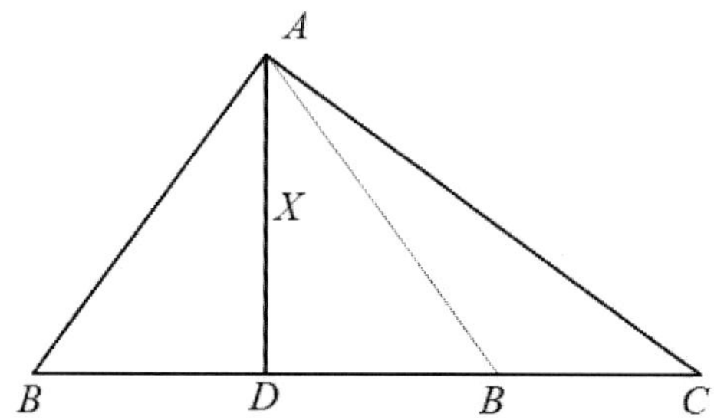

Figure 2: Construction of a triangle.

In triangle ADB, X is the side other than hypotenuse then

$$AB = \frac{1}{2}\left[\frac{X^2}{a} + a\right] \text{ and } BD = \frac{1}{2}\left[\frac{X^2}{a} - a\right]$$

In triangle ADC, X is the side other than hypotenuse then

$$AC = \frac{1}{2}\left[\frac{X^2}{b} + b\right] \text{ and } DC = \frac{1}{2}\left[\frac{X^2}{b} - b\right]$$

And, $BC = BD + DC = \frac{1}{2}\left[\frac{X^2}{a} + \frac{X^2}{b} - a - b\right]$

In triangle ADB, if AD = 12 then BD = 5 and AB = 13, also in triangle ADC, AD = 12 then DC = 9 & AC = 15. Then the triangle with sides 13, 14, 15 has altitude 12.

Segments of the base and perpendicular in a triangle[9]

An interesting result in Brahamasphutasiddanta is related with length of segments of the base and perpendicular in a triangle. It is exemplified in Fig. 3.

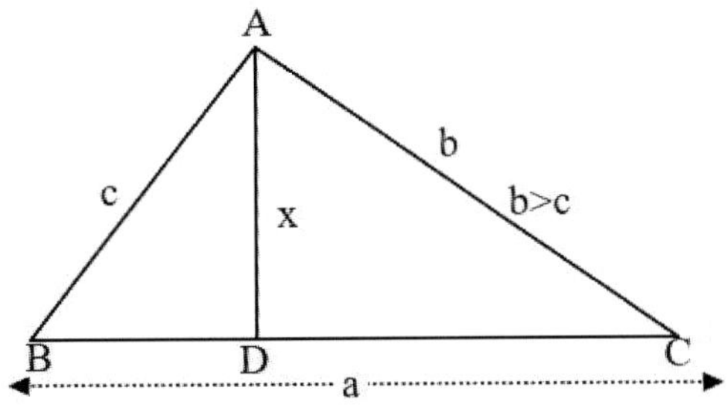

Figure 3: Segments of base and length of perpendicular in a triangle.

Segments: $CD = \frac{a + \frac{b^2 - c^2}{a}}{2}$, $BD = \frac{a - \frac{b^2 - c^2}{a}}{2}$, **Perpendicular:** $AD = \sqrt{c^2 - BD^2} = \sqrt{b^2 - CD^2}$

Proof: $BD^2 = c^2 - AD^2 = c^2 - (b^2 - CD^2)$, $CD^2 - BD^2 = b^2 - c^2$, $(CD - BD)(CD + BD) = b^2 - c^2$. But $(CD + BD) = a$, $(CD - BD) = {b^2 - c^2}/a$

Hence $CD = \frac{a + \frac{b^2 - c^2}{a}}{2}$, $BD = \frac{a - \frac{b^2 - c^2}{a}}{2}$, Also $AD = \sqrt{c^2 - BD^2} = \sqrt{b^2 - CD^2}$.

Brahmagupta's theorem[10,11]

Brahmagupta stated that 'The product of any two sides of a circumscribed triangle is equal to the product of its circum-diameter and altitude drawn on the third side'. It is illustrated in Fig. 4.

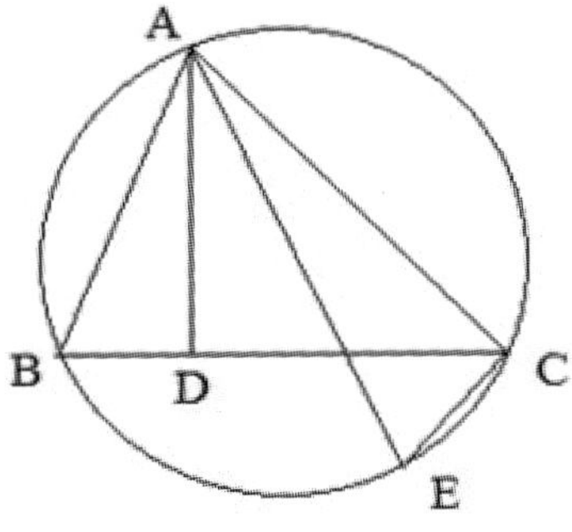

Figure 4: Brahmagupta's theorem

i. e. $AB \times AC = AE \times AD$

Proof: In triangle ABC, AD is the altitude to the base BC and AE is its circum-diameter. Join CE. Then triangles ACE and ADB are similar.

Hence $^{AC}/_{AE} = {}^{AD}/_{AB}$ or AB × AC = AE × AD

This result is useful for finding the circum-diameter of triangle. AB and AC are two sides of a circumscribed triangle and AD is the perpendicular on the third side then the diameter of circum-circle is $^{(AB \times AC)}/_{AD}$ and radius of circum-circle is $^{(AB \times AC)}/_{2 \times AD}$.

This is useful in the construction of cyclic quadrilaterals for the verification that constructed quadrilateral is cyclic or not.

A. Area of cyclic quadrilateral[12,13,14]

Brahmagupta was the first to give the exact formula for the area of cyclic quadrilateral in terms of sides. The square root of the product of four factors formed by half the sum of sides diminished by each side is the exact area (of cyclic quadrilateral). i.e.

$$\text{Area} = \sqrt{(s-a)\,(s-b)\,(s-c)} \text{ where } s = {}^{(a+b+c)}/_{2}$$

B. Brahmagupta's expression for diagonals of a cyclic quadrilateral[15,16,17]

The Brahmagupta's expression for the diagonals cyclic quadrilateral states that "The sums of the product of the adjacent sides about diagonals are both divided by each other. Multiply (the quotients obtained) by the sum of the products of the opposite sides. The square roots (of the results) are diagonals". It is explained in Fig. 5.

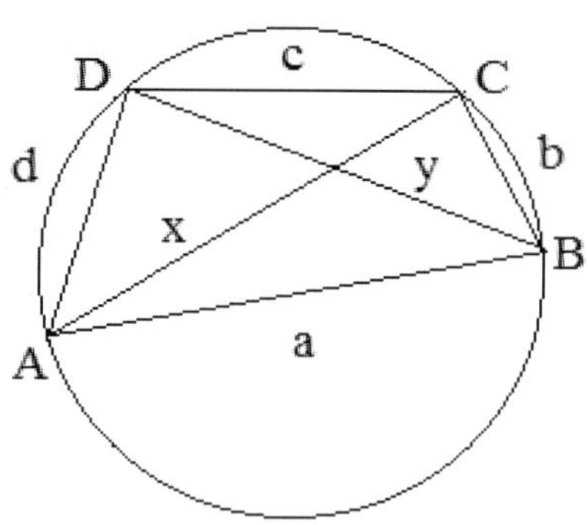

Figure 5: Digonals of a cyclic quadrilateral.

ABCD is a cyclic quadrilateral. If the length of sides AB, BC, CD, DA are a, b, c, d separately and diagonals are AC = X and BD = Y then according to Brahmagupta's expression-

$$AC = X = \sqrt{\frac{(ad + bc)\,(ac + bd)}{(ab + cd)}} \text{ and } BD = Y = \sqrt{\frac{(ad + cd)\,(ac + bd)}{(ad + bc)}}$$

The two results of cyclic quadrilateral and expression for the diagonals cyclic quadrilateral are remarkable and excellent in the Hindu geometry.

C. Construction of cyclic quadrilateral or Brahmagupta's quadrilateral[18]

Brahmagupta gave a method of construction of cyclic quadrilateral. In this construction, cyclic quadrilateral has integer sides, integer diagonal and integer area. "*The kotis and bhujas of two jatyas* (Right-angled triangle) multiplied by each other's hypotenuse are the four sides in a *Vishma* (irregular) quadrilateral. The longest is the base, the least is the face, and the remaining two sides are the flanks". It is exemplified in Fig. 6.

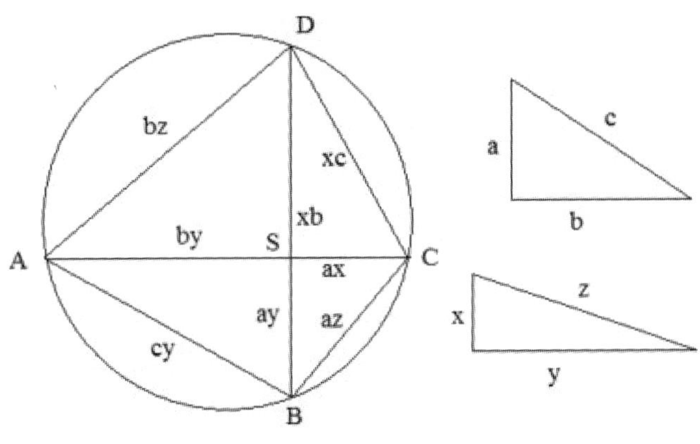

Figure 6: Construction of cyclic quadrilateral.

Method: Let (a, b, c) and (x, y, z) are any two non-similar right-angled triangles where c and z are the hypotenuses. Construct the triangle CSD having sides (ax, bx, cx) and another triangle BSC having sides (ax, ay, az). Now on the other side of BD, construct triangles ASB with sides (ay, by, cy) and ASD with sides (bx, by, bz). Thus, we obtain a quadrilateral ABCD with sides cy, az, cx and bz in order.

The diagonals AC and BD intersect at right angle.

The circum-radius of triangle BCD = $\frac{\text{azxc}}{\text{2ax}} = \frac{\text{cz}}{2}$

And the circum-radius of triangle ABD = $\frac{\text{bcyz}}{\text{2by}} = \frac{\text{cz}}{2}$

The circum-radius of ABD and BCD are (cz/2) so that their circum- centre is same. So, points A, B, C and D lies on the same circle. Hence the quadrilateral ABCD is cyclic. If we consider two right angled triangle with sides (3, 4, 5) and (5, 12, 13) then the above method gives the quadrilateral with sides (39, 52, 60, 25) and the circum-diameter of this quadrilateral is 65. The cyclic quadrilaterals constructed by Brahmagupta has perpendicular diagonals.

D. Solution of equation $Nx^2 + 1 = y^2$ or Varga Prakṛti[19]

The solution of the second order indeterminate equation of the form $Nx^2 + 1 = y^2$ was the most remarkable and significant contribution of Brahmagupta to algebra. This method is called as *Bhāvanā*. The problem is to find the value of x and y in integer satisfying the equation $Nx^2 + 1 = y^2$ for given constant integer N. This equation is called *Varga Prakriti*. Here N is called *Prakṛti*, x is *Kaniṣtha* and y is *Jyeṣṭha*. Brahmagupta gave a method for the solution of the above equation. This method was perfected by Bhaskara-II.

i. Result 1

Suppose $x = \alpha$ and $y = \beta$ is the solution of the equation $Nx^2 + k = y^2$ and x $= \alpha_1$ and y $= \beta_1$ is a solution of the equation $Nx^2 + k_1 = y^2$ then x $= \alpha\beta_1 \pm \alpha_1\beta$ (*Kaniṣtha* of new equation), and $y = N\alpha\alpha_1 \pm \beta\beta_1$ (*Jyeṣṭha* of new equation) is a solution of the equation $Nx^2 + kk_1 = y^2$.

Equivalently if $Na^2 + k = \beta^2$ and $Na_1^2 + k_1 = \beta_1^2$ then -

$$N (\alpha\beta_1 \pm \alpha_1\beta) + kk_1 = (N\alpha\alpha_1 \pm \beta\beta_1)^2$$

ii. Result 2

If $x = \alpha$ and $y = \beta$ is the solution of the equation $Nx^2 + k = y^2$ then $x = 2\alpha\beta$ and $y = N\alpha^2 + \beta^2$ is also the solution of $Nx^2 + k^2 = y^2$. Equivalently if $N\alpha^2 + k = \beta^2$ then $N (2\alpha\beta)^2 + k^2 = (N\alpha^2 + N\beta^2)^2$.

iii. Result 3

If $x = \alpha$ and $y = \beta$ is solution of $Nx^2 + k^2 = y^2$, then $x = \alpha/\beta$, $y = \beta/k$ is a solution of the equation $Nx^2 + 1 = y^2$.

Using these three results the solution of $Nx^2 + 1 = y^2$ in integers.

The above results are called *Bhāvānā*, which are categorized as follows.

(i). Samāsa Bhāvānā (i.e. addition)
(ii). Antara Bhāvānā (i.e. subtraction)
(iii). Tulya Bhāvānā when the Bhāvānā is made with two equal sets of roots
(iv). Atulya Bhāvānā when the Bhāvānā is made with two unequal sets of roots

Pi ***(π)***

In verse 40 of *Brahmasphutasiddhanta*, he gave the values of π,

The diameter and the square of each radius multiplied by 3 are respectively the practical circumference and the area of a circle. The accurate values are the square-roots from the squares of those two multiplied by ten. He used 3 as a "practical" value of π, and $\sqrt{10} \approx 3.1622$ as an "accurate" value of π, with an error less than 1% (verse 12.40).

Concept of Gravity

In 628 CE, he first described gravity as an attractive force, using the term "Gurutvākarṣaṇam":

The earth on its sides is the same; all people on the earth stand upright, and all heavy things fall down to the earth by a law of nature, for it is the nature of the earth to attract and to keep things, as it is the nature of water to flow ... If a thing wants to go deeper down than the earth, let it try. The earth is the only low thing, and seeds always return to it, in whatever direction you may throw them away, and never rise upwards from the earth (Wikipedia. org).

Trigonometry

In Chapter 2 of his *Brāhmasphuṭasiddhānta (planetary True Longitudes)*, he presented a sine table. He also devised and used a special case of the

Newton–Stirling interpolation formula of the second-order to interpolate new values of the sine function from other values already tabulated (Wikipedia.org).

Contribution to Astronomy

His important contributions in astronomy include his methods for calculating the position of heavenly bodies over time, their rising and setting, and the calculation of solar and lunar eclipses. He rebutted the idea that the Moon is farther from the Earth than the Sun by explaining the illumination of the Moon by the Sun. He explained that since the Moon is closer to the Earth than the Sun, the degree of the illuminated part of the Moon depends on the relative positions of the Sun and the Moon, and this can be computed from the size of the angle between the two bodies. Likewise works relating to the longitudes of the planets, diurnal rotation, lunar and solar eclipses, risings and settings, the moon's crescent and conjunctions of the planets, are discussed in *Khandakhadyaka* (Wikipedia.org).

Epilogue

Indian mathematicians played a significant role in the development of mathematics. Brahmagupta was one of the great Indian astronomer and mathematician. He was head of the astronomical observatory in Mathematical Centre at Ujjain, India. Without his ideas and formulas geometry and number theory would not be the way we know it today. The science historian George Sarton described Brahmagupta as "one of the greatest scientists of his race and the greatest of his time."

Bibliography

1. Chatterjee, B. (1975) Al-Biruni and Brahmagupta. Indian J History Sci 10 (2), 161-165.
2. Jha, S. (1978) A critical study on Brahmagupta and Mahaviracharya and their contributions in the field of mathematics. Math Ed (Siwan) 12 (4), 66-69.
3. Datta, B. (1930) Brahmagupta. Bull Calcutta Math Soc 22, 39-51.
4. Pranesachar, C. R. (2012) Brahmagupta, mathematician par excellence. Resonance 7(3), 247-252.

5. Prakash, S. (1986) A critical study of Brahmagupta and his works: The most distinguished Indian astronomer and mathematician of the sixth century A.D., Govindram Hasanand, Delhi.
6. Dutta, A.K. (2005) Brahmagupta's Bhāvanā: Some Reflections. In: Emch, G.G., Sridharan, R., Srinivas, M.D. (eds.) *Contributions to the History of Indian Mathematics*. Culture and History of Mathematics (Vol 3), Hindustan Book Agency, Gurgaon. https://doi.org/10.1007/978-93-86279-25-5_4.
7. Gupta, R. C. (1972) Brahmagupta's rule for the volume of frustum-like solids. Math Education 6, B117-B120.
8. Rao, S. B. (2000) Indian Mathematics and Astronomy: Some Landmarks, Jnana Deep Publication, Bangalore.
9. Srinivasiengar, C. N. (1988) The History of Ancient Indian Mathematics, The World Press Pvt Ltd, Calcutta.
10. Arya, S. P. (1991) On the Brahmagupta- Bhaskara equation. Math Ed 8 (1), 23-27.
11. Parameswaran, S. (1998) The Golden Age of Indian Mathematics, Swadeshi Science Movement, Kochi, Kerala.
12. Bhalla, G. S. (1986) Brahmagupta's quadrilateral. Math. Comput Ed 20 (3), 191-196.
13. Kak, S. C. (1989) The Brahmagupta algorithm for square rooting, Ganita Bharati 11 (1-4), 27-29.
14. Heroor, V. D. (2006) The History of Mathematics and Mathematicians of India, Vidya Bharthi, Karnataka, Bangalore.
15. Datta, B. B., Singh A.N. (1962) History of Hindu Mathematics (Part I and II), Asia Publishing House.
16. Gupta, R. C. (1974) Brahmagupta's formulas for the area and diagonals of a cyclic quadrilateral. Math Education 8, B33-B36.
17. Pottage, J. (1974) The mensuration of quadrilaterals and the generation of Pythagorean triads: a mathematical, heuristical and historical study with special reference to Brahmagupta's rules. Arch History Exact Sci 12, 299-354.
18. Dani, S. G. (2012) Ancient Indian Mathematics- A Conspectus. Resonance 17(3), 236-246.
19. Chaurasya, P. K. (2011) History of Mathematics. Campus Books International, New Delhi.
20. https://en.wikipedia.org/wiki/Brahmagupta

AUTHOR PROFILE

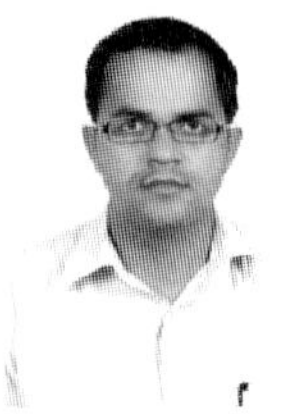

Raghav Prasad Parouha is Assistant Professor at Department of Mathematics, Indira Gandhi National Tribal University, Amarkantak, M. P., India. He did Ph. D. from National Institute of Technology (NIT), Silchar, Assam, India. His areas of research are - computational intelligence including algorithm design, real world application, etc. He received Young Scientist Award (YSA) by International Academy of Physical Sciences (IAPS), Allahabad (U.P.), India. He has published 39 research articles, attended about 42 and organized around 10 workshops/ seminars, etc.

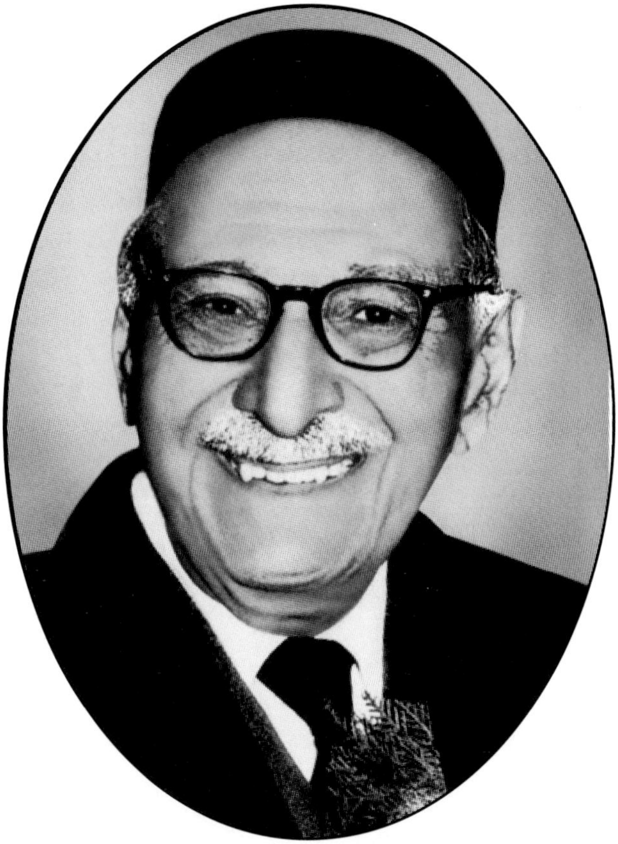

Darashaw Nosherwan Wadia

(23 October 1883-15 June 1969)

DARASHAW NOSHERWAN WADIA: A LONELY KHAKI-CLAD FIGURE SILENTLY HITTING EVERY STONE IN THE NEIGHBOURHOOD

Kapesa Lokho

Prof. Darashaw Nosherwan Wadia (henceforth D.N. Wadia) known as the "Father of Geology in Post-Independent India," was one of the forerunners, who made significant contributions to the geological history of the world's youngest fold mountain, the Himalayas. He had climbed and studied peak after peak of the Himalayas while carrying out extensive fieldwork, mapping high altitudes of about 26,000 feet on the scale of one-inch to one-mile, mostly in the region of Kashmir, Hazara, Poonch, Chilas, Nanga Parbat and Gilgit to understand its geological structure and dating of the rock formations. He was instrumental in shaping the development of Indian geology. He is fondly called the *voice of India* among the geological fraternity overseas (Nolan, 1965). He was the Indian star of Himalayan Geology during British India, the first and the only Indian employee to join the Geological Survey of India who had a degree from an Indian University. He was also responsible for setting and formulating the national policies of geological activities and its natural resources with the dawn of India's independence.

Prof. Wadia made a remarkable contribution to establishing the various geoscientific institutions in the country. It was because of his determined initiative and calculative efforts that the Institute of Himalayan Geology, Dehradun was established in 1968 and he was the Founder Director of it from 1968-69. In honor of his worthy contribution, the Institute was renamed as Wadia Institute of Himalayan Geology (WIHG) in 1976 and celebrated its Golden Jubilee in 2018. He was also hugely responsible for the establishment of reputed research institutions such as the National Geophysical Research Institute (NGRI) Hyderabad, the National Institute of Oceanography (NIO) Goa, The Indian Bureau of Mines, and The Atomic Minerals Division among others.

He was also incredibly responsible in establishing a large number of geoscientific professional societies. In 1964, when the 12th International Geological Congress (IGC) was held in Delhi, Prof. Wadia was the president of the event. It was a great success and a moment of achievement for the Indian geologists (Figs. 1A-D). After a gap of 56 years, the 36th IGC (2020) was scheduled to be held in New Delhi with the theme "Geosciences-the basic science for a sustainable future." Due to the unprecedented, historic global pandemic Covid-19, the Congress was held virtually in 2022 with Prof. V.P. Dimri as the president. Prof. Wadia authored about one hundred original research papers and monographs on various geological topics. Among others, his acclaimed textbook "Geology of India" was published in 1919. As a token of appreciation for his voluminous contribution, a commemorative volume of Prof. Wadia was released in 1965 by the Mining, Geological, and Metallurgical Institute of India. The volume contains a total of 57 popular papers contributed by prominent geologists from across the world.

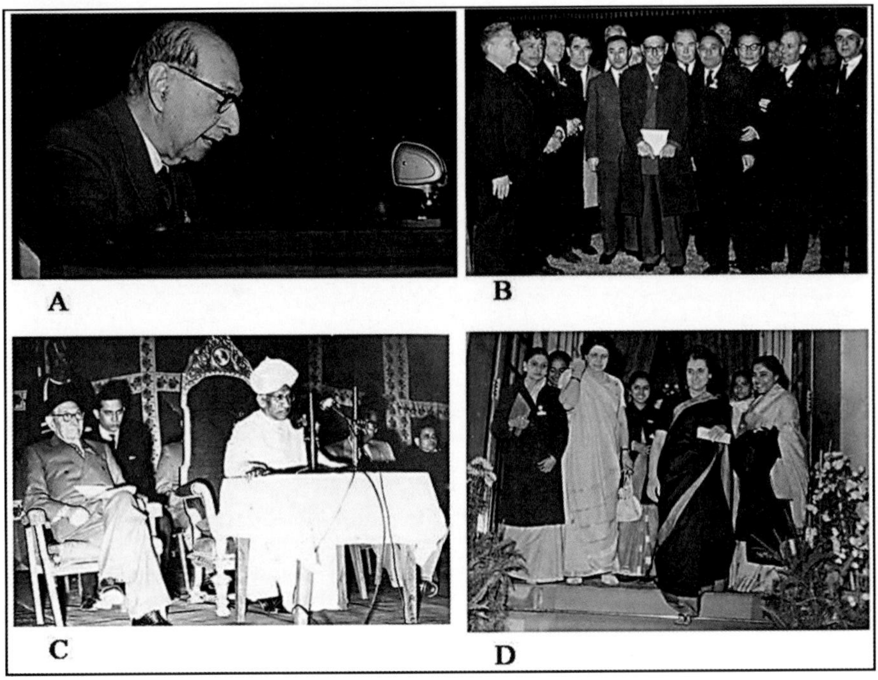

Figure 1: 12th International Geological Congress (IGC) held in Delhi (1964). (A): Prof. Wadia delivering the presidential address. (B): Prof. Wadia with the IGC delegates. (C): *Dr. S. Radhakrishnan* the then President of India. (D): Mrs. Meher Wadia in white saree with Mrs. Indira Gandhi in black saree, the then Minister for Information and Broadcasting Govt. of India, and ladies of IGC delegates.

For his superb contributions, he has been honored with numerous international and national awards as listed at the end of the chapter. He was awarded various honorary posts including honorary doctorates from University of Delhi in 1947 and Aligarh Muslim University in 1967 respectively. In recognition of his contributions to Indian geology and systematizing the geoscientific role for the nation, The Indian Posts & Telegraphs Department, Government of India (GoI) released a commemorative postage stamp on the centennial of his birth anniversary in 1984 (Fig. 2).

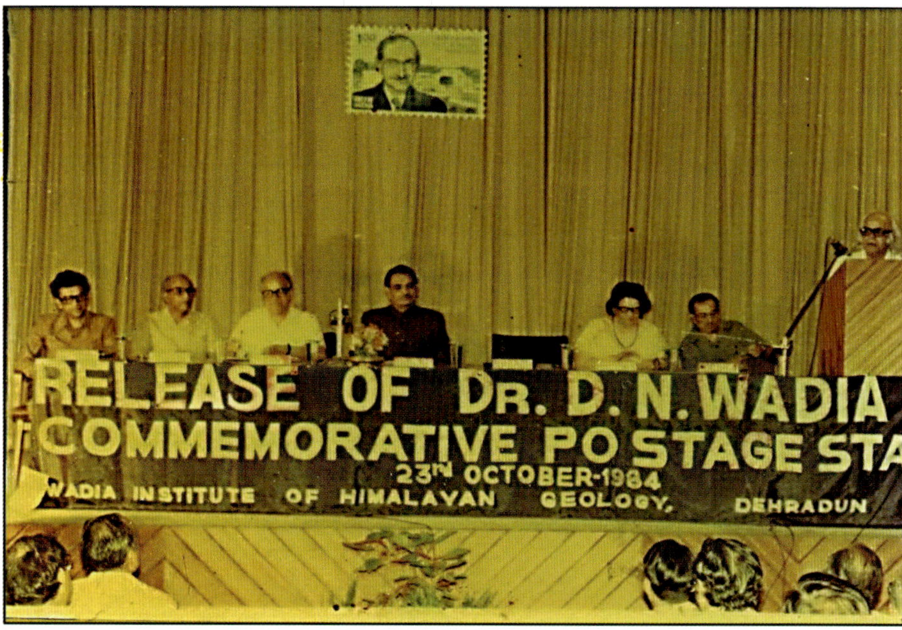

Figure 2: Prof. Yash Pal, Secretary Department of Science and Technology, Government of India speaking at the occasion of the release of Prof. Wadia Commemorative Stamp on 23rd October 1984 at the function organized at INSA, Delhi in the presence of Mrs. Meher Wadia.

Family Background and Early Years

Prof. D.N. Wadia was born on 23rd October 1883 in Surat, Gujarat. He was the fourth child of nine children of Nosherwan and Gooverbai Wadia. The family of Wadia was from a widely respected and educated Parsi family. Name and fame were added to Wadia's clan as Ardeseer Cursetjee (1808-1877), a naval architect and a marine engineer was the first Indian to be elected FRS on 27th May 1941 (Stubblefield, 1970, p. 544). His father worked as a station master in the Indian Railways at Bombay, Baroda, and Central India, and presumably lived in the railway's premises. As there were no good schools around the railway premises, "Dara" as Prof. Wadia was affectionately called in the family, stayed at Surat with his maternal grandmother with noble care and discipline. He studied his primary education in a private Gujarati school, and then joined the Sir J.J. English School in Surat. In 1894, when he was just 11 years old, his family moved to Baroda and he joined the Baroda High School. At Baroda, Wadia came under the influence of his elder brother, Munchershaw N. Wadia, a reputed educationist from whom he got inspired for science and knowledge with a rational outlook on human relationships, which ultimately bore fruit later in his life.

After his schooling, Wadia joined Baroda College, which was then affiliated with Bombay University, Bombay. He obtained his B.A. and B.Sc. degrees in arts and science with natural science, botany, and zoology in 1905 (Editorial note of PSI, 1957, Virdi, 1983). He completed his M.A. in geology in 1906. At Baroda College, Prof. Wadia was encouraged and motivated by Prof. Adarji M. Masani, a naturalist, and Prof. Aravind Ghosh, a great philosopher, and a mystic. His degree in M.A. Geology was at his own effort and enthusiasm as in those days, geology was taught only at the Universities of Calcutta (Kolkata) and Madras (Chennai). His geological studies were greatly helped by the geological collections of rock samples and specimens hosted in the Museum of Arts and Sciences at Baroda (Editorial note of PSI, 1957, Stubblefield, 1970). This museum was built by Maharaja Sayajirao Gaekwad, the ruler of Baroda State who was passionate for a progressive education.

Teaching and Social Life (1906-1920)

In 1907, Wadia was appointed as a lecturer at the Prince of Wales College, Jammu. It stated that "The Prince of Wales College, Jammu, had been built to commemorate a visit to that city in 1905 by King George V while he was Prince of Wales. It is now called the Mahatma Gandhi College and forms a part of the University of Jammu and Kashmir" (Stubblefield 1970, p. 545). The builder of the college was Maharaja Pratap Singh. Wadia found the college favorable and the consecutive principals of the college Sir Frame Dadina and Sir S. Robinson bestowed him with ample encouragement and support. The college location also provided an ideal environment for his geological research in the northwest Himalayas and this has paid him a ransom in his later profession on the structure and stratigraphy of the region. In recognizing his talents and capabilities, he was entrusted with the responsibilities of the Department of Geology. He taught the English language apart from his favorite discipline of Geology. He was also good at sports. Under his abled stewardship, the department gradually blossomed, and developed facilities for full-fledged graduate and postgraduate courses.

During his 14 years of stay at the Prince of Wales College, Jammu, he spent the vacations carrying out geological fieldwork familiarizing himself with the rocks and their structures. He collected minerals, rocks, and fossils to assist in teaching and gradually framed better ideas on the evolution and tectonics of the Himalayas. In the course of his research, he met Sir C.S. Middlemiss, F.R.S., the then Superintendent of the staff of GSI from whom he acquired and gained a good amount of knowledge on the stratigraphy of the Himalayas. Sir Middlemiss worked in GSI for 34 years and retired in 1917, then he was hired as the superintendent of the mineral survey by the Maharaja of Jammu and Kashmir (Sorkhabi, 2019, p. 28).

Geological Survey of India, GSI (1921-1938)

At the age of 38, Prof. Wadia joined GSI as an Assistant Superintendent in 1921, after serving as a lecturer of English and Geology for 14 years at the Prince of Wales College, Jammu. In GSI, he continued his research with determined perseverance and unrelenting vigor, mapping the NW Himalaya in the princely states of Kashmir, Hazara, Waziristan, and Gilgit. Most of the original findings that brought him laurels were the publications made while he was in GSI. Other than the research on mapping, structure, stratigraphy, and fossils, he also described the Joya Mair dome (1929) in the Jhelum district of Punjab, wherein he predicted the presence of petroleum in the dome structure, which proved correct. He delivered a number of lectures at the Presidency College, Calcutta then under the University of Calcutta (Kolkata) when he visited the Geological Survey headquarters at Calcutta. He became a Palaeontologist in GSI in 1928 after the retirement of Sir G.E. Pilgrim (F.R.S), a British Palaeontologist and Superintendent of the GSI till 1935.

While in GSI, Prof. Wadia accomplished three overseas tours. In 1926-1927, he availed study leave and worked on vertebrate fossils that were collected from the Siwalik strata of the Potwar and Kashmir at the British Museum

(Natural History) and visited geological institutions and universities in Germany, Austria, and Prague. Around this time, he also pursued a course in Alpine geology in the Swiss Alps organized by the University of Geneva. Secondly, in 1935, he was given an opportunity to represent India at the 3rd International Congress of Soil Science, held at Oxford, and participated in the field excursion to England, Wales, and Scotland to study soil profiles arranged by the Congress. Thirdly, he made another educational tour in 1935 to China, Japan, and the USA, while visiting Universities and Geological Surveys thereby establishing valuable contacts with prominent geologists from Yale, Berkeley, Stanford, Pasadena, Peking, and Tokyo (Editorial note of PSI, 1957, p. 3). He was with the GSI until his retirement in 1938 as an Assistant Superintendent. He was crowned with the Back Award of the Royal Geographical Society, London in 1934 in recognition of his work on the tectonics and trend lines of the Himalayan axis. He was in the GSI for 17 years and retired as an Assistant Superintendent. Even though he worked for the organization with many good findings, publications and awards, he retired with the same post. This is something which every one of us would feel disappointed yet ups and downs are a part of life. In his later years, he has been honored with many more awards and positions.

External Service in Ceylon (1938-1944)

In 1938, Prof. Wadia accepted the offer of Mineralogist by the Government of Ceylon (Sri Lanka), after his retirement from the GSI. He studied extensively the Geology of Ceylon, during his six years of stay on the island, which he considered a graceful pendant of the Indian Peninsula (Editorial note of PSI, 1957, p. 3). With his usual zeal and enthusiasm, he studied the unique geology of the island (Valdiya, 2003). Based on his in-depth research, he recommended that a systematic geological survey of the island be made for a complete and accurate geological map. The recommendation was gracefully accepted by the Ceylon Government (Stubblefield, 1970). In many articles and reports, the results of his research dealing with economic mineralogy, structure, physiography of Ceylon, and the making of the island were published. In Ceylon, he delivered various Presidential addresses. Prof. Wadia produced the first geological sketch map of Colombo (Vigyan Prasar, undated). The Royal Asiatic Society of Ceylon conferred him its prestigious fellowship in recognition of his contributions to the country.

Back to India from Ceylon in 1944 Till Leaving for His Heavenly Eternal Abode (External Services)

After his return from Ceylon, in 1944, Prof. Wadia was appointed Geological Advisor to the Government of India and a member of the Board of Scientific and Industrial Research. In those years, the country lacked a mineral policy to safeguard its mineral interests. In 1947 after the country's independence, due to the partition of the then Indian sub-continent, minerals like salt and gypsum were in short supply (Searle, 2009). Wadia's immense efforts and broad vision made the government aware of the proper conservation and utilization of the country's mineral resources. Accordingly, he initiated and formulated a mineral policy for the country in 1947 and thereby established the Indian Bureau of Mines, with him as its first Director (Editorial note, PSI, 1957; Stubblefield, 1970). Under his Directorship, the Bureau drafted the *Mines and Minerals Act,* of 1948, the *Mineral Concession Rules* of 1949, and the *Petroleum Concession Rules* of 1949 (Stubblefield, 1970, p. 552; Searle, 2009). As the nation was in the transition period with the dawn of Independence, he took serious concerns with the progress of science in India and its role in a new world. In his presidential address on 'India in Transition' in 1947 at New Delhi, he stated how we should tackle 'to tap the basic sources of wealth and well-being, yet imperfectly tapped in the land, man-power, its rivers, forests, minerals, and electric power' (Stubblefield, 1970, p. 552).

As atomic energy had gained worldwide importance, the Atomic Energy Commission (AEC) of the GoI, established its Atomic Minerals Division in 1949 with Dr. Bhabha as the Chairman of the Commission with a view to explore domestic resources of radioactive raw materials. Wadia was given a lead role in the commission. Under his leadership, the Indian AEC grew into a well-knit unit comprised of 470 geologists and geophysicists, and mining and drilling personnel (Stubblefield, 1970). From 1961 until his demise, he was the Chairman of the Programming Board of the Departments of Geology and Mining (Ministry of Mines & Metals), where he coordinated the programs of the Atomic Energy Raw Materials Division, the GSI Rare Minerals Section, and those of various State directorates of geology and mining. Further, he was an enthusiastic advocate of a national policy for the search, utilization, and conservation of mineral resources including gas, oil, and water. Thus, he had a hand in establishing almost all of India's post-war minerals and natural resources policies.

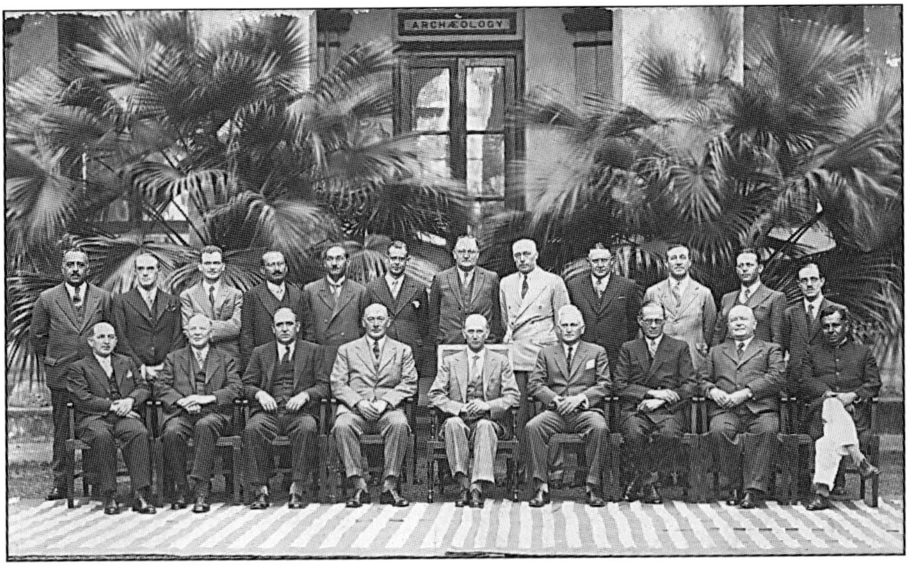

Figure 3: Some of the members of the Council of the Mining and Geological Institute of India, 1932-33 and 1933-34. Sitting from left 1. J. Thomas, 2. G. Miller, 3. D. Penman, 4. H. Lancaster (President, 1932-33), 5. F.G. Percival (President, 1933-34), 6. W.H. Bates (Vice-President, 1933-34), 7. L.L. Fermor (Hons. Treas., 1932-33, 1933-34), 8. R. Purdy (Vice-President, 1932-33), D.D. Thacker. Standing from left 1. G.G. Carapiet, 2. A.M. Heron (Hons. Treas., 1932-33), 3. J.A. Dunn, 4. J.K. Dholakia, **5. D.N. Wadia,** 6. A.L. Coulson (Jt. Hon. Secy.), 7. A. Farquhar (Jt. Hon. Secy.), 8. F.B. Kerridge, 9.W. Cooksey, 10. H.M. Sale, 11. N. Barracloiugh, 12. C. Forrester.

Realizing the need for more geologists in the country, he effectively contributed to increasing and establishing the departments of geology in India. Wadia (1964) informed that at his request, as many as 20 of the 35 universities of India had introduced departments of geology, out of which many of them teach pure and applied geology up to a doctorate degree. In 1960, the GoI set up the Indian National Committee on Oceanic Research with Prof. Wadia as its chairman. India started to participate in the International Indian Ocean Expedition in 1962. He also served as an adviser to the Egyptian Government's atomic minerals programme and made an extensive tour of the desert zones of Egypt. Being a zealous lover of science and nature, he took great interest in the dissemination of scientific information by serving as editor and member of the editorial board of various journals.

He was a council member of different geoscientific organizations and here is one of his photographs (Fig. 3).

Personal Life and Retirement

Prof. Wadia's life spanned from British India to Independent India. He was a star of Himalayan Geology at par with the renowned geologists of his time like Sir Charles Stewart Middlemiss (1859-1945) F.R.S. the then Superintendent of GSI; Sir John Bicknell Auden (1903-1991) elder brother of the poet W.H. Auden and Sir William Dixon West, Director of the GSI from 1945 till India's Independence to mention some few (Sorkhabi, 2019, p. 29). I would like to quote a beautiful description of Prof. Wadia by Sir W.D. West in Prof. Wadia's Commemorative Volume, *"To have lived for over 80 years and still to be engaged in fruitful activity is not a common lot of mankind. But to do great things a man must live as though he had never to die and this is the image, we have of Darashaw Nosherwan Wadia, a doyen of Indian Geology*" (West, 1965, p.1). In fact, for Prof. Wadia, retirement from active service in 1938 marked an era of a real professional career. Physically, he was above average height, wiry looking rather than robustly built, and enjoyed good health. He was a lover of trekking and outing as all his holidays were spent carrying out fieldwork in the Himalayas. His favorite dictum was, "The best work is done with the least number of amenities" (Editorial note of PSI, 1957, p. 4). Although crowned with many laurels and important portfolios in various ministries and departments, he remained a humble person all through his life.

He was blessed with a blissful married life in 1909 with Mrs. Alan G. Contractor, daughter of G.P. Contractor, an engineer from Gujarat, but saddened by the untimely demise of their one and only daughter in her infancy and his beloved wife in the 1930s. Wadia, a widower married Mrs. Meher G.K. Medivala in 1940 who was a graduate and a mineralogist from the University of Bombay. His wife, Mrs. Meher Wadia published a book on the *Minerals of India* in 1966.

Describing his usual life, in 1942, he was reported to the police in Namunukala, Ceylon, as *"a lonely khaki-clad figure silently hitting every stone in the neighborhood*" (Editorial note of PSI, 1957, P. 5). This was an amusing event that happened during the course of Prof. Wadia's geological fieldwork in Ceylon. Moreover, he was an avid reader, a skilled writer, and an excellent observer. It wasn't a surprise for visitors, meeting him was like a geological pilgrimage and an open book. His attitude to life and work was strictly rational, be it criticism or compliment, he considered it as a continuous scientific process. For him simple or great, life process is a scientific engagement in itself. He never allowed the politics of science in his life and career. He was a pure swadeshi Indian scientist with an open heart to all irrespective of race, caste, gender and creed. A great lesson for all of us from his simple but truly an exemplary life.

After giving his best for the nation and the world, he left for his heavenly abode on 15th June 1969 at the advanced age of 86, leaving behind his much loved and caring wife Mrs. Meher Wadia. She was his soul mate and like a personal secretary who accompanied him on all his tours be it in India or abroad. His demise marked the end of an era and a huge void was created which is not at all easy to be filled. The legacy he left behind remains fresh and communicative even after 53 years of his departure, especially in the lives of the scientists and staff of the Wadia Institute of Himalayan Geology, Dehradun. As a geological custodian, Prof. Wadia's contribution to the field will go a long way from generation to generation not only for the Indians but for the whole world.

Science Contributions

1. Unravelling the geological structure

Prof. Wadia's original work on the syntaxis of the northwest Himalayas is a monumental classic achievement and an enduring contribution to geology.

a). The Geology of Poonch State (Kashmir) and the adjacent portion of Punjab

Prof. Wadia's first important contribution was the geology of Poonch State and adjacent portions of Punjab published in 1928. The unique observation of the V-like loops at the Poonch area (Fig. 4) was one of his greatest contributions to the structure of the Himalayan syntaxis (Wadia, 1928). In this paper, he described detailed stratigraphy and structure of rocks extending in age from Purana of Dogra Slate to sub-Recent to Pleistocene age of glacial moraines and river terraces. This work rectified the views of Lydekker (1876) on the structure and stratigraphy of the Pir Panjal range. Furthering on this work, led to the publication of his 1931 monumental paper.

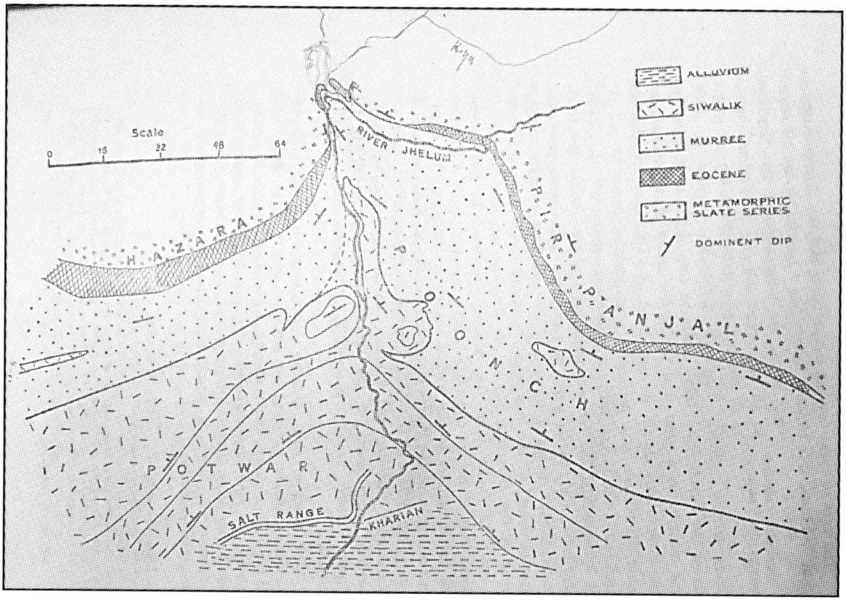

Figure 4: The syntaxial folds along the Jhelum Valley.

b). The syntaxis of the north-west Himalaya

The paper on syntaxis of the north-west Himalaya, published in 1931 is considered as one of the most fundamental contributions to our knowledge of Himalayan tectonics. His finding dealt with acute, knee-bend of the entire Himalayan belt around a pivotal point of Nanga Parbat, brought him international and national fame. In recognition of this finding, he was awarded the Back Award by the Royal Geographical Society of London (1934), and the Lyell Medal by the Geological Society of London (1934) (W.D. West, 1965, p. 2). He was also awarded Fellow of The Royal Society, particularly on this matchless contribution (Dr. V. C. Thakur, personal comm. on 15.08.2022).

The areas of the Hazara-Kashmir syntaxial zone were characterized by a deep knee-bend in the geological strike of the north-west Himalaya forming a unique feature in the orography (Fig. 5). The inflection affects some hundreds of miles depth of the mountains, extending from Assam to Kashmir. In an attempt to find an explanation for this unique mountain feature of the northwest Himalayas, the renowned Swiss geologist Sir Edward Suess gave a hypothesis that the syntaxis was a convergence

(*Schaarung*) point of two distinct mountain systems, the Himalayas and the Hindukush. He regarded this syntaxis as originating in the effort of the fold-system belonging to these two orographic areas of northern India to adjust themselves to each other. But there was no sufficient evidence to substantiate the claim and his hypothesis remains inconclusive (Wadia, 1931, p. 191). However, Prof. Wadia's extensive research of Poonch state (1928) led him to conclude that the syntaxis is created by pressures acting from the north driving successive folds as they rose from the Himalayan geosynclinal belt against the northern promontory of the Gondwana foreland. On colliding the shoulders of the triangular horst, the northerly pressure resulted in two components. The tongue of the foreland had acted as the *bloc* and divided the orogenic wavefront into two arcs. Such tectonic interpretation of the western Himalayan syntaxis by Prof. Wadia has been universally accepted and further research in structural, tectonics, metamorphism, and geo-bio-chronological dates of the region has corroborated his interpretation.

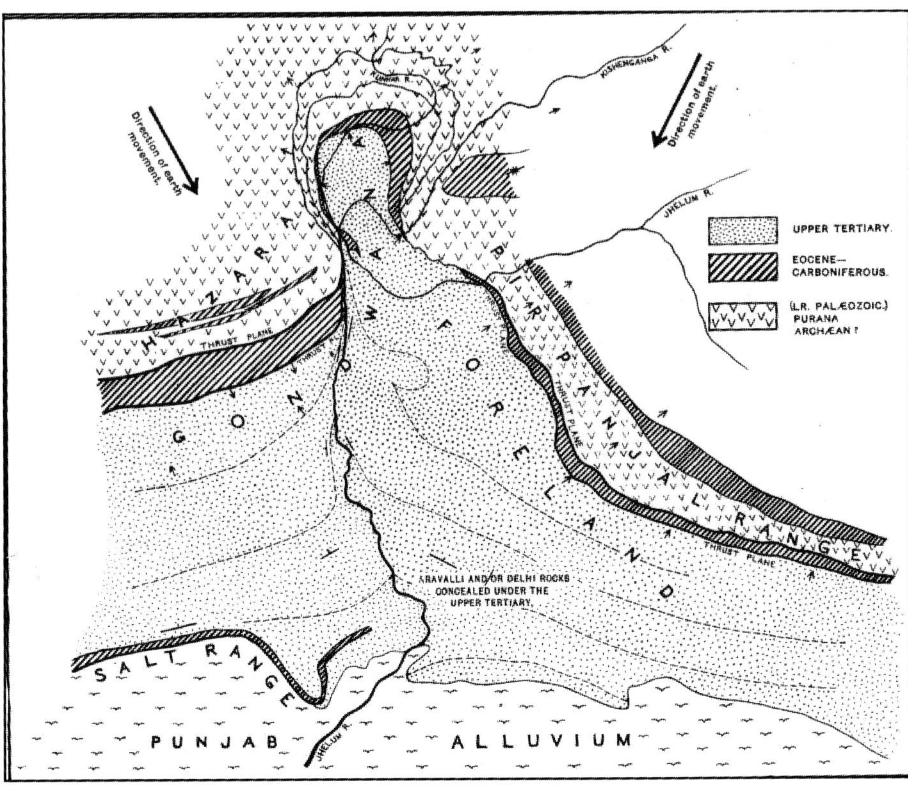

Figure 5: The Himalaya knee-bend around the pivot of the Nanga Parbat.

c). The trend-line of the Himalaya with its north-west and south-east limits

After several years of research in NW Himalaya (Wadia 1928; 1929; 1931; 1932), Wadia (1936) suggested a similar explanation for the acute knee-bend in the eastern Himalayas, where it had been thought that the Himalayan axis extends eastward to China. Though detailed surveys in this rather largely inaccessible area has not been made, he believed that the chain to turn sharply, through Assam and Burma, at the high mountain of Namche Barwa on the Brahmaputra, to take a south-westerly and southerly course, molded by the Assam tongue of the Gondwanaland bloc (Fig. 6). His hypothesis has been proved right with firm establishment of Namche Barwa Syntaxis or Eastern Himalayan Syntaxis to this day.

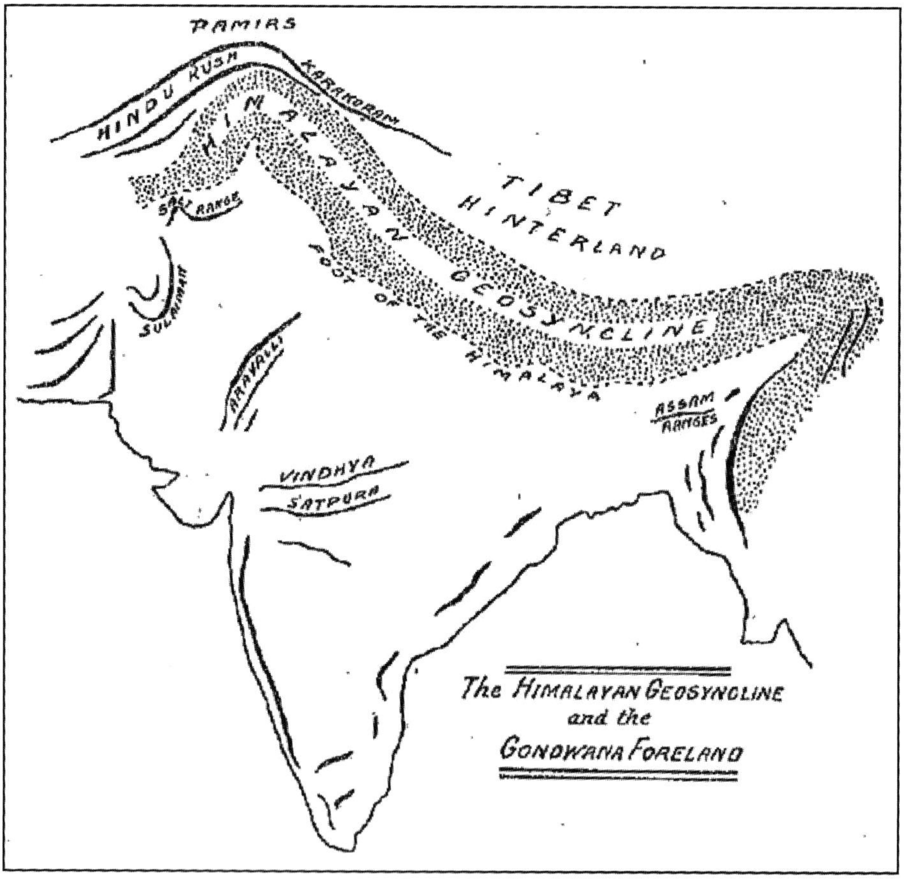

Figure 6: The Himalayan geosyncline and the Gondwana Foreland showing the trend of NW and NE Himalayan syntaxis.

2. Paleontological findings

Prof. Wadia, while carrying out extensive fieldwork to map the geology and structure, made significant fossil discoveries which include plant fossils, vertebrates, and microfossils. They throw a breaking light on the stratigraphy of rock formations. Two important findings amongst others are:

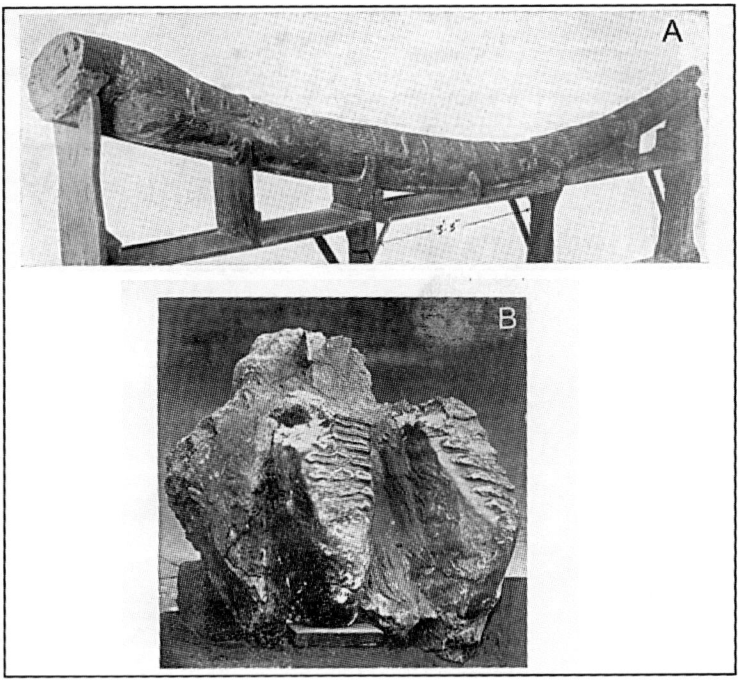

Figure 7A & B: The tusk as viewed obliquely (A), and the two upper molars (B).

a). Stegodon ganesa from Siwaliks of Jammu

The remains of the extinct elephant *Stegodon ganesa* (Figs. 7A, B) described by Prof. Wadia consist of a tusk of extraordinary length measuring over 10 ft., together with the maxillary part of the cranium, near the village of Jagti (long. 74° 57', lat. 32° 47') in the north of Jammu. The fossils are housed in the Geological Museum of the Prince of Wales College, Jammu (Wadia, 1925, P. 1). On the basis of *Stegodon ganesa* and other vertebrate fossils, the horizon yielding the specimens was equated with the standard rock formation known as the Tatrot or Pinjor Formation of the Upper Siwalik (Wadia, 1925).

In commemoration of the Geological Survey of India's centenary on the 13th January 1951, the Indian Postal Department released a postage stamp of *Stegodon ganesa*, the first ever reconstruction of a prehistoric animal on a stamp (Fig. 8) with a value of two-anas. Prior to 1956, ana was used as a currency/coin in India. http://www.paleophilatelie.eu/description/stamps/india_1951.html.

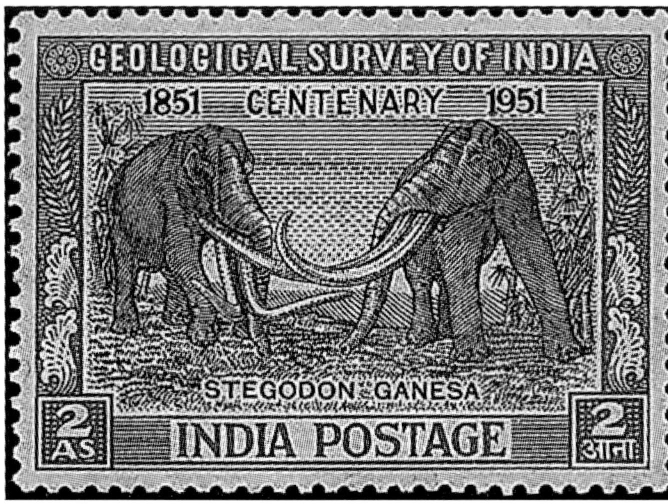

Figure 8: Postage stamp with two individuals of *Stegodon ganesa.*

b). On the Cretaceous and Eocene Volcanic Rocks of the Great Himalaya Range in North Kashmir

The discovery of fossil foraminifers in the metamorphic and volcanic rocks occupying the Burzil valley of North Kashmir by Prof. Wadia had brought altered the description of this strip, which he presented in his 1934 paper 'Cambrian-Trias sequence of North-West Kashmir.' This finding led to revise the geological map of Burzil valley, NW Kashmir (Fig. 9) of Wadia (1935). According to his observations, the Chechri-Minimarg belt consists of volcanic ash-beds, tuffs, agglomeratic slates, and lava flow with intrusions of gabbro, pyroxenite, and serpentine. In the outcrop of the same volcanic series, he found thin lenticular limestone intercalations with fossil foraminifera provisionally identified as belonging to the genera *Dictyoconoides, Orbitolina, Orbitoides,* etc. These fossils determined the age of the Cheechri-Burzil volcanic series to be Upper Cretaceous to Eocene. (Wadia, 1935, p. 420).

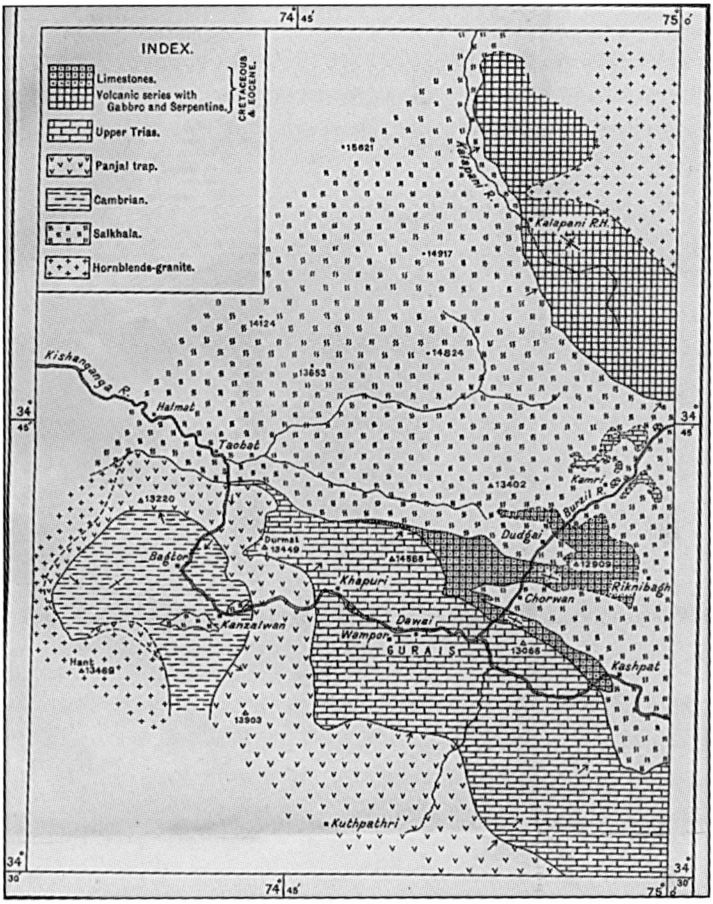

Figure 9: The revised geological map of Gurais and Burzil area, Kashmir state.

3). Geological investigations contributed in Ceylon

In 1938, when Wadia arrived Ceylon to head the Mineralogy Department, he found practically no structure in existence; no staff, clerk and peon. He started from scratch to improve the department and train the staff. Prof. K. Kularatnam, who was the first Assistant Geologist in 1939 in Ceylon Government, trained by Wadia stated, "Wadia infused new life and vigor into the dept. and set it functioning as an active living organism during his years of heading" (Kularatnam, 1965, p. 11). Prof. Wadia initiated a series of geological investigations as a mineralogist to the Ceylon Government. His notable contributions were - systematic geological maps of the islands and geological investigations concerning water supply, dam sites, and other engineering projects. Some of the notable articles he published were: *the making of Ceylon*; *Ceylon and North India-a geographical antithesis* (Fig. 10); *the occurrence of pumice on the east coast of Ceylon; the geology of Colombo and its environs; and the ring of waterfalls in Central Ceylon* (Wadia, 1940, 1941).

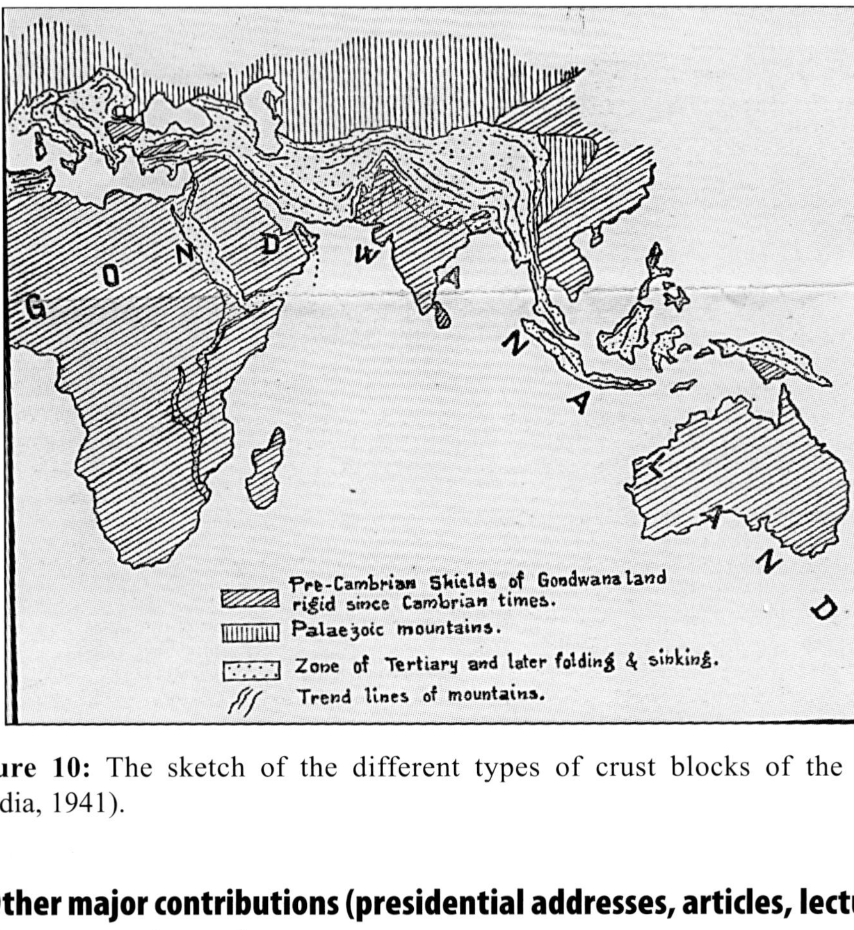

Figure 10: The sketch of the different types of crust blocks of the earth (Wadia, 1941).

4. Other major contributions (presidential addresses, articles, lectures and correspondences)

a). Geological Foundations of the Soils of India

Prof. Wadia and his colleagues from GSI published the first soil map of India in 1935 making a remarkable influence on the agricultural development of the country. In 1929, Sir Edwin Pascoe received a request from the International Association of Soil Science to compile a soil map of Asia including India. He constituted a sub-committee to collect information in order to prepare the soil map of India comprised of the Directors of Agriculture in India, the Director of the Imperial Agricultural Research Institute, Pusa, and the President of the Imperial Forest Institute, Dehradun, and some geologists including Prof. Wadia from GSI. He along with his GSI colleagues M.S. Krishnan and P.N. Mukherjee, prepared the first 'Soil Map of India', which was published in 1935 (Fig. 11). It was a landmark achievement that paved the way for the later soil map of India (Wadia, 1935; Wadia, 1945; Thakur, 2003).

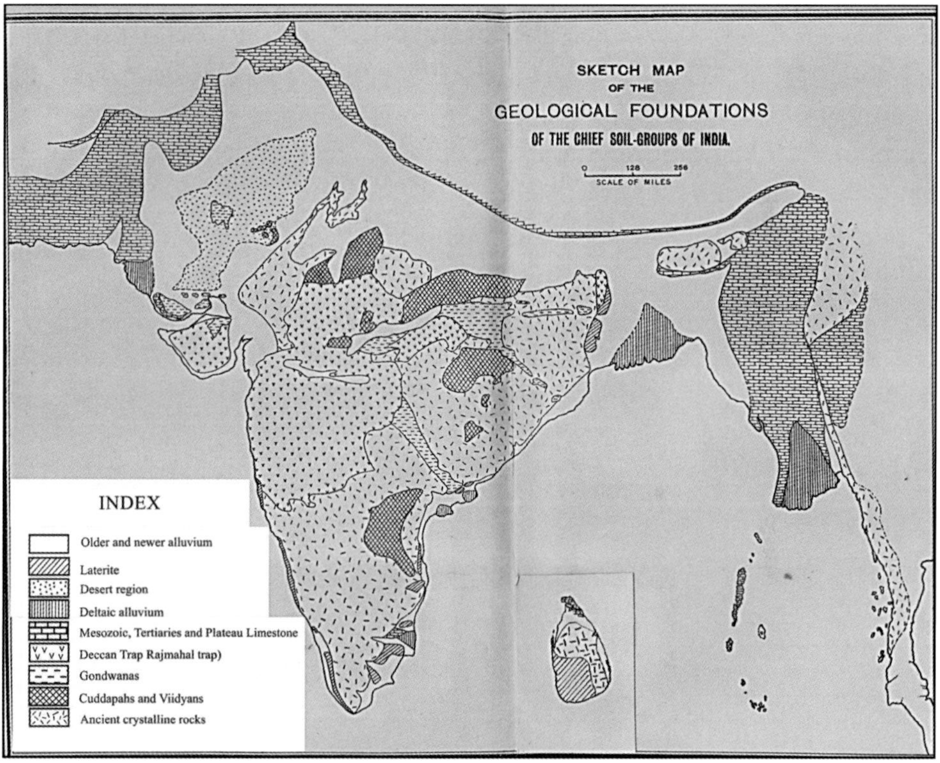

Figure 11. The first Soil Map of India, 1935.

b). Wartime correspondences

It was in 1938, Indian Science Congress held in Calcutta that paved the paths of two great geologists of their respective countries came across; the Indian D.N. Wadia (Fig. 12A) and the South African A.L. du Toit (Fig. 12B). This acquaintance was soon followed by exchanging their works and ideas, through letters and books during the WWII (1939-1945). Their letters were well documented and discussed by Master (2020). While Wadia was one of the foremost geologists from India, du Toit was well known for his advocacy of the then-fresh Continental Drift theory. Besides their expertise, there was evidently much common between the two, especially with the World War in full swing during this period. Both of them were invariably involved in finding strategic minerals for the then-British Empire, under which both India and South Africa were a part. Their correspondence starts with exchanging their books. On his return from India, du Toit wrote in his diary in February 1938 "sent book to Wadia" (Master, 2020), most probably referring to his famous book, "Our Wandering Continents" (du Toit, 1927). In response, Prof. Wadia sent a copy of the second and revised edition of his monumental book "Geology of India" (1939), wherein, du Toit already had a copy of the first edition with him. This was much appreciated by du Toit, who called it a "fine revision" in his letter dated 19th April 1939.

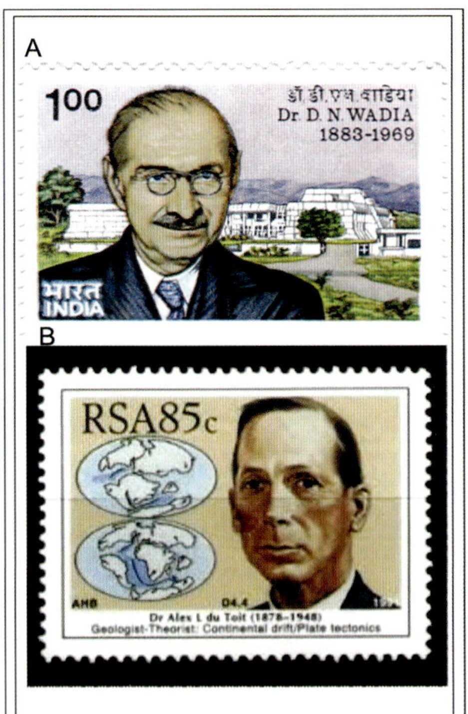

Figure 12: Two great personalities of geology. A postage stamp issued in 1984 shows Prof. D. N. Wadia, and the Wadia Institute of Himalayan Geology, named after him (A), and A South African postage stamp, issued in 1991 shows Dr. A.L. du Toit, and his palaeocontinental reconstructions (B) (Master, 2020).

Although they did not publish any scientific papers together, one can easily see how passionate they are about each other's works, and how much they must have benefitted from each other. Prof. Wadia retired in 1938 and subsequently, he was appointed as mineralogist by the Government of Ceylon, and the correspondence continued from Colombo, where he was based. In the late 1939 letters, they exchanged ideas on the geological origin and structure of the island. Their discussions were often punctuated with anticipation of ending the war. In 1945, Wadia returned to India as Mineral Adviser in the Planning and Development, GoI. They continued to correspond. Post WW II, and were looking forward to meeting each other at the International Geological Congress, which was to be held in London in 1948. But sadly, du Toit passed away before they could meet a second time. The duet, du Toit-Wadia letters showed how the geologists were actively involved even during wartime in finding strategic minerals and how the war had badly affected research. One is left guessing as to what more they could have achieved had they met again in London and collaborated more than just exchanging letters and books.

c). Metals in relation to living standards

Since the advancement of human civilization, metals have been important resources for mankind (Wadia, 1950, p.3). Overuse of metals and depletion of metal reserves over the years caused serious concern and geologists cannot shy away from their bonded duty to understand the matter. For equitable development, there is a need to move beyond colonial policy as erstwhile colonies and the weaker nations were exploited to meet the interest of the colonial masters and relatively developed countries (Wadia, 1950, p.3-4). When the metal reserves are not even across, those suppliers who happened to be weaker nations hardly get their returns proportionately. To mine the metals effectively and scientifically, among others there is an urgent need for trained geological and mining personnel (Wadia, 1950, p.5). In terms of metal reserves, the Indian sub-continent together with China and the Far East constitutes one of the largest metal reserve regions in the world. The mineral economy should be used for human welfare and overall development, and UNESCO needs to take a call on how to narrow the gap between the supplier and the consumer nations (Wadia, 1950, Geological Adviser, Dept. of Scientific and Industrial Research).

d). Honorarium lectures

From 1952-1953, The Maharaja Sayajirao University of Baroda invited Prof. D.N. Wadia to deliver lectures. Accordingly, he delivered six lectures on the topics namely: *The age and origin of the Himalayan mountains, their place in the structure of Asia; Minerals and War; Modern concepts about the earth's interior; Sub-recent changes in the geography of India; the Mineral wealth of India and The Geology and Mineral Resources of India with reference to Gujarat and Bombay.* The students and faculties highly appreciated the lectures for the wealth of information enriching their knowledge.

e). Evolution of the arid zone of Asia

Prof. Wadia was requested to write an article on *The post-glacial desiccation of central Asia: Evolution of the arid zone of Asia* to UNESCO's Arid Zone Programme. The reports were desired to be written by different experts in their respective fields. He explained the historical aspects of desert evolution and stated that the conversion of millions of square miles into semi-deserts to deserts in Asia post-late Pleistocene glacial age **(Fig. 13)**. The geological evidence shows that the arid zone of the Afro-Asia was once a belt of agriculture, which was well forested, the idea was very much supported by archaeological and historical facts. A number of conflicting theories have been put forward regarding the causes of desiccation in Asia. Prof. Wadia suggested that one of the consensus theories is that geographical change is competent to bring about unwelcome climatic change affecting the continent. Ice Age is thought to have been caused by geographical changes in conjunction with astronomical causes that brought the last great refrigeration of the earth. After the retreat of the ice, the immediate region to the south was converted into the arid zone in the Northern Hemisphere. The end of the Ice Age approximately dated 10,000-15,000 years ago, and the commencement of desiccation of the Afro-Asia arid zone is from the early history to proto-historic times. The transformation of highlands, plateaus, and mountains into peneplains resulted in the dislocation of water and air circulation. However, he mentioned that there are no factual records of dates and events as well as weather observations. The alteration of climate or the nomad life of these de-populated lands is mostly unwritten history. The main sources of knowledge on the subject are from the medieval books on history and the literature on travel and exploration, and their pages have been the sole source of information that remained long devoid of laboratories, observatories, or research institutions of any description (Wadia, 1960).

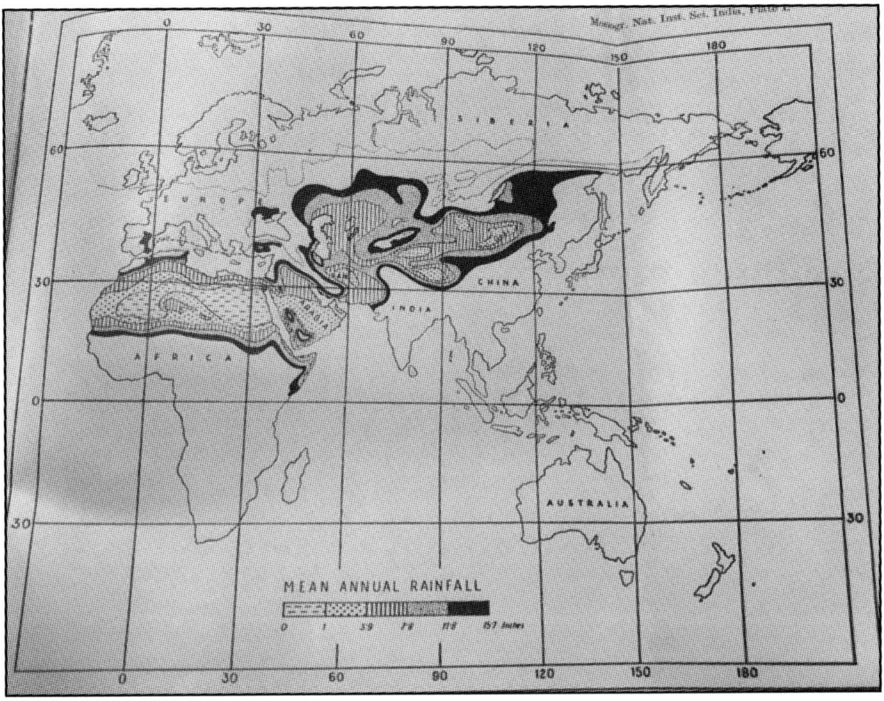

Figure 13: Arid Zone of Central Asia and North Africa.

f). The biography of a pebble (First article of Prof. Wadia, 1913)

As a classic writer, Prof. Wadia composed an amazing popular science article illustrated with an artistic drawing in the Story of a Stone. The abstract of the article is reproduced here:

> *"God worketh slowly: and a thousand years*
> *He takes to lift his hands off. Layer on Layer*
> *He made the earth, fashioned it and hardened it*
> *Into the great bright useful thing it is:*
> *Its seas life-crowded and soul-hallowed lands*
> *He girdled with the girdle of the sun." (Wadia, 1913, p.1).*

The article conveys various valuable lessons of geology such as its processes that are undertaken all through whilst keeping us fascinated in its autobiography, and one will feel the true sermon in a stone (Fig. 14). In his biographical sketch in Editorial note of PSI (1965) it narrates, "*while referring to Ceylon early in 1913, as a graceful pendant of the Indian Peninsula in his very first geological article, 'The story of a stone' perhaps the only one where he indulges in a popular style of writing-little did he imagine that he would, one day, be called upon to unscramble the structure of that very region!*"

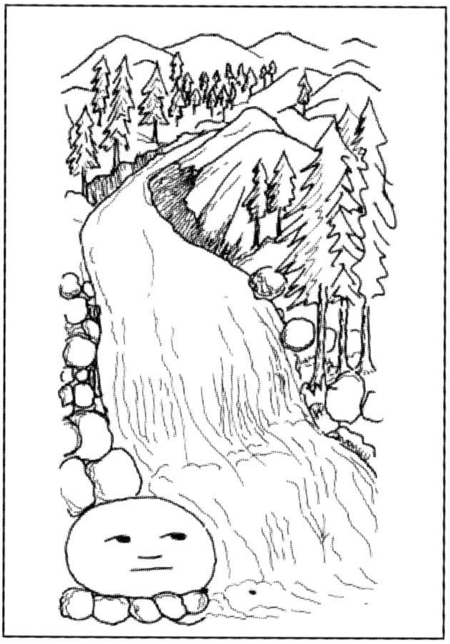

Figure 14: Illustration of a pebble at its infancy.

g). "The Geology of India" (1919)

Prof. Wadia in this book (Fig. 15) recalled his days at Prince of Wales College, Jammu, and stated, *"as a lecturer in Geology to students preparing for the Panjab University examinations I have constantly experienced great difficulty in the teaching of the Geology of India, because of the absence of any adequate modern book on the subject"* (Wadia, 1919, p. vii). Earlier, the only study material was by Sir Medlicott and Sir Blanford which was published by GSI in 1887, the same was revised by Sir Oldham in 1893. However, the voluminous size of the manual was not suitable for the students and the book was out of print. Researchers, faculties, and students were all compelled to collect information from the *Records* and *Memoirs* of the GSI. It was an inconvenient exercise for the students and faculties. Thus, he summarizes "*Much valuable scientific information contained in these admirable publications was, for the most part, unassimilated by the student class and remained locked up in the shelves of a few libraries in the country"* (1919, p. vii). The objective of the book was to provide the remedy for the above-mentioned problems in the form of a standard textbook, which summarized all the main facts along with geological maps, field photographs, and tables. He acknowledged Sir Thomas Holland, F.R.S., D.Sc., and Sir C.S. Middlemiss, C.I.E., F.R.S., the doyen of Indian Geology for their guidance, advice, and checking of illustrations and proofs. He completed the manuscript of the book in 1916 and was published by Macmillan in 1919. The book was so popular and in high demand that it went through several reprints with the 6th edition in 1969. It is worth noting that the revision of the 6th edition was completed just a few months before his sudden demise in June 1969. Mrs. Meher Wadia gratefully thanked K.K. Dar, the then Director of the Atomic Minerals Division, Department of Atomic Energy, GoI, for the support and help. Finally, the 6th edited version was published and dedicated to, "A. and F. in heaven, these pages are inscribed."

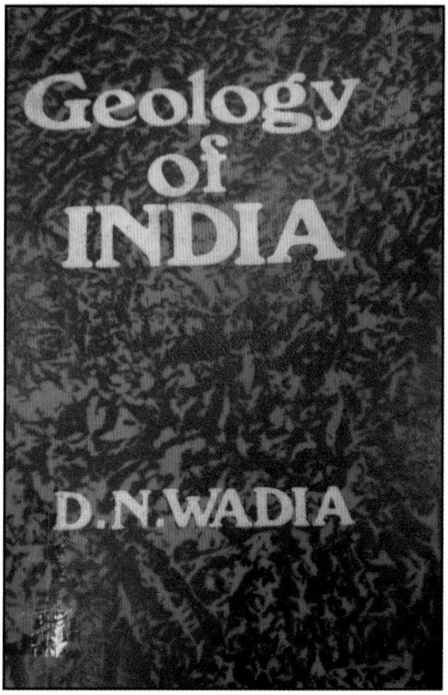

Figure 15: *Geology of India* (1919).

It is one of the most resourceful books as of today on the subject and it is still in high demand and can be found in every library of the geological institute, college, and university in the country. While, complimenting on the book, Sir W.D. West, another doyen of Indian Geology, wrote, *"Written, as are all his contributions, in matchless, and in places almost Churchillian style, it has had a profound influence on generations of students of geology, attracting them where others might have repelled, and stimulating them to take a keen interest in the subject of Indian Geology"* (W.D. West, 1965, p. 5).

h). Problems of Himalayan Geology and the inception of the Wadia Institute of Himalayan Geology, Dehradun

Prof. Wadia (1963) attributes that the Survey of India (SI) and the Geological Survey of India (GSI) had made noteworthy contributions in elucidating physical, stratigraphic, palaeontological, tectonics as well as physiographic aspects of the Himalayan geology and geography. However, he noted that certain vital problems of Himalayan Geology are yet to be resolved or have been partially answered. Some problems that he identified include (Wadia 1963, p.3):

1. The extent and limits of the Himalayan geosynclines and their axial continuation at either extremity.
2. The geographical extent of the Tethys Sea, beyond India, particularly its southeastern continuation towards Malaya and Indonesia, its connection with Malayan Island Arc, and its termination to the southeast.
3. The significance of the arcuate trendline of the chain from the northwest to southeast and its acute syntaxial bend at the Kashmir-Hazara extremity to the northwest and the Assam-Burma extremity southeast.
4. From some restricted sites in Kashmir, Shimla, and Garhwal encouraging solutions have been received with regard to the significance of the thrust or nappe structures in the geotectonic of the Himalayas.
5. The fifth problem of Himalayan geology is the isostasy and gravity observations which need explanation related to the foundation and support of the Himalayas.

6. The crustal warp theory was first proposed by Col. Glennie in the 1930s whereby the surface crust produces uplifts and depressions due to conventional currents in the sima. (Wadia, 1963, p.3-6)

Based on the above-stated problems, Prof. Wadia suggested the idea of having an institute devoted exclusively to all-encompassing comprehensive studies of the Himalayas. Accordingly, in June 1963 in a seminar sponsored by the Education Ministry, GoI, held at Shimla, a memorandum on this account was submitted by Prof. D.N. Wadia to Professor Humayun Kabir, the then Minister for Scientific Research and Cultural Affairs, GoI, and President of the Indian Science Congress Association. The proposal was approved by the GoI on 1st March 1968. Subsequently, the Memorandum of Association and Rules and Regulations of the Institute of Himalayan Geology Society was registered on 29th June 1968 in Delhi (Valdiya, 2018). On this very auspicious day, the Institute came into being. Presently the Wadia Institute of Himalayan Geology has its in-house journal 'Himalayan Geology' published bi-annually, and conducts various National and International seminars and conferences (Fig. 16). Presently, the institute has been pursuing basic research to unravel the orogeny of majestic Himalayas and to provide an improved understanding of seismogenesis, geodynamics, climate-tectonic interaction, biotic evolution, ores/minerals forming processes, glacial dynamics, fluvial system, geo-hazards (landslides, flash floods, avalanches, earthquakes), geo-resources (minerals, ore bodies, hydrocarbons, cold/hot springs), anthropogenic impact, etc. for the well-being of the population and safeguarding the properties and structures in the Himalaya and adjoining areas. It is also equipped with sophisticated analytical facilities like LA-MC-ICP-MS, Stable Isotope Mass Spectrometer, EPMA, ICP-MS, XRF, SEM, XRD, Raman Spectrometer, TL/OSL, Magnetic Susceptibility meter, etc. The analytical and laboratory facilities are being utilized by the scientists of WIHG and researchers from other universities, institutes, and organizations. The institute serves as a National Centre of excellence in Himalayan Geoscience Education and Research. It provides summer/winter training to over 100 students; produces an average of 10 Ph.Ds. as trained manpower and publishes over 120 research papers in quality journals every year; collaborates with Universities, Industries, and other Institutes on Himalayan Geosciences; maintains a modern Geological Museum decorated with varieties of rocks, minerals, and fossils of Himalaya for Education; conducts outreach programs for Science Education and Geo-hazards awareness.

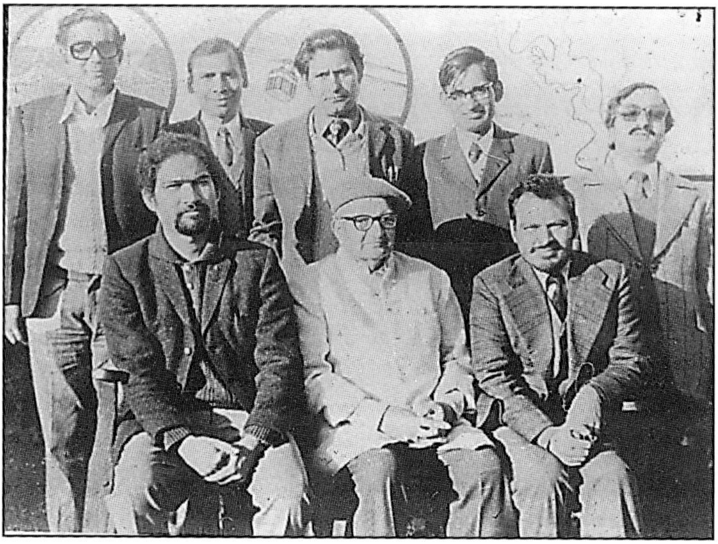

Figure 16. Post VI Himalayan Geology seminar field excursion at Mussoorie in 1975. Sitting from left 1st Dr. V.C. Thakur; 2nd Prof. A.G. Jhingran, the then Director, Wadia Institute of Himalayan Geology, Dehradun; 3rd Dr. S.K. Tandon. Standing from left 1st Dr. A.C. Nanda; 2nd Dr. D. Pal; 3rd Dr. K.K. Sharma; 4th Dr. N.S. Mathur; 5th Dr. T.N. Bagati.

Education and Career Achievements

- 1894: Sir J. J. English School, Surat.
- 1903: B.Sc. degree in Zoology and Botany from Baroda College (then affiliated with Bombay University).
- 1906: M.Sc. degree in biology and Geology from Baroda College (then affiliated with Bombay University).
- 1907 to 1920: Lecturer in Geology and English, Prince of Wales College, Jammu (J&K).
- 1921 to 1938: Asstt.Superintendent, Geological Survey of India.
- 1926-1927: Visited the British Museum, London, Germany, Austria, and Czechoslovakia.
- 1938: Mineral Advisor to the Ceylon Government.
- 1947: Director of Indian Bureau of Mines.
- 1949: Head of Atomic Minerals Division of the Atomic Energy Commission.

Awards

- 1934: Back Award of the Royal Geographical Society, London.
- 1943: Lyell Medal of the Geological Society, London & Honorary Fellowship of the Royal Asiatic Society of Ceylon.
- 1944: Joyakishan Medal from the Indian Association for the Advancement of Science.
- 1947: Honorary degree of D.Sc., from the University of Delhi.
- 1947: Jagdish Bose Memorial Medal from the Royal Asiatic Society of Calcutta.
- 1950: The Nehru Medal from the National Geographic Society, Banaras.
- 1951: Indian postage stamp with *Stegodon ganesa* was released to commemorate the centenary of the Geological Survey of India.
- 1951: Meghnad Saha Medal from the National Institute of Sciences, India.
- 1957: Fellow of the Royal Society F.R.S.
- 1957: Palaeontological Society of India dedicated a jubilee volume of its journal to mark 50 years of Prof. Wadia's geological career.
- 1958: Padma Bhushan, Govt. of India.
- 1960: Leopold von Buch Plakette of the German Geological Society.
- 1963: First National Professor of Geology by the Govt. of India.
- 1964: The Khaitan Gold Medal of the Asiatic Society, Calcutta.
- 1964: The Sarvadhikari Gold Medal from Calcutta University.
- 1965: Commemorative Volume of Dr. D.N. Wadia edited by The Mining, Geological and Metallurgical Institute of India.
- 1967: Honorary D.Sc. degree from the Aligarh Muslim University.
- 1984: Commemorative postage stamp bearing his image by Govt. of India.

Service to Professional Bodies

- 1932-1935: Council Member of Mining, Geological and Metallurgical Institute of India.
- 1936-1937: Vice-President of Mining, Geological and Metallurgical Institute of India.
- 1938: President Calcutta Geographical Society.
- 1938: Mineral Advisor to the Ceylon Government.

- 1938 and 1939: First Chairman of the National Planning Committee.
- 1942 and 1943: Two terms of General President of the Indian Science Congress.
- 1945 and 1946: President of the National Institute of Sciences of India (now Indian National Science Academy).
- 1945: Geological Advisor to the national government of Jawaharlal Nehru.
- 1947: First Director of Indian Bureau of Mines.
- 1949: Head of Atomic Minerals Division of the Atomic Energy Commission.
- 1949 until his death: Geological Adviser to the Indian Atomic Energy Commission.
- 1949 and 1950: President of the Indian Society of Soil Sciences.
- 1950 -1951: President of the Geological, Mining, and Metallurgical Society of India.
- 1951 and 1952: President of the Geological Society of India.
- 1954 to 1957: Chairman of the Central Board of Geophysics Indian Government.
- 1955: Chairman of the Council of Scientific and Industrial Research of India.
- 1958 to 1964: President of the Geological Society of India.
- 1960: Chairman of The Indian National Committee on Oceanic Research (INCOR).
- 1961 till demise: Chairman of the Programming Board of the Departments of Geology and Mining (Ministry of Mines & Metals).
- 1964: President of the 12th International Geological Congress, New Delhi.
- 1967: First Chairman of the Executive Committee of National Geophysical Research Institute, Hyderabad.
- 1968 until his last breath: First Chairman of the Governing Body of the Institute of Himalayan Geology (now Wadia Institute of Himalayan Geology).

Acknowledgments

Author gratefully acknowledge Dr. Kalachand Sain, Director, Wadia Institute of Himalayan Geology, Dehradun for the permission to contribute to this chapter (WIHG/Publication No. 0262), Dr. V.C. Thakur, formerly Director of WIHG and Padma Shri awardee for his precious time to discussions and reviewing the manuscript wherein the manuscript has immensely enhanced, Dr. B.N. Tiwari (retired Scientist G, WIHG) who enthused the author to take up this piece of work and Dr. Vikram Pratap Singh, IGNTU, Amarkantak who spotted the author amongst the many for the invitation to contribute this chapter. She expresses her gratefulness to her colleagues namely Dr. Khayingshing Luirei, Dr. M. Prakasam, Mr. N.K. Juyal (Senior Technical Officer of SEM Lab.), Ph.D. scholar Mr. Sunny Sohel Biswas for the help extended in various ways. She is indebted to the library staff namely Dr. Balram, Mr. S.S. Bhandari, Mr. Bharat Rana, Raj Kiran, S.K. Gupta, and Mrs. Deveshwari Rawat for their support in finding and locating the research papers and materials of Prof. Wadia, to the museum staff viz. Mr. Prateek Negi, Ms. Deepti Pandey, Amit Bhandari (photographer) and Nitesh Kumar (Field cum Lab attendant) for their valuable. Dr. Athikho Kaisii (husband of the author) Jamia Millia Islamia, New Delhi and Dr. Kezhakielie Whiso, formerly ONGC, Dehradun, Writer, and Independent Researcher is thanked in reviewing and editing the article. A sincere acknowledgement to the Royal Society of London and the Palaeontological Society of India for retrieving much of the information of Prof. Wadia from their publication amongst others.

References

1. D.N. Wadia - A biography, Reminiscences of golden days (1968-2018), 2018. Wadia Institute of Himalayan Geology Dehradun, 7-9.
2. Editorial note of the *Palaeontological Society of India.* D.N. Wadia: a biographical sketch, 1957. Journal of the *Palaeontological Society of India (PSI)*, Vol. 2, 2-8.
3. Geology of India. Rev. ed. D. N. Wadia. London: Macmillan; New York: St Martin's Press, 1953. 552 pp. Illus. + plates.
4. http://www.paleophilatelie.eu/description/stamps/india_1951.html.
5. https://scientistsinformation.blogspot.com/search/label/Dr.D.N. Wadia %281883 –1969%29.
6. Kularatnam, K., 1965.Wadia's contribution to the study of the geology of Ceylon.Wadia commemorative volume. P.10-13.
7. Lydekker, R.,1876. Notes on the geology of the Pir Panjal and neighbouring districts. Rec. Geol. Sur. Ind., vol. ix, p. 155.

8. Master, S., 2020. The wartime correspondence (1939-1945) between South African A.L. du Toit and Indian Geologist D.N. Wadia. Indian Journal of History of Science. 160-172.
9. NIO memory lane https://www.nodc.noaa.gov/archive/arc0001/9900162/2.2/data/0- data/jgofscd/htdocs/memorylane/pre1966.html.
10. Nolan, B.D., 1965. Director, United States, Geological Survey. In: Dr. D. N. Wadia Commemorative Volume. Kolkata: Mining, Geological and Metallurgical Institute, 1965.
11. Report of the Indian participation in the International Indian Ocean Expedition, New Delhi, 1976.
12. Report. Proc Indian Nat. Sci. Acad. 78, No. 3 September 2012, pp. 565-576.
13. Searle, M., 2009. Nanga Parbal-an uplifting tale. Geoscientist. The magazine of the Geological Society of London.Vol. 19, No.8.
14. Sorkhabi, R., 2019. Life and legacy of D.N. Wadia. Science Reporter, 28-29.
15. Stubblefield, C.J. 1970. Darashaw Nosherwan Wadia, 1883-1969. Biographical Memoirs of Fellows of the Royal Society, Vol. 16, PP. 543-562. https://www.jstor.org/stable/769604.
16. Thakur, V. C., 2003. Resonance – Journal of Science Education, Vol. 8(2), 65-67.
17. Valdiya, K.S. 2003. Resonance, Journal of Science Education. Vol. 8(2), 2-3.
18. Valdiya, K.S. 2003. As I remember. Reminiscences of golden days (1968-2018), 2018. Wadia Institute of Himalayan Geology Dehradun, 63-64.
19. Vigyanprasarhttps://vigyanprasar.gov.in/darashaw-nosherwan-wadia.
20. Virdi, N.S., 1983. D.N. Wadia - A biography.
21. West, R. D. "D. N. Wadia-An Appreciation" in Dr. D. N. Wadia Commemorative Volume. Kolkata: Mining, Geological and Metallurgical Institute, 1965.

Bibliography

The following publications are referred directly in the text. A full bibliography is available at https://royalsocietypublishing.org/doi/10.1098/rsbm.1970.0023.

1. 1913. The story of a stone: the biography of a pebble. Jammu also reprinted *Calcutta Geogr. Rev.*1, 1936, 39-49.
2. 1919. *Geology of India for Students*, xx+398 pp. London: Macmillan. 2nd edit. 1939; 3rd edit. 1953, xx+531 pp. with col. map dated 1949; 5th edit. 1961.
3. 1925. *Stegodon ganesa* (Falc. and Caut.) in the outer Siwaliks of Jammu. *Rec. Geol. Surv. India,* 56 (4), 352-355.
4. 1928. Geology of the Poonch State (Kashmir) and adjacent portions of the Punjab. *Mem. Geol. Surv. India*, 51 (2), 185-370.
5. 1931. The syntaxis of the north-west Himalaya: its rocks, tectonics and orogeny. *Rec. Geol. Surv. India*, 65 (2), 189-220.
6. 1932. Notes on the geology of Nanga Parbat (Mt Diamir) and adjoining districts of Ghilas, Kashmir. *Rec. Geol. Surv. India*, 66 (2), 212-232.
7. 1935. On the Cretaceous and Eocene volcanic rocks of the Great Himalaya Range in north Kashmir. *Rec. Geol. Surv. India*, 68 (4), 419-421.
8. 1935. (With M. S. Krishnan & P. N. Mukerjee.) Introductory note on the geological foundations of the soils of India. *Rec. Geol. Surv. India*, 68 (4), 363-391, pis.24, 25.
9. 1935. (With M. S. Krishnan & P. N. Mukerjee.) Introductory note on the geological foundations of the soils of India. *Rec. Geol. Surv. India*, 68 (4), 363-391, pis.24, 25.
10. 1936. The trend-line of the Himalayas—its north-west and south-east limits. *Himal. Jl*, 8, 63-69.
11. 1937. Nanga Parbat. *Calcutta Geogr. Rev.* 1, 81-82.
12. 1937. An outline of the geological history of India, pp. 43-69, in *An Outline of the Field Sciences of India.* Calcutta: Indian Sci. Congr. Assoc.
13. 1941. Ceylon and North India- A geographical antithesis. *Sci. Cult.* 6 (11), 624-628.
14. 1941. Ceylon and North India- A geographical antithesis. *Sci. Cult.* 6 (11), 624-628.
15. 1945. Soils of India. *Jl. Sci. Ind. Res. Delhi*, 3 (8), 359-367.
16. 1953. Maharaja Sayajirao Gaekwad Honorarium Lectures. The Geology and Mineral Resources of India with reference to Gujarat and Bombay State.

17. 1950. Metals in relation to living standards (in industrially under-developed countries). From the proceedings of the U.N.S.C., on conservation and utilization of Natural Resources.
18. 1960. The post-glacial dessication of Central Asia. Report for UNESCO Arid Zone programme. *Mon. Natn. Inst. Sci. India*, 1960, 1-25.

AUTHOR PROFILE

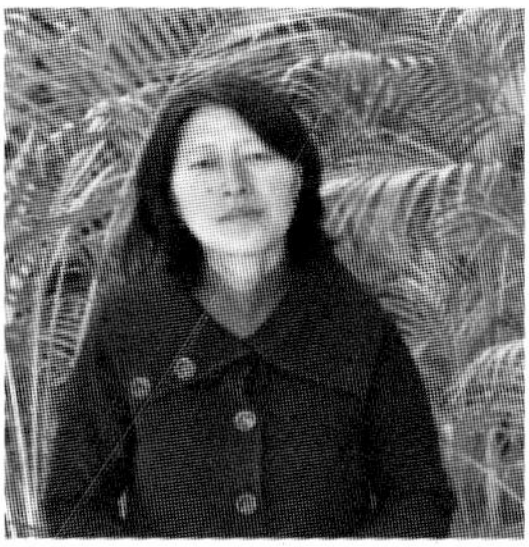

Dr. Kapesa Lokho joined the Wadia Institute of Himalayan Geology, Dehradun in 2002 and is currently Scientist-E in Biostratigraphy Group and Associate Professor of AcSIR. Her progressive educations were: schooling at the Don Bosco School, Mao, Manipur, PUC from Krupanidhi College, Karnataka Board, Bangalore, B.Sc. from Science College Kohima and M.Sc. from Nagaland University (NU), Kohima. She was awarded Ph.D. in 2006 in Micropaleontology from NU. Her research interests include high-resolution biostratigraphy of Paleogene and Neogene sediments; paleoenvironment, paleogeography, and collisional tectonics of the Indo-Myanmar Range. She was formerly Head of the Biostratigraphy Group, Wadia Institute of Himalayan Geology; Executive Member of the Indian Geological Congress 2019-2020; Executive member of the Palaeontological Society of India (PSI), 2020-2022; re-elected for the term 2022-2024. Presently, she is the Liaison Officer of Scheduled Caste (SC) and Scheduled Tribe (ST); Chairperson of the **Women Harassment Prevention Committee** in the Institute, Officer in charge of the Scanning Electron Microscope (SEM) and Micropalaeontology laboratories. She is a Life Member of Himalayan Geology, Indian Geological Congress, Palaeontological Society of India and a Fellow of the Geological Society of India.

Email: kapesa@wihg.res.in

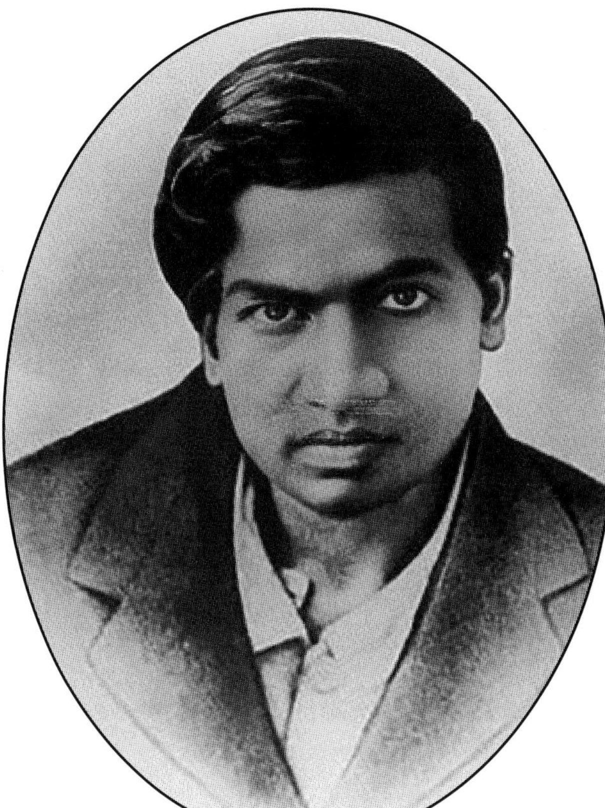

Srinivasa Aiyangar Ramanujan

(22 December 1887 – 26 April 1920)

SRINIVASA AIYANGAR RAMANUJAN: A MATHEMATICAL GENIUS

Ajit Kumar Rai

Srinivasa Ramanujan was one of the greatest mathematical geniuses. In his short life, he contributed substantially to the analytical theory of numbers, elliptic functions, continued fractions, and infinite series.

Early Life and Education

Ramanujan was born on 22 December 1887, in his maternal grandfather's house at Erode village (about 400 km southwest of Madras), in the then Madras presidency (now Tamil Nadu). His parents K Srinivasa Aiyangar, an accountant in a saree shop, and Komalatammal who use to sing in temples) were poor. The young Ramanujan was very close to his mother. In December 1889 he contracted smallpox. His family was orthodox and God-loving, fully devoted to the goddess Namagiri of Namakkal. Ramanujan, while asleep, had a divine vision where many elliptic integrals appeared before him, which, he used to record on paper after coming out of sleep without knowing anything about them.

He joined Kangayan Primary School in Kumbakonam at the age of five, and in 1898 joined Town High School (an English medium School). He performed well in all the subjects but was extraordinarily gifted in mathematics. In 1900, he started working independently on many mathematical problems such as cubic equations (1902), the quartic, and the quintic (but failed). He passed high school with a first class and was awarded a scholarship for further studies. In 1904, he enrolled in the FA course at the Government College, Kumbakonam. While still in high school, he accidentally got a copy of *A Synopsis of Elementary Results in Pure and Applied Mathematics* (1880) by Shoobridge Carr. The book was a compilation of notes for students taking competitive exams in mathematics in Cambridge and London. It contained theorems, formulae, short proofs, and an index to papers on pure mathematics published in the European Journals of Learned Societies. Carr did not solve all the theorems and problems and gave only the results at the end. Students had to solve them on their own. This book heightened the mathematical curiosity of Ramanujan.

By 1904, he began researching the series $\sum(1/n)$, calculated Euler's constant to 15 decimal places, and studied Bernoulli numbers. As the paper was costly, he used a large slate to solve the problems, and noted down only the final solutions on paper. His obsession with mathematics took a toll on other subjects, he failed in English which resulted in the termination of his scholarship. Meanwhile, he constructed magic squares - a grid of numbers that gave the same total in whichever way the numbers were added and also worked on prime numbers pattern. The sock brought in by the failure and termination of the scholarship was unbearable for Ramanujan, he ran away from home to Vizagapatnam about 650 km north of Madras, but was traced and returned home. In 1906, he retook admission to First Arts (FA) course at Pachiyappa's College in Madras. But he failed in Physiology, and retried but failed again. Thus, ends his hope of getting a college degree. He tried to tutor high school students but achieved little success. On 14 July 1909, he got married to 10-year-old S Janaki Ammal, probably under pressure from his mother.

Despite the disappointments, he continued working on complex mathematical problems like hypergeometric series, relations between integrals and series, elliptic functions, etc. He became seriously ill and underwent an operation in April 1909, which took considerable time to recover. In 1910, he worked out relations between elliptic modular equations, and in 1911, published his work on Bernoulli numbers in the *Journal of the Indian Mathematical Society* which gave him some recognition. In 1911, he got his first job, a temporary post in the Accountant General's Office in Madras. He further approach Ramachandra Rao who was a Collector at Nellore and a founder member of the Indian Mathematical Society. He noted -

A short uncouth figure, stout, unshaven, not over clean, with one conspicuous feature-shining eyes- walked in with a frayed notebook under his arm. He was miserably poor. ... He opened his book and began to explain some of his discoveries. I saw quite at once that there was something out of the way, but my knowledge did not permit me to judge whether he talked sense or nonsense. ... I asked him what he wanted. He said he wanted a pittance to live on so that he might pursue his researches.

He told him to return to Madras and tried, unsuccessfully, to arrange a scholarship for Ramanujan.

In March 1912, he got appointed as a clerk in The Port Trust of Madras, on the recommendation of E W Middlemast, professor of mathematics. He wrote -

I can strongly recommend the applicant. He is a young man of quite exceptional capacity in mathematics and especially in work relating to numbers. He has a natural aptitude for computation and is very quick at figure work.

Gradually, his stature as a gifted mathematician started getting some sort of recognition, his bosses at the Port Trust like Sir Francis Spring and Mr. Narayana Rao, and Mr. S N Aiyar (who published an article on Ramanujan's work in 1913- *On the distribution of primes*) played an important role in strengthening his reputation as a mathematician. Prof. C.L.T Griffith of the Madras Engineering College who knew the genus of Ramanujan wrote to Prof. M.J.M Hill, professor of mathematics at the University College London along with copies of Ramanujan's work, particularly his 1911 paper on Bernoulli numbers, Hill took little cognizance. Ramanujan himself wrote to E.W. Hobson and H.F. Baker at Cambridge University but received no response. What came next was one of the most romantic quests in the history of mathematics. Ramanujan had studied G.H. Hardy's book *Orders of Infinity,* and in January 1913, wrote a ten-page letter to Hardy enclosing his works. He wrote to Hardy -

I have had no university education but I have undergone the ordinary school course. After leaving school I have been employing the spare time at my disposal to work on mathematics. I have not trodden through the conventional regular course which is followed in a university course, but I am striking out a new path for myself. I have made a special investigation of divergent series in general and the results I get are termed by the local mathematicians as 'startling'.

Further, the letter contained about 120 statements of theorems on infinite series, improper integrals, continued fractions, and number theory. Hardy and his colleague J.E. Littlewood, studied the long list of theorems. On 8th February 1913, in an encouraging reply to Ramanujan, Hardy desired to see the proofs to be able to evaluate the work.

I was exceedingly interested by your letter and by the theorems which you state. You will however understand that, before I can judge properly of the value of what you have done, it is essential that I should see proofs of some of your assertions. Your results seem to me to fall into roughly three classes: (1) *there are a number of results that are already known, or easily deducible from known theorems;* (2) *there are results which, so far as I know, are new and interesting, but interesting rather from their curiosity and apparent difficulty than their importance;* (3) *there are results which appear to be new and important...*

Ecstatic Ramanujan wrote back *"I have found a friend in you who views my labors sympathetically. . . I am already a half-starving man. To preserve my brain, I want food, and this is my first consideration. Any sympathetic letter from you will be helpful to me here to get a scholarship either from the university or from the government."* Hardy's endorsement of Ramanujan's work opened the doors that were shut due to his inability to clear the FA examination hurdle. In May 1913, the syndicate of the Madras University in an extraordinary bending of rules gave him a research scholarship of Rs. 75/- per month, for two years. For the first time in his life, Ramanujan had a well-paying job and could do what he was destined to do.

Hardy was eager to get Ramanujan to Cambridge. He requested his Cambridge colleague Prof. E.H. Neville who was on a lecture tour in India, to meet Ramanujan. Prof. Neville, impressed by Ramanujan's mathematical virtuosity, did everything to get Ramanujan to Cambridge University. Including, persuading Ramanujan who was an orthodox Brahmin and a strict vegetarian. His religion should have prevented him from traveling abroad. He also convinced Ramanujan that he could follow his religious practices and remain a vegetarian without any difficulty. Ramanujan was initially averse to accepting Hardy's offer. Only a divine intervention could change his mind. The command to go to Cambridge came from Namagiri in his dream

Life at Cambridge

On 13 March 1914, Ramanujan sailed from Bombay by the P&O Liner Nevasa. He arrived in London on 14 April 1914, met Neville, and after spending a couple of weeks in Neville's home reached Trinity College on 30th April, to begin an extraordinary collaboration. Initially, Hardy was unsure how to approach the problem of Ramanujan's lack of formal education.

What was to be done in the way of teaching him modern mathematics? The limitations of his knowledge were as startling as its profundity.

He requested Littlewood to teach Ramanujan rigorous mathematical methods. However, he said -

... that it was extremely difficult because every time some matter, which it was thought that Ramanujan needed to know, was mentioned, Ramanujan's response was an avalanche of original ideas which made it almost impossible for Littlewood to persist in his original intention.

Due to the severe winter, Ramanujan felt ill and could not publish anything for five months. In 1914, he published only one paper: *The modular Equations and Approximations to Pi,* based mostly on his work in India, in the *Quarterly Journal of Mathematics.* In 1915, he published around 20 papers some of which he co-authored with Hardy. The most notable one was about partition numbers. They gave a reliable formula for calculating *partition numbers* by adopting the circle method. They surprised mathematicians by arriving at the exact formula for calculating $p(n)$, the number of partitions possible for any integer. He propounded Ramanujan's Congruence, a monumental contribution to number theory. In June 1914, he was allowed to enroll despite not having the proper qualifications. On 16 March 1916, he graduated from Cambridge with a Bachelor of Science by Research (Fig.1). His dissertation was on *Highly composite numbers* and consisted of seven of his papers published in England.

Ramanujan fell seriously ill in 1917. Loneliness (he had no communication with his family in India) further worsened his health, he spent most of his time in various nursing homes. He tried to commit suicide by jumping in front of a speeding train but was miraculously saved by the guard on the train. In February 1918, Hardy wrote -

Batty Shaw found out, what other doctors did not know, that he had undergone an operation about four years ago. His worst theory was that this had been for the removal of a malignant growth, wrongly diagnosed. In view of the fact that Ramanujan is no worse than six months ago, he has now abandoned this theory - the other doctors never gave it any support. Tubercle has been the provisionally accepted theory, apart from this, since the original idea of gastric ulcer was given up. ... Like all Indians he is fatalistic, and it is terribly hard to get him to take care of himself.

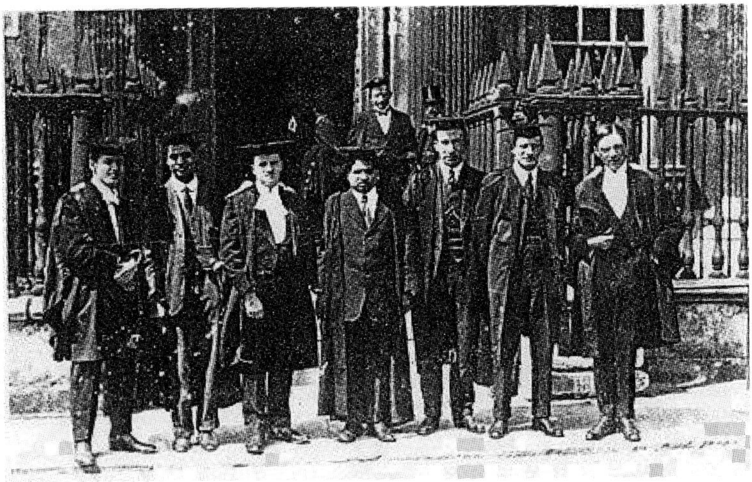

Figure 1: Ramanujan (center) at Cambridge.

At the age of 30, on 18 February 1918 Ramanujan was elected as a Fellow of the Cambridge Philosophical Society and then three days later, as a Fellow of the Royal Society of London (FRS), one of the youngest to be elected as FRS. On 10 October 1918, he was elected as a Fellow of Trinity College Cambridge, along with a fellowship for six years. This good news had a positive impact on his health. Hardy wrote in a letter

I think we may now hope that he has turned to corner, and is on the road to a real recovery. His temperature has ceased to be irregular, and he has gained nearly a stone in weight. ... There has never been any sign of any diminuation in his extraordinary mathematical talents. He has produced less, naturally, during his illness but the quality has been the same. ....

Hardy often visits him in the hospital, on one occasion, to cheer up Ramanujan, he said that he came by taxi with a very ordinary plate number 1729. However, Ramanujan exclaimed that "on the contrary, it is a very special number since it is the smallest number which was the sum of cubes of two numbers":

1729

$$1^3 + 12^3 = 9^3 + 10^3$$

(The Hardy-Ramanujan number)

$1^3 + 12^3 = 1 + 1728 = 1729$ and $9^3 + 10^3 = 729 + 1000 = 1729$. This number is known as the Ramanujan-Hardy number. This shows how the number is related to elliptic curves and $K3$ surfaces.

Return to India

He started his journey back to India (by P&O Liner SS Nagoya) on 27 February 1919 and arrived on 13 March. Hardy wrote -

He will return to India with a scientific standing and reputation such as no Indian has enjoyed before, and I am confident that India will regard him as the treasure he is. His natural simplicity and modesty has never been affected in the least by success - indeed all that is wanted is to get him to realise that he really is a success.

However, his health remained poor. Upon his return to India, he found that relation between his mother and wife was not cordial. For the first time, he rebelled against his mother. Tuberculosis (new findings suggest it to be amoebiasis) and depression had brought him severe physical and mental trouble. But he continued to work. On 20 January 1920, he wrote to Hardy for the first time since coming back to India. He informed Hardy about his discovery of Mock Theta Functions. He explained a new class of functions that were not theta functions but had crucial similarities, and how they could be constructed. The theta function lies at the heart of string theory in physics. On 20 April 1920, he breathed his last.

Ramanujan left three notebooks of unpublished work carried out between 1904-1914 (Notebooks 1 and 2). In Notebook 3, he recorded his work after his return to India. G N Watson, Mason Professor of Pure Mathematics at Birmingham, published 14 papers under the general title *Theorems stated by Ramanujan,* in total he published 30 papers inspired by Ramanujan's work. Hardy passed on to Watson the large number of manuscripts of Ramanujan that he had, both written before 1914 and some written in Ramanujan's last year in India before his death. Ramanujan's collected papers were later published by Cambridge University. American mathematician Bruce C. Berndt has written a multi-volume study of notebooks.

Honours & Recognitions

- Paul Erdös believed that if mathematicians were rated based on the pure talent on a scale from 0 to 100, Hardy would get 25, Littlewood 30, Hilbert 80, and Ramanujan 100.
- Journal Nature has listed Ramanujan as a mathematician on a "Calendar of Scientific Pioneers" who had achieved eminence.

- Tamil Nadu government celebrates 22 December (Ramanujan's birthday) as 'State IT Day'.
- Department of Post, Government of India issued commemorative postal stamps on Ramanujan in 1962, 2011, 2012, and 2016.

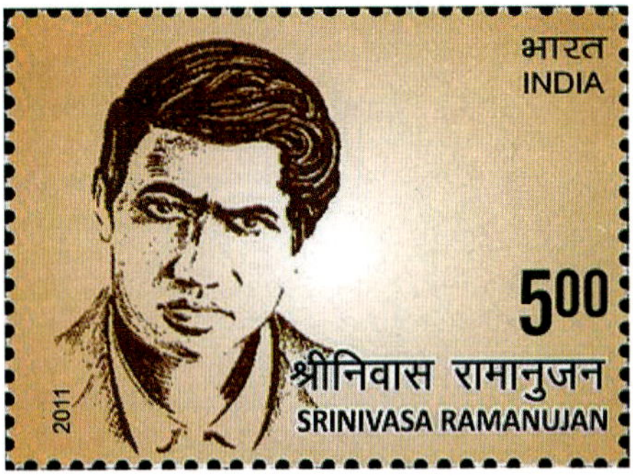

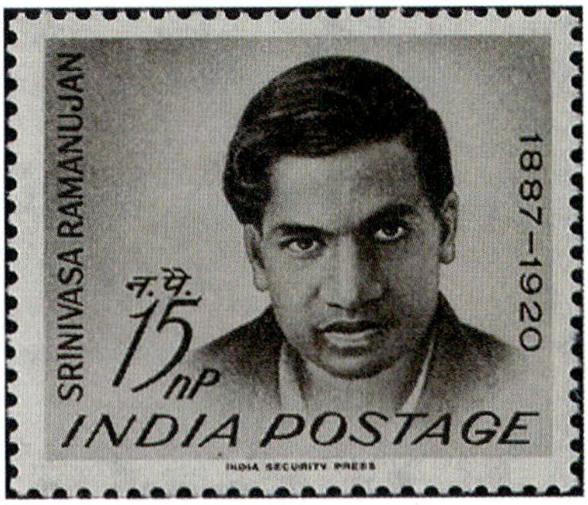

- To mark the 125th birth anniversary of Srinivasa Ramanujan, the then Prime Minister Dr. Manmohan Singh announced that December 22, would hereafter, be celebrated as National Mathematics Day.

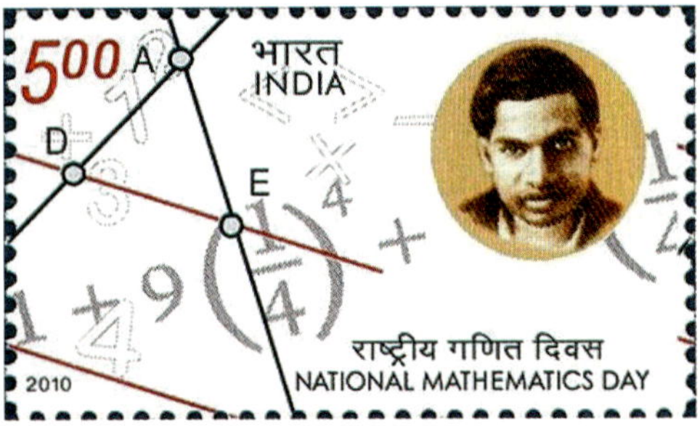

- The International Centre for Theoretical Physics (ICTP) has created a prize in Ramanujan's name for young mathematicians from developing countries in cooperation with the International Mathematical Union, which nominates members of the prize committee.
- SASTRA University, Tamil Nadu, has instituted the SASTRA Ramanujan Prize of US$10,000 to be given annually to a mathematician not exceeding age 32 for outstanding contributions in an area of mathematics influenced by Ramanujan
- *'The Man Who Knew Infinity'* is a 2015 film on the life of Ramanujan based on Kanigel's book of the same name.

- Written and directed by Gnana Rajasekaran, '*Ramanujan*,' is an Indo-British collaboration film chronicling the life of Ramanujan.
- Nandan Kudhyadi directed documentary films '*The Genius of Srinivasa Ramanujan*' (2013) and *Srinivasa Ramanujan: The Mathematician and His Legacy* (2016) portrays the life of Ramanujan
- In 1997 *The Ramanujan Journal* (published by Springer) was launched to publish work "in areas of mathematics influenced by Ramanujan".

Bibliography

1. *Hardy, G. H. (1978). Ramanujan. New York: Chelsea Pub. Co.* ISBN *978-0-8284-0136-4.*
2. Kanigel, R. (1991). The Man Who Knew Infinity: A Life of the Genius Ramanujan. New York: Charles Scribner's Sons. ISBN 978-0-684-19259-8.
3. Leavitt, D. (2007). The Indian Clerk. London: Bloomsbury. ISBN 978-0-7475-9370-6.
4. Narlikar, J. V. (2003). Scientific Edge: The Indian Scientist from Vedic to Modern Times. Penguin Books, New Delhi, India. ISBN 978-0-14-303028-7.
5. Ono, K., et al. (2016). My Search for Ramanujan: How I Learned to Count. Springer. ISBN 978-3319255668.
6. Rao, C.N.R., Rao, I. (2021) Founders of Modern Science in India, India Academy of Sciences, Bengaluru. p. 103.
7. Writings of Bruce C. Berndt on Ramanujan.
8. https://en.wikipedia.org/wiki/Srinivasa_Ramanujan.

AUTHOR PROFILE

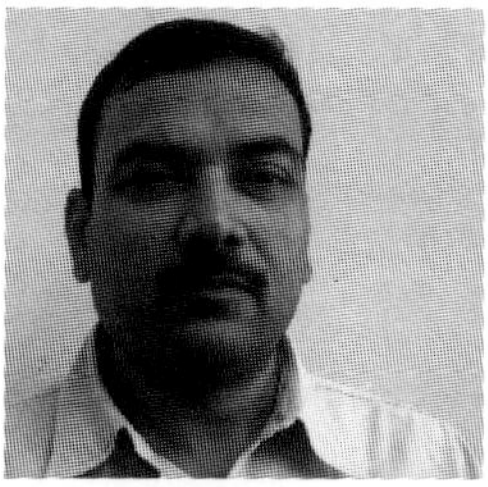

Dr Ajeet Kumar Rai is an Assistant Professor in education at the Faculty of Education (K), Banaras Hindu University, Varanasi, India. He is specialized in Pedagogy of Science at Secondary Level and have published 30 papers and several chapters in diverse areas of science education and curriculum studies both nationally and internationally.

Email: ajeetk.rai5@bhu.ac.in

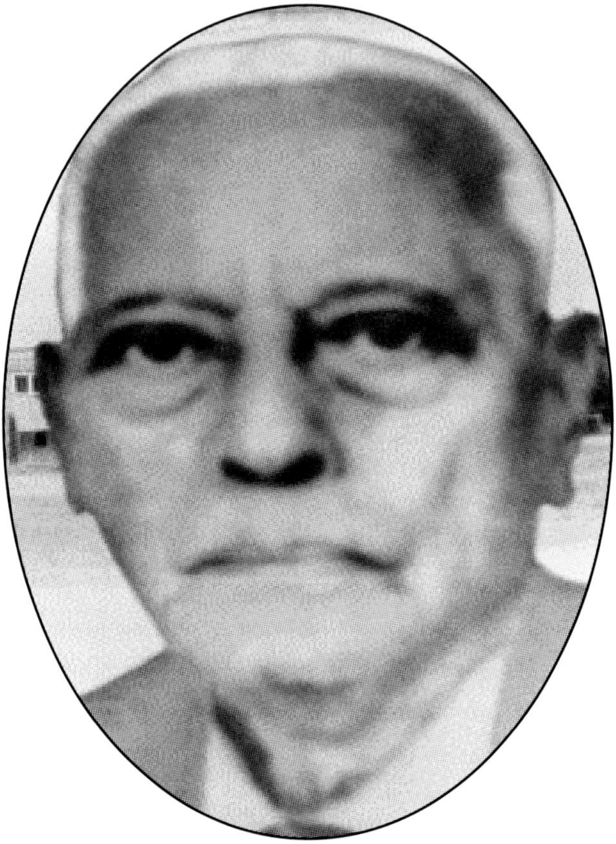

Pranakrushna Parija

(1 April 1891 – 2 June 1978)

PRANAKRUSHNA PARIJA: FOUNDER OF BOTANICAL STUDIES IN ODISHA

Siba Prasad Adhikary

Early Life and Education:

Pranakrushna Parija was born on 1st April 1991 in a middle-class family in Icchapur village in the Ballikuda area, 36 miles from Cuttack in Odisha state, India. He lost his father Biswanath Parija at the age of 12 and soon after mother Jayanti Devi passed away. Hence, he was dependent on other members of his extended family. After their initial education in a vernacular school in the village, he joined the minor school in April 1901 at Ballikuda at a distance of about two miles for which he had to walk four miles each day. As he was very good in studies, he got double promotion thrice, completed middle school in 1904, stood first in Orissa, got a fellowship of monthly four rupees and free ship, and joined Ravenshaw Collegiate School at Cuttack for further studies. He stood 1st from Orissa in the Entrance examination (called Matriculation from 1910 onwards) and then joined Ravenshaw college and secured 4th position in 2011 under Calcutta University which covered Bengal, Bihar, Orissa, and Assam at that time. For the B.Sc. course, he joined Presidency College, Calcutta, and studied Physics, Chemistry, and Mathematics. His classmates were the famous scientists Satyendra Nath Bose and Meghanad Saha, and Acharya Jagdish Chandra Bose and Acharya Prafulla Chandra Ray were his teachers. He passed with Mathematics Honours in 1913 and received Joynarayan Prize for standing 1st in Sanskrit in the University. While as a Postgraduate student in Mathematics, the Government of Bihar and Orissa decided to send three students to England for higher education for which Pranakrushna Parija was selected. He proceeded to England on a ship from Bombay on 14th August 1914, reached after 20 days of the voyage, and joined Christ College under Cambridge University with the subjects in Natural Science in the 1st Tripos. He took Botany (Hons.) in the 2nd Tripos course in 1916 and joined under the guidance of Prof. F. F. Blackman, the famous Professor of Botany. He secured 1st class in 2nd Tripos and received the Frank-Smart Prize and fellowship and joined as a research student at Cambridge School of Botany. He worked there on the mechanism of respiration in the leaves of evergreen plants and related aspects of Apple until the end of July 1921.

Contribution to Science

At Cambridge University, UK (September 1914 – July 1921)

Prof. Parija initiated his research at the Cambridge School of Botany under the guidance of Prof. F. F. Blackman on the respiration of evergreen leaves which continue to exist in a state of maturity for very long periods. Subsequently, he studied the drift in respiration of apples maintained in a refrigerator for storage. The objective was to find out the senescence mechanism, the dominant stage of ontogeny in the ripening fleshy fruits so that they can be stored for longer periods to meet the food requirement during the 1st world war in which England was involved at that time. The research was also intended to find out whether the two types of organs, the evergreen leaves, and ripening fruits, so strikingly different from each other, manifest the same fundamental principles of respiration. The findings of this study were published in 1928 [1]. In the paper, F.F. Blackman and P. Parija demonstrated that respiration in the apple in a current of ordinary air is an integration of two independent and opposed processes that are at work in senescence. One is the starvation drift at 22^{0}C, tending continually to lower the respiration, while the other, tends to accelerate the respiration by lowering organization resistance, expressed as the rise in hydrolysis. The second paper in the series presented the behavior of several individual species alternatively in air and nitrogen[2]. It showed carbon dioxide production in oxygen respiration (OR) is less than in nitrogen respiration (NR). The total carbon loss was three or more times more in nitrogen than in air. The question that remained to answer was what happens then to the deficit of carbon in the air? The answer was presented later by him in a book by F.F. Blackman in 1954 through a scheme of reactions comprising the respiration sequence of several catalyzed reactions[3]. It starts with carbohydrate reserves in the apples through hydrolysis to hexoses, then by activation to hetero-hexoses, then by glycolysis to methyl-glyoxyl, etc. The reactants in the last stage have an alternative fate either binding with the presence or absence of oxygen. In nitrogen, the final products were carbon dioxide + alcohol in the usual ratio. In the air and other concentrations of oxygen, the final products were eater + carbon dioxide. No final carbon derivative accumulates in the tissue during OR. Hence the logical conclusion derived was that in the air part of the last stage, reactants were somehow worked back into the system continuously by oxygen as oxidative anabolism (OA).

At Ravenshaw College, Cuttack, Odisha, India (August 1921 – January 1945)

During his time at Cambridge, he was selected for Indian Education Service, returned to India in July 1921, and joined Ravenshaw College, Cuttack as a Professor of Botany on 4th August 1921. He devoted fully to strengthening botany teaching and research at Ravenshaw and opened Botany at B.Sc. pass level in 1924 and Botany (Hons) in 1930. Soon after, Ravenshaw became an active center for research in botany in India. Prof. Parija worked on problems both of fundamental and applied nature particularly, in the field of physiology of rice during salinity, drought, and waterlogging.

Water hyacinth and other aquatic weeds

At the beginning of the twentieth century the water hyacinth, *Eichhornia crassipes* brought to India due to its beautiful violate flowers, could establish itself quickly and go on spreading at a fast pace in water bodies posing a threat due to its water-clogging behavior. An all-India expert committee was set up to study the life history, cause of rapid establishment, and method of control of this obnoxious aquatic weed. Prof. Parija received a grant from the Imperial Council of Agricultural Research to study this problem in Orissa. A team of research scholars from various parts of India joined the project. They reported that seeds of water hyacinth remain dormant at least for one season and retain their viability for several years. The type of germination of its seeds is like that of the date and *Borassus*. Light hastens the floating of the seedlings. The weed can flourish in a wide range of pH with optimum growth at 6 to 8 pH. It can also resist drought to a considerable extent. Copper sulfate was found as the most effective weedicide for water hyacinth and for *Pistia* and *Salvinia* as well[4,9,10,11].

Experimental morphology of angiosperms plants

Prof. Parija along with his students, P. Mishra, P. Mallick, K. Samal, and B. N. Misra worked on experimental morphology of several species of angiosperms plants like *Bridelia pubescent*, *Impatiens balsamina*, *Tecoma capensis*, *Momordica dioica*, *Ipomoea crassicaulis*, *Cucurbita maxima*,

Scirpus articulates, Datura alba, Helianthus annus, Ixora undulate and *Amaranthus* species. They established that the thorns that arise on the stem of *Bridelia pubescens* are morphologically roots. These root thorns are apo-geotropic and grow as long as the atmosphere is humid, and light did not affect the direction of plant growth[6]. Parija and Mallick proved experimentally that turgescence in the cells of the fruit wall is not the only cause of the bursting of the Balsam fruit[12]. Suberization of the cell wall at the sutures of the five carpels of the fruits in longitudinal furrows also supplements turgidity. They also reported that dryness alone did not induce cuticle formation in *Ficus religiosa*. Rather, dryness is coupled with light-induced cuticle formation. Red light is ineffective while blue light-induced the cuticle formation[13]. Further, they found oily seeds resist the effect of high temperature better than starchy ones. Among the oily seeds the greater the oil content, the higher the temperature they can resist[17]. The distribution, structure, and development of glandular hairs and extra-floral nectaries were also studied by Parija and Samal in *Tecoma capensis*[14]. They proved that the extra-floral nectaries of the plant are from glandular hairs. These petaliform glands help in the self-pollination of the flowers by keeping the unwelcome ants fully fed with the profuse secretion of honey from these glands and thereby preventing them to visit other flowers which would have facilitated their cross-pollination. Parija also observed growth of the ovary of *Momordica dioica* when the flowers were pollinated with the pollen of *Luffa acutangular*[27]. His student B.N. Mishra worked on the topic "Autecology of *Ipomoea crassicaulis* (Benth.) Robinson obtained Ph.D. from Utkal University in 1965. Parija and Saran worked on respiration in the leaves of *Aralia* [7,8]. They reported that short exposures to light raised the rate of respiration and red light had no effect, while blue and violet light affected the respiratory rate in the same way as white light. They postulated that an increase in the rate of respiration was due to hydrolysis of the reserve, activation of the enzyme system, or change in the permeability of the cells. With Samantarai, Parija reported the march of transpiration in a leaf from its measurable stage to its fall[16]. They found a characteristic curve of transpiration for each leaf with a rise and then a fall to a steady value and finally a decline in *Datura alba, Helianthus annus,* and *Ixora undulate*.

Research on algae

Prof Parija studied the life history of aquatic weeds and their role in the prevalence of malaria around Chilika lake, the largest brackish water lagoon of Asia located in Orissa state. He also studied the algal succession on a Charaiguha rocky island on the way to Kalijai[23]. Diatoms were found dominant and appear maximally twice a year. The red alga *Polysiphonia* occurs from January to May and requires moderate salinity. Another red alga, *Ceramium* occurs from February to April under higher salinity levels of the lake. *Grateloupia* species does not grow at the water edge but occupies the lowermost zone to avoid damage by waves and requires higher salinity for its profuse growth. Diatoms and red algae grow in the deeper waters of the lake even in feeble light due to chromatic adaptation. In addition, the green algae *Chaetomorpha* and *Enteromorpha* also occur in the lake. Indian Council of Agricultural Research funded a project on "Mass culture of Algae" in 1968, Prof. Parija along with Prof. H. Pattnaik and his students surveyed blue-green algae in soils of Cuttack[30,31], and studied the effect of growth and change of pigmentation in a few blue-green algae under different light intensities and temperature[29].

Plant physiology, especially in rice

The Government of Orissa, under the Department of Agriculture, sanctioned a Rice Research Scheme in April 1937 in which Prof. Parija was entrusted to work on the physiological aspects of rice plants in Ravenshaw college. The project continued after its completion in 1941 with fresh funding from the Imperial Council of Agricultural Research and continued till March 1945. Prof. Parija and his team worked on this rice project for eight continuous years and contributed several new findings[19]. They reported that flood resistance was induced in rice plants by pre-sowing of the seeds at a low temperature (2-5^{0}C) for 6 days, and anaerobiosis for three days or anaerobiosis for three days plus low temperature for three days. The treated plants survived submersion better than the control plants and yielded higher. The flood-resistant varieties of rice revealed peculiar anatomy as the presence of a sclerenchymatous band around the cortical lacunae in their stems. Drought resistance was further inducted in the rice plants by pre-sowing seeds at a high temperature (40 to 42^{0}C). Likewise, salt resistance in rice was induced by pre-sowing seed with 1.7% of common salt solution. Such varieties revealed the presence of highly suberized exodermis in the roots[18,20,21,22,24]. He achieved dormancy break in winter paddies through seed treatment with smoking, drying, de-husking, and soaking in the juice of germinated grains[19].

Since these works were carried out at Ravenshaw College, Cuttack, Orissa became a center for rice research. The Government of India established a Central Rice Research Institute (CRRI) at Cuttack, later named as National Rice Research Institute, NRRI, in which Prof. Parija played a key role. In recognition of his contribution to developing drought, flood, and saline-resistant paddy seeds, one of the high-yielding strains of paddy developed at CRRI was named after him. Orissa is an agriculture-based state, at that time was prone to frequent floods and droughts, his research triggered the state Government to establish the Orissa University of Agriculture and Technology in Bhubaneswar, the second oldest agriculture University in India.

Prof. Parija was the President of the Indian Botanical Society held at Allahabad University in 1930. He was also the General President of the Indian Science Congress (47th Indian Science Congress) held in Bombay in 1960, where he delivered the Presidential lecture titled "Impact of Society on Science"[25]. He had written several popular science articles, one of which was published in Everyman's Science[26], the rest were mainly in Odia language. In 1960 he was awarded the Birbal Sahani Gold Medal by the Indian Botanical Society; Prof. Sahani was a close friend since his Cambridge days. In a joint expedition near Nagpur, he picked up a fossil fruit not known earlier, which Prof. Sahani named *Enigmocarpon parijae* in his honor. Upon subsequent discoveries of the flowers and seeds of this fruit, Prof. Sahani changed the name to *Sahianthus parijae*, associating with both of them. Prof Parija was a member of the Governing body of Birbal Sahani Institute of Paleobotany at Lucknow founded by Prof. Sahani.

Educator, Academic Legacy, and Achievements

Prof. Parija joined Ravenshaw College, Cuttack, India as a Professor of Botany in August 1921, and worked for 24 years until 1945. He was the Founder Fellow of the National Academy of Sciences, Allahabad, and National Institute of Science of India; Fellow of the Royal Asiatic Society, Calcutta, and Berkely Memorial Gold Medal (1966); awarded Order of the British Empire (1943); received Birbal Sahani Gold Medal by Indian Botanical Society (1960), and Doctor of Science (Honoris Causa) from Patna University (1944), Utkal University (1949), Sri Venkateswara University (1962), and Sambalpur University (1972).

Academic Administration:

He served as the Principal of Ravenshaw College, Cuttack from 1936-1945, Vice-Chancellor of the Utkal University (1943-48), (1955-65) for three terms (Fig. 1-3), Pro-Chancellor of Utkal University (1951-55), and Pro-Vice Chancellor, Banaras Hindu University for 3 years (1948-51).

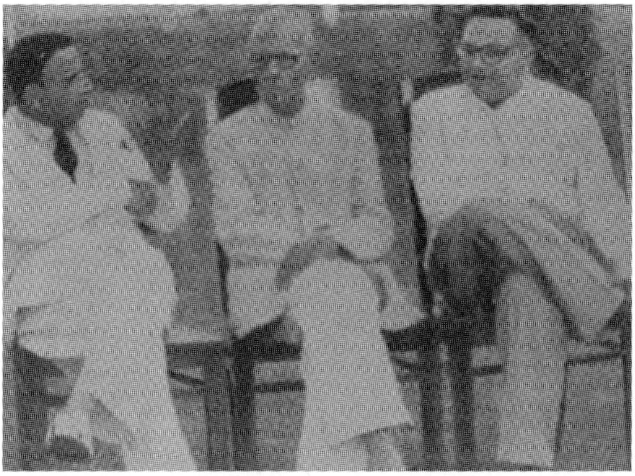

Figure 1: Prof. P. Parija (center) with Sri Chintaman Deshmukh, Chairman, UGC (left), and Prof. Panchanan Maheswari, Vice-Chancellor, University of Delhi (right) in 1957.

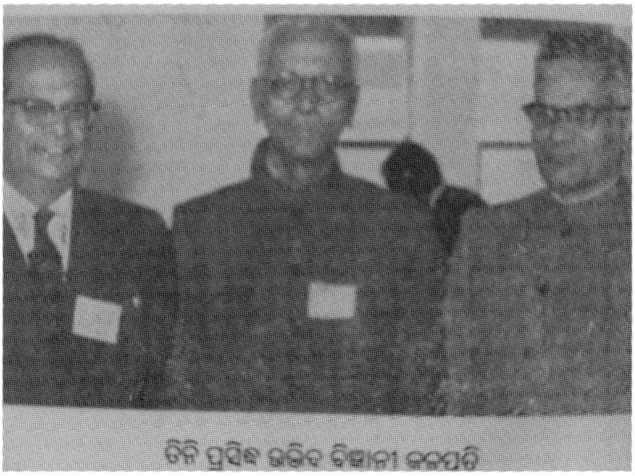

Figure 2: Prof. Sriranjan, Vice-Chancellor, Allahabad University (left), Prof. P. Parija, Vice-Chancellor, Utkal University (center), and Prof. Amarchand Joshi, Vice-Chancellor, Punjab University (right) in 1957.

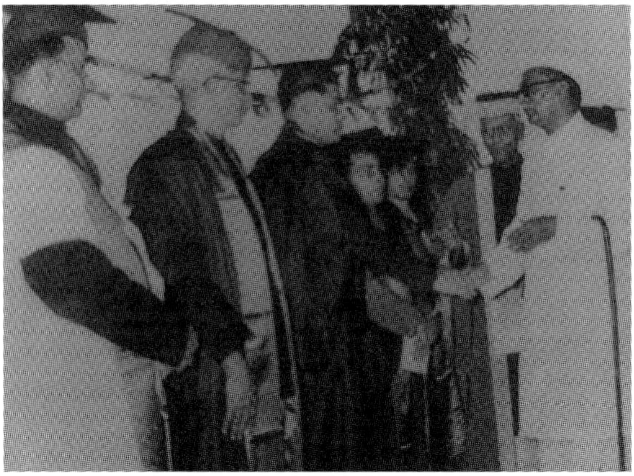

Figure 3: Prof. Parija with Dr. Rajendra Prasad, the then President of India during a convocation at Utkal University.

Service to Professional Bodies:

He was Elected as President of the Indian Botanical Society in 1930 (Fig. 4), General President of the Indian Science Congress in 1960 (Fig. 5-7), Vice-President of the International Botanical Society twice in 1959 and 1964, and Served as the Editor of the Journal of Indian Botanical Society (1935-42).

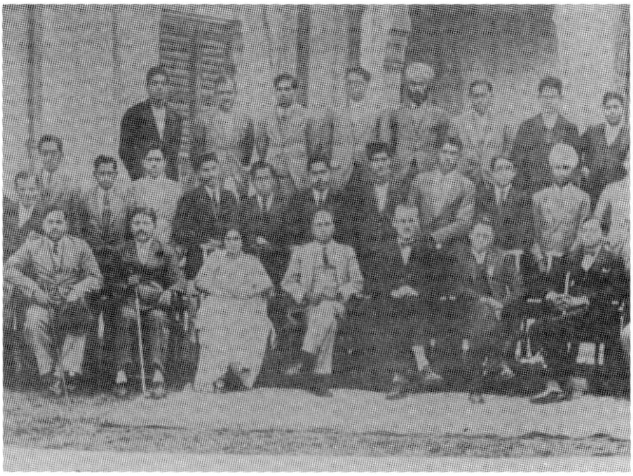

Figure 4: Prof. P. Parija (Sitting, 2nd from right), President of the 9th Annual Conference of the Indian Botanical Society at Allahabad University in 1930.

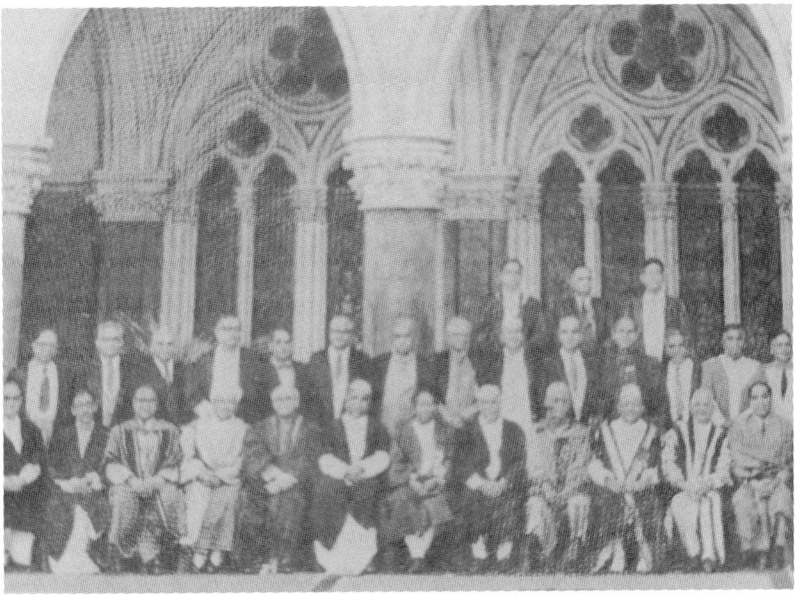

Figure 5: Prof. P. Parija, President of the 47th session of the Indian Science Congress at Bombay with Pt. Jawaharlal Nehru, Prime Minister of India (both sitting in the center) with scientists and delegates in 1960.

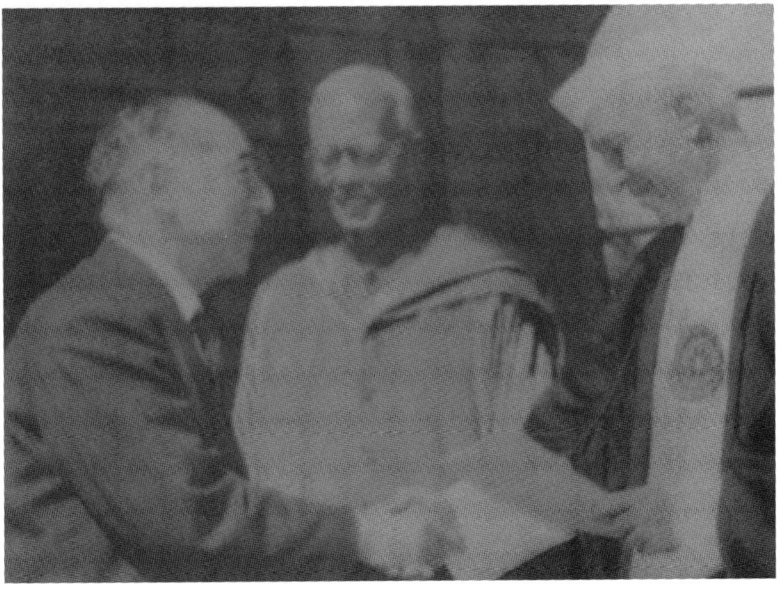

Figure 6: Prof. P. Parija (center) with Pt. Jawaharlal Nehru (right) at the 47th Indian Science Congress, Bombay in 1960.

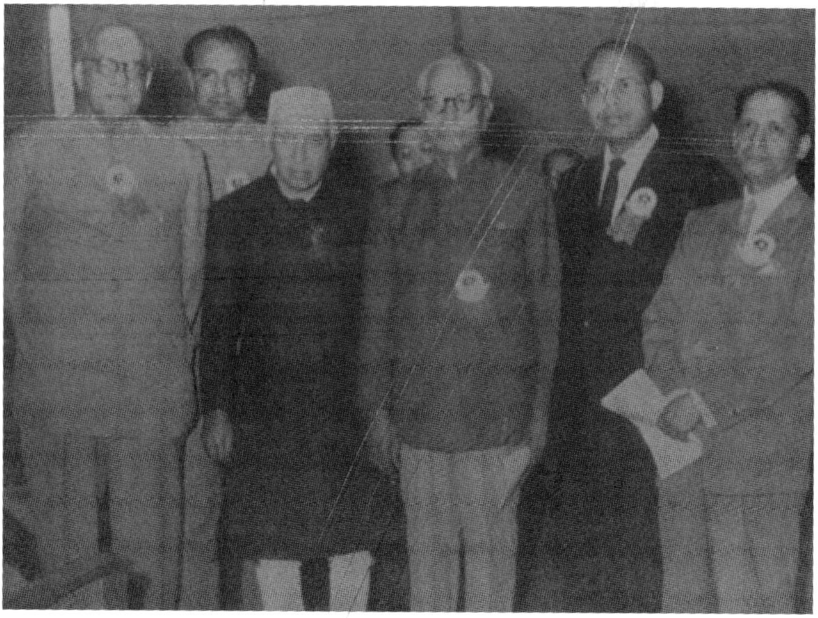

Figure 7: Group photograph of the 49th session of the Indian Science Congress at Ravenshaw College, Cuttack. L-R. Sri Sukhantkar, Governor of Orissa, Sri. Bijayananda Patnaik (Biju Patnaik), Chief Minister, Orissa, Pt. Jawaharlal Nehru, Prime Minister of India, Prof. P. Parija, Vice-Chancellor, Utkal University, Prof. Radhanath Ratha, Professor of Psychology, Utkal University, and Prof. Bansidhar Samantarai (Professor of Botany, Ravenshaw College) in 1962.

External Services and Social Life

- Director of Agriculture, Government of Orissa in 1945
- Member of the Central Advisory Board of Forest Utilization by the Government of India, 1949
- Chairman of the Expert Committee of the Ministry of Food and Agriculture by the Government of India in 1953
- Member of the Official Language Commission (1955-56) by the Government of India
- Chairman of the Geological Education Committee of the Government of India, 1946
- Member of the University Formation Committee in 1938 by the Government of Orissa, which leads to the formation of Utkal University as the 17th University of India in 1942

- Chairman of the General Education Committee of the University Grants Commission,1963
- Chairman of the Inter-Universities Board comprising Vice-Chancellors of India and Ceylon, 1961
- President of Utkal Sahitya Samaj (1934-38)
- Elected as Member of the Orissa Legislative Assembly (MLA) as an independent candidate from Ballikuda Constituency of Orissa in 1952;
- Awarded Padma Bhusan by the Government of India, 1955 (Fig. 8).

Besides, while at Cambridge, he served as the President of the Indian Majilis Society and "Unit League", a form of Indian students whose aim was the unity and integrity of India. Some of the well-known Indian students of these societies were - Srikrishna Memon, George Mathai, Rabindra Nath Banerjee, Subhas Chandra Bose (Netaji), Y. J. Taraporabala, R. S. Inamdar, Kamta Prasad, C.V. Hanumata Rao, K.M. Khadiae, Birbal Sahani, T. Ekambaram, K. C. Mehta, C. D. Deshmukh, D. M. Bose, S. P. Agharkar, who later established themselves as Professor, Scientist, ICS officer, Lawyer, Ministers and Patriots working for the Independence of our country. When the British Government formed the Lord Lytton Committee in 1918 to examine the difficulties and problems of Indian students in England, he was among the three persons (Khadia, Subhas, and Parija) selected by the Indian Majlis to speak on their behalf. When Lokamanya Bal Gangadhar Tilak visited Cambridge, he stayed with Parija in his lodge and addressed Indian Majlis.

He was well-loved and respected in the botanical and scientific fraternity Besides, political figures like Netaji Subhas Chandra Bose (born in Cuttack and studied at Ravenshaw Collegiate school), Chakrabarty Raj Gopalchari, Smt. Sarojini Naidu were his guest while he was the Principal of Ravenshaw college. Although he was in Government service, he was a passionate patriot. The freedom fighters of that era have recorded how Prof. Parija's house was a safe meeting place for Congress party meetings even when British rules declared the Party as an illegal organization. He used to give monetary assistance to many impoverished freedom fighters, reflecting his commitment to the cause of the Nation.

Acknowledgments

I feel it a great honor to write about Prof. Pranakrushna Parija, the founder of Botany teaching and research in the state of Odisha. I have consulted two books (in Odia language) to write the article. These are - Pranakrusha Parija, by Dr. Debakanta Mishra, National Book Trust, India, 2005, 150 pp; and Sikhayabit Pranakrushna Parija, Edited by. Dr. Gadadhar Mishra, Bidyapuri, Cuttak, 2000, 344 pp.

N.B. In the article Orissa, Calcutta and Bombay were mentioned in place of Odisha, Kolkata, and Mumbai which are new names, to maintain the naming as such, while he was a student and working as a professor and academic administrator. In the references, the research publications of Prof. Parija are listed year-wise, and the number is cited in the text wherever appropriate.

Bibliography

1. Blackman, F.F., Parija, P. (1928) Analytic studies in plant respiration. I. The respiration of a population of senescent ripening apples. Proc Royal Society, B 103, 412-445.
2. Parija, P. (1928) Analytic studies in plant respiration. II. The respiration of apples in nitrogen and its relation to respiration in air. Proc Royal Society, B 103, 446-490.
3. Parija, P. (1954) Analytic studies in plant respiration. Part IV to IX. F.F. Blackman, Cambridge University Press.
4. Parija, P. (1930) A preliminary note on the physiology of the seedlings of water hyacinth, *Eichhornia crassipes*. Agr J India 25, 386-391.
5. Parija, P. (1931) The law of modifications. Presidential address, 11th Annual session of the Indian Botanical Society, Nagpur. J Indian Bot Soc 10, 63-71.
6. Parija, P., Misra, P. (1933) The root thorn of *Bridelia pubencens* Kutz. J Ind Bot Soc 12, 227-233.
7. Parija, P., Saran, A.B. (1933) Variability of the osmotic strength of the sap of *Cuscuta reflexa*, Roxb. J Indian Bot Soc 12, 271-276.
8. Parija, P., Saran, A.B. (1934) The effect of light on the respiration of starved leaves. Ann Botany 48, 347-354.
9. Parija, P. (1934) Physiological investigations on water hyacinth *Eichhornia crassipes* in Orissa with notes on some other aquatic weeds. Indian J Agr Sci 4, 399-429.

10. Parija, P. (1934) A note on the reappearance of water hyacinth seedlings in cleared tanks. Indian J Agr Sci 4, 1049.
11. Parija, P. (1934) Water hyacinth. Agr and Livestoc in India 5, 124-125.
12. Parija, P., Mallick, P. (1936) The mechanism of the bursting of the fruits of *Impatiens balsamina* Linn. J Indian Bot Soc 15, 59-61.
13. Parija, P., Mallick, P. (1936) The formation of cuticles in relation to external conditions. J Indian Bot Soc 15, 63-70.
14. Parija, P., Samal, K. (1936) Extra floral nectaries in *Tecoma capensis* Lindl. J Indian Bot Soc 15, 241-246.
15. Parija, P., Samantarai, B (1939) March of transpiration of a leaf since its measurable stage to its fall. J Indian Bot Soc 18, 65-77.
16. Parija, P., Mallik, P. (1940) Nature of the reserve foods in seed and their resistance to high temperature. J Indian Bot Soc 19, 223-229.
17. Parija, P. (1943) On the pre-sowing treatment and phasic development. Curr Sci 12, 88-89.
18. Parija, P. Physiological studies in rice. In: Progress report of the Orissa Rice Research Scheme for 1937-38; 1938-39; 1939-40; 1940-41, 1941-42, and 1942-43, Orissa Govt. Press, Cuttack. 1939, 1940, 1941, 1942, 1943, and 1944.
19. Parija, P., Pillay, K.P. (1944) Inducing flood resistance in paddy by pre-sowing treatments. Curr Sci 13, 183-185.
20. Parija, P. (1945) Report of the Research scheme. Physiology of rice plant with particular reference to Hood, Salinity, and Drought, Orissa Govt. Press.
21. Parija, P, Pillay, K.P. (1945) Effect of pre-sowing treatment on the drought resistance in rice. Proc Natl Acad Sci India 15, 6-14.
22. Parija, P., Parija, B. (1946) Algal succession on a rocky island named Charaiguha in the Chilika lake. J Indian Bot Soc 25, 375-379.
23. Parija, P. (1960) Physiological studies in rice. J Indian Bot Soc 39, 335-350.
24. Parija, P. (1960) Impact of Society on Science. Presidential Address, 47th Indian Science Congress, Proc. Indian Sci. Congress, Part-11. 1-7.
25. Parija, P. (1967) Science, its basis and its impact on human thought. Everyman's Science 2, 20-24.
26. Parija, P. (1967) Xenocarpy in *Momordica dioica* Roxb. Curr Sci 36, 106-107.
27. Parija, P. (1968) Problems of Agriculture. Indian Agriculturist 12, 7-11.
28. Parija, P., Pattnaik, H., Rao, S.D. (1968) Effect of growth and change of pigmentation in blue-green algae in different light intensities and temperature. Proc Orissa Ass Adv Sci 1, 98-99.

29. Parija, P., Pattnaik, H., Mishra, R.K. (1968) Morphological studies of a new *Fischerella* species. Proc Orissa Ass Adv Sci 1, 106-107.
30. Parija, P., Pattnaik, H., Rao, S.D. (1969) Blue-green algae in soils of Cuttack. Prakruti, Utkal Univ J Sci 6, 183-186.

AUTHOR PROFILE

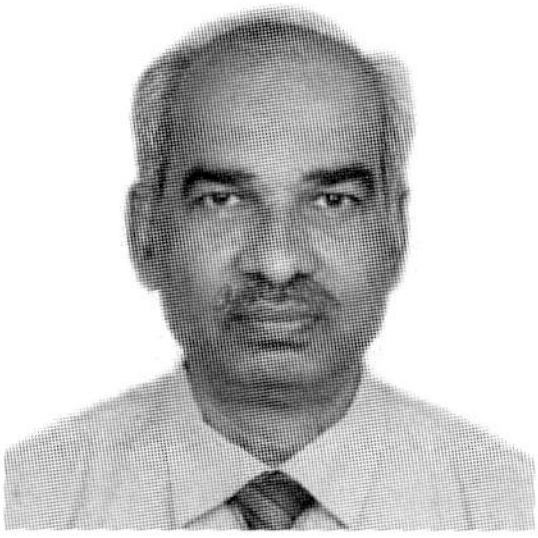

Prof. Siba Prasad Adhikary (M.Sc. Botany, Gold medalist of Berhampur University; Ph.D. and D.Sc. in Botany), had taught and administered in the University system for 39 years; Professor from 2002 to June 2009 at Utkal University, Professor of Biotechnology from July 2009 to April 2019 at Visva-Bharati, Santiniketan and Vice-Chancellor of F. M. University in Odisha. He Carried out research on (1) Nitrogen fixation and biofertilizers; (2) Biodiversity, Genomics, and bioprospecting of algae and cyanobacteria in extreme environments, and (3) Biodeterioration of stone monuments of India and technology for their conservation. Worked as a Postdoc as well as visiting Fellow in Germany, Japan, Czech Republic, Italy, Slovakia, and Hungary at different times from 1982 to 2014. He has supervised 27 students for their Ph.D. and has published 172 research papers in peer-reviewed journals, 62 chapters in edited books, and authored five books. He received the Samanta Chandra Sekhar Award in Life Sciences by Orissa Bigyan Academy, Government of Odisha, 1999; UGC Research Award, 1999; Lifetime achievement Award in Algae by KIA, Chennai, 2012; Dr. B.P. Pal National Environmental Fellowship Award on Biodiversity in 2012 by MOEF-CC, Government of India, 2012; Fellow of Indian Botanical Society, 1986 and Fellow of the National Academy of Agriculture Sciences, 2008. He served as President of Orissa Botanical Society (2016-17) and President of Probir Chatterjee Research Foundation, Kolkata (2010-2018).

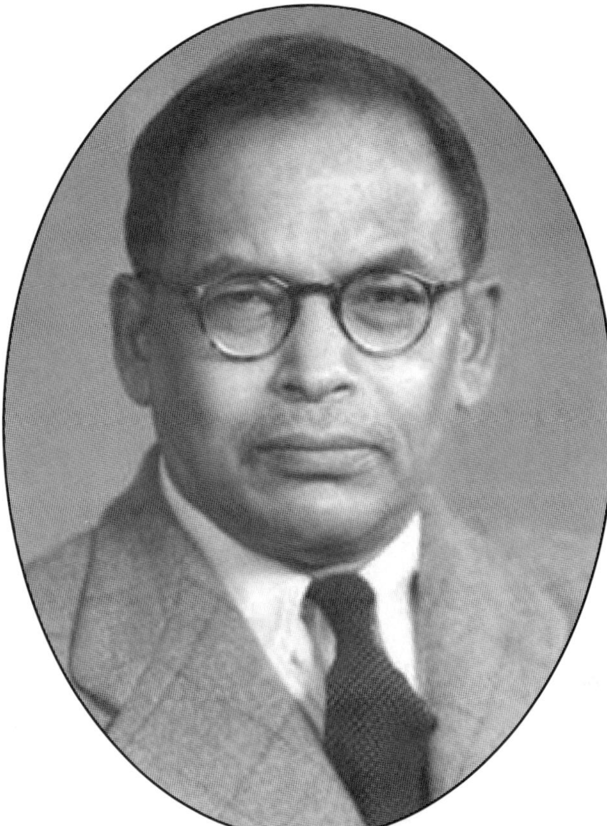

Meghnad Saha

(6 October 1893 - 16 February 1956)

MEGHNAD SAHA: AN EXTRAORDINARY ASTROPHYSICIST

Sheo Kumar Mishra

Early Life

India has a rich scientific heritage. Among many great Indian Scientists of modern times, Prof. Meghnad Saha has a special place. He was born on 6 October 1893 in Shiortali, a village about 45 km from Dhaka (Capital of the present-day Bangladesh) in the then-undivided Bengal province of India, to Jagannath Saha and Bhuvaneshwari Devi. He was the fifth child of his parents [2]. His childhood was full of struggle. His father was a general shopkeeper and could not afford the education of his children. None of his siblings could go beyond primary education, his father wanted Meghnad to assist in running the shop.

Education

In 1900, he joined his native primary school at the age of seven, always worried about the continuation of his studies. Fortunately, he was supported by a local doctor, Mr. Ananth Kumar Das. He stood first in the entire Dhaka district and was awarded a monthly scholarship of Rs. 4. In 1905, he went to Government Collegiate School for further studies. Besides the scholarship, he used to receive five Jainath and two rupees Purva Banga Baishya Samiti, per month. In 1905, the British Government decided to partition Bengal which invited widespread opposition from across the Bengal. The Governor of East Bengal Bamfilde Fuller came to visit the school, along with his friends he boycotted this tour and was expelled from the school, and the scholarship was withdrawn. Fortunately, he got admitted to the Kishori Lal Jubilee Vidyalaya with a fee waiver and a small amount of stipend. He secured the first position in the entire East Bengal. In 1911, he passes his intermediate examinations from the Dhaka College, Dhaka. There he learned German from Prof. Nagendra Nath Sen, who had done his doctorate in Vienna.

In 1913, he received a Bachelor of Science degree with honors in Mathematics (B.Sc.) from the Presidency College, Kolkata securing the second position. Satyendra Nath Bose got the first position. In 1915, he did his Masters in

Applied Mathematics from the same college, both Saha and Bose stood first in their respective subjects *viz*. Saha in Applied Mathematics and Bose in Pure Mathematics. Besides Satyendra Nath Bose, Gyan Ghosh and JN Mukherjee were his classmates; and Jagdish Chandra Basu and Prafulla Chand Rai were his teachers. While studying at Presidency College, Saha also joined Anushilan Samiti to take part in the freedom movement. He met nationalist leaders like Subhash Chandra Bose and Rajendra Prasad. Amiya Chandra Banerjee, a famous mathematician at Allahabad University, was very close to him.

In 1916, he was appointed lecturer at the Department of Applied Mathematics, and subsequently also to the Department of Physics, at the University College of Science. Though never studied physics beyond under-graduation due to hard work and self-motivation, he succeeded in teaching physics to post-graduate students but developed a lifelong interest in astrophysics, particularly in the theory of thermal ionization.

Contributions to the Science

In 1919, he wrote a paper on 'Selective Radiation Pressure' explaining the selective role of radiation pressure on the atoms, negating the action of gravity. But due to financial reasons he could publish his article as a short note in the Astrophysical Journal; and a detailed article in the Science Journal of Calcutta University. Later on, in the same year he published two more papers in the Philosophical Magazine and Physical Review. Those days Calcutta University did not offer Ph.D. degrees. He submitted his papers for the Doctor of Science degree, which was conferred to him in 1919. He aha received The Premchand Roychand Scholarship from Calcutta University for his dissertation on the 'Harvard Classification of Stellar Spectra.', which allowed him to work with Alfred Fowler in London for the first five months and Nernst's laboratory in Berlin for the remaining 19 months.

In 1920, he published four outstanding papers in astronomy - 'Ionisation of the Solar Chromosphere'; 'On the Harvard Classification of Stars'; 'On Elements in the Sun'; 'On the Problems of Temperature-Radiation of Gases;' and 'Origin of Lines in Stellar Spectra.' He received Griffith Prize (1920) from Calcutta University. Later on, he published his famous paper 'Theory of Thermal Ionization of elements' using thermodynamics and quantum theory. The theory allowed the interpretation of stellar spectra. He developed the Saha Ionization equation that can be used to determine the temperature of stars and the estimation of the amount of chemical elements present in stars. It became possible to predict the spectral classes of stars based on their actual temperatures.

In 1921, he returned to India from Europe. He joined the University of Calcutta as the Khaira Professor of Physics. But due to a lack of funds, required infrastructure, and research opportunities, he moved to Allahabad University in 1923 as professor and head of the Department of Physics. From 1923 to 1938, he served at Allahabad University. However, the situation at Allahabad University was far worse than at Calcutta University. He wrote his '*A textbook of Heat* (with B N Srivastava) in 1931; a concise version of the book for graduate students was published as '*Junior Textbook of Heat*'. In 1927 he became a Fellow of the Royal Society. He returned to Calcutta University in July 1938 as the Palit Professor. He served there as head of the department of physics and dean of the faculty of science. He remained there till his death in 1956. He was the President of the Indian Science Congress of 1934.

Besides, science, he had a deep interest in the History of Ancient India, Biology, and Archeology. Prof Saha translated the works of Einstein. Like him, he was in favor of the positive use of nuclear power.

Saha and New Indian calendar

India is geo-culturally a vast nation, prior to independence the country was following the Gregorian calendar, which suffers from shortcomings such as – the inability to evenly split the 365 into halves or quarters, no day-date connections, leap years, etc. Further, it has no respect for its cultural heritage and regional date-management systems. While local calendars were unscientific – misestimation of the duration of the year by 0.01656 days – which meant that every 1,400 years, the New Year will arrive 23.2 days ahead of the Gregorian calendar. After independence, in 1952, a "Calendar Reform Committee", was constituted under the chairmanship of Prof. Meghnad Saha. By November 1955, after studying more than 30 local variations, the committee submitted its report to the government, outlining the revised, accurate, uniform 'Indian National Calendar' to "re-create a new element of unity in India." In this work, he was assisted by several experts from abroad - Harold Spencer Jones, Britain's Astronomer Royal, and Donald Sadler of the UK's Royal Observatory. They offered precise solar and lunar data to help with recalculation. Austrian-American astronomer Otto Neugebauer helped to clear up the suspicions on date-keeping history around the world. Saha's team recommended an updated version of the Saka Era calendar, one that Indian astronomers have been using since 500 CE. They suggested it be put into effect on March 21, 1956, which lined up with the first day of Chaitra, 1878. To help with the switch, "the last month of the year, 1877, the month of Phalguna, which has a normal length of 30 days, will have an extra 6 or 7 days," the report advised. The Calendar aimed to fix the dates of religious observances and standardize date documents in rural areas.

Founder of Research Institutions and Associations

He founded two important institutions named Saha Institute of Nuclear Physics (the year 1951) and the Indian Association for the Cultivation of Science. He also founded the National Academy of Sciences established at Allahabad (now Prayagraj), and the Indian Physical Society. He played an active role in the foundation of the International Association of Astronomy. In 1953, he became the director of the Indian Science Association. To make science accessible to common people in simple language, he started the publication of a magazine called Science and Culture. He initiated the study of nuclear physics at the University of Calcutta.

Saha as Social Worker

When Bengal was partitioned, he worked hard for the resettlement of the people affected by the partition. During his childhood, he witnessed the horrors of floods. He studied the causes and prevention of floods and became a collaborator in many dam and power projects.

Saha in as a Parliamentarian

He contested the first Lok Sabha election from Calcutta in 1952 as an independent, winning it with an overwhelming majority. He worked on the National Planning Committee with Prime Minister Jawaharlal Nehru.

Honors and Awards

He was a fellow of the Royal Society (1927), the Indian National Science Academy, and the Indian Academy of Sciences. He was a winner of the J C Bose Medal.

1. Chairman, Indian Calendar Reform Committee of the CSIR
2. Member, University Education Commission
3. President, Indian Science Congress (1934)
4. President, Indian Association for the Cultivation of Science (IACS)
5. President, National Academy of Sciences in India (NASI), Allahabad (1932-1934)
6. President, Asiatic Society (1944-1946)
7. President, Indian National Science Academy (INSA) (1937-1938)
8. The INSA established a 'Meghnad Saha Medal' in his honour

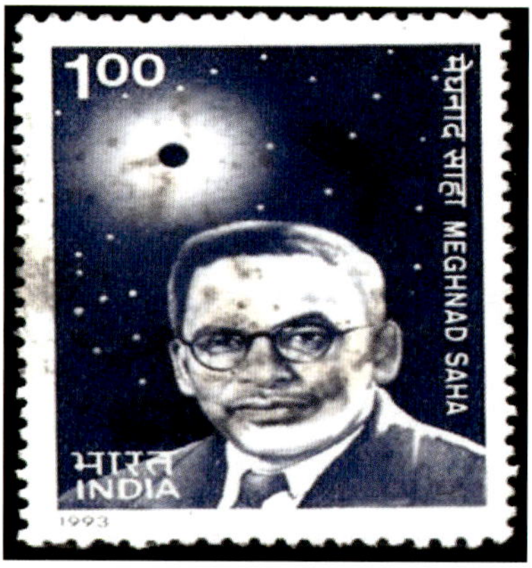

In 1993, to commemorate the birth centenary of Prof Saha, the Department of Posts, the Government of India, issued a postal stamp.

Personal Life

On 16 June 1918, Prof. Saha married Radharani, with whom he had three sons and three daughters.

Death

On 16 February 1956, on his way to the Rashtrapati Bhavan to attend a meeting of the Planning Commission, he collapsed and passed away due to heart failure. Paying homage to his mentor, Prof. D. S. Kothari said -

"The life of Saha was in a sense an integral part of the growth of scientific research and progress in India...His dedication to science, his forthrightness and utter disregard of personal comforts in the pursuit of his chosen vocation will long remain an inspiration and an example"

Bibliography

1. Kothari L.S., Vardya, M.S. (2002) Meghnad Saha, NCERT, New Delhi.
2. Ray, K. (1968) The Life and Work of Meghnad Saha, NCERT, New Delhi.
3. Sen, S.N. (1954) Meghnad Saha- His Life, Work and Philosophy, Sixtieth Birth Committee, Calcutta.
4. Joshi, M.M. (1993) Meghnad Saha: Centenary Souvenir, Allahabad University, Allahabad.
5. Lopez, R. (2021) Lend me your years: How the Indian National Calendar came into being, Hindustan Times, 02 January 2021.

AUTHOR PROFILE

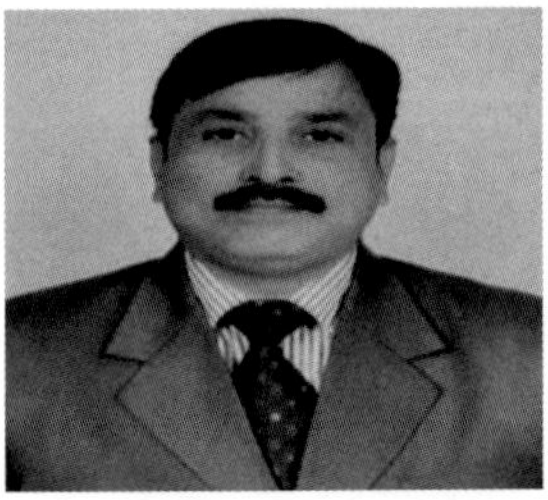

Dr. Sheo Kumar Mishra is an Associate Professor at the Department of Physics, Indira Gandhi national tribal university, Amarkantak, India. He completed his doctorate in Experimental Condensed Matter Physics/ Nanoscience from the J.K. Institute of Applied Physics and Technology, Department of Electronics and Communication, University of Allahabad; and did his post-doctoral training at the Saha Institute of Nuclear Physics, Kolkata, India, and from the University of Johannesburg, South Africa. To date, he has published 50 research articles in reputed journals.

Email: sheokmishra@igntu.ac.in

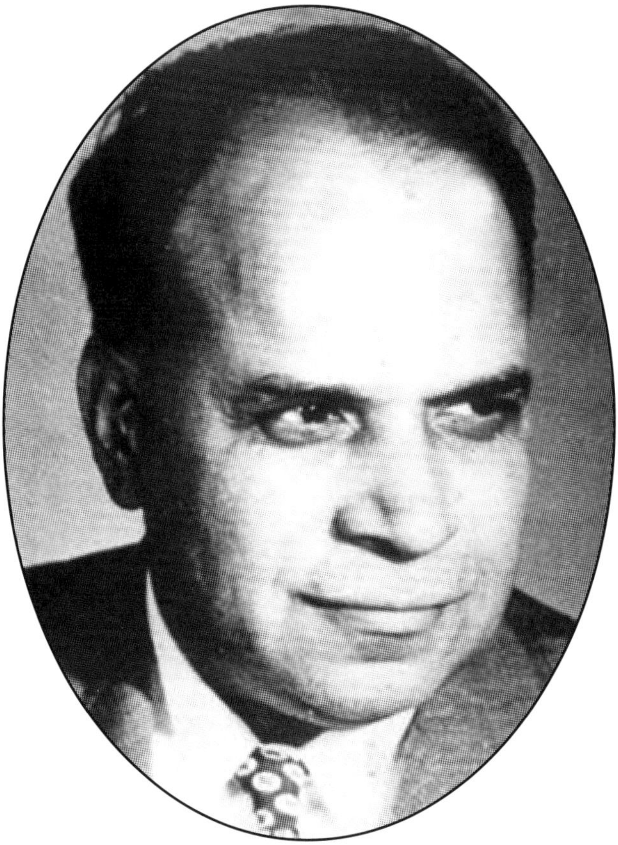

Yellapragada SubbaRow

(12 January 1895- 9 August 1948)

YELLAPRAGADA SUBBAROW: A SCIENTIFIC SAINT

Tantravahi Srinivasan

Prof. SubbaRow's life exemplifies how a dreamer, unfazed by life's obstacles, achieved for the greater good what humanity most needed at the time through his ceaseless efforts. He is a visionary with unyielding determination, which has allowed him to realize his dreams despite switching between fields. He has a strong desire for fame, but he has never promoted himself and is always generous in sharing or giving credit for scientific achievements. The field of science has possibly transformed him and revealed his true personality to the world. As evidenced by his publications, he has sacrificed his rights to phosphorus research for the career advancement of his supervisor and has always promoted his co-workers. He has always prioritized scientific progress over his own needs and desires. Here, I describe the journey of a dreamer who became a selfless achiever and leader whose contribution to science and humanity has yet to receive the recognition it deserves.

Personal Life

SubbaRow was an optimistic and determined individual. Since his childhood, he has encountered numerous challenges, but he was always able to find a solution at his level. In his youth, he adapted his thoughts and actions to the circumstances, but after realizing his life's purpose, he has become a man of resolve. Every event in his life illustrates how one may transform themselves and succeed. Problems that develop throughout a process might be viewed as impediments that prevent further progress, or as chances to improve one's thinking and performance. SubbaRow has achieved what the majority of others only dream of.

Childhood: A period of exposure and experience

Yellapragada SubbaRow was born into a traditional Brahmin family on January 12, 1895, in Bhimavaram, West Godavari district, Andhra Pradesh. He was the fourth of seven children, four boys, and three girls. His father, Jagannatham, was a revenue inspector, and his mother, Venkamma, was a traditional housewife. The salary of a revenue inspector could not be sufficient for a family of nine and he was brought up under difficult circumstances[1,2]. These experiences have motivated him to find a solution to his family's problem and execute it. Thus, SubbaRow planned to overcome poverty at thirteen by selling bananas in Varanasi, a famous pilgrim town. He left home secretly, but his absence was soon noticed and he was brought back. This incident has curtailed his freedom and his mother has kept a close watch on his activities. She also saw that he went to school and focused on his studies. SubbaRow completed his pre-high school education in Narasapur and Rajahmundry and his high school education at Hindu High School, Madras (now Chennai)[1]. He passed through a traumatic period in his schooling days due to the premature death of close relatives by disease. His father also passed away in 1913, when SubbaRow was 18. These experiences of SubbaRow may have changed his way of thinking and given him the idea to comprehend the losses and sufferings. Additionally, this probably impacted his academic performance, as it took him three attempts to pass the matriculation exam. He did his intermediate studies at Madras Presidency College [1,3]. Around this time, SubbaRow's future plans may have been influenced by maturity and thought. He had lost interest in worldly life and desired to join the Ramakrishna Mission as an ascetic. Again, his mother intervened and did not permit this deviation. The Mission advised him to pursue medical studies; by becoming a doctor, he could achieve the same goal of serving society and people as he would be joining the mission as an ascetic. He was probably partially convinced and followed his mother's directives. At about this time, he studied Hindu scriptures, the Bible, the Quran, and other religious literature[1,4]. This might have kept his balance between worldly life and understanding the world.

Young age: A period of comprehension, maturation, and dreams

Following the directives of his mother and the Ramakrishna Mission, he joined Madras Medical College in 1915. This was also made possible by the contributions of his friends and Kasturi Suryanarayana Murthy, a distant relative. In his early years as a student of allopathic medicine, he had a close call with death due to sprue, but ayurvedic treatment helped him recover. This has revealed to SubbaRow the inadequacies of western medicine in the early 20th century. He discovered that his miraculous recovery was attributable to herbal juices containing *Eclipta alba* as their primary ingredient. This has led him to become interested in the ayurvedic theory of pathogenesis and he has also contemplated combining the best aspects of western medicine and Ayurveda[4]. Mr. Murthy had a good understanding of SubbaRow and offered his daughter's hand to him. In 1919, two years before completing his medical studies, SubbaRow married Seshagiri, the 15-year-old younger daughter of Murthy[1].

The Indian Independence Movement had gained considerable momentum at the time. The vast majority of high school and college students participated either directly or indirectly. Under Gandhiji's influence, SubbaRow abandoned British surgical dress in favor of khadi surgical attire. This earned him the ire of his surgery Prof. M. C. Bradfield, who punished SubbaRow by undervaluing his surgery performance, as a result, he was awarded an LMS diploma instead of an MBBS degree in 1921[1,3]. Therefore, he was unable to join the Madras State Medical Service. He exercised the next best option by joining Dr. Lakshmypathi's Ayurvedic College as a lecturer in Anatomy and Physiology in the same year. After accepting a position at Ayurveda College, which paid him a very modest salary, he rented a small house where he, his wife, and his mother lived frugally[1]. His allopathically educated mind was exposed to Ayurveda to a greater degree. He endeavored to make the most of the available opportunity. During this period, he had the opportunity to meet Dr. Kenrick of Philadelphia University, who was in Madras on the Rockefeller Foundation's anti-hookworm campaign. After witnessing SubbaRow's boundless energy and desire to discover cures for diseases, the doctor advised him to enroll at Harvard Medical School (HMS) in Boston. This cue was enough to motivate the enthusiastic SubbaRow to work out a way to achieve it. He got admission to Harvard's School of Tropical Medicine that same year (1921), but tragically, both of his brothers contracted and died from Tropical Sprue that summer[1,5]. This unexpected and tragic event prevented him from enrolling at the Harvard School of Tropical Medicine that year. In addition, his earlier near-death experience with a sprue and his brothers' deaths from sprue profoundly impacted his inquisitive nature and the doctor in him. He made it his life's mission to find an effective remedy to cure tropical sprue. When he tried the second time, the admission was denied. However, his persistent request made Harvard Medical School relent and let him in a second time in 1923. This time, his wife is pregnant with their first child. His family members, including his father-in-law, initially opposed his attempt but later understood his life ambition. Mr. Murthy not only permitted him to go but also bore his travel and initial expenses[1].

Middle age: A period of realization of dreams

SubbaRow had to begin sacrificing his personal life in order to continue his education and make ends meet. His persistent efforts began to bear fruit, allowing him to conduct ground-breaking research and realize his dreams. He prioritized humanity over his family and strived to find cures for various diseases.

At the School of Tropical Medicine

SubbaRow traveled to the USA via London by steamer. His lack of funds prevented him from purchasing even a third-class ticket, so he was forced to travel in steerage. He managed the month-long voyage between September and October of 1923 without any problems. He arrived in Boston on October 26, 1923, and enrolled in a diploma program at the Harvard School of Tropical Medicine. This was necessary for him to gain admission to the medical school, as his Indian degree was deemed insufficient for his admission there. He did not get a scholarship or an internship because his LMS certificate course did not qualify him for one. Prof. Richard Strong, the Director of the Harvard School of Tropical Medicine, was very helpful and provided him with working facilities in the laboratory and a scholarship. After attending classes from 9 a.m. to 5 p.m. Monday through Friday, he worked from 7 p.m. to 1 a.m. at the Peter Brent Bright Hospital in Boston to supplement his income. Very little time remained for sleep or other activities. He was compelled to labor in order to survive and advance. SubbaRow used to write lengthy letters to his relatives regularly, particularly to his wife (in Telugu) and father-in-law (in English), reporting on his life in the United States and inquiring about his people in India[1,3,4].

On April 12, 1924, Seshagiri gave birth to a baby boy in Anaparthi, her parents' place. SubbaRow was not very excited about it. He was a great believer in astrology, fate, the existence of the soul, etc. His astrological calculations predicted that his son would not survive long after birth. Unfortunately, the prediction came true and on December 24, 1924, the boy succumbed to Erysipelas (Sarpi), less than nine months after birth[1,2]. During this time, SubbaRow was also working in Strong's laboratory to realize his goal of finding a cure for tropical sprue. After working for one year, SubbaRow switched over to biochemistry as he was not happy with his background in chemistry[6].

At the Department of Biochemistry

In June 1924, after earning his diploma in tropical medicine, SubbaRow joined under the supervision of Dr. Cyrus Hartwell Fiske for a Ph.D. at the Department of Biochemistry, Harvard Medical School[1,4]. Thus began the phase of discovery in his career. Along with Cyrus Fiske in 1925, he developed the Fiske-SubbaRow method for estimating phosphorus concentrations in body fluids and tissues[7]. In 1927 and 1929, Fiske and SubbaRow discovered phosphocreatine[8] and adenosine triphosphate (ATP)[9], respectively. Fiske and SubbaRow could not get the due credit for identifying ATP as Karl Lohmann announced similar findings at the 13th International Physiological Congress held in Boston, where Fiske and SubbaRow were also present. Lohmann used the Fiske–SubbaRow method for phosphate analysis. Lohmann had some discussions earlier with Fiske on this, from which Lohmann gained much. However, Fiske saw that SubbaRow also presented their work at the same conference[1]. SubbaRow earlier presented his work on ATP to the New York Academy of Sciences on the isolation of ATP from muscle extract, a compound of adenosine containing three phosphates, one of which is linked to ribose. However, the abstract was not published in the proceedings. Had the abstract been printed in the proceedings, Fiske and SubbaRow perhaps could have shared the Nobel Prize with Lohmann[6]. In 1930, SubbaRow earned a Ph.D. in biochemistry from Harvard Medical School for his ground-breaking work in phosphorus biochemistry, which he documented in six seminal papers.

As an employee at Harvard Medical School

Soon after receiving his doctorate, SubbaRow was appointed as a Teaching Fellow at Harvard Medical School, a junior teaching position that allowed him to conduct independent research. However, he was denied Ph.D. students, a separate laboratory and analytical facilities, the opportunity to collaborate with other scientists on research, etc., usually enjoyed by higher faculty members. This severely restricted his creative genius. He had to be satisfied with working alone and hard at a time when it was common for a scientist of his calibre to have research projects, research assistants, and collaborators. During the early 1930s, SubbaRow continued to work on phosphorus compounds extracted from the spleen, liver, pancreas, and kidney and isolated 7–8 compounds. As he was still formally under the supervision of Fiske, the latter had taken the responsibility of writing up the work for publication. But Fiske, inexplicably, never did it. In this context, George Hitchings, (1988 Nobel Prize in Medicine), who was SubbaRow's colleague in Fiske's laboratory, is believed to have remarked in 1965, that "SubbaRow had isolated several phosphorus compounds which were most likely nucleotides associated with RNA synthesis, and they had to be rediscovered by other scientists because he was not allowed to publish that work"[1,2,3]. This shows how SubbaRow's efforts were in vain, possibly delaying the understanding of RNA considerably.

In 1935, SubbaRow had to face a very unusual situation. Fiske was being considered for promotion from Associate Professor to Full Professor. For this, the work on phosphorus, phosphocreatine, and ATP was being taken as the basis, but the entire planning of the research and the imaginative ideas leading to it had to be Fiske's. It was known then that SubbaRow's share of credit for these discoveries was probably more or at least equal to Fiske's. Nevertheless, to save the day for Fiske, SubbaRow declared that he did not contribute to the ideas but provided a pair of hands to implement Fiske's ideas in the laboratory. It was a terrible sacrifice because SubbaRow could never fulfill his dream of becoming a full faculty member and having his own research team at HMS. He was appointed as an instructor in 1936 and an associate in 1938, which were still not completely independent teaching positions[1,5].

A career at Lederle Laboratories

The liver extract work attracted the medical community's attention at the time because it was recognized as a cure for several deficiency diseases, including some forms of anaemia. Extraction, concentration, and purification of organ constituents require a high level of expertise and extensive experience. SubbaRow had both in abundance. William Bell, the President of American Cyanamid, the parent company of Lederle Laboratories at Pearl River, New York State, had noticed the unequalled expertise of SubbaRow and had enlisted his services to guide them in making liver and other organ preparations. SubbaRow used to spend his weekends at Lederle Laboratories (Pearl River is about 340 km from Boston). Lederle had a rabbit farm to make sera and vaccines and use the animals to test new medicinal preparations[1,10].

SubbaRow's intelligence, dedication, hard work, and honesty were all recognized by the Lederle management, who felt he was underappreciated in the HMS. William Bell took advantage of the situation and offered him a position at Lederle Laboratories. This ultimately resulted in SubbaRow relocating as the Associate Director of Research in May 1940. The Department of Biological Chemistry at HMS gave SubbaRow a grand farewell party with speeches of plaudits and a dinner befitting a well-established faculty member. In 1942, he was elevated to the position of Director of Research. During his tenure at Lederle, he was instrumental in identifying and isolating compounds of immense importance to human well-being, such as folic acid, antifolates, antibiotics, etc.[1,2,3,4,5,6,11].

Contributions to science

Individually and as a member of a team, he made significant contributions to science that are still utilized in the modern healthcare system. Modern medicine was in its infancy when he began his studies and his discoveries have propelled modern science forward by leaps and bounds. In India, the once-famous Ayurveda is now considered an alternative medicine system, whereas allopathy or modern medicine is the predominant medical system.

Fiske – SubbaRow method

SubbaRow is a doctoral student under the supervision of Dr. Cyrus Hartwell Fiske, Department of Biochemistry, Harvard Medical School. The department under the headship of Prof. Otto Folin was working on the development of methods for quantitative and qualitative analysis of blood, urine, and tissue constituents. In the process, a method for the estimation of phosphorus in tissues was developed where hydroquinone was used to reduce the phosphate derivative to blue color. It was a slow procedure that was affected by many different substances. SubbaRow was tasked with assisting Cyrus Fiske in resolving the issues with the phosphorus technique. Fiske has directed SubbaRow to find a chemical that, in small amounts, would completely convert the phosphorus in the prepared tissue into a blue substance in as little time as possible. In addition, he also instructed that the chemical should not interact with other tissue components or pre-treatment chemicals, nor should phosphorus digestion with sulphuric acid be required[12].

The first indication of the success of the SubbaRow protocol was when it produced nearly 20% more color than the previously designed protocol containing hydroquinone. However, it required 30 minutes of incubation to produce the maximum color. His next significant success occurred when he substituted hydroquinone with 1,2,6-amino-naphthol-sulphonic acid. In less than a minute, the bright blue color was achieved, which is significantly more intense than the color achieved using the hydroquinone protocol. SubbaRow wasn't satisfied because 1,2,6-amino-naphthol-sulphonic acid was difficult to prepare. He continued his research and discovered an isomer of 1,2,6-amino-naphthol-sulphonic acid that was widely available under the trade name 1,2,4-acid (1,2,4-amino-naphthol-sulphonic acid) (1,7,12,13). He then identified the protocol as a highly sensitive and accurate colorimetric method for estimating the levels of inorganic phosphorus, organic phosphorus, organic phosphates, and lipoid phosphorus in human tissues. SubbaRow proudly claimed that the protocol, "is correct to 1/100,000th of a grain". Fiske and SubbaRow demonstrated the new phosphorus method at the annual meeting of the American Society of Biological Chemists on December 29, 1924. This study was published in the Journal of Biological Chemistry as "The Colorimetric Determination of Phosphorus." (Fiske, C. H., and SubbaRow, Y. (1925) J. Biol. Chem. 66, 375–400). This publication is one of the most cited in the history of biochemistry and is mentioned in biochemistry textbooks in the same year[1,2,3,5,12].

Phosphocreatine and ATP

SubbaRow was analyzing different biological samples for phosphorus and was also trying to understand the relationship between blood sugar and insulin. He concurrently recalled the work of Frederick Banting, which demonstrated that insulin injections control blood sugar and save the lives of diabetics. He investigated further for 18 months, but without success. The work of German biochemist Embden, who stated that blood sugar and phosphorus combine to form a hexose phosphoric ester that breaks down glycogen in the muscle to lactic acid, provided the impetus to focus on muscular contraction. By that time, Hill and Meyerhof's work, which won them the 1922 Nobel Prize for medicine and physiology, had led people to think that glycogen is the source of energy that muscles need to contract[14].

SubbaRow worked on muscle filtrates for the estimation of phosphorus and demonstrated that there was a delayed formation of blue color with the muscle filtrate. He inferred that certain compounds may release phosphorus as a chemical reaction progresses. The mysterious color-delaying substance was found to be a compound that contains an equimolar amount of creatine and phosphate which was named phosphocreatine. It accounted for two-thirds of the phosphorus in the resting muscle and was depleted when the muscle became functional, giving rise to inorganic phosphorus. It reformed as the muscle relaxed[8]. When it was first presented by Fiske in front of the American Society of Biological Chemists at Rochester in April 1927, this work caused quite a stir in the scientific community. This study was published in the Science and Journal of Biological Chemistry in 1927[14].

SubbaRow further studied the inorganic phosphorus that increased as phosphocreatine decreased and identified it as a chemical in which adenylic acid is linked to two extra molecules of phosphoric acid. He completely studied the catabolism of phosphocreatinine and proved that one or two phosphate groups break away from ATP by hydrolysis during muscle contraction, which releases energy and results in the formation of adenosine diphosphate (ADP) or adenosine monophosphate (AMP). ATP is regenerated from these molecules by the reaction with phosphocreatinine[9]. This is the energy cycle that drives biochemical reactions in living organisms. These findings were published in 1929 in the journal "Science," which helped SubbaRow in getting his doctorate as well as disproved the claims of Hill and Meyerhof on muscular contraction, for which they were even awarded the Noble Prize. Moreover, this also led to the award of a fellowship to SubbaRow by the Rockefeller Foundation[14].

SubbaRow and Fiske did not receive full credit for their ATP work because Karl Lohmann had announced similar findings just before SubbaRow and Fiske. Lohmann got the Nobel Prize for this discovery. Currently, Lohmann, Fiske, and SubbaRow are all recognized as co-discoverers of ATP, despite the fact that only Lohmann's name is mentioned in most of the books. Both groups published their work at about the same time in 1929[1,6].

Folic acid

During his doctoral studies, SubbaRow interacted frequently with Gordon Alles, an assistant to Edwin Cohn working on the isolation of antipernicious anaemic factor (APAF). Gordon Alles valued SubbaRow's recommendations greatly because of his expertise in removing protein from liver tissue. Alles was unable to continue the work and moved to California for another diabetes-related assignment, where he tragically passed away. SubbaRow took over Alles' unfinished task of isolating APAF. In addition, pernicious anaemia and sprue were believed to share the same treatment due to their similar symptoms. The fact that he survived the sprue while his brother did not has also motivated him[2,15].

SubbaRow made several liver extracts, and Bernard Jacobson, a medical student, assisted him with the APAF animal experiments. Later, Jacobson established himself at Massachusetts General Hospital, where he tried on patients the promising liver fractions from animal experiments. In patients, the most promising 3 mg fraction proved ineffective. Later, SubbaRow precipitated the promising extracts, which were then administered to patients to their advantage. During the subsequent purification procedure, charcoal was used to decolorize the fractions, and the resulting concentrate or crystals were less active. He hypothesized that the principal active components may have been absorbed by the charcoal and experimented with several extraction methods to retrieve them. He eventually achieved success with ethyl alcohol, which once again demonstrated potential efficacy in patients. In May 1935, Jacobson was able to demonstrate to the Society for Clinical Investigation that a tiny brown 1 cc water solution of three crystalline liver portions effectively treated pernicious anaemia[15].

Informally, Guy W. Clark of Lederle Laboratories began working on liver extracts with SubbaRow. Over the weekend, SubbaRow utilized the Lederle Laboratories' facilities to process liver and during the week, he used to fractionate it. These fractions were tested on patients by Jacobson. They were able to discover an extract referred to as Fraction I that had the maximum blood regeneration. Thus, the fraction containing APAF was detected, but the factor could not be isolated. SubbaRow joined Lederle Laboratories, where he had access to a multitude of resources. Approximately at the same time, Jacobson tested the APAF-rich fraction on a sprue patient with positive results. SubbaRow opted to conduct clinical trials on patients with pernicious anaemia and tropical sprue for each liver fraction. Since sprue is uncommon in the United States, he established the sprue inquiry program in Puerto Rico with Dr. Ramon M. Suarez at the Mamiya Hospital in Santurce. The promising extracts identified in the Suarez investigation were further processed to identify the sprue factor. After two years, Lederle's team could only recognize previously reported B-complex vitamins from the fractions. SubbaRow was doing a parallel investigation on chicken liver fractions in which a growth-promoting component was found. Dr. E. L. R. Stokstad, who initially identified the "chicken growth factor" in yeast, was recruited to concentrate the fraction. His efforts were somewhat fruitful; he was only able to concentrate it by 17 times but still with impurities. The factor was identified as folic acid. SubbaRow's knowledge of organic chemistry procedures came into play as he transformed the compound into an ester form and dissolved away the contaminants in the water. Stokstad has concentrated it further. Later, on April 5, 1943, SubbaRow converted it back to its original form, and it was declared to be free of folic acid. Folic acid was extracted; however, the procedure was not cost-effective and therefore the research was abandoned[1,3,5,15].

SubbaRow continued his work, and he and Henry Piersma inadvertently hypothesized that folic acid may also be produced during riboflavin fermentation by the same microbe. Al Dornbush was assigned to conduct the investigation, and he reported that a contaminant microbe in the fermentation process is capable of producing folic acid. SubbaRow promptly requested Dr. Brian Hutchings to isolate the microbe and standardize the fermentation technique for folic acid synthesis. He was successful in the isolation of the organism (*Cornybacterium* sps.) and standardization of large-scale production of folic acid but was not successful in its isolation[4]. Around October 1943, Nestor Bohonos, a biochemist taken off from another project could successfully crystalize folic acid. This was successful in increasing the yields but was still not economical. SubbaRow has parallelly instructed his organic chemists to synthesize folic acid and they were successful by this time. This was the most economical approach of all. It is published in the August 31, 1945 issue of Science. Other researchers investigated folic acid in both pernicious anaemia and sprue patients, observing a complete cure in the case of sprue but not pernicious anaemia. In cases with pernicious anaemia, the blood volume increased, but the accompanying nerve condition did not improve. Further, there were relapses also. Careful studies however established that folic acid cures the blood disorder in pernicious anaemia but has no effect on the associated nervous disorder. With folic acid, SubbaRow found a cure for tropical sprue, one of his life's objectives[15].

Aminopterin

The studies on folic acid fortuitously led to an entirely new line of cancer research, thanks to SubbaRow's ever-probing and analytical mind. His team discovered teropterin, a precursor form of folic acid in a fermentation broth containing three molecules of glutamic acid. It is converted into folic acid, which contains one glutamic acid, by treating it with hydrochloric acid. Teropterin suppressed and even destroyed cancer cells in mice, whereas folic acid encouraged the development of cancer cells. Jim Boothe synthesized teropterin in 1947 in response to an increasing demand from cancer researchers. SubbaRow established a full evaluation program of teropterin with his old friend Dr. Sidney Farber at Boston's Children's Hospital. Cancer patients have experienced an alleviation of symptoms and a greater sense of well-being. The study found that teropterin is a palliative[16]. Further, Dr. Faber reported that it has escalated the leukemic process. It was hypothesized that teropterin is a folic acid analog and antifolates might decelerate the disease[1,4,17].

SubbaRow and his colleagues synthesized all feasible chemical compounds resembling folic acid and test them for vitamin or anti-vitamin qualities. In the process, aminopterin was made, which has an amino radical replacing the hydroxy radical in the vitamin[18]. Dr. Farber administered aminopterin to a youngster with leukemia and he improved within a month[3,19]. It gave for the first time a form of treatment for leukemias and launched the chemotherapeutic technique to treat widespread tumors or cancers that cannot be treated surgically. Lederle Laboratory sold aminopterin, the "first-ever anticancer medication," for the treatment of pediatric leukaemia from 1953 to 1964. Aminopterin's impressive outcomes were accompanied by toxicity. Farber requested a less toxic but more potent anti-folic from SubbaRow. SubbaRow tasked his colleagues with synthesizing a compound that was as harmless as teropterin yet as potent as aminopterin[1,4,17].

Methotrexate is a derivative of aminopterin with a methyl group linked to the nitrogen atom in the 10th position[20, 21]. It is one-fifth as toxic as aminopterin but requires a five-fold higher dose. Combined with other medications, it has extended the lives of children with acute leukemia by up to five years. Considering how quickly children previously passed away, doctors consider these treatments to be near-cure. Later on, methotrexate was found to treat disorders other than cancer. It has become a very common medicine used to treat rheumatoid arthritis and psoriasis, two chronic debilitating illnesses affecting the joints and skin. Furthermore, it is also used to treat ectopic pregnancy, chronic ulcerative disorders, and asthma. Methotrexate remains on the World Health Organization's list of essential medications for a basic health system, where it is mostly used to treat cancer and autoimmune illnesses. In 1951, SubbaRow's Harvard colleague George Hitchings independently found that purine antagonists augment folic antagonists in leukemia treatment. In 1988, 37 years later, he was awarded the Nobel

Prize. If the Nobel committee had approved posthumous prizes, SubbaRow would have likely shared it[1,4,17].

Aureomycin

Subaarow was a doctoral student at the time penicillin was discovered; therefore, he has first-hand knowledge of the medical revolution it sparked. During this time in World War II, the United States government was making preparations to safeguard its troops against the tropical illnesses they would encounter. This has enabled SubbaRow to design and conduct one of the greatest scientific experiments to date. His group looked for possible antibiotics in soil samples that had been collected from all around the world. It has led to the development of the world's first broad-spectrum antibiotic that is more effective than the existing antibiotics, penicillin, and streptomycin. Additionally, this was the first tetracycline antibiotic[1,2].

Actinomycetes were preferred over aspergilli, penicillin, etc. The screening program was initiated in 1944 by amateurs. SubbaRow brought in a retired plant pathologist, Benjamin Minge Duggar, through Ed Backus, one of his mycology group members. Duggar was inspired to participate in this study because he believed it was more important to human well-being than his well-known work on mushroom cultivation. On April 1, 1944, he began screening samples with code A for actinomycetes and code B for bacteria. In August 1945, he was able to extract golden-colored actinomycetes from a soil sample from the University of Missouri. The A-377 actinomycetes were capable of inhibiting infections resistant to sulfates and existing antibiotics but were not effective against the tuberculosis pathogen. A-377 was authorized further for fermentation studies along with other promising actinomycetes to Edwin Ball[22]. Meanwhile, Duggar was more enthusiastic about A-491, which possesses antituberculosis properties, but SubbaRow was not, as A-491 injections were harmful to the examined animals. Infected guinea pigs, however, responded favorably to A-377 broth that had been partially purified. In June 1946, SubbaRow appointed Joseph Niedercorn, a synthetic chemist, to purify the broth. All isolation and purification techniques of penicillin and streptomycin were unsuccessful in isolating antibiotics from A-377. SubbaRow insisted Niedercorn do a more comprehensive examination of the A-377 mold's nutrient requirements. Niedercorn then prepared an alkaline medium by adding lime water, which resulted in the precipitation of antibiotics without affecting the growth of the mould. To further boost the production of the antibiotic, mutation studies of A-377 were assigned to Ed Backus. Two of the mutant strains, A377-899 (the 899th mutant of A-377) and A377-2920-3 (the 3rd mutant of 2920 mutant), had antibiotic production that was 2-3 times and 15 times higher, respectively[3,23].

In April 1947, the prototype plant was constructed and the fermentation of the antibiotic began. At the beginning of 1948, all fermentation-related issues were overcome, and crystalline antibiotic was isolated. Charles Pidacks was tasked with developing the solvent form of the antibiotic; he was initially unsuccessful, but after teaming up with George Krupka, they were able to develop the desired product. During this phase of the study, the company executives were not ready to fund this expensive project further as the country was stuck in a recession. SubbaRow stood by the project and convinced the management to permit them to work as it is in the last leg of a promising endeavor. A series of animal studies were conducted on multiple infections like typhoid, paratyphoid, erysipelas, rickettsia, viruses, etc. The molecule was very successful and was designed to be given orally. SubbaRow's scientific and administrative expertise brought to light the efforts of his whole team[24]. On July 21, July 1948, SubbaRow unveiled the drug to the medical world at a conference in New York[3].

In the meantime, Duggar identified A-377 mould as a member of the same streptomyces group of actinomycetes and named it *Streptomyces aureofaciens*, the golden mould. The antibiotic crystals were golden yellow in color and were named "Aureomycin" the golden antibiotic. The aureomycin is chlortetracycline as it has a chlorine atom attached to the tetracycline molecule. It heralded a golden era in the history of antibiotics[25].

Hetrazan (diethylcarbamazine citrate).

This drug was also produced as a part of SubbaRow's program to protect American soldiers from tropical diseases during the Second World War. Both malaria and filariasis are prominently found in the Pacific region. During his time in India, he also observed that filariasis was one of the greatest causes of suffering. Early in 1944, SubbaRow was able to establish a parasitology group and appointed Dr. Redginal Irving Hewitt to test various chemicals against the malaria-infected ducklings. Hewitt was shifted to the project of studying filariasis, whose preliminary research was conducted by SubbaRow at Ayurvedic College in Madras. SubbaRow sent Hewitt all of the chemicals he came across, including organic dyes, sulphonamides, quinolines, sulphones, cyanamides, and piperazines. In April 1945, Hewitt discovered that a potential painkiller synthesized by a Calco Chemist reduced the number of filarial larvae in cotton rats. This is effective against young worms but not against adult worms. The molecule was identified to be a piperazine and SubbaRow has asked for the synthesis of all possible piperazines. In total 35 piperazine molecules were produced by substituting the methyl side-chain with other alkyl groups, but none were as effective as the earlier tested molecule. Therefore, the derivatives were produced from the other carbethoxy chain. The antifilarial activity is shown by a compound related to the carbamic acid derivative. It encouraged SubbaRow to get all possible chemicals related to this "carbamine" synthesized. A compound, Diethyl-carbamyl-4-methyl piperazine (diethylcarbamazine), made by substituting the two end hydrogen atoms with ethyl groups, was unmatched in its antifilarial activity[1]. In 1947, it was synthesized by Dr. Sam Kushner in SubbaRow's group and could immobilize filarial worms in rats, dogs, and frogs[2,3]. The compound was found to be low in toxicity. Hewitt identified the antifilarial compound by screening 517 molecules using cotton rats[26].

Dr. Jose Oliver-Gonzales of San Juan's School of Tropical Medicine was given the compound for further testing on humans. It was reported that the young and adult worms died and the compound didn't cause any serious side effects. The diethylcarbamazine (DEC) with the generic name of Hetrazan was tested extensively between 1955 and 1959. Initially, the suggested high dosages had some side effects but now WHO has suggested hetrazan as the key drug in the treatment of filariasis[3,26].

Other contributions

SubbaRow's efforts to find an antipernicious anaemia factor have led to the discovery of folic acid, which could address the issue of tropical sprue but not pernicious anaemia. Hence, SubbaRow continued his studies to isolate the APAF from the liver. His team could get an APAF-rich fraction, which had shown promising results in pernicious anaemia patients. His team was in the further process of isolation and purification of APAF, but on April 16, 1948, Merck Research Laboratories announced that it could isolate a crystalline product that acted as APAF and is Vitamin B12. It was isolated from fermentation broths of the antibiotic grisein. Thus, SubbaRow's efforts to isolate APAF had been partially successful[2,15].

In the process of the discovery of aureomycin, Benjamin Minge Duggar isolated a bacterium (B-71) from the soil sample of Colorado. It was identified to be *Bacillus polymyxa* and was handed over to John Porter so that Duggar could concentrate on the actinomycetes. Eventually, Porter and his team were able to isolate the antibiotic polymyxin. It was initially found effective against undulant fever, whooping cough, and meningitis, but was stopped as it was harmful to the kidneys[22]. Presently, polymyxin antibiotics are used as a last resort in the treatment of multiple drug-resistant gram-negative bacteria[27]. Dr. SubbaRow authored over 100 papers that have been published. There are several unpublished works[3].

Honours and Awards

It is fact that SubbaRow didn't get any awards or recognition during his lifetime. Neither Lederle laboratories nor the remaining scientific world of his time recognized his contributions and honour him when he was alive. The Nobel Prize eluded him during his lifetime and posthumously his portrait was placed in the "Karolinska Institute" in Stockholm, an institute that awards the Nobel Prize in physiology and medicine. However, Lederle laboratories after his death recognized his contributions and honored him in numerous ways. A library block on Lederle campus was named after him and a fungus was named in his honor as *Subbaromyces splendens*. A tetracycline antibiotic was called subamycin. Although India could not bestow the Bharat Ratna on him, the centenary of his birth in 1995 was commemorated in India through conferences and talks, and the Government of India released a commemorative stamp (**Fig. 1**). Scientific journals and newspapers paid tributes. The best tribute to date is possibly from a news reporter, Doron Antrim of Argosy magazine in 1950. He wrote "*You've probably never heard of Dr. Yellapragada SubbaRow. Yet, because he lived, you may be alive and are well today. Because he lived you may live longer*"[1-6].

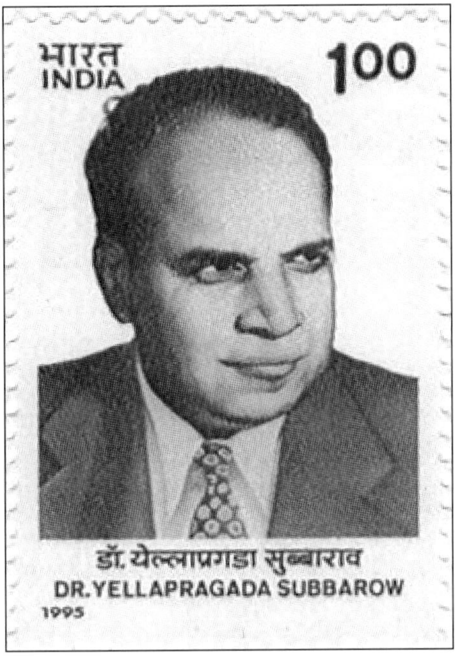

Figure 1: The stamp of Yellapragada SubbaRow released by Government of India in his centenary year. Source / Courtesy: File: Yellapragada Subbarow 1995.jpg. (2022, August 20). *Wikimedia Commons, the free media repository*. Retrieved 12:14, September 2, 2022, from https://commons.wikimedia.org/w/index.php?title=File:Yellapragada_Subbarow_1995.jpg&oldid=683766043.

Demise

Dr. SubbaRow was not found at work on Monday, August 9, 1948. Since he was such a workaholic, his colleagues noticed his absence. Upon entering his home, he was discovered dead from a massive heart attack. He was an avid smoker, which may have contributed to his untimely demise on the night of August 8, 1948, at the age of 53[1,3]. He never returned to India, possibly due to the research facilities available in the United States, as he was so motivated and obsessed with research. Even in his last days, he said, "*If God will spare me another couple of years, maybe we can cure another disease*." He gave up his personal life to the point where he never saw his wife again. SubbaRow could pay back the money borrowed, possibly with interest, to his father-in-law when he was going through challenging times in 1946–1947. It might be the only satisfactory moment in his family life[1].

Epilogue

By observing the impact of poverty, SubbaRow may have considered gaining wealth and reputation. The influence of his father's death on him as a youngster and his exposure to poverty may have prompted him to investigate their causes, leading him to engage in religious activities and read the Gita, the Bible, the Quran, etc. His near-death experience and the loss of his brothers to sprue may have led him to think of an ascetic lifestyle. Later, it also motivated him to find solutions for human suffering. SubbaRow moved from a worldly person to a highly realized person due to different experiences in life. He was not pained even to leave his pregnant wife to pursue his dream of finding cures for the deadly diseases of those times. Moreover, he donated his earnings to institutions of different beliefs as well. As an adult, he lost interest in fame and fortune. He has given credit for his efforts to others and has labored ceaselessly to alleviate human misery. This is the essence of all religions and sacred texts. He is a realized man and the world has just realized the significance of his work and not his actual accomplishments as a scientific saint.

Bibliography

1. Nagendrappa, G. (2012) Yellapragada SubbaRow. Resonance 17, 538–557.
2. Kamath, P., Shenoy, K.A. (2013). Yellapragada Subba Row: The Unsung Hero. Muller J Med Sci Res 4(2), 130-132.
3. Dixit, V. S. (2018) Unknown facets of "not so well-known scientist" Dr. Y Subbarow: A great scientist, who did not receive the Nobel Prize. J Mar Med Soc. 20(2), 141-144.
4. Gupta, S.P., Bansal, S., Ramesh, V. (2013) Remembering Yellapragada SubbaRow. International journal of dermatology 52(7), 882–886.
5. Bhargava, P.M. (2001) Dr. Yellapragada SubbaRow (1895-1948) He Transformed Science; Changed Lives. Journal, Indian Academy of Clinical Medicine. 2: 96-100
6. Rao. E.V. (2015) Visionary chemist – Dr Yellapragada Subba Row. Current Science, 109(1), 213.
7. Fiske, C.H., Subbarow, Y. (1925) The colorimetric determination of phosphorus. Biol Chem, 66, 375-400
8. Fiske, C. H., Subbarow, Y. (1925) The nature of the "inorganic phosphate" in voluntary muscle. Science 65, 401–403.

9. Fiske C.H., Subbarow Y. (1929) Phosphorus compounds of muscle and liver. Science 70, 381–382.
10. Yellapragada Subbarow Archives Online. Available from: https://www.ysubbarow.info/folicacid.html. [Last accessed on 2022 Aug 28].
11. Yellapragada Subbarow Archives Online. Available from: https://www.ysubbarow.info/con_research.html. [Last accessed on 2022 Aug 28].
12. Yellapragada Subbarow Archives Online. https://www.ysubbarow.info/ph.html. [Last accessed on 2022 Aug 28].
13. Valiathan, M. S. (1998) Healing plants. Current Science 75(11), 1122–1127.
14. Yellapragada Subbarow Archives Online. https://www.ysubbarow.info/atp.html. [Last accessed on 2022 Aug 28].
15. Yellapragada Subbarow Archives Online. https://www.ysubbarow.info/folicacid.html. [Last accessed on 2022 Aug 28].
16. Farber, S., Cutler, E.C., Hawkins, J. W., Harrison, J. H., Peirce, E.C., 2nd, Lenz, G.G. (1947). The Action of Pteroylglutamic Conjugates on Man. Science (New York, N.Y.), 106(2764), 619–621.
17. Yellapragada Subbarow Archives Online. https://www.ysubbarow.info/anti.html. [Last accessed on 2022 Aug 28].
18. Seeger, D.R., Smith, J.M. Jr., Hultquist, M.E. (1947). Antagonist for pteroylglutamic acid. Journal of the American Chemical Society 69(10), 2567.
19. Farber, S., & Diamond, L. K. (1948). Temporary remissions in acute leukemia in children produced by folic acid antagonist, 4-aminopteroyl-glutamic acid. The New England Journal of Medicine 238(23), 787–793.
20. Smith J.M., Cosulich D.B., Hultquist M.E., Seeger D.R. (1948) The chemistry of certain pteroylglutamic acid antagonists. Trans N Y Acad Sci 10, 82–83.
21. Seeger D.R., Cosulich D.B., Smith J.M., Hultquist M.E. (1949) Analogs of Pteroylglutamic Acid. III. 4-Amino Derivatives. J Am Chem Soc 71,1753–1758.
22. Yellapragada Subbarow Archives Online. https://www.ysubbarow.info/tet.html. [Last accessed on 2022 Aug 28].
23. Yellapragada Subbarow Archives Online. https://www.ysubbarow.info/tet1.html. [Last accessed on 2022 Aug 28].
24. Yellapragada Subbarow Archives Online. https://www.ysubbarow.info/tet2.html. [Last accessed on 2022 Aug 28].

25. Yellapragada Subbarow Archives Online. https://www.ysubbarow.info/tet3.html. [Last accessed on 2022 Aug 28].
26. Yellapragada Subbarow Archives Online. https://www.ysubbarow.info/fil.html. [Last accessed on 2022 Aug 28].
27. Wikipedia contributors. (2022, June 6). Polymyxin. In Wikipedia, The Free Encyclopedia. Retrieved 18:01, August 28, 2022, from https://en.wikipedia.org/w/index.php?title=Polymyxin&oldid=1091846238

AUTHOR PROFILE

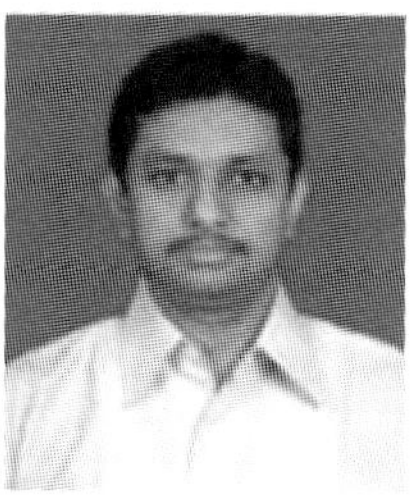

Dr. T. Srinivasan is a Professor in the Department of Botany at the Central Tribal University of Andhra Pradesh, Vizianagaram (A.P.). His areas of expertise include bioprospecting and plant stress biology. He has isolated a few compounds of microbial and plant origin showing antimicrobial, immunostimulatory, and anticancer activities. He is a recipient of the Sirohi Award from the Indian Society of Plant Physiology, India.

Email: saveplants@gmail.com

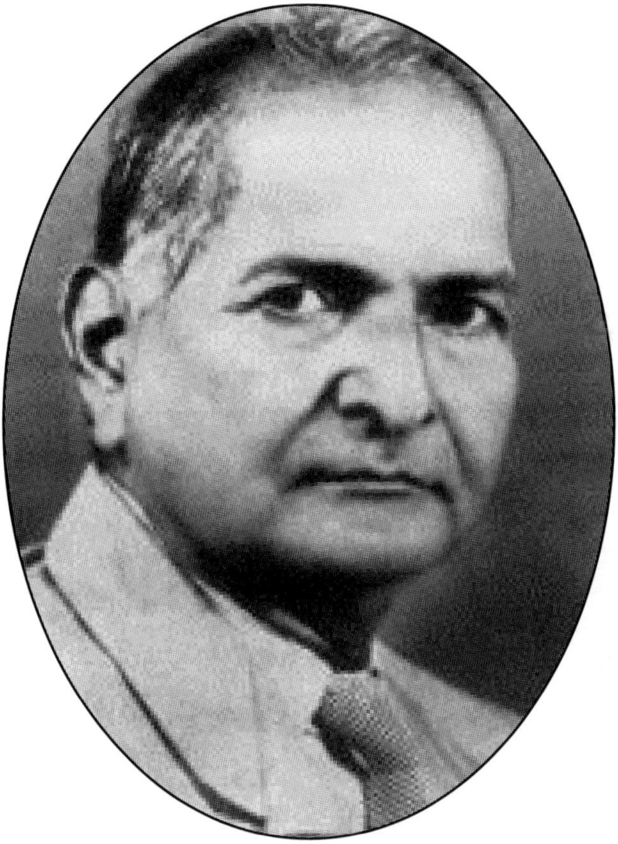

Maharajapuram Seetharaman Krishnan

(24 August 1898 – 24 April 1970)

MAHARAJAPURAM SEETHARAMAN KRISHNAN: THE FIRST INDIAN DIRECTOR OF THE GEOLOGICAL SURVEY OF INDIA

Vikram Pratap Singh

Santhanur, a tiny village in Perambalur district of Tamil Nadu, suddenly found itself as the new artefact for global attention in 1940 when an 18 m long, 120-million-year-old fossil tree trunk (fig.1) was discovered by a great geologist Dr. Maharajapuram Seetharaman Krishnan (hereafter Dr. M S Krishnan). Dr. Krishnan had the unique distinction to be the first person holding a doctorate degree to join as a Geologist in the Geological Survey of India (GSI) and later being the first 'Indian' to be appointed as the Director of GSI in 1951. He was a geologist par excellence and held vast experience in various fields of geology. Dr. Krishnan was a great institution builder and academic administrator who headed some of the leading organizations like GSI, Indian Bureau of Mines (IBM), Indian School of Mines (ISM), and played a key role in establishing institutes like National Geophysical Research Institute (NGRI) and Department of Atomic Energy.

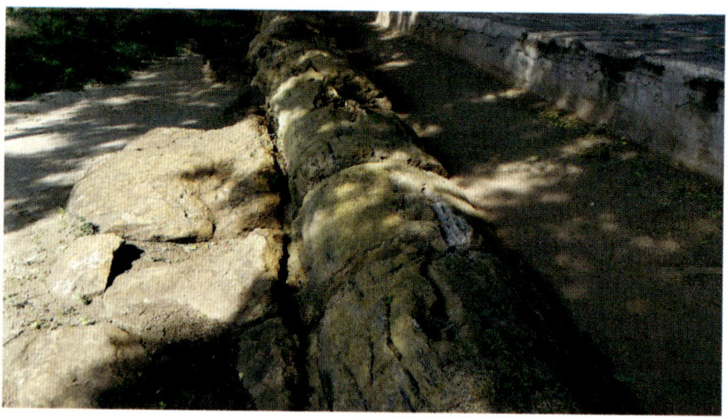

Figure 1: The fossil tree trunk at National Fossil Wood Park, Santhanur discovered by MS Krishnan in 1940 (image courtesy: wikipedia.org)

Early Life and Education

Dr. M S Krishnan was born on the 24th August 1898, in Maharajapuram Village of Tanjore of Madras Presidency of British India, in a humble family of scholars. After completing his school education was from

Tanjore, Krishan proceeded to Tiruchirappalli to continue his education. He graduated with B.A. (Hons.) Degree in Geology with distinction from the Presidency College, Madras in 1919 and earned the M.A. Degree in Geology from the Madras University in 1921. Later in 1921, M S Krishnan was awarded a fellowship to join the Imperial College of Science and Technology, London for higher studies, rarely given to Indians during the British era. In 1922 he received the Associateship of the Royal College of Science (A. R. C. S.) and then Diploma of the Imperial College of Science in the year 1923. Dr. Krishnan was awarded the Ph.D. Degree in Geology from London University in the year 1924 at the age of 26 years. His doctoral work was on the rocks from the Girnar and Osham hills in Kathiawar, supervised by Prof. W.W. Watts and Dr. J.W. Evans, the then greats in the field of petrology. Dr. M S Krishnan also received special training in mining geology at the Imperial College of Science and Technology, which added another dimension to his academic personality.

During 1935-36, Dr. M S Krishnan revisited Imperial College of Science and Technology to take a full course in applied geophysics, followed by USA where, he worked in several laboratories, mines and geological surveys. Dr. Krishnan was an ardent admirer of innovation in geological techniques and familiarised himself with the then modern mineralogical techniques at the Harvard and Wisconsin Universities, and techniques of petrofabric analysis at Innsbruck, Austria.

Professional Life and Contribution to the Indian Geological Studies

Dr. Krishnan started his professional career working for some time in the Indian Stall of the London Exhibition prior to being selected for the superior service in the Government of India (Secretary of State Services). He was the member of the Coal Commission appointed by the Government of India in 1937-38, to cater to the problems of the coal industry. Dr. Krishnan showed exemplary courage in recording his dissent note in the final report pleading for nationalisation of the coal industry (Sankaran,1998).

Dr. M S Krishnan was geologist in the GSI from 1924 to 1943 and later the Superintending Geologist till 1948. Indian economic geology, then, was in its nascent stage and owes a lot to Dr. Krishnan for its advancement. He used to guide large field-party surveys and trained young geologists of the GSI. He, as Superintending Geologist, initiated the Southern Circle Office in Madras. He carried several important expeditions and work to refine the stratigraphic sequences in the Indian sections. One such work was on the Precambrian Gangpur rocks in Odisha, where he could demarcate a definite stage. In his honour it was renamed as the 'Gangpur Stage of Krishnan'. This work was notably published as the *GSI Memoir 71* (1937).

In 1948, Dr. Krishnan was appointed Director of the Indian Bureau of Mines (IBM). His stint as the Director till 1951 led to discovery of several important and viable economic mineral deposits. In 1951, he was appointed the permanent Director of GSI, being the first Indian to head the organisation since its inception more than a century ago.

Dr. Krishnan carried out many field investigations in economic mineral deposits of the then Madras Presidency, notably iron ores, manganese ores, gypsum, mica, limestone and a host of other mineral resources. These exhaustive works have been published in the voluminous *GSI Memoir 80* (1952). His investigations on radioactive and rare-earth minerals were instrumental in the establishment of the Department of Atomic Energy.

It wasn't before Dr. Krishnan's initiative and pioneering work in 1940s that the Neyveli Lignite project was launched. He, owing to his vast knowledge, experience and vision, successfully persuaded the then Advisor to the Governor of Madras to start drilling to delineate the lignite field. He was also instrumental in the resurrection of the gold mining in Karnataka, particularly the mining operation in Hutti gold field.

In 1955 Dr. Krishnan was appointed as Mineral Advisor to the Government of India in the Ministry of Natural Resources and Scientific Research, post which he held till 1957. He took up the post of Director of Indian School of Mines and Applied Geology, Dhanbad, in May 1957 on special request of the Government, but relinquished the post and voluntarily retired in 1958 to pursue his true love of teaching. He was revered by the teachers and students not only in India but also in Western Europe, Russia, Japan, North America and Australia.

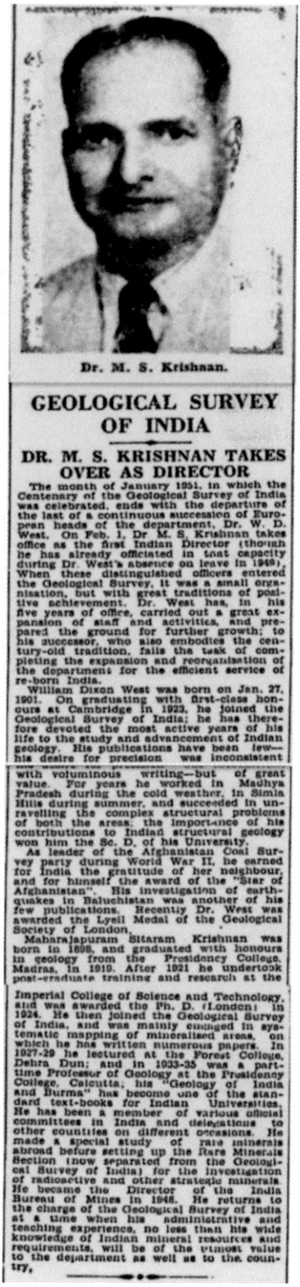

Dr. M. S. Krishnan.

GEOLOGICAL SURVEY OF INDIA

DR. M. S. KRISHNAN TAKES OVER AS DIRECTOR

The month of January 1951, in which the Centenary of the Geological Survey of India was celebrated, ends with the departure of the last of a continuous succession of European heads of the department, Dr. W. D. West. On Feb. 1, Dr M. S. Krishnan takes office as the first Indian Director (though he has already officiated in that capacity during Dr. West's absence on leave in 1949), When these distinguished officers entered the Geological Survey, it was a small organisation, but with great traditions of positive achievement. Dr. West has, in his five years of office, carried out a great expansion of staff and activities, and prepared the ground for further growth; to his successor, who also embodies the century-old tradition, falls the task of completing the expansion and reorganisation of the department for the efficient service of re-born India.

William Dixon West was born on Jan. 27, 1901. On graduating with first-class honours at Cambridge in 1923, he joined the Geological Survey of India; he has therefore devoted the most active years of his life to the study and advancement of Indian geology. His publications have been few—his desire for precision was inconsistent with voluminous writing—but of great value. For years he worked in Madhya Pradesh during the cold weather, in Simla Hills during summer, and succeeded in unravelling the complex structural problems of both the areas; the importance of his contributions to Indian structural geology won him the Sc. D. of his University.

As leader of the Afghanistan Coal Survey party during World War II, he earned for India the gratitude of her neighbour, and for himself the award of the "Star of Afghanistan". His investigation of earthquakes in Baluchistan was another of his few publications. Recently Dr. West was awarded the Lyell Medal of the Geological Society of London.

Maharajapuram Sitaram Krishnan was born in 1898, and graduated with honours in geology from the Presidency College, Madras, in 1919. After 1921 he undertook post-graduate training and research at the Imperial College of Science and Technology, and was awarded the Ph. D. (London) in 1924. He then joined the Geological Survey of India, and was mainly engaged in systematic mapping of mineralised areas, on which he has written numerous papers. In 1927-29 he lectured at the Forest College, Dehra Dun; and in 1933-35 was a part-time Professor of Geology at the Presidency College, Calcutta; his "Geology of India and Burma" has become one of the standard text-books for Indian Universities. He has been a member of various official committees in India and delegations to other countries on different occasions. He made a special study of rare minerals abroad before setting up the Rare Minerals Section (now separated from the Geological Survey of India) for the investigation of radioactive and other strategic minerals. He became the Director of the India Bureau of Mines in 1948. He returns to the charge of the Geological Survey of India at a time when his administrative and teaching experience, no less than his wide knowledge of Indian mineral resources and requirements, will be of the utmost value to the department as well as to the country.

Figure 2: The Feb 1, 1951 edition of Indian Express published the news of Dr. M S Krishnan being appointed as the Director of GSI (source: https://news.google.com/newspapers?id=qANFAAAAIBAJ&sjid=Z7cMAAAAIBAJ&pg=4631%2C34523)

Dr. Krishnan had several brief stints of teaching earlier at various institutions like Presidency College Madras (1920-21), Forest College Dehradun (1928-30), Presidency College Calcutta (1933-35). He then joined the Andhra University in 1959 and remained there till 1961, teaching and training the budding geologists and geophysicists. In 1961, the Council of Scientific and Industrial Research (CSIR) invited him to be the first Director of the National Geophysical Research Institute (NGRI) at Hyderabad, earlier known as the Central Board of Geophysics. He headed the institute till his retirement in 1963.

Dr. Krishan realized the problem faced by the students in studying Indian geology due to lack of a comprehensive textbook. On the suggestion of C. S. Fox, a great contemporary geologist in GSI, Dr. M S Krishnan brought out an amazing piece of work named *Geology of India and Burma* in 1943. This book was arguably the most important contribution of M S Krishnan to geology education. It became so popular among the academia and industry that it was quoted as 'bible' of Indian geology. The impact of this book can be gazed from the fact that even after almost eight decades it is one of the most sought-after literatures for the detailed Indian geology and runs out of stores almost immediately as it is placed. It was also translated in Russian language.

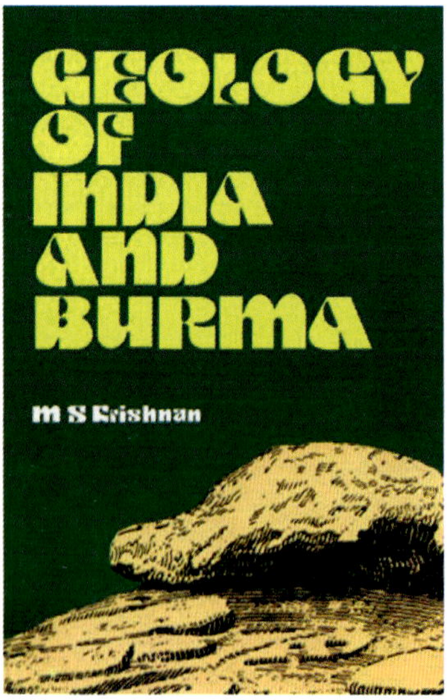

Figure 3: The book Geology of India and Burma written by Dr. M S Krishnan in 1943 remains as one of the most comprehensive textbooks for the Indian geology even after eight decades

This book is still considered as the most authentic book on the geology of India by many geologists in UK and USA. Dr. Krishnan later published a concise version of this textbook named *Introduction to the Geology of India* for the undergraduate and engineering students and for those where knowledge of geology is required. Such was the importance of this book that it was translated in Hindi in 1955, making it probably the first book on technical subject to be translated in Hindi (Sankaran, 1998).

Dr. Krishnan has authored several monographs and published 400 papers in various national and international journals. His keenness for publishing quality work was such that he completed his last two papers just days before his demise.

Amongst his other significant contributions were his commentary on the orogenic trends of the Archean rocks in different parts of India as mentioned in the *GSI Memoir 81* (1953). He had immensely contributed to the studies on various volcanic episodes, petrography of rocks, laterization of khondalites, mineral resources of the Central Provinces and Berar (presently part of Madhya Pradesh), Deccan Traps etc.

Awards and Honors

Dr. Krishnan had been a leading member and chair of most learned societies dealing with earth sciences in this country and abroad. Dr. M S Krishnan was recipient of many accolades and awards.

- He was sectional President of the Indian Science Congress in 1935 and its General President in 1958.
- He delivered the' Ripon' lectures of the Indian Association for the Cultivation of Science in 1954 on the ' Iron ores of India'.
- He was a member of Geological Society of London (1939-41), American Institute of Mining and Metallurgical Engineers (1954-56).
- As a mark of his outstanding contributions to geological science, the Geological Society of London honoured him with a Commonwealth fellowship in 1967.
- In 1967, the Mineralogical Society of America made him a life fellow.

- He was a member of the Society of Economic Geologists, was its Vice-President on several occasions and had been an associate editor of the Journal 'Economic Geology' for the last twenty years.
- He was a 'Foundation Fellow' of the Geological Society of India, and was one of its Vice-Presidents ever since its inception in 1958.
- A Gold Medal of the Geographical Union has been instituted in his memory.
- As a mark of recognition of his vast contributions to Indian Geology, the Royal Asiatic Society of Bengal awarded him the P. N. Bose Medal.
- He was invited to deliver a lecture on Salt tectonics of the Punjab and Northwest India in 1962 at the Salt Symposium at Houston in U.S.A.
- The Commonwealth Foundation, London, invited him to undertake a lecture tour to Australia and New Zealand in March-July 1969 as distinguished lecturer.
- His lectures at all across New Zealand and Australia are a testimony of his scholarly attainments in all aspects of geology and the respect he commanded from the geological community.
- In 1970 Dr. M S Krishnan was conferred India's third highest civilian award the Padma Bhushan.

Personal Life and Demise

Apart from being an eminent geologist, Dr. M S Krishnan had a vast knowledge of English and French literature. He was a scholar of the Vedas and a connoisseur of Karnatic music and also appreciated good European music.

On 24th April 1970, Dr. Krishnan breathed his last after a major abdominal surgery. He is survived by his three daughters.

In popular culture

The youth of Santhanur village observe the birth anniversary of Dr. M S Krishnan at the National Fossil Wood Park campus every year since 2017 to commemorate his findings and the fame he brought to the village.

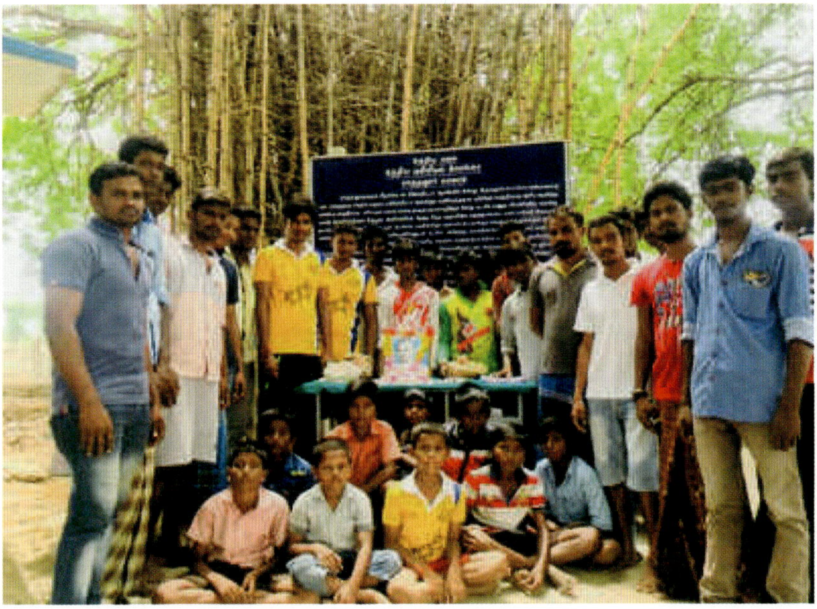

Figure 4: Youths paying floral tribute to the portrait of M S Krishnan (https://timesofindia.indiatimes.com/city/trichy/tamil-nadu-village-observes-birth-anniversary-of-geologist-m-s-krishnan/articleshow/65544284.cms)

Bibliography

1. Sankaran, A.V., (1998). M. S. Krishnan: Geologist par excellence. Current Science, v. 75 (10), 1084-1085.
2. https://www.insaindia.res.in/detail.php?id=N35-0395
3. http://www.portal.gsi.gov.in/portal/page?_pageid=127%2C529552&_dad=portal&_schema=PORTAL
4. www.wikipedia.org
5. Geological Survey of India: 'M.S.Krishnan, Pen Portrait', GSI News, Vol.4, No.6,June 1972, p. 5-10
6. Krishnan, M.S., (1943). Geology of India and Burma. Associated Printers, Madras
7. https://www.geosocindia.org/index.php/jgsi/article/download/71925/56027
8. https://timesofindia.indiatimes.com/city/trichy/tamil-nadu-village-observes-birth-anniversary-of-geologist-m-s-krishnan/articleshow/65544284.cms

9. Indian Science Congress Association, Volume II - Presidential Address (2003). *The Shaping of Indian Science: 1948-1981*. Hyderabad: Universities Press. p. 769.

AUTHOR PROFILE

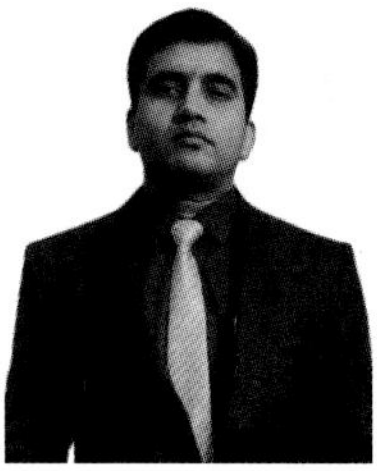

Dr. Vikram Pratap Singh is an Assistant Professor in the Department of Geology at Indira Gandhi National Tribal University, Amarkantak (M.P). His research interests include marine micropaleontology, biostratigraphy, paleoceanography and paleoclimatology. He has also worked as Geologist in hydrocarbon exploration at Reliance Industries Limited.

Email: vikram.singh@igntu.ac.in

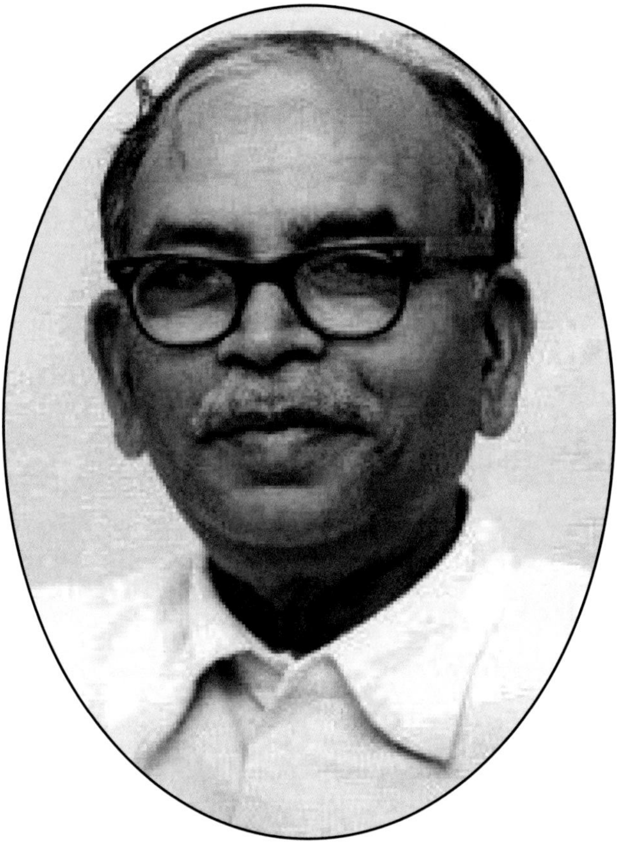

Daulat Singh Kothari

(6 July 1906 – 4 February 1993)

DAULAT SINGH KOTHARI: A GREAT INSTITUTION BUILDER

Aalok Pandya

These days, the 'National Education Policy 2020 (NEP 2020)' are very much in discussion. In Independent India, *Radhakrishnan Commission* (1948-49) was the first initiative to make the higher education system more effective and relevant, this was followed by *Mudaliar Commission* (1952-1953) and *Kothari Commission* (1964-1966). Dr D. S. Kothari who headed the *Kothari Commission* submitted its report with the title- '*Education and National Development*'. Report of another committee for the education reforms was released in the year 1986, the document that was prepared under the leadership of Prof. Yash Pal and referred to as 'New Education Policy (1986)'. On this occasion, someone asked Prof. D.S. Kothari, "What tagline would you like to associate with this report?" Prof. Kothari immediately replied, "I would like to dedicate the document of New Education Policy by title- *Education for Character Building*." This reaction of Prof. Kothari was in the background of mega-scams that created a huge political noise and turmoil in India during the mid-80s. But his comments are relevant even today[1].

Childhood and Early Life

Daulat Singh Kothari was born on 6th July 1906 in the city of Udaipur. His father Fateh Sigh Kothari was the Head-Master of the Maharana's High School, he died at a very young age in 1918. Due to the untimely demise of his father, Daulat Singh's family was left with fewer means. Having completed his High School education in Udaipur, he had to move to Indore for Intermediate studies in the year 1923. He stood first in the entire Central Board (known as Madhya Bharat Board of Central Province those days). This was brought to the knowledge of Maharana (Ruler) of Udaipur by some well-wishers of his family. Maharana of Udaipur generously granted him a scholarship for pursuing higher studies. He joined the University of Allahabad for a Bachelor of Science in the year 1924.

University of Allahabad[2]

D.S. Kothari did his B.Sc. and M.Sc. from the University of Allahabad. Those days, the Department of Physics at Allahabad University was headed by none other than Prof. Meghnad Saha who made a pioneer contribution in the field of Astrophysics that was known by his name- '*Saha's Ionisation Equation*'. During his master's, he caught the attention of Prof. Meghnad Saha which changed the course of his life. For M.Sc. Final practical examination, Prof. C.V. Raman was appointed examiner by the University. Prof. C.V. Raman while interrogating young Kothari during the *Viva-Voce* was left with a profound impression, which he expressed to Prof. Meghnad Saha. He told Meghnad Saha, "Please make sure that justice is done with the talent of this student and that he continues to do science and Physics." Later Prof. Meghnad Saha recommended D.S. Kothari for pursuing PhD degree at Cambridge University.

Cambridge University Days

In Cambridge D.S. Kothari joined PhD under the guidance of Nobel Laureate Lord Ernest Rutherford who had discovered the nucleus of an atom. However, Lord Rutherford left for York University and so within a year, the thesis advisor of D.S. Kothari was changed. His second thesis advisor was Prof. Ralph Fowler who too was a Nobel Laureate and an illustrious faculty of Cambridge. In 1933 Kothari completed his PhD. Kothari worked on the physics of ionisation in stars, the work that he had already started with Prof. Meghnad Saha in Allahabad. However, Kothari also applied quantum mechanics and statistical thermodynamics in his doctoral thesis. Quantum Mechanics was taking shape in those days and Cambridge University was a prominent hub of this development. It was because of Prof. P.A.M. Dirac who really shaped and presented Quantum Mechanics as a branch of Mechanics and Physics to the world of science. It was also the time 'Atomic Theory' was developing in Cambridge and other prominent centres in Europe.

At that time, four Indian students were pursuing their PhD in Cambridge, S. Chandrashekhar, Homi Jahangir Bhabha, D.S. Kothari and R.C. Majumdar. All of them made a significant contribution to Fundamental Physics. Bhabha worked in Particle Physics, D.S. Kothari and R.C. Majumdar worked on the Statistical Thermodynamics of Astrophysics and S. Chandrashekhar made a seminal contribution to the theoretical aspects of Black Holes and condensed stars for which he was conferred the Nobel Prize. Subramaniam Chandrashekhar and R.C. Majumdar moved to the US after completing their PhD and made great strides in advanced research in Physics. Bhabha and Kothari returned to India and became institution builders as they are known now. D.S. Kothari completed his PhD from Cambridge during 1930-1933.

University of Delhi

Having completed his PhD, Dr Kothari returned to India and joined the University of Delhi as Associate Professor in the year 1933. He was entrusted with the responsibility of building the Department of Physics and Astrophysics of the University in its early days. He shaped the Department, but, did not stop there only. He was instrumental in appointing many eminent scientists and scholars at Delhi University. This included some luminaries such as Prof. R.C. Majumdar, Prof. Panchapakesan, Prof. T.R. Sheshadri and Prof. Panchanan Maheshwari among others. He invited some of the most eminent scientists in the world to deliver lectures at Delhi University. Notable among these were Albert Einstein, Neils Bohr, P.A.M. Dirac, P.M.S. Blackett, Pauli Wolfgang, Russian physicists Pyotr Kapitza and Ilya Prigogine

Contributions: Defence Ministry

Prof. Kothari was appointed Defence Advisor to the Government of India in 1948, the duty which he discharged till 1963. Though India in 1947 had inherited a Defence Science Organization (DSO) from Imperial Government, but it took its present shape only after Prof. Kothari took charge of it. He was the founder of the Defence Research and Development Organization (DRDO) which now has a chain of laboratories. It started with a DRDO laboratory in Jodhpur and today there are 52 DRDO laboratories in India.

He envisaged eight major divisions in DRDO labs *viz.*, (i) Armaments, (ii) Ballistics, (iii) Explosives, (iv) Operational Research, (v) Rockets and Missiles, (vi) Naval Technologies, (vii) Engineering; and (viii) Food and Life Sciences. Even today the line of research in Defence Science is continuing along the same lines. And Defence Science in India grew further under the able leadership of Dr Nagratnam, Prof. M.G.K. Menon and Dr A.P.J. Abdul Kalam in the following years. Dr A.P.J. Abdul Kalam, ex-Director of DRDO labs and Defence Advisor to the Government of

India rose to the highest office of President of India, he often referred to Prof. Kothari as an institution builder and visionary and his *Role Model* who ever inspired him.

Prof. Kothari as Defence and Scientific Advisor to the Government of India was entitled to get a salary of Rs. 4200, which he never drew. Instead, he took only One Rupee from the organization and continued to draw Rs 1200 as a professor's salary from the University of Delhi. This set an example that many others followed. Prof. Satish Dhawan, Professor in the Aerospace Department of Indian Institute of Science (IISc Bangalore), when appointed Chairman of the Indian Space Research Organization (ISRO) after the demise of Prof. Vikram Sarabhai drew only one rupee from ISRO and continued to draw the salary of professor from IISc, which was far less than that of ISRO Chairman.

Documentation of Defence Records

Prof. Kothari constituted a committee headed by a Major General of the Indian Army to explore the means and importance of documentation of wars and strategic conflicts. The committee observed that there was no record or document in the court of Pratap related to the historical battle of *Haldi Ghati* fought between the Army of Maharana Pratap of Mewar and the Mughal Army of Emperor Akbar. Interestingly, there was an excellent record of the battle and its background in the court of Emperor Akbar. Two months prior to the battle of *Haldi Ghati* which took place on 18th June 1576, while the tension was still mounting between the two sides, every day a messenger used to rush from the ground zero and report to the Mughal Emperor in his court in the evening. Learning lessons from the past, Indian Army has recorded all its battles afterwards. The limited war of Kargil which took place in 1999, was video recorded and Indian Army has been using it for its review and analysis.

The University Grants Commission (UGC)

In 1961 Prof. Kothari was assigned the additional responsibility of the Chairman of the University Grants Commission (UGC). Prof. Kothari restructured UGC which was founded in 1956. In fact, he was the Principal Architect of the organisation who envisaged all its functions. With minimal resources, the most generous and valuable funding schemes were launched and supervised by the UGC under his visionary leadership.

Today the organization has evolved and has launched many more funding and assistance schemes for education and educationists. Prof. Kothari persuaded many eminent non-resident Indian scientists who shined in Europe and USA to come back to India and lead science and technology in their homeland. This included Prof. E.C. George Sudarshan who served IISc for about five years and created a Centre for Theoretical Studies (CTS) IISc Bangalore.

He also played an important role in shaping National Council for Education Research and Training (NCERT) in its early days. Prof. Kothari was also Chairman of the Indian Academy of Sciences (INSA) in the year 1973-74 and Indian Science Congress during its Golden Jubilee year 1963.

In the Vanaprastha

Prof. Kothari always advocated the promotion of 'Value Based Education' and 'Science for Sustainable Development' and his thoughts on science and education referred can be observed in Convocation Addresses delivered by him in various IITs, Central Universities and other institutions, which are always relevant. He left for his heavenly abode on 4th February 1993. One of his contemporaries rightly commented on his persona: *Prof. D.S. Kothari was not just man of few words, but was man of few wants too.* Another rich tribute paid to him was by noted bureaucrat, culturist and art critic Dr. Kapila Vatsaayan, in her words '*Dr. D. S. Kothari was a saint amongst scientists and a scientist amongst saints*'. The government of India released a postal stamp in commemoration of his contributions and accomplishments.

Awards and Accolades

He was conferred Padma Bhushan in the year 1962, and the second highest civilian award Padma Vibhushan in the year 1973 by the Government of India.

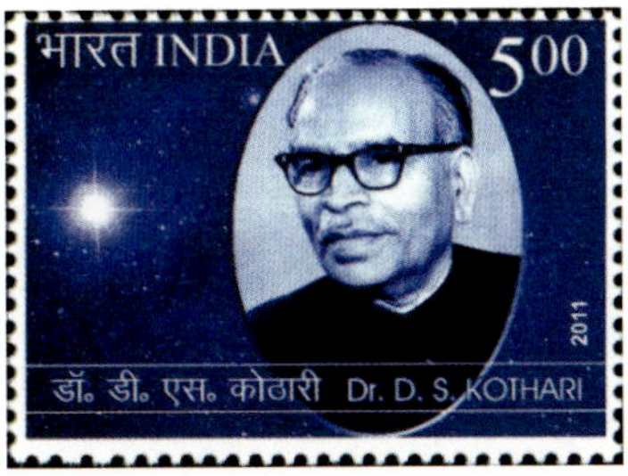

Figure 1: The postal stamp was released to commemorate the contributions of Prof. Kothari.

He was also conferred the 'Atma Ram Award' by the Central Hindi Directorate in 1990. He played an important role in shaping the National Council for Education Research and Training (NCERT) in its early days. He acted as the Chairman of the Indian National Science Academy (INSA) in the year 1973-74, and Indian Science Congress during its Golden Jubilee year 1963. He has been proudly listed as "Allahabad University Alumni Association".

Bibliography

1. Arora R. K., Kothari, L.K. (2006) *Vision and Values: Essays in Honour of Dr. D. S. Kothari*, Paragon Publication, New Delhi.
2. Mehrotra R.C., Arora R. K. (1994) *Education, Science and Human Values: Essays in Honour of Prof. D.S. Kothari*, Wiley Eastern.

Box 1. Prof. D. S. Kothari and Motilal Jain.
In those days Prof. Kothari (1906-1993) was the defence and scientific advisor to the Government of India and chairman of the University Grants Commission (UGC). However, he continued to live on the Delhi University campus where he once served as Professor. It was well known that he was a teetotaller, a Gandhian and a Jain by faith. One day, a grown-up puppy made its way to Professor Kothari's bungalow at Delhi University. Like any other Indian household, here too, the puppy was offered food, leftover or otherwise. Very soon the puppy befriended the kids in the family and soon became a member of the family. The kids of the family named it- *Moti*. The dog was so lovable that it drew Prof. Kothari's attention too and won his heart. An old-fashioned Prof. Kothari started calling the dog- *Motilal*. *Motilal* used to move around Prof. Kothari or sit close to his feet

as long as Prof. Kothari stayed at home. Otherwise, it used to be in the company of children. By then Motilal was well known all over the Delhi University campus. Whenever the dog moved around the campus, people on the Delhi University campus used to give all possible eatables to it. The next-door neighbourhood of Prof. Kothari included families of Prof. Das and Prof. Khan and there were many other Bengali families too on the campus. Very often all of them fed the dog. Occasionally, it was given fish and other non-vegetarian items too. Someone interestingly noticed that *Motilal* did not eat non-vegetarian food. People on the Delhi University campus then started calling the dog- *Motilal Jain*.

It is said that *Motilal* remained a *Jain* till it breathed last.

AUTHOR PROFILE

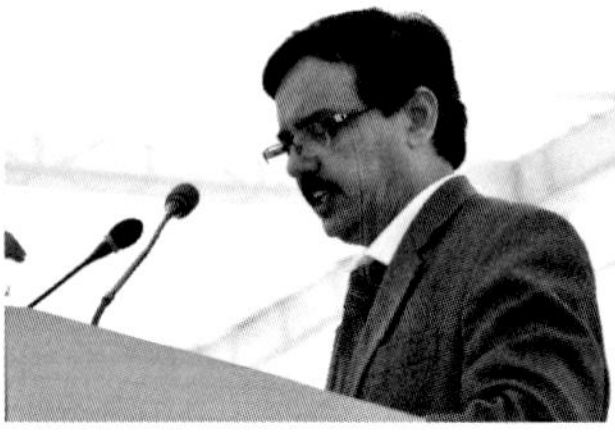

Dr Aalok Pandya is a Professor and Head of the Department of Physics at Indira Gandhi National Tribal University, Amarkantak.

Email: aalok.pandya@igntu.ac.in

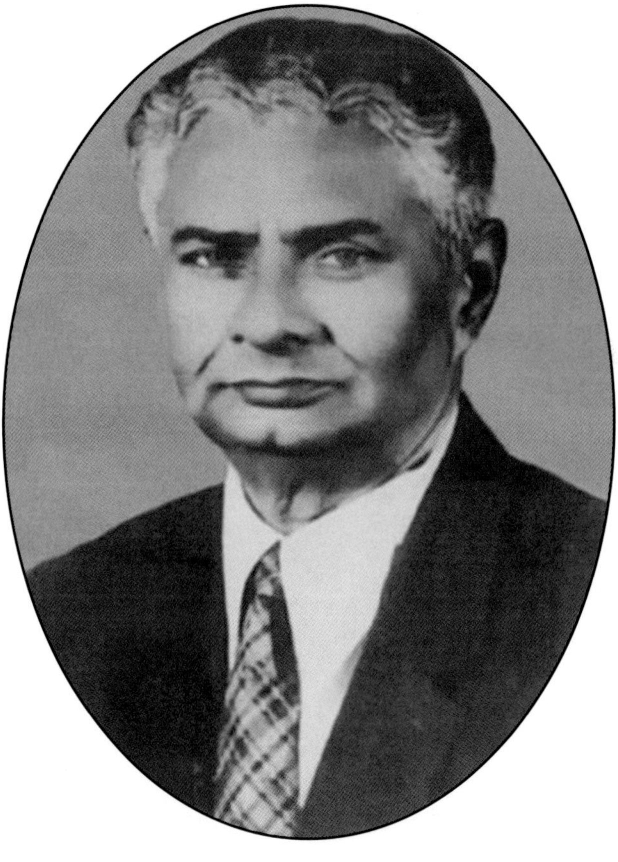

Sachi Prasad Ray-Chaudhuri

(15 September 1907- 15 February 1994)

SACHI PRASAD RAY-CHAUDHURI: THE FATHER OF ANIMAL CHROMOSOME RESEARCH IN INDIA; A SHORT MEMOIR

Sen Pathak

Ray-Chaudhuri was a rare architect in the field of Biology. He not only started animal cytogenetics but also cancer cytogenetics in India. He was a great scientist and scholar with many virtues.

Early Life and Education[1]

Sachi Prasad Ray-Chaudhuri was born on 15 September 1907, in the small village of Kulkathi in East Bengal (now Bangladesh). He received his early education in Calcutta (now Kolkata) and did his master's degree in Zoology from Calcutta University in 1930. In 1937, he went to the Institute of Animal Genetics, University of Edinburg, for his Ph.D. degree on silkworms under F.A.E. Crew, but he advised H. J. Muller (a Nobel laureate), who was to join the institute from Moscow. Ray-Chaudhuri started a Ph.D. project under Muller's supervision and completed the degree on the effects of radiation on the fruit-fly *Drosophila*, in 1939.

After his return from Edinburg to Calcutta, he found that the condition was not suitable for *Drosophila* research. He took training in cytogenetics under P. C. Koller, formed a small group of students in the zoology Department at Calcutta University, and started working on chromosomes of grasshoppers, ladybird beetles, dragonflies, spiders, and Indian heteropteran insect species. His group worked mainly on the structure and behavior of chromosomes in the natural population of these insects. As well as on sex-determining mechanisms, cytotaxonomy, the effect of radiation and chemicals on animal chromosomes, radiation genetics in *Drosophila*, and cytology of malignant human cervical tissues. He used electron microscopy to study the chromosome structure.

In 1960, he joined the Department of Zoology, at Banaras Hindu University (BHU). He introduced modern branches such as genetics, cytogenetics, and biochemistry to the department. There is an interesting story of his appointment in BHU narrated by his daughter, Ratna, who is my contemporary: "Sometimes in 1960 my father was then a reader in Zoology Department of Calcutta University; Prof J.L. Bhaduri, the Professor and Head of Zoology in Calcutta University at that time went to BHU as a member of the selection committee for the appointment of the Professor. Everyone in the dept in Calcutta was waiting eagerly to know who was selected because in those days' professors' post was rare, and everybody used to keep an eye over the appointment of professors in reputed universities all over India. When Prof Bhaduri came back, my father along with all others asked him "whom did you appoint?" He was silent. Then my father repeated "Sir, tell me who has become the Professor at BHU?" He then replied, "It is you." My father was taken aback and said, "Sir, are you joking? I am not even an applicant!" Prof Bhaduri narrated that the committee met in the presence of the Vice Chancellor (VC) Justice H.N. Bhagawati and after prolonged discussions among the members, one name was finalized. When the VC was sure that the name was unanimously approved, he said "Now that you have decided finally, I have to tell you something before you sign." Then he brought out a piece of paper from his pocket and said, "Here is a name suggested by the outgoing Prof A. B. Misra (who was persuaded to return from Oxford University, by Malviya ji to establish the Zoology department at BHU), for the consideration, which is S. P. Ray-Chaudhuri. I did not tell you earlier as I did not want to introduce any bias in your selection. Now you tell me what do you think of him?" Seeing the name, each and everyone said that if Ray-Chaudhuri accepts, he will be undoubtedly far above all other candidates. After narrating this, Prof Bhaduri told my father "So, Ray-Chaudhuri, now you know, if you accept, you are the next Professor and Head of the Zoology Department, BHU." He retired from the department in 1971 and went back to Calcutta University and joined there as Emeritus Scientists. In between, he joined many Indian universities as Visiting professor and trained young students and researchers. He was a great patriot and did not believe in brain drain.

His Contributions: My Recollections

Prof. Ray-Chaudhuri is credited for establishing two of the most modern disciplines of biology within the Zoology Department - *Drosophila* genetics and vertebrate including human cytogenetics studies. During my B.Sc., I decided to study plant cells and their ecology (say Botany). Unfortunately, because I fell short of two marks, I was not selected for botany. Chemistry was not my favorite subject and, therefore, I was dumped into Zoology for my master's degree. In 1962, I began my 5th-year master's degree program in the newly constructed Zoology Building, tucked behind the university library. Prof Ray-Chaudhuri conducted a series of lectures on cytogenetics and since then, the study of chromosomes has become my "bread and butter" (Pathak 2000). A teacher can make the subject either interesting or uninteresting for a student. In the very first motivational lecture, he gave to our class he said, "When I visit many academic institutions in India and am introduced to faculty members, most of them are trained in different universities but hardly anyone from the BHU. That makes me wonder what is wrong with BHU. Either the faculty members there are not doing good teaching or maybe the students are not serious about their training. If you only wish to add three letters, M.Sc. or Ph.D. after your name then do whatever you want to do, but if you want to do real justice with the subject then start working very hard from the beginning. One more thing! Your M.Sc. or Ph.D. is only a certificate after which many in India think that they have attained the highest degree and nothing else is left for them to learn and, therefore, stop doing further research. Your actual research contribution starts after that." The professor's inspiring remarks and future lectures made me think seriously about following his instructions throughout my academic life. These lessons and decisions ultimately made me who I am today.

When Ray-Chaudhuri joined BHU, the first thing he did was to establish *Drosophila* genetics and the cytogenetics laboratories of various insect species including grasshoppers and mantids. He wanted to expand the cytogenetics lab further and became interested in studying mammalian chromosomes including humans. Fortunately, I was the first to be drafted for this task. I finished my M.Sc. in 1963 and was accepted as his first Ph.D. student for the study of chromosomes of the Old-world bats. Since blood culture and other tissue culture techniques were not established in India, we decided to use the bone marrow cells for cytogenetic preparations. With great difficulties and several complaints, I finally established the procedure for chromosome preparation from the bone marrow of the locally caught bat species to study somatic chromosomes. One day in 1964, Ray-Chaudhuri came to the cytogenetics lab to examine the chromosomes of a bat. These were the very first metaphases prepared on vertebrate chromosomes in his newly established cytogenetics lab in BHU. He was very happy and used his favorite two words," very good, very good." While we all were enjoying our discussions with him, Gajananda Babu, the senior clerk of the department, came upstairs with a bundle of papers for Ray-Chaudhuri's signature. Being a true scientist, Ray-Chaudhuri was not very happy because the joy of scientific discussion was interrupted. After signing those papers, he told me, "Pathak! Never accept the position of a chairman in your future career; you would become a glorified clerk." His cytogenetics lab became so well-equipped that every research scholar, about 10 at that time, was assigned his/her own microscope. The Zeiss Photomicroscope that I had used in the lab for the past 10 years was bought into the famous "Mecca of Mammalian Cytogenetics" lab of TC Hsu at The University of Texas MD Anderson Cancer Center in Houston in 1974. Ray-Chaudhuri being a professional magnet had received grants not only from the Government of India but also from abroad, including the USA. One morning, in the hallway of our department, I was opening a big wooden box of shipments received from the USA. It was an international centrifuge machine that was purchased from his Rockefeller Foundation grant. Ray-Chaudhuri had just arrived on a Rickshaw and saw me working on the box. He exclaimed, "Pathak! There will be no scarcity of equipment and supplies in the lab here, but one day there will be a scarcity of workers." By that time Ray-Chaudhuri's daughter, Ratna Ray-Chaudhuri (married name Dr. Ratna Nandi), arrived from Kalyani University to work on the chromosomes of birds for her Ph.D. degree. At that time, modern techniques used in Cytogenetics were not established anywhere in India. So, whenever examiners from other universities visited the BHU Zoology lab, they were always requesting microphotographs. Later, the human blood culture technique was established by Surabhi Kakati who worked on the effect of radiation on human chromosomes for her Ph.D. dissertation. Ray-Chaudhuri and his student G. K. Manna were the first in India to start a cancer cytogenetics laboratory at Chittaranjan Cancer Centre in Calcutta.

Ray-Chaudhuri became instrumental in hiring M. S. Kanungo as a biochemist and G.P. Agarwal as a parasitologist to add these disciplines to the department. He also provided T. Sharma a permanent faculty position in Zoology to assist and carry on his legacy of cytogenetics. A couple of years later, the Annual Meeting of the Zoological Society of India was held in BHU and Professor AB Misra was the President of the Society. Prof MA Moghe of Nagpur, who had done incredible research on the endocrinology of various bat species, also attended the meeting. Ray-Chaudhuri had a separate meeting with Prof Moghe and since I was working on the chromosomes of bats, he asked me to join. In that meeting, Prof Moghe said, "Every zoology department in India must copy the prospectus of BHU's zoology department." He was very impressed and happy to see for the first time the chromosomes of local bat species and promised to help procure other species found in Nagpur and Nanded areas in the State of Maharashtra.

Ray-Chaudhuri was a born teacher and a great scientific storyteller. He used to teach us genetics and cytogenetics by narrating incidents in the labs of Prof HJ Muller and Prof PC Koller. One of his many pet projects was focused on chemical protection against radiation damage, on which most of his students did their Ph.D. dissertations. Surabhi Kakati was his first student who used the newly purchased Picker X-Ray Machine to study the effect of radiation on human chromosomes. By that time, Ratna was working on avian cytogenetics, Surabhi on human chromosomes, Sen Pathak on chiropteran chromosomes, P.V. Ranjini, a senior teacher in Women's College, on Mongoose chromosomes. Lalji Singh, who was then a master's degree student in the department, started to work on snake chromosomes. One day Najju Mia, an animal supplier, brought a non-poisonous snake for Lalji to prepare its chromosomes. Lalji was waiting for T. Sharma to show him the technique of snake chromosome preparation but he never showed up. Late in the evening, I went to help this M.Sc. student who waited almost a whole day to learn the methodology. Since I was familiar with the chromosome preparation from the very small thin bones of *Pipisrellus* sp., I suggested taking out the ribs of the snake and making chromosomes. This is where "Lady Luck" first smiled on Lalji and we both saw many metaphases of the snake's macro- and micro-chromosomes under the microscope, a characteristic shared with reptilian and avian species.

One day when both of us (Lalji) were working on the answer books of students in his office, Alagoo brought tea for us. While we took a break and started taking tea, he told me the story of how he was able to get a *Drosophila* lab at Calcutta University. For that, he was grateful to one of his Ph.D. thesis examiners, Professor John Burdon Sanderson Haldane. Prof Haldane was a famous biochemist, geneticist, mathematician, journalist, classical scholar, and politician from the University College in London. Around 1957, Haldane and his wife, Helen, migrated to India and decided to stay in Calcutta. He used to give a series of talks at the Indian Statistical Institute (ISI) in Calcutta, where Professor Prasanta Chandra Mahalanobis was the Director. One day, Haldane asked Ray-Chaudhuri about his research on *Drosophila*. Ray-Chaudhuri did not have a *Drosophila* genetics lab because no one was interested in that subject at the time. Haldane wrote a letter to Sir JC Ghosh, then VC of Calcutta University, with a copy to the Head of Zoology, regarding joining the department as a Visiting Professor and his immediate need for an air-conditioned *Drosophila* lab where Ray-Chaudhuri could maintain the stocks of flies that he will ship from London.

Realizing that such a distinguished scientist will be joining Calcutta University, an air-conditioned lab was immediately established where Ray-Chaudhuri started maintaining the *Drosophila* stocks that he had received from London. Several months passed but there was no trace of Haldane. One day Ray-Chaudhuri met with Haldane at the ISI and told him, "Sir! We are all eagerly waiting for your arrival to work in the newly established *Drosophila* lab, and I am taking care of those stocks. When will you be back Sir?" Haldane replied, "That lab is for you to carry on research on *Drosophila* genetics and I am not joining there." Ray-Chaudhuri was shocked, but this is the way he was able to get a *Drosophila* research lab in the Zoology Department of Calcutta University. Mr. P.G. Kale, a former M.Sc. student of Professor MA Moghe from Nagpur, who had just registered for his Ph.D. under Ray-Chaudhuri, became instrumental in bringing the stocks of flies from his Calcutta *Drosophila* lab to BHU.

Ray-Chaudhuri was not only a distinguished geneticist, and a great mentor, but he also knew how to smoothly administer a department of such magnitude. He often put the requirements and demands of his colleagues before his own. One summer day, I was in his office discussing some project when a junior faculty member with an earthen pot (Surahi) entered Ray-Chaudhuri's office and said in an angry tone, "How come, there is nobody assigned to fill up water for me, whereas, other faculty members in the department have someone to help them." Ray-Chaudhuri got up from his chair, took the earthen pot in his own hand, and said "I will fill up water for you." I was shocked to witness the scene. Later, he told the faculty member that no one in the department has been given special privileges for this task. Only some faculty members who have their own grants can hire a lab assistant for such tasks. This illustrated another humane characteristic of Ray-Chaudhuri. A few years later, another incident took place in the department. Six assistant professor positions were advertised in Zoology and there were seven local applicants including me. Due to my first-class-first ranking in M.Sc., publications, and Ph.D. under Ray-Chaudhuri, every faculty member of the department and even some of my fellow applicants and classmates started congratulating me before the interview date. My interview went on very smoothly and I replied satisfactorily to most questions asked by the experts. When the appointment result was announced, guess what happened? Everyone was appointed except me. I felt very ashamed, but I never asked Ray-Chaudhuri why I was not appointed. About nine months later, Ray-Chaudhuri and I were walking toward the central office to clear some bills. He then asked me, "Pathak! Do you know why you were not appointed?" I said, "No Sir." he replied, "All experts had unanimously agreed to appoint you, but I told them to appoint the students of all my colleagues and I sacrificed my own student. I wanted to keep my colleagues happy by appointing their students." From this incident, I learned a great lesson in my life. God had something else planned for me. I came to the USA and join The University of Texas MD Anderson Cancer Center in Houston. Dr. S.P. Shukla, a former Professor of Zoology once told me, "One great thing that had happened in the history of this Zoology Department is that two former students of Prof Ray-Chaudhuri, Sen Pathak and Lalji Singh, were not appointed here." Of course, Shukla was right. Lalji and I, who hailed from the villages of India, went in our own ways in our future endeavors. I can tell with great honesty that by following the humane instructions of my teacher Prof Ray-Chaudhuri, I am who I am today.

In 1980, I invited Ray-Chaudhuri (Fig. 1) for a distinguished seminar series at MD Anderson Cancer Center in Houston while he was in Maryland visiting his daughter. Prof TC Hsu was immensely impressed by Ray-Chaudhuri's talk and told me during a reception, "Sen! Now I know who has trained you not only in cytogenetics but also in being a true human being." After visiting his students in various places in the USA, Canada, and Europe and returning to India, in one of his hand-written letters dated June 3, 1981, Ray-Chaudhuri wrote, "(Pathak)! You can imagine how pleased I was to see you people so well-liked and respected in your place of work. What else can a true teacher ask for from his students? I am proud of my students and will have a peaceful death." Ray-Chaudhuri passed away at the age of 87 in his hometown of Calcutta after a short illness on February 15, 1994. He was a visionary, who successfully established one of the best zoology departments in India and shared his success in the form of stories with his students and colleagues. He was always involved and had forward-thinking about the entire zoology department. He found many ways to encourage the young generation to advance their scientific aptitudes and work to the best of their capabilities. Without any reservation, I would call him "The Father of Animal Cytogenetics and *Drosophila* Genetics Research" in India. He was elected a Fellow of the National Institute of Science of India in 1950 and was the President of the Zoological Section of the Indian Science Congress in 1960.

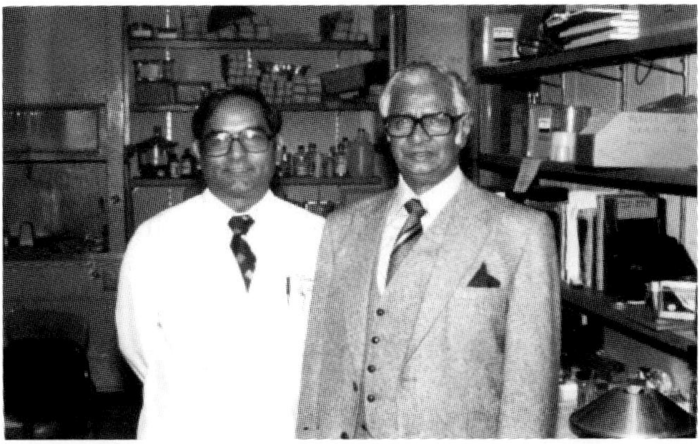

Figure 1: Author with Prof. S.P. Ray-Chaudhuri.

Bibliography

1. Pathak, S. (2000) Prof. S.P. Ray-Chaudhuri (1907-1994): An architectural scientist. Current Science 78(11), 1392-1394.

AUTHOR PROFILE

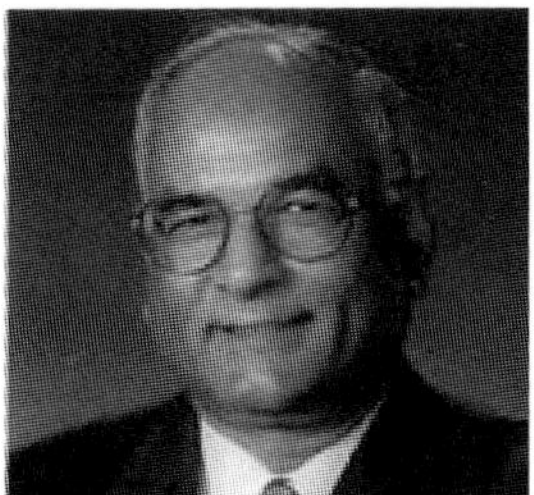

Dr. Sen Pathak is a Distinguished Professor Emeritus at the University of Texas MD Anderson Cancer Center, Houston, Texas, USA.

Emails: spathak@mdanderson.org ; spathak@gmail.com

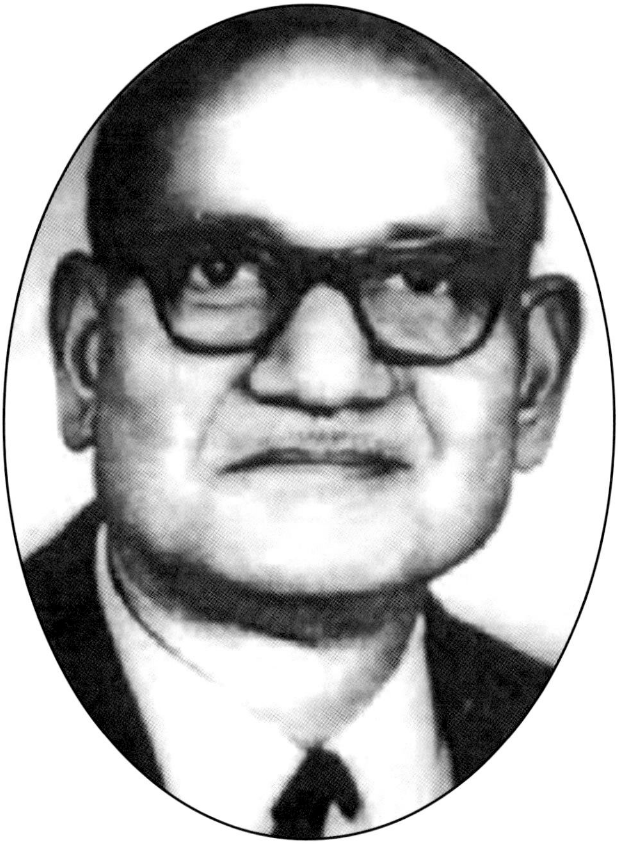

Ramdeo Misra

(26/08/1908 – 25/06/1998)

RAMDEO MISRA: FATHER OF ECOLOGY IN INDIA

Gopa Pandey

India's outreach in mainstreaming ecology in biological sciences has expanded through the decades of the fifties, sixties, and seventies during the last century. The subject was largely introduced in Indian universities by the knowledge emerging from the Botany Department of Banaras Hindu University, Varanasi, under the guidance of Ramdeo Misra. Popularly known as the Father of Ecology in India, Prof Misra started teaching and research in ecology way back in the forties. His research laid to the understanding of tropical communities and their succession, environmental responses of plant populations, productivity, and nutrient cycling in tropical forest and grassland ecosystems. He established teaching and research in ecology at the Department of Botany of the Banaras Hindu University, Varanasi; and formulated the first postgraduate course in ecology in India. He played a pivotal role in the establishment of the Ministry of Environment and Forests.

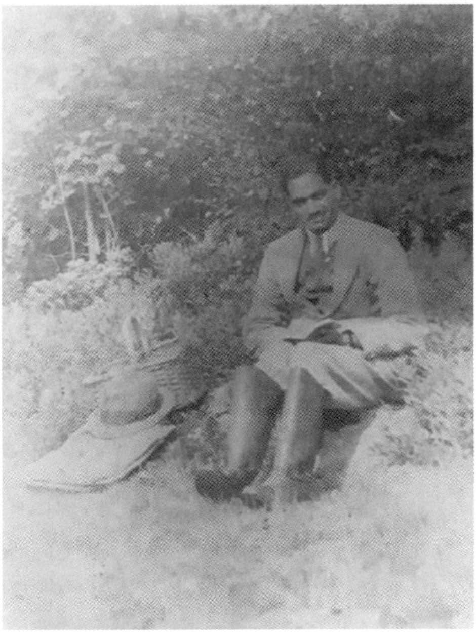

Figure 1: Prof Ramdeo Misra during his Ph.D. days at Leeds University (1934-36).

Early Life and Education

Ramdeo Misra was born on August 26, 1908, in Dobhi, Jaunpur district of Uttar Pradesh, India. He had his early education in Varanasi and obtained Bachelor of Science (B.Sc.) and Master of Science in Botany (M.Sc.) degrees from Banaras Hindu University. Subsequently, he joined the Department of Botany as a lecturer, but soon afterward went to England where he did his Ph. D. in Ecology under Prof. W. H. Pearsall, FRS, from Leeds University in the UK, in 1938 (Fig.1). He showed the importance of edaphic factors in growth and distribution of macrophytes in English Lakes.

Return to India and Contribution to Science

After completing his Ph. D, he returned to India and helped in establishing a school of ecology teaching and research at the Department of Botany, Banaras Hindu University (BHU). For a brief period of time (1946-55) he moved to the Department of Botany, University of Saugor, Sagar (Madhya Pradesh, India) as a Reader and served as the Head of the Department. He returned to the Department of Botany, BHU as a Professor. He served as the Head of the Department (1954-71) (Fig.2), Dean of Faculty, and Vice-Chairman of the Academic Council, BHU, Varanasi. He continued to work as Professor Emeritus at BHU till his death. Prof. Misra is credited to formulate the first postgraduate course in ecology (in 1941) in India.

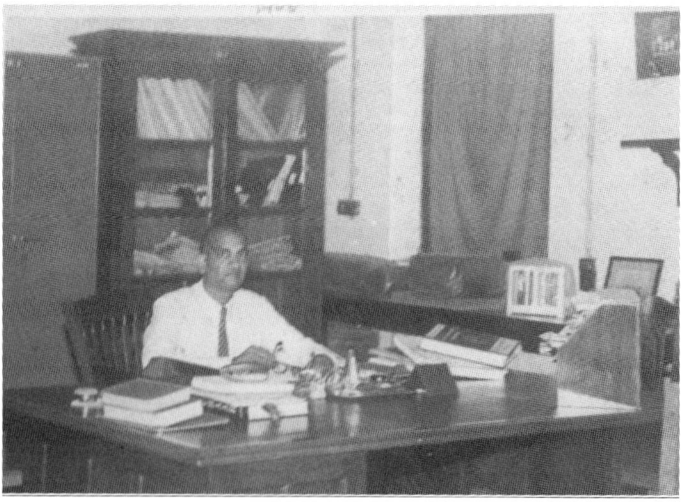

Figure 2: Prof Misra working in his office at the Department of Botany, BHU.

Upon his return from England, he made extensive studies on the vegetation of the Upper Gangetic plains and initiated an experimental approach in ecology to make it objectively verifiable. He surveyed and classified the aquatic, marshy, and terrestrial plant communities and described their environmental relationships. He was instrumental in getting projects to support his researchers leading to classic works in temperate, tropical, and arid zone climes. To name a few- the PL 480 in the sixties and UNESCO Man and Biosphere Program in the seventies which assisted integrated study of ecosystem components by over a dozen research scholars in each program. At Sagar University, he worked on the ecology of forests and grasslands. His research laid the foundation for the understanding of tropical communities and their succession, environmental responses of plant populations, productivity, and nutrient cycling in tropical forests and grassland ecosystems. Under his leadership, the Department of Botany, BHU, gained international recognition for research on the ecology of tropical ecosystems (forests, grasslands, ponds, lakes, etc.). He used innovative ways to measure soil redox potential and studied plant adaptations along soil-moisture gradients. He developed the theory of body biomass build-up, demonstrated ecotypic differentiation; discussed synecological and autecological hypotheses, and promoted environmental education in India (refer to INSA fellow citation).

He supervised 60 students for their Ph.D., who spread out to various institutions across the country and established vibrant centers of ecology at their respective places. The introduction of ecology as a course in universities and institutions is primarily because of the efforts of Prof. Misra. He organized several short-term summer schools/professional courses on ecology for teachers, planners, administrators, etc. Organized several national and international seminars and symposia. He had published about 150 research papers and authored and edited 10 books.

Due to his efforts, the Government of India established the National Committee for Environmental Planning and Coordination (NCEPC) in 1972, which paved the way for the establishment of the Ministry of Environment and Forests (1984). He was a member of the committee (1969-72) and the chairmanship of Dr. Pitambar Pant, to prepare India's contribution to the UN Conference on the human environment (Stockholm Conference of 1972). He drafted the speech of Prime Minister Indira

Gandhi for the conference. In 1956, along with Dr. G.S. Puri and Dr. F.R. Fosberg (Smithsonian Institute USA), he founded the International Society for Tropical Ecology, with its headquarters at BHU, which has played a significant role in addressing ecological issues of tropical areas. He served as the treasurer and president, and chief editor (1960-85) of its journal *Tropical Ecology*. In 1974, he started the journal *International Journal of Ecology & Environmental Sciences* and acted as its chief editor (1975-88). He was on the editorial board of several journals, notably, *Agroecosystems* and *Applied Ecology Abstracts*. He was associated with the formation of the Indian Council of Ecological Research and its journal *Indian Ecologists*. He also helped in the establishment of the National Institute of Ecology. He developed content on ecology and population ecology for XII standard NCERT book. Besides, Prof Misra served as –

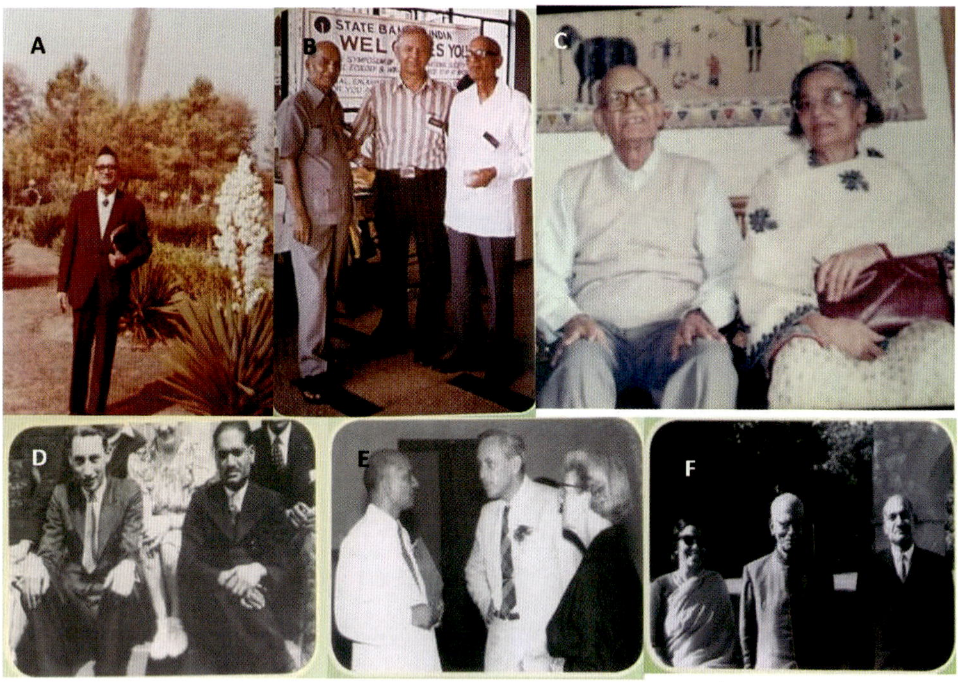

Figure 3: Prof. Misra (a); with Prof. K.C. Misra (left) and Frank B. Golley (center) (July 1982) (b); with his wife (c); with Prof. W.H. Pearsall (1936) (D); with Prof K.V. Thimann and Mrs. Thimann (Delhi, 26 August 1957) (E); and with his wife and Prof. Parija 1959) (F).

- Vice-Chairman of the International Coordination Council to UNESCO's Man and Biosphere Programme.
- Chairman of the International Commission for Training & Research Ecology (1967).
- Member, Governing Body of Wildlife Institute of India (1986-1995),
- Advisory Board of Botanical Survey of India (1970-73),
- Vice-Chairman, MAB National Committee (1972-75)
- Member, INSA Council (1981-83).
- President, Botany Section, Indian Science Congress (1958).

Awards and Honours

- Founder Fellow, National Institute of Ecology
- Indian Botanical Society (President, 1959)
- Fellow, National Academy of Sciences India, Allahabad
- Fellow, Indian National Science Academy (INSA), New Delhi (1955)
- International Society for Tropical Ecology (President, 1971-75).
- Birbal Sahni Gold Medal (1967)
- Jawaharlal Nehru Gold Medal (Madhya Pradesh Vigyan Academy) (1974);
- Bronze Medal International Society for Tropical Ecology (1979);
- Sanjay Gandhi Award for Environment and Ecology (Government of India) (1984);
- Professor TS Sadasivan Endowment Lecture (INSA) (1984)
- Swami Pranavanand Saraswati Award (UGC) (1986).
- Delivered the Malaviya Memorial Foundation Lecture (BHU) (1986)
- Platinum Jubilee Lecture Indian Science Congress (1991).

Commemorative medals have been instituted in honor of Ramdeo Misra, e.g., the Founder's Medal by the International Society for Tropical Ecology (instituted in 1979) and; Ramdeo Misra Gold Medal by the Indian Environmental Society (instituted in 1980).

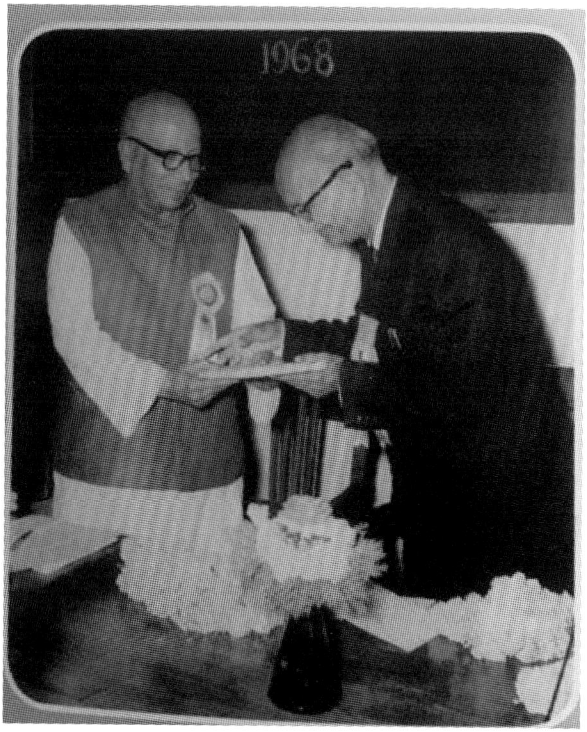

Figure 4: Prof. Misra is being felicitated by Prof. Trigun Sen, Education Minister of India (1968).

Personal Life

Prof. Misra was married to Sunanda Misra who studied at BHU and was the daughter of Pt. Ramavatar Sharma, a professor in Sanskrit at Patna University. They had four daughters and a son.

Epilogue

He was a stalwart in radiating knowledge. An extremely charming presence due to his soft-spoken style coming from a Gandhian personality and simple language without prefixes, he had the ability to attract the full attention of the audience. He used to wear khadi. He laid strong foundations for the subject and left behind a legacy in international ecology understanding in India. He had a passion to relate simple things in nature to ecological principles. Often, he would quote relevant lines from Vedas to correlate forms, factors, and functions in the ecosystem, making it easier to comprehend. He parted from his roots in mother earth saying goodbye forever on June 25, 1998 in New Delhi. The candles of ecology lighted by him in every nook and corner of the country will always enlighten the lives and times of people studying ecology.

AUTHORS PROFILE

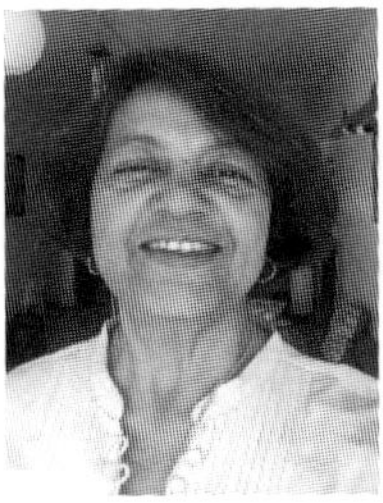

The author is a member of the Indian Forest Service (IFS) and has served in the Government of Madhya Pradesh during 1984-2015. She is a Ph.D. in grassland ecology from BHU, in 1980.

Email: pandeyg121@gmail.com

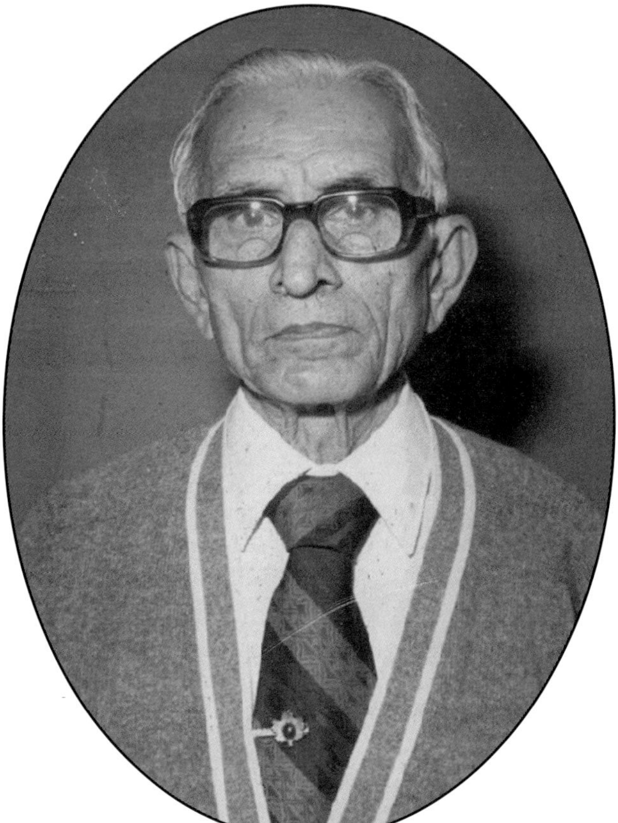

Ratan Nadirshaw Sukheswala

(1 December 1910 to 3 June 1992)

RATAN NADIRSHAW SUKHESWALA: THE CARBONATITE MAN OF INDIA

Ashwin Pundalik & Hrishikesh Samant

Dr Ratan Nadirshaw Sukheswala (hereinafter Dr R N Sukheswala) was a researcher and an academic who contributed substantially to the advancement of Geology during the days when Geology, as well as Earth Sciences education, was in its nascent stages in India (Tolman 2006). Dr. Sukheswala's pioneering research on the Igneous Rocks of the Deccan Traps of Western India, the Igneous Rocks of Mumbai Volcanic Complex, and alkaline-carbonatite magmatic complexes associated with Deccan Traps are a benchmark for researchers.

Early Life and Education

Dr. R N Sukheswala was born on 01st December 1910 in Valsad, Gujarat. He received his primary education at Seth R.J.J.A.V. School and Bai Avabai High School, Bulsar. He passed his Matriculation examination in the year 1928. He won the Pirojaha P. Dhanbhoora gold medal for standing first in the school in the matriculation examination (Sethna 1992). In those days, Geology was not a career option for most of the youngsters, and prime geological organizations like the Geological Survey of India were not keen on hiring Indian geologists (Tolman 2006). However, young Ratan had a passion for studying nature; especially to understand the origin and evolution of the Earth. For a serious study of Geology, he came to Mumbai (erstwhile Bombay) and joined Wilson College, Mumbai, from where he cleared the First Year Science examination. For his Intermediate Science examination, he joined St. Xavier's College, Mumbai which was the only institution in Western India offering Geology as a subject since 1895, at the Under-Graduate level, through the erstwhile University of Bombay (now University of Mumbai). After passing the B.Sc. examination with Geology and Chemistry, in 1932, he then registered for M.Sc. with research under Dr A. S. Kalapesi, and with the help and guidance of Prof. S.K. Chhapgar and Dr. Kalapesi, he determined the age of the Deccan Traps in Mumbai area, by Pb/U ratio. Based on the Pb/U ratios of basalts and andesites collected from Colaba, Goregaon, Borivali and Cambala, they assigned the age of 68.4 My to 45.6 My to these rocks (Kalapsei et al. 1941). He continued this work for his Ph. D degree, which had just started at the University of Mumbai. In 1938, he was awarded his Ph. D degree, making him the first to be awarded a Ph. D. at the University of Mumbai in Geology (Sukheswala, 1938; Kalapesi et al. 1941; Sethna 1992). The Ph.D. thesis of Dr. Sukheswala was examined by the great geologist and later the director of Geological Survey of India, Cyril S. Fox (Fig.1), who considered the work to be worthy of being awarded for the degree of D.Sc.

Professional Career and Contribution to Science

After getting the doctoral degree, Dr Sukheswala joined the Department of Geology, St. Xavier's College in 1939 as a Lecturer (Sethna 1992). Apart from his work on volcanic rocks of Mumbai, he took a keen interest in the intertrappean sedimentary rocks of Mumbai Island and discovered a fossil of a tortoise (*Testudo leithii*) from the Worli Hills, Mumbai (Sukheswala 1947) which is now in the collection of the Indian Museum at Kolkata (Webb 1980). In 1953, he described some of the volcanic and intertrappean rock types of Mumbai, and the fossil fauna of the Intertrappean bed of Worli Hill (Sukheswala 1953; Sethna 1992).

In 1954, Dr. Sukheswala took over as the Head of the Geology Department and in 1955, he joined Columbia University as a post-doctoral research fellow and continued his research on the petrology of igneous rocks of Mumbai. Under the guidance of Dr. Arie Poldervaart, he prepared the first-ever detailed geological map of Mumbai which is a standard reference for geologists working in the area (Sukheswala and Poldervaart 1958). Based on the petrography and geochemistry of rocks such as albite-basalt, olivine basalt, rhyodacite, rhyolite, monchiquite, pitchstone and oceanite, Sukheswala and Poldervaart (1958) stated that the basalts in Mumbai region have undergone rapid cooling and incomplete crystallisation, while rhyodacitic rocks are formed due to magmatic differentiation and diffusion of volatiles.

After returning from the U.S.A. in 1956, Dr Sukheswala introduced an M.Sc. course by papers in Geology and took up the task of modernizing the department with limited resources and grants from the UGC. In June 1957, the M.Sc. course by papers in Geology was first introduced at Mumbai University (Sethna 1992) and the department expanded considerably. Till 1965, he was the only recognized post-graduate teacher in geology at the University of Mumbai.

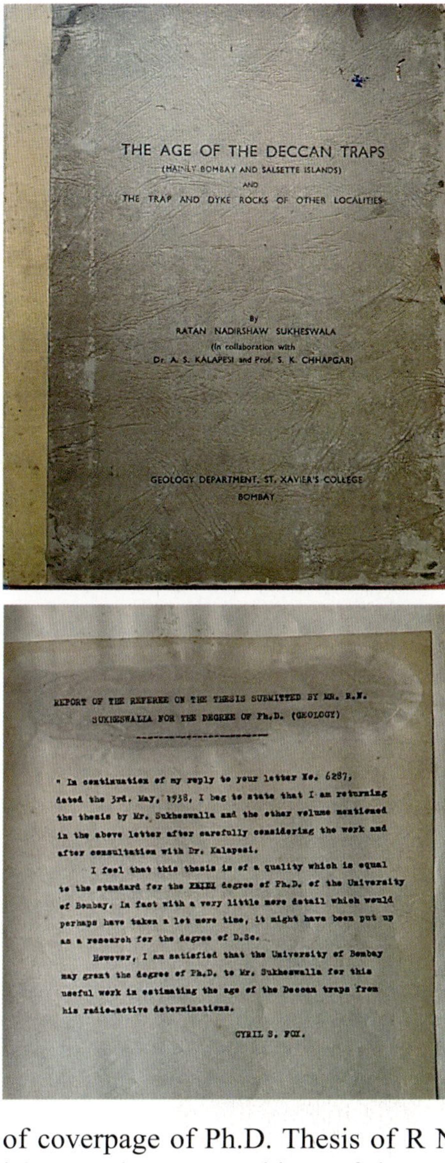

THE AGE OF THE DECCAN TRAPS
(MAINLY BOMBAY AND SALSETTE ISLANDS)
AND
THE TRAP AND DYKE ROCKS OF OTHER LOCALITIES

By
RATAN NADIRSHAW SUKHESWALA
(In collaboration with
Dr. A. S. KALAPESI and Prof. S. K. CHHAPGAR)

GEOLOGY DEPARTMENT, ST. XAVIER'S COLLEGE
BOMBAY

REPORT OF THE REFEREE ON THE THESIS SUBMITTED BY MR. R.N. SUKHESWALLA FOR THE DEGREE OF Ph.D. (GEOLOGY)

" In continuation of my reply to your letter No. 6287, dated the 3rd. May, 1958, I beg to state that I am returning the thesis by Mr. Sukheswalla and the other volume mentioned in the above letter after carefully considering the work and after consultation with Dr. Kalapesi.

I feel that this thesis is of a quality which is equal to the standard for the degree of Ph.D. of the University of Bombay. In fact with a very little more detail which would perhaps have taken a lot more time, it might have been put up as a research for the degree of D.Sc.

However, I am satisfied that the University of Bombay may grant the degree of Ph.D. to Mr. Sukheswalla for this useful work in estimating the age of the Deccan traps from his radio-active determinations.

CYRIL S. FOX.

Figure 1: The photo of coverpage of Ph.D. Thesis of R N Sukheswala and the review report by Cyril S. Fox. (Source: archives of the Department of Geology, St. Xavier's College (Autonomous), Mumbai)

Because of its composition consisting of a variety of basic, felsic-intermediate volcanic rocks, intrusive igneous rocks and large volumes of tuffs, the geology of Mumbai is unique as compared to the main Deccan Traps (Sheth et al. 2001; Duraiswami et al. 2019). Dr Sukheswala pioneered the research on the petrological complexity of these volcanic and intrusive rocks. He described repetitive series of green and black ashes occurring at Malabar and Worli hills (Sukheswala 1956), and similar facies occurring around Jogeshwari (Sukheswala and Awate 1957). He opined that the regional volcanic activity made the Mumbai region geologically inhospitable for life during Deccan volcanism. He stated that the volcanic and pyroclastic units were substantially reworked, eventually becoming clay and organic matter-rich, as reflected in a transition from tuffs and rhyolites to dark, fossiliferous shales in the Malabar and Worli hills (Sukheswala 1956; Cripps et al. 2005). The chemical analysis of trachytes and rhyolites carried out by him proved them to be sub-acidic differentiates of the theoleiitic magma, originating due to diffusion of volatiles (Sukheswala and Poldervaart 1958; Sukheswala and Sethna 1962). Further, he recognised that the differentiation of the Deccan Traps theoleiitic magma culminated into acidic fractions represented by the rhyolite lavas which occur at Manori, west of Malad and at Gorai, west of Borivali in Northern Bombay (Sukheswala and Awate 1957; Sukheswala and Poldervaart 1958). Similar acidic fractionation of the Deccan Traps theoleiitic magma was also traced by him in collaboration with H.N. Siddique in deep sea drilling project site 219 on the Laccadive Ridge (Siddique and Sukheswala 1976). Sukheswala and Avasia (1966) reported the occurrence of nepheline syenite dyke at Jawhar near Mumbai. He identified three zeolite zones (laumontite, scolecite, and heulandite) within Deccan Traps and suggested that the different zones of zeolite mineralization are the result of increasing depth and the action of circulating fluids on the rocks (Sukheswala et al. 1974). He also reported spilite pillows in Mumbai Volcanic Complex, at Bhoiwada in Parel and at Kurar at Malad in the Northern Metropolitan Region, thereby suggesting the subaqueous nature of volcanism in the Mumbai region (Sukheswala 1974). He described the presence of glass blebs in basalts at Antop Hill, Mumbai (Sukheswala et al. 1979). Dr. S. J. Najafi, a Ph. D student of Dr. Sukheswala carried out the geochemical analysis of basaltic lava flows from the Mahabaleshwar-Mahad section and laid the foundation for the concept of chemo-stratigraphically differentiating lava flows (Najafi et al. 1981).

Dr. Sukheswala put India on the international carbonatite map. He discovered Carbonatite complex at Amba Dongar region, Gujarat (Fig. 2). The carbonatite plug intrudes the Deccan lavas which are overlain by the Bagh Beds of the Upper Cretaceous age (Sukeshwala and Udas 1963; Yellur 1968). This is a ring structure with carbonatite breccia, sovite and ankeritic carbonatite (Sukheswala and Udas 1963, 1964; Viladkar 1981).

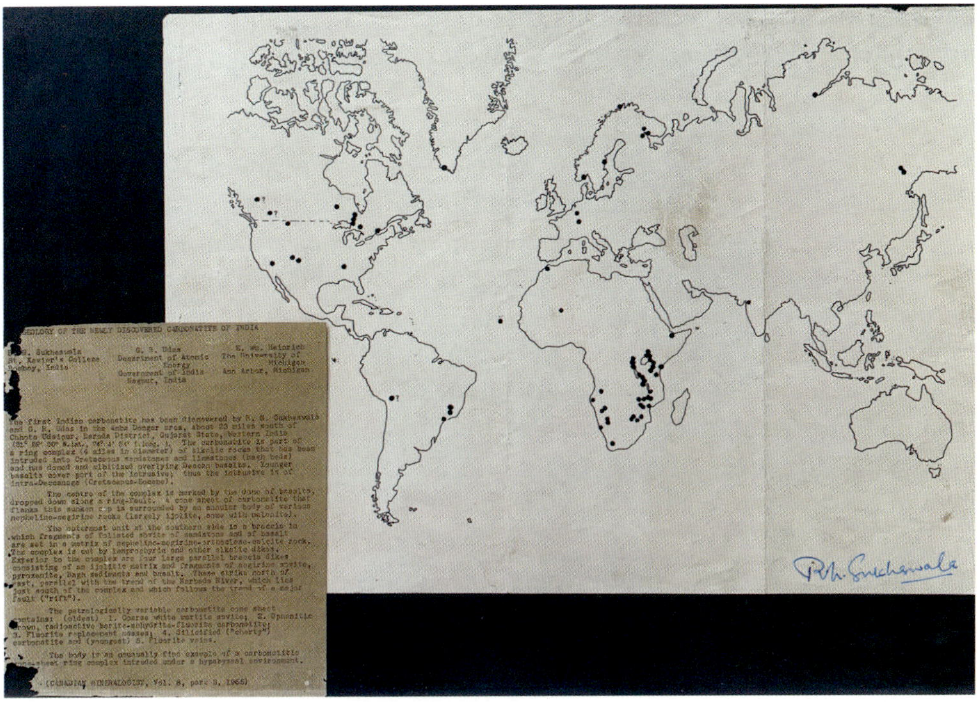

Figure 2: The original map showing the location of carbonatite from Amba Dongar in Gujarat, drawn by Dr. Sukheswala and concept note (inset) about the geology of the area. This was the first discovery of carbonatites from India, which added a new dimension to India's geological studies.

At that time, carbonatite was known from only at a few places in the world, most of them being in the major rift zones within the earth's crust, the most prominent of them existing in the African rift valley (Oldoinyo Lengai) and in the Rhine Graben rift (Kaiserthul) in Germany (Sukheswala 1976). The volcanic to subvolcanic type Amba Dongar carbonatite-alkalic complex exhibits not only the structural disturbances due to the emplacement of carbonatites, such as doming and radial faulting but also the explosive activity in the form of large circular outcrops of volcanic fluidized breccia in between the sovite and the central core basalt (Sukheswala and Udas 1963, 1964; Sukheswala 1976; Sukheswala and Viladkar 1981). The Amba Dongar carbonatite was rich in Fluorite mineralisation which sustained the largest mines in India (Subramaniyam and Parimoo 1963; Sukheswala and Udas 1967). Dr. Sukheswala's research proved that fluorspar was genetically related to carbonatite magma. He further reported carbonatite-alkaline complexes at Panwad-Kawant (Gujarat), Chota Udaipur (Gujarat), with his associates, R.K. Avasia and S.G. Viladkar, which gave new insights about this unique alkaline magmatism. (Sukheswala and Avasia 1971; Dean et al. 1973; Sukheswala and Borges 1975; Sukheswala and Viladkar 1981). Dr. Sukheswala further continued his research on alkaline magmatism, particularly in Western India along with his colleagues and research students. He described Phenai Mata hill as a composite plug which is successively filled by basalt, gabbro, granophyre and nepheline syenite, and later described the characteristics of layered gabbro within it (Sukheswala and Sethna 1964, 1969). Sukheswala and Sethna (1967) reported Pseudoleucite bearing tinguaite dyke near the village of Ghori near Phenai Mata, Chhota Udaipur. The pseudoleucite-bearing tinguaite is one of many dykes in a dyke cluster trending ENE, intrusive into the Cretaceous Bagh Beds. Sukheswala et al (1971) gave a detailed account of this dyke cluster.

Administrative Responsibilities

Prof. Sukheswala retired in 1976, but he continued to guide research students as a Professor Emeritus and delivered lectures to post-graduate students until 1984 (Sethna 1992). He was the first Director of the Caius Laboratory for Interdisciplinary Research at St. Xavier's College, Mumbai. In November 1979, in conjunction with Prof. K.V. Subbarao of I.I.T., Mumbai, he successfully organized an International Symposium on 'Deccan Volcanism and Related Basalt Provinces in other parts of the World', held partly in Mumbai and partly in Khandala, with field excursions in between, which was attended by a number of foreign earth scientists (Sethna 1992).

Awards and Honours

Prof. Sukheswala served St. Xavier's College, Mumbai ardently and educated several hundred students to achieve their careers in Geology and the allied fields. For his long and exceptional service to the Catholic church by being an exceptional teacher in St. Xavier's College - Bombay, India, and a researcher in the field of Geology, he was awarded the prestigious Benemerenti Medal by Pope Paul VI on 26th September 1968, an honour bestowed on just a couple of Indians in the entire history of the Vatican Church (Fig. 3).

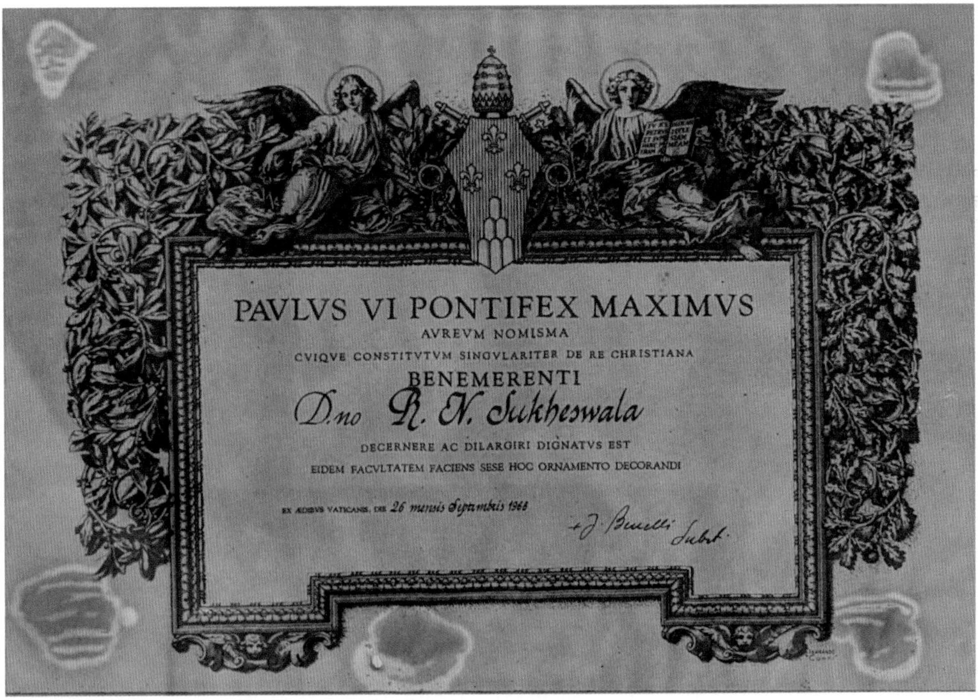

Figure 3: Benemerenti Medal by Pope Paul VI was awarded to Dr R N Sukheswala on 26th September 1968, he was the first Indian to receive the honour.

He was a Corresponding Member of the Sub-commission on Systematics of Igneous Rocks, IUGS; and was a Member of the Indian National Committee for the International Geological Correlation Programme. He was awarded Pramatha Nath Bose Memorial Medal by the Asiatic Society in 1978. He was elected a Fellow of the Geological Society of India; Indian Society of Earth Sciences; Geological, Mining and Metallurgical Society of India (also served as Vice-President); Earth Science Society of India (also elected President); Indian National Science Academy (INSA) and Maharashtra Academy of Sciences.

Demise

Prof. Sukheswala passed away after a brief illness on 3rd June 1992. He will be remembered for his ever-lasting contribution to igneous petrology and the geology of the Deccan Traps. During his time, when a majority of researchers were interested only in mineralogy and petrology, he chose a different path and added new dimensions to the petrology and understanding of magmatic processes. His pioneering work on alkaline-carbonatite complexes, intricacies of the geology of the Mumbai Volcanic complex and stratigraphy of Deccan Traps have become benchmarks for future researchers.

Acknowledgements

This article is based on the drafts sent by Dr S.F. Sethna and Dr R.K. Avasia. The article has benefitted immensely through the editorial support from Ms Jyoti More, a faculty member from the Language Lab, St. Xavier's College-Mumbai.

Bibliography

1. Cripps, J. A., Widdowson, M., Spicer, R. A., Jolley, D. W. (2005) Coastal ecosystem responses to late stage Deccan Trap volcanism: the post K–T boundary (Danian) palynofacies of Mumbai (Bombay), west India. Palaeogeography, Palaeoclimatology, Palaeoecology 216(3-4), 303-332.
2. Deans, T., Sukheswala, R. N., Sethna, S. F., Viladkar, S. G. (1973) Discussion and contributions: Metasomatic feldspar rocks (potash fenites) associated with the fluorite deposits and carbonatites of Amba Dongar, Gujarat, India. Transactions of the Institutions of Mining and Metallurgy 82, 33-40.
3. Duraiswami, R. A., Jutzeler, M., Karve, A. V., Gadpallu, P., Kale, M. G. (2019) Subaqueous effusive and explosive phases of late Deccan volcanism: evidence from Mumbai Islands, India. Arabian Journal of Geosciences 12, 1-21.
4. Kalapesi, A. S., Chhapgar, S. K., Sukheswala, R. N. (1941). A note on the "Lead Ratio" method for determining the age of Deccan Traps. Current Science 10(12), 526-528.
5. Najafi, S. J., Cox, K. G., Sukheswala, R. N. (1981) Geology and geochemistry of the basalt flows (Deccan Traps) of the Mahad-Mahableshwar section, India. Memoir-Geological Society of India (3), 300-315.
6. Sethna, S. F. (1992) RN Sukheswala (1910-1992). Geological Society of India 40(3), 291-292.

7. Sheth, H. C., Pande, K., Bhutani, R. (2001) 40Ar-39Ar age of a national geological monument: The Gilbert Hill basalt, Deccan Traps, Bombay. Current Science 80(11), 1437-1439.
8. Siddiquie, H. N., Sukheswala, R. N. (1976) Occurrence of rhyolytic tuffs at deep sea drilling project site 219 on the Laccadive Ridge. Jour. Geol. Soc. India, v.17 (4), 539-546.
9. Subbarao, K. V., Reddy, V. V., Reddy, G. R., Sukheswala, R. N. (1979) Rare Earth Element Geochemistry of Basalt-Spilite Association of Bombay and Carlsberg Ridge-A Preliminary Study. Geological Society of India 20(10), 517-519.
10. Subramaniam, A. P., Parimoo, M. L. (1963). Fluorspar mineralization related to Deccan basalt volcanism at Amba Dongar, Baroda district, India. Nature 198, 563-564.
11. Sukheswala, R. N. (1938). Age of the Deccan Traps (mainly Bombay and Salsette Islands) and the trap and dyke rocks of other localities. Ph.D. Thesis, Bombay University.
12. Sukheswala, R. N. (1947). A fossil tortoise (*Testudo leithii*) from the intertrappean of the Worli Hill, Bombay. In Proceedings of the Indian Science Congress, 33rd Session, p. 97.
13. Sukheswala, R. N. (1953) Notes on the field occurrence and petrography of the rocks of the Bombay Island, Bombay. Transactions of the Indian Institution of Mining and Metallurgy 50, 101-126.
14. Sukheswala, R. N. (1974). Gradation of tholeiitic Deccan basalt into spilite, Bombay, India. In Spilites and spilitic rocks. Springer Berlin Heidelberg, pp. 229-250.
15. Sukheswala, R. N. (1976) Carbonatite kimberlite complexes of India. *Geological Society of India* 17 (4), 429-438.
16. Sukheswala, R. N. Poldervaart, A. (1958) Deccan basalts of the Bombay area, India. Geological Society of America Bulletin 69(12), 1473-1494.
17. Sukheswala, R. N., Avasia, R. K. (1966) Nepheline syenite in the Deccan traps of Jawhar, Bombay. Geological Society of India 7, 86-91.
18. Sukheswala, R. N., Avasia, R. K. (1971) Carbonatite-alkalic complex of Panwad-Kawant, Gujarat, and its bearing on the structural characteristics of the area. Bulletin Volcanologique 35(3), 564-578.
19. Sukheswala, R. N., Avasia, R. K., Gangopadhyay, M. (1974) Zeolites and associated secondary minerals in the Deccan Traps of Western India. Mineralogical Magazine 39(306), 658-671.

20. Sukheswala, R. N., Avasia, R. K., Master, D. J. (1971) Dyke cluster of Phenai Mata region, Chhota Udaipur, Gujarat. Studies in Earth Science (West Volume) 608-616.
21. Sukheswala, R. N., Awate, G. S. (1957). Correlation of the ash beds occurring in the western parts of Salsette Island, Bombay. *Journal of University of Bombay*, 48-52.
22. Sukheswala, R. N., Borges, S. M. (1975) The carbonatite-injected sandstones of Siriwasan, Chhota Udaipur, Gujarat. Indian Journal of Earth Sciences 2(1), 1-10.
23. Sukheswala, R. N., Sethna, S. F. (1962) Deccan Traps and associated rocks of the Bassein area. Geological Society of India 3, 125-146.
24. Sukheswala, R. N., Sethna, S. F. (1967). Giant Pseudoleucites of Ghori, Chhota Udaipur, India. *American Mineralogist: Journal of Earth and Planetary Materials*, *52*(11-12), 1904-1910.
25. Sukheswala, R. N., Sethna, S. F. (1969) Layered gabbro of the igneous complex of Phenai Mata, Gujarat State. Geological Society of India 10(2), 177-187.
26. Sukheswala, R. N., Sethna, S. F., Merchant, H. (1979) Acid glass blebs in the basalt of Antop Hill, Bombay. Bulletin of Earth Sciences 7, 1-4.
27. Sukheswala, R. N., Udas, G. R. (1963). Note on the carbonatite of Ambadongar (Gujarat State) and its economic potentialities. Science and Culture 29, 563-568.
28. Sukheswala, R. N., Udas, G. R. (1964). The carbonatite of Ambadongar, India-some structural considerations. Abstracts, International Geological Congress Report of the XXII Session, India, 109.
29. Sukheswala, R. N., Udas, G. R. (1967). Fluorspar mineralization related to carbonatite-alkalic complex at Amba Dongar, Gujarat State. Current Science 36(1), 14-16.
30. Sukheswala, R. N., Viladkar, S. G. (1981) Fenitized sandstones in Amba Dongar carbonatites, Gujarat, India. Geological Society of India 22(8), 368-374.
31. Sukheswala, R.N. (1956) Notes on the field occurrence and petrography of the rocks of the Bombay Island, Bombay. Transactions of Mineralogical, Geological and Metallurgical Institute of India 50, 101 – 126.
32. Tolman, A. B. (2016) *Geologists and the British Raj, 1870-1910*. Utah State University, p. 89.

33. Viladkar, S. G. (1981) The carbonatites of Amba Dongar, Gujarat, India. Bulletin of Geological Society of Finland 53, 17-28.
34. Webb, R. G. (1980) Gray, Hardwicke, Buchanan-Hamilton, and drawings of Indian softshell turtles (family Trionychidae). Amphibia-Reptilia 1(1), 61-74.
35. Yellur, D. D. (1968). Carbonatite complexes as related to the structure of Narmada valley. *Geological Society of India*, *9*(2), 118-123.

AUTHORS PROFILE

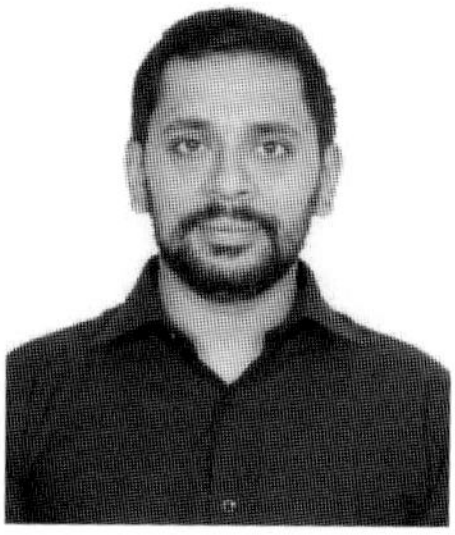

Dr. Ashwin Pundalik is an Assistant Professor in Geology at St. Xavier's College, Mumbai. He did his M.Sc. and Ph.D. in geology from Savitribai Phule Pune University, Pune. His research interests include Sedimentology, Structural Geology and Quaternary Geology. He worked in the Geological Survey of India before joining academics. Dr. Pundalik has vast experience in geological fieldwork in India.

Email: ashwin.pundalik@xaviers.edu

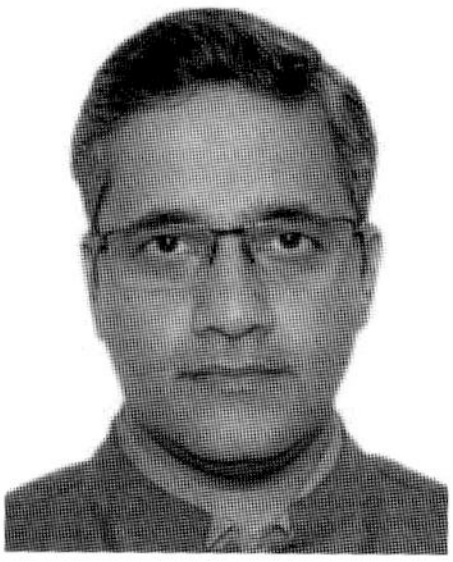

Dr. Hrishikesh Samant is Associate Professor in Geology and Vice-Principal (Science) at St. Xavier's College, Mumbai. He obtained his M.Tech. and Doctorate from IIT Bombay. His research interests include Geomorphology, Remote Sensing and GIS. He has published several papers on these aspects. Dr. Samant has been associated several educational programmes with many institutions of India. Before joining academics, he had a stint as a geologist at Mineral Exploration Corporation Ltd., Ministry of Mines, Govt. of India.

Email: Hrishikesh.samant@xaviers.edu

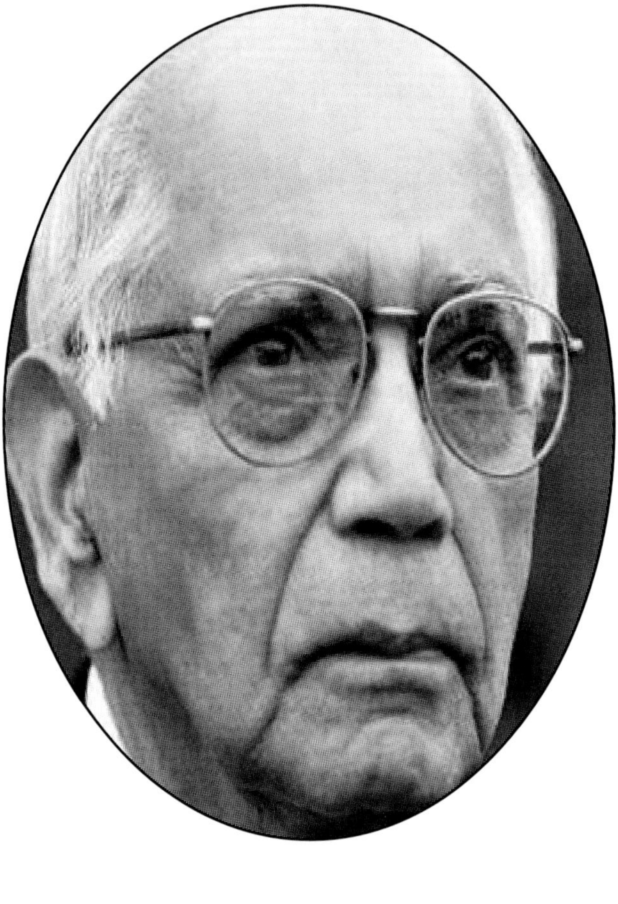

Calyampudi Radhakrishna Rao

(b. 10 September 1920)

CALYAMPUDI RADHAKRISHNA RAO: A LEGEND IN STATISTICS

R. Vishnu Vardhan and S. Balaswamy

Prof. C. R. Rao is an exemplary personality who had a great vision for the future of statistics in various disciplines, particularly in Big-data, Genetic engineering, Signal processing, etc. His views about statistics and statisticians are that "*the job of the statisticians is not something out of the world and it influences many disciplines*". His services at Indian Statistical Institute (ISI) were notable and gave great opportunities to many researchers to dwell in emerging areas to gain good exposure. He made ground-breaking contributions in the field of statistics and expanded their applications to social, biological, and psychological fields. Prof. Rao inspired many with his approach and humbleness, and still inspires many researchers, and students around the world.

Early Life and Education

Calyampudi Radhakrishna Rao was born on September 10, 1920, in Huvanna Hadagali, the then Madras Province, in present-day Karnataka state. His parents Sri C.D. Naidu and Smt Lakshmi Kanthamma were blessed with ten children. Rao is their eighth child and was named Radhakrishna. His parents recognized the interest of their son in mathematics and encouraged him to pursue a career in the same field. His mother instilled virtues such as discipline, and work ethic in him, which made him an extraordinary person with a bright career. Rao pursued a Master's degree in Mathematics from Andhra University in 1940. This was the time when the world was facing the second world war. He faced difficulty in finding a job and planned to apply for a position in the Department of Survey for which he traveled to Kolkata. The travel to Kolkata changed his future course of life. On the journey, he met a young man who was traveling to Kolkata to join a training program in statistics at the Indian Statistical Institute. He went to ISI to know about its activities and after interacting with the people there, he got a clear idea about what to do next. He also envisioned that ISI would be a good place to pursue research. After several discussions with his parents at Vishakhapatnam, Rao moved to and joined ISI on 1st January 1941.

The founder of ISI Prof. Prasanta Chandra Mahalanobis had a significant influence on Rao's thought process. Mahalanobis was known as a "*Professor*" at ISI rather than by his name. His expertise in applying statistical tools and techniques to various domains enabled Rao to understand that Statistics is an emerging area. Fortunately, when he was about to complete his training at ISI, Calcutta University launched a Master's program in Statistics, and Mahalanobis was appointed as Head of the Department. Rao successfully completed and obtained M.A. in Statistics in 1943.

Notable Contributions to the Science

Prof. Rao has been a world leader in statistics for the past eight decades. His research, scholarship, and professional services have had a profound impact on the theory and applications of statistics. He discovered his famous inequality in 1944 when a student asked about the existence of a strict inequality for the smallest difference attainable by an unbiased estimator. These brief papers of his opened up new fields of research and coined many technical terms that appear in the specialized literature, such as Heisenberg's principle, Kramer-Rao bound, and many more. His influence on multivariate statistical analysis is exemplary. By means of spectral and singular value decomposition of matrices, he explained the special basis of already known and newly introduced methods. He defined the generalized inverse of a matrix and demonstrated its use in the study of linear models and singular multiple distributions. Over the past decades, he also touched on non-linear methods, resampling methods, neural networks, data mining, estimation theory, and differential geometry. His research in multivariate analysis is useful, for example, in financial planning, weather forecasting, medical diagnosis, tracking the movements of spy planes, and monitoring the movements of spacecraft. His works have been widely used in physical, biological, economic, and engineering sciences in the 20th century, and data science and big data in the 21st century. His early work with Mahalanobis helped in anthropometric measurements used by anthropologists to measure the probability distribution between two populations called Mahalanobis distance (MD). This work eventually led to the development of the concepts of Cramer-Rao bound (CRB) or inequality, Rao-Blackwellization, Fisher-Rao metric, and Rao distance. These concepts have found applications in signal detection, tracking aircraft, and object recognition by patterns. Rao made important contributions to combinatorial mathematics; orthogonal sequences have been useful for designing experiments. He also introduced the concept of 'quadratic entropy' - a variation measure used to analyze variation in any sequence.

Rao under the guidance of Mahalanobis contributed to the establishment of many statistical bureaus across India, establishing one of the best statistical systems in India. He established a statistical institute in his name '*CR Rao Advanced Institute of Mathematics, Statistics and Computer Science (AIMSCS)*' at the University of Hyderabad, India. He is a Senior Policy and Statistics Advisor for the Indian Heart Association, a non-profit organization that focuses on raising awareness of heart disease in the South Asian community. During his tenure at ISI, Rao developed several courses in numeracy, which were later converted into bachelor's and master's degrees at ISI.

He received the *Shanti Swarup Bhatnagar Award* in 1963, and donated the entire prize money to the National Defense Fund, saying "*the need of the nation is greater than that of an individual scientist*". He has always emphasized that statistical research should largely arise from real life problems. He has spent his entire career promoting statistics and their usefulness in society. He said that "*If there is a problem to be solved, seek statistical advice instead of appointing a committee of experts*". His career is full of remarkable achievements. Two of Rao's papers, written in the 1940s, were reproduced in the book Progress in Statistics, edited by Kotz and Johnson (1990). One of these papers was "*Information and Accuracy Achievable in the Estimation of Statistical Parameters*" and the other "*Large Sample Tests of Statistical Hypotheses Concerning Many Parameters with Applications to Problems of Estimation*" (1945). In this, he proposed a differential geometric foundation for statistics by introducing a quadratic differential metric in the space of probability measures. The idea of connecting statistics and differential geometry was very early at that time. However, half a century later, his idea developed into one of the most active and important aspects of information science, linking statistics, information theory, control theory, and statistical physics. The concept of distance between two probability measures introduced by Rao using differential geometric concepts is called Rao distance.

Educator, academic legacy, and career achievements

Statistician, Professor Bradley Efron once said, "*Rao really was Fisher's student, in the sense of carrying on the Fisherian statistical tradition*". After his stay at Cambridge genetics lab for five years with Prof. Fisher, Rao returned to ISI in 1948. In 1949, he was offered a professorship. At ISI, he was instrumental in building research potential by interacting with experts across the globe. By 1949, Mahalanobis had established the institute as a world-class institution. He encouraged young minds to pursue research, giving proper training in statistical methodologies and how they can be applied in other domains. In 1950, Rao started guiding Ph.D. students; Basu was his first Ph.D. student who worked in the area of statistical inference.

At any given point in time, he was working with 5 to 6 Ph.D. students in different areas of Statistics. Notably, survey sampling, characterization, quality control, design of experiments, and directional data. He used to tell to his students to give a complete view of the topics they are working on, with his intuition. He referred to the period of 1930 – 1960 as the "*Golden Age of Statistics*". Rao always encouraged Ph.D. students to interact and exchange their views and ideas with experts who were regularly visiting ISI. To name a few, Norbert Weiner, Ragnar Frisch, John Kenneth Galbraith, J. B. S. Haldane, Walter Shewhart, A.N. Kolmogorov and J. L. Doob.

He realized the need for statistics in the industry, therefore, revamped the training program, and introduced courses on quality control and industrial statistics. With the great support of a Japanese engineer, Genichi Taguchi, he contributed significantly to the field of statistical quality control. One such contribution was the works on "*Orthogonal Arrays*". Rao's efforts for knowledge sharing and proper training brought partnerships with the reputed International Statistical Institute. This partnership played a critical role in capacity building and training young minds and interested researchers across the globe. In 1953, he brought computational facilities to ISI. This was based on his visit to the University of Illinois where he took courses on programming using machine language. In 1960, ISI started many programs like Bachelor's, Master's, and Ph.D., and for all these courses, Rao's innovative cum interdisciplinary curriculum focused on both mathematical foundations and applications. In 1972, after the death of Mahalanobis, Rao became Director of the ISI. After five years he stepped down, soon after, he received an invitation from the University of Pittsburgh and thereafter a visiting professor at Ohio State University.

Rao, in one of his plenary talks, entitled "Perspectives in Statistics" at an international conference in 1971, suggested that the future of Statistics lies in its integration with mathematics and computer science. Today, we can see this in form of machine learning and data science. Secondly, he spoke about three types of errors in Statistics. The first type is in making or training a Statistician with good theoretical and practical knowledge. The second is about knowledge dissemination and the exchange of ideas between two statisticians and the third is about the gap between the Statistician and the experts in other domains. He strived hard to bridge the gap in all these three types of errors.

Academic Administrator

Rao worked in Cambridge for two years from 1946 to 1948 as a visiting scholar at the Cambridge University Museum of Archeology and Anthropology and developed new methods of multidimensional analysis of data. In 1955 as an outcome of his work on the skeletal material was published by Cambridge University Press as *The Ancient Inhabitants of Jebel Maya*. He returned to the ISI in 1948 and was appointed junior professor at the age of 28. He served ISI for 40 years in various capacities - Head and Director of Research and Training School, ISI Director, Jawaharlal Nehru Professor, National Professor, etc., and retired at the age of 60. He established various research departments at ISI to work in economics, sociology, psychology, genetics, anthropology, geology, etc. The basic idea was to encourage the application of statistical methods in other fields and to enable interactions between statisticians and scientists to develop new statistical methods motivated by real problems.

After his retirement from ISI, he moved to the United States (1982), and he established the Center of Multivariate Analysis at the University of Pittsburgh. He joined Pennsylvania State University in 1988. After his retirement, he accepted distinguished professorships in the United States with minimal teaching responsibilities. He held an appointment as a university professor at the University of Pittsburgh for eight years and the Eberly Chair of Statistics at Pennsylvania State University for 13 years, continuing his research in diverse areas of statistics. He retired from Penn State at the age of 81 but continued his research until 2008 as director of the Center for Multivariate Analysis at Penn State. Nearly forty years after his retirement, Rao published another 274 papers. He has authored and co-authored several books and more than 400 research papers. His book Linear Statistical Inference and its Applications, published in 1965, has been translated into six languages and has remained one of the most cited books in science.

Honors and Awards

He received many honorary doctoral degrees from various universities across the world. The Government of India honored him with the second highest civilian award that is Padma Vibhushan in 2001 in recognition of his services to the field of statistics. The Royal Statistical Society, UK recognized him as a *Fellow of the Royal Society*. On June 12, 2002, he was presented the National Medal of Science by United States President George W. Bush for his pioneering contributions to the statistical sciences. He also received the Indian Science Prize in 2010. The American Statistical Association described him as a *living legend* whose work has influenced not just statistics, but also various disciplines. Besides, he received many other prestigious awards in India and abroad, to name a few – the Guy Medal (2011), the International Mahalanobis Prize (2003), the Srinivasa Ramanujan Medal (2003) of the Indian National Science Academy and the Sardar Patel Lifetime Achievement International Award (Sardar Ratna) (2014) by Sardar Patel International Foundation, India. The Department of Post, Government of India released a special postal cover with his photograph on 29th December 2009, at an International Conference (AIMSCS), Hyderabad. To honor his extraordinary contributions, the Ministry of Statistics and Programme Implementation (MoSPI), the Government of India has constituted a *National Award in Statistics* in his name. The Pennsylvania State University has established C.R. Rao and Bhargavi Rao Prize in Statistics. The road from IIIT Hyderabad to the Central University of Hyderabad, crossroads to Alind Factory, Lingampally, has been named after him. Prof. CR Rao has been recently awarded International Prize in Statistics (2023), equivalent to Nobel prize in the field for his contributions.

Services to Professional Bodies

He has been the president of all prestigious statistical associations, the International Statistical Institute, the Institute of Mathematical Statistics, USA, and the International Biometric Society. He has been a member of several government committees on the development of national statistical systems, statistical education, and research in India. He was Chairman of a Committee on Statistics (1962-69), Chairman of Population and Communication for Population Control (1968-69), Chairman of the Mathematics Committee, the Atomic Energy Commission, AEC (1969-78), Member of the Committee on Science and Technology (1969-71), and was a member of the Justice Sarkar Committee to inquire into the overall functioning of the Council of Scientific and Industrial Research (CSIR) in India. He had all his education in India and did most of his research on his own without any guidance from others, and is not just a statistician. His other interests include music and dancing, and he pursues his passion for photography and gardening. When he moved to Delhi from Calcutta in 1970 to stay at ISI Delhi, he was surprised that there was no dance school to teach Kuchipudi, which has not attained the popularity of Bharatanatyam, Kathak, Kathakali, and Odissi. He started the Kuchipudi Dance Academy in Delhi and was its first president. The academy held regular exhibitions at Kuchipudi and he was its president until 1979 when he moved to the USA.

Personal Life

Prof. Rao and Bhargavi were married on 9th September 1948, in Chennai, India. They were blessed with a son and daughter. Their daughter, Tejaswini pursued Ph.D. in Nutrition from the Pennsylvania State University and worked as a Professor in the Dietetics and Nutrition Department of SUNY College, Buffalo. She is also an accomplished Indian classical dancer and the director of a dance school called Natya. Their son, Veerendra is an electrical engineer and computer scientist. He has a computer consultancy business in Pittsburgh. Prof. Rao has two grandchildren.

Bibliography

1. Ramesh, S. (2020) Legendary statistician CR Rao, credited with restructuring field of statistics, turns 100. The Print.
2. Prakasa Rao, B.L.S. (2020) C.R. Rao: A Life in Statistics. 4(1). Bhavana – The Mathematics Magazine.
3. Majumder, P.P. (2020) C. Radhakrishna Rao, a living legend. The Hindu.

AUTHORS PROFILE

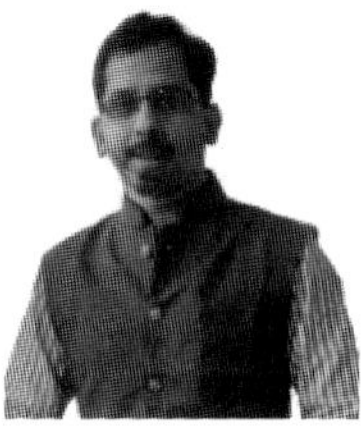

Dr. R. Vishnu Vardhan is currently working as an Associate Professor of Statistics at Pondicherry University, Puducherry. His areas of research interest are Biostatistics - Classification Problems, Statistical Process Control, and Statistical Computing. He has published more than 75 research papers in journals of national and international repute.

Email: vrstatsguru@gmail.com

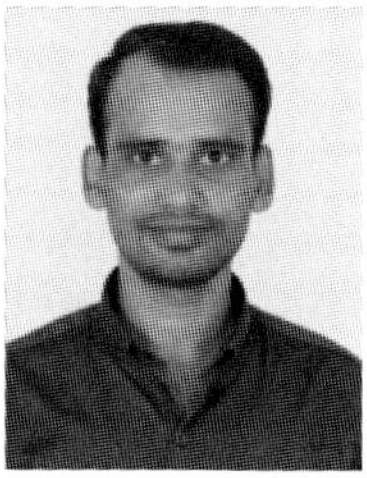

Dr. S. Balaswamy is currently working as an Assistant Professor of Statistics at Indira Gandhi National Tribal University, Amarkantak, Madhya Pradesh. His areas of research interest are Biostatistics and Statistical Computing. He has published more than 20 research papers in journals of national and international repute.

Email: balaswamy@igntu.ac.in

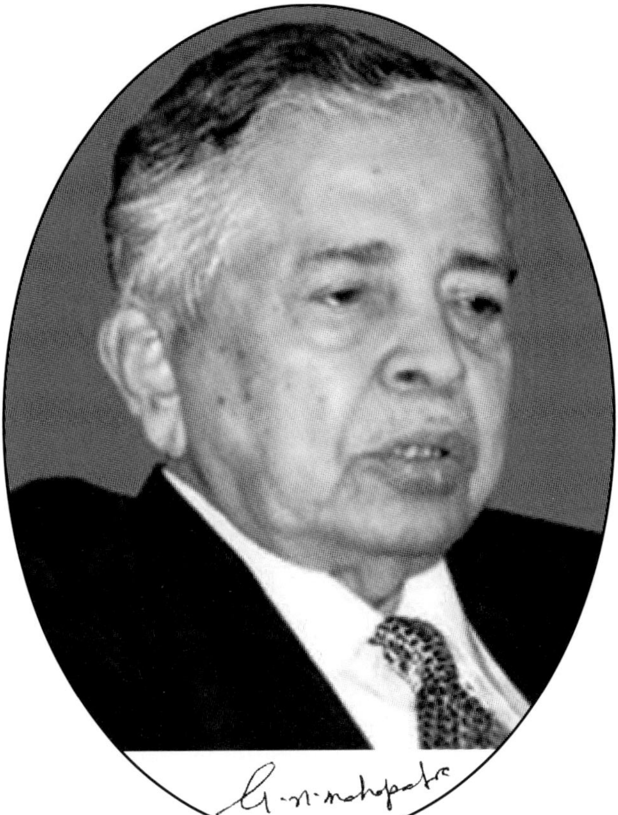

Gokulananda Mahapatra

(24 May 1922 - 10 July 2013)

GOKULANANDA MAHAPATRA: THE H. G. WELLS OF ODISHA

Chitta Ranjan Mishra

Prof. (Dr.) Gokulananda Mahapatra, popularly known as 'The H. G. Wells of Odisha', is an iconic personality in the field of chemical education and research in the country. He is widely recognized for his outstanding contributions to DNA structure elucidation and public outreach of science in his mother tongue Odia. He was the brain behind the formation of 'Odisha Bigyan Prachar Samiti' on 7th August 1949 at Cuttack, which has been working relentlessly for the dissemination of scientific temper among the common man. This was the second scientific society in the Country after 'Bangiya Bigyan Parishad' of Kolkata formed on 25th January 1948 by Dr. Satyendra Nath Bose. He has written more than 100 books on the popularization of science, including science fiction, novels, essays, travel delights, children's stories, articles in print media and magazines, etc., which captured the imagination of Odia readers. He was the first science fiction and school textbook writer in Odia. He occupies a very special place in the Odia intelligentsia and is a household name in Odisha.

Family Background, Early Life and Education

Prof. (Dr.) Gokulananda Mohapatra was born to Smt. Fuka Dei and Sri Bijay Govinda Mahapatra on 24th May, 1922 in the village of Kuansa in the district of Bhadrak, Odisha. He had three sisters (Parashamani, Kshetramani, and Netramani) and two brothers (Nityananda, and Gokulananda). He was the youngest in the family. He spent his childhood on the banks of the river Salandi. He had his schooling at Kuansh U.P. School. He lost his father when he was in third standard. He continued his studies at the nearby Narayan Chandra Middle English School. He completed his Matriculation from Bhadrak High School in the year 1941 with 1st Class and ranked No. 2 in the District.

After that, he first applied for admission in arts (I.A.) at Ravenshaw College, Cuttack, with Mathematics, Logic, and Sanskrit as subjects. In those days, there was a common feeling amongst students that if you read science, it will be very difficult to pass the examination. Afterward, he got admission to science (I. Sc.) at Ravenshaw College. He stayed there with his elder brother-in-law Sri Kishori Mohan Mohanty. When Sh. Mohanty got transferred to Koraput, he stayed at West Hostel. Prof. Bama Charan Mohanty was his Hostel Superintendent. I the college, he was taught by Prof. Brahmananda Mishra, Prof. Golak Banerjee, and Prof. Haribandhu Mohanty (Physics); Prof. Balabhadra Prasad (Chemistry); Prof. Ramanath Mohanty (Mathematics), and Prof. Bansidhar Samantaray (Botany). In 1941, the study of Biology commenced at Ravenshaw College. Prior to that, only Botany was taught there. In 1943, his immediate elder sister Netramani died. He did not get good marks in I. Sc. examinations. He did his B.Sc. (Hons.) in Chemistry in 1945 from Ravenshaw College. Prof. Sukumar Aditya (a retired professor of Chemistry at Calcutta University), and the Late Prof. Harihar Patnaik (Professor of Botany, and Former Vice-Chancellor of Berhampur University) were his classmate at Ravenshaw College. He got married in the same year (1945) to Kumudini and his father-in- law helped him in further studies.

Subsequently, he took admission to the Presidency College, Calcutta, for M. Sc in Chemistry. During 1946-47, Hindu-Muslim riot took place in Calcutta. He witnessed severe blood baths and large-scale massacres in front of the main gate of the college. He and his friends hid within the four walls of the hostel with great fear and panic. At that time, there was an exchange program between Calcutta Science College and Presidency College for theory and practical classes. Prof. Priyada Ranjan Ray and Prof. J. C. Bardhan were noted professors of chemistry at Calcutta Science College. In 1945, Prof. M.Q. Khuda, who was a professor of Chemistry at the Presidency College, visited Ravenshaw College as an external examiner to conduct B.Sc. (Hons.) practical examinations, Dr. Mahapatra appeared in examination, and was asked to prepare an organic derivative compound, but he failed. The derivative prepared by him was so negligible that it was not possible to record its melting point. Prof. Khuda gave him fewer marks (probably 4-5 marks out of 20), and as a result, he secured second class but stood first in his class. He completed his M.Sc. (Chemistry) from Calcutta University in the year 1947. Though, due to the Hindu-Muslim riot, the 1947 examination was held in the year 1948. After completing his master's at Presidency College, Calcutta, Dr. Mohapatra came back to Odisha. He was appointed as Assistant Demonstrator in the Ravenshaw College, Cuttack, at a salary of Rs. 100/- per month.

Early Academic Carrier (1948- 1980)

Besides many problems, Dr. Mohapatra devoted his career to teaching and research in Chemistry at Ravenshaw College, Cuttack. Where M.Sc. (Chemistry) classes started in the year 1947, Prof. D.V. Ramana Rao and Prof. Sukumar Aditya were his colleagues in the department. He did his doctorate in Chemistry from Utkal University, Bhubaneswar in the year 1958 on "Synthesis of new heterocyclic compounds and their mercurial derivatives and testing their biological activities" under the guidance of Prof. Mahendra Kumar Rout. His research paper based on his Ph.D. thesis work was appreciated as the Best Research Paper in organic chemistry for which he received the Cooper Memorial Gold Medal by the Institution of Chemists (India), Kolkata in the year 1959. He also presented his research paper at the 46th Indian Science Congress Association (ISCA) annual conference held in New Delhi. In 1961, he was awarded with the fellowship of the Institution of Chemists (India), Kolkata.

Post-Doctoral studies at Brandeis University, USA (1961-1963)

In 1961, he received a fellowship and joined Brandeis University, Boston, USA under Prof. Orrie M. Friedman, as a post-doctoral research associate. He and his family stayed there from June 1961 to November 1963. At that time, the fare for visiting the USA from India was Rs. 3500/- per ticket. He took a loan of Rs 6000/- from the Government of Odisha for the visit. He worked on DNA structure elucidation, specifically on the elucidation of the structure of de-oxyguanosine.

Scientific Contribution

He returned to India in November 1963 and continued working as a faculty in the Department of Chemistry at Ravenshaw College, Cuttack. For a brief period (1970-1972), he was deputed as Director of Odisha State Bureau of Textbook Preparation and Production, Bhubaneswar for preparing college-level textbooks in science, arts, and commerce subjects in Odia. He superannuated as Professor and Head of the Department of Chemistry, Ravenshaw College on 31st May 1980. He supervised 10 students for their Ph.D. and published more than 70 research papers in various national and international journals. He visited the USA, Canada, the UK, France, Switzerland, and Italy for various research and academic purposes.

Chemistry was his profession, passion, mission, and obsession, while the popularization of science was his mind, heart, and soul.

Contribution as a Popular Science Writer

After his return from the USA, he published his experiences in a series of weekly articles entitled 'Neela Chakrabala Separe' (Beyond The Blue Horizon) in 'Kalinga', for a period of 2 years. Kalinga was a daily Odia newspaper published from Cuttack, and was a brainchild of Biju Patnaik. Afterward, collection of the articles was published in form of two books. Likewise, articles on his USA and Europe experiences entitled 'Memoirs of West' were also published in the daily newspaper 'The Samaja'. In 1945, when he was doing his masters, there was no magazine in Odisha. Due to the wartime and shortage of printing papers, all publications came to a halt in Odisha. 'The Samaja' was published only in two pages. Dr. Mohapatra started writing popular science articles in the Odia language. At that time, the literary magazine 'Sankha' was published from Deogarh, the capital of Bamanda State, and was edited by famous poet Dr. Mayadhar Mansingh. In December 1945, Dr. Mohapatra sent one popular science article 'Atom Bomb' for publication in 'Sankha' magazine. It was misplaced somewhere and lost. In July 1946, he wrote another article on the "Contribution of Pitch to Modern Day Science" and sent that to 'Sankha' for publication, which was published, and is considered the first popular science article in Odia. From that very day onwards his career as a science writer began. It was Sri Balakrushna Kar, the then Editor of Sahakar, who constantly encouraged and motivated him for writing. At that time, there was no Radio Station in Odisha. Odia programs were broadcasted from All India Radio (AIR), Calcutta daily for half an hour (9.30 -10 PM). A large number of his popular science articles were broadcasted in the said program. For each talk, he was getting Rs.10/- from AIR. 'Sankha' was giving him Rs.5/- for each article.

In 1949, Dr. he wrote 'Bigyana Bismaya', published by Bharati Bihar, Cuttack, the first popular science book of Odisha. The price of the book was one rupee and four anas. Noted physicist Prof. Brahmananda Mishra wrote the preface of the book. The articles in the book were earlier published in different Odia magazines. Dr. Mohapatra has penned more than 100 popular science books in Odia language notably, Bigyana Bismaya (1949), Success of Science (1950), Discovery of Atom Bomb (1951), Man Beyond Earth (1952), Flying Saucer (1955), and Artificial Satellite (1957). The

'Man beyond Earth' was the first scientific novel in Odia Language. Nobel Laureate Sir C.V. Raman has written only one popular science book (Aspects of Science) in his lifetime. It was translated into Odia by Dr. Mohapatra during the year 1957-58 as 'Vision of Science' published by National Book Trust, New Delhi. In a lucid style, he portrayed the impact of science on human civilization and human life. His fiction played a significant role in the consolidation of the contemporary scientific imagination. He had a good sense of scientific realism and knew the art of combining it with fantasy. He is popularly known as the H.G. Wells of Odisha.

Besides popular science books, Dr. Mahapatra has contributed to a great extent in writing textbooks of chemistry in English for college students. In 1957, organic chemistry was introduced as a subject in the I.Sc. curriculum in Odisha. He wrote the book 'Intermediate Organic Chemistry', the first organic chemistry book for college students of Odisha. Subsequently, he wrote another book 'Intermediate Chemistry', published by The New Students Store (now Grantha Mandir), Cuttack. He has written more than 20 textbooks and practical manuals starting from the sixth standard to undergraduate courses, both in Odia and English. In total, he had written more than 100 books including popular science books, textbooks in chemistry, and general science in Odia for school children.

Birth of the Bigyan Prachar Samiti

A man of many virtues, Dr. Mohapatra has left an indelible mark in the history of science popularization in Odisha. He was one of the nine founder members (Dr. Radhanath Rath, Dr. Shyamananda Patnaik, Prof. Sukumar Aditya, Sri Krushna Charan Dani, Prof. Mahendra Chandra Mishra, and Prof. Rai Krushna Mohanty) who formed 'Bigyan Prachar Samiti', the oldest scientific society of Odisha, on 7th August 1949, in a meeting held at the residence of Prof. Gopal Chandra Patnaik, Principal, SCB Medical College, Cuttack, under the Chairmanship of Prof Sadasiva Misra, an eminent economist. The initially proposal was to name it as 'Utkal Bigyan Parishad', however, to avoid any corollary with 'Bangiya Bigyan Parishad, this idea was dropped. There is an interesting story behind the naming of 'Bigyana Prachar Samiti'. In 1918, Mr. Atul Chandra Ganguli, a student of Sir Prafulla Chandra Ray, the father of chemistry in India and the founder of the Indian Chemical Society, joined Ravenshaw College as a lecturer in chemistry. He also took a keen interest in setting up a chemical plant in Odisha in collaboration with some Odia businessmen. In line with the 'Bengal Chemical & Pharmaceutical Works' set up by Sir P.C. Ray in Bengal, the new company was named 'Utkal Chemical & Pharmaceutical Works'. Mr. Atul Ganguli, being a technical man, was looking after the production activities of the company. However, his businessmen colleagues pocketed all profits leading to the insolvency of the company. Mr. Ganguli had to sell his Cuttack house to pay back the loan and returned back to Calcutta with utmost agony and discontentment. Taking a lesson from this incident, members of the presidium were unanimous in naming the organization as 'Bigyan Prachar Samiti', not 'Utkal Bigyan Parishad'.

In Odisha, initially the medium of teaching in high schools was English. In 1944, it was changed to Odia. However, there were no science books available in the language. So, the need for an association like 'Bigyan Prachar Samiti' and writing science books in Odia was very much felt. Mr. Raghunath Padhi, a science teacher at Khallikote High School, published the first science notebook in Odia. College teachers were reluctant to take up this job, even when Dr. Mahapatra and Dr. Harihar Patnaik jointly wrote the first science book in Odia for school children of Odisha, they were criticized by their fellow colleagues. The 'Bigyan Prachar Samiti' was touted as 'Bigyan Apaprachar Samiti'. However, subsequently, it was recognized by the Government of Odisha. Ten years after its formation, Dr. Balabhadra Prasad, the then Director of Public Instruction (DPI), Odisha, took a personal interest and recognized Samiti as an Educational Society of Odisha. Membership in the Samiti was introduced vide the Confidential Character Report of the College Teachers, wherein college teachers have to mention the Samiti membership in their Confidential Character Reports (CCRs).

Since then, 74 years have passed. 'Bigyan Prachar Samiti' has been operating at the 'Amrapalli', the residence of Prof. Gokulananda Mahapatra at Dolamundai, Cuttack. Scientific meetings, twice a month, preferably on the second and fourth Sundays of the month, are regularly organized wherein a large number of scientists, technocrats, engineers, doctors, professors, teachers, students, publishers, guardians, and common men participate. The Samiti is a nodal science communication forum in the state to disseminate scientific knowledge and propagate scientific temper amongst the masses. Encouraged by the success of the Samiti, its members have instituted large numbers of awards over the years presented regularly to leading scientists, science writers, and other professional stalwarts of the state for their outstanding contribution to science and science popularization. 'Bigyan Ratna' is the highest award conferred by the Samiti to a living legend for his/her outstanding contribution to the field of scientific research and science popularization. Prizes are also given to school children through various competitions organized by the Samiti. Other notable awards conferred by the Samity include - Dr. Balabhadra Prasad Samman (for Physics and Chemistry), Dr. Prana Krushna Parija Samman (for Biology), and Jyotsna Dei Samman (for Medical Sciences). The Odisha Bigyan Academy, a Government of Odisha organization under the Department of Science & Technology, was borne out of Bigyan Prachar Samiti.

Other contributions

Prof. Mahapatra instituted the 'Bijay-Govinda Memorial Charitable Trust', which annually confers the Bijay-Govinda Memorial Award to renowned scientists and science popularizers of Odisha below the age of fifty. He also instituted the 'Nityananda Memorial Award' in honor of his elder brother Nityananda Mahapatra, which is given once in three years to popular science writers of the state. And, the 'Fuka Devi Memorial Children's Literature Award' in loving memory of his mother Fuka Devi, which is given annually to one of the most popular children litterateurs in the state. He also formed the 'Fuka Devi Memorial Charitable Trust' at Bhadrak, his home district, in the year 1992. The trust awards 'Kabi Sekhar Chintamani Puraskar' in the field of literature; and the best student and the best sports person awards to the students of the Kuansh School, Bhadrak, where he had his schooling. He also formed 'Gokulananda - Nityananda Mahapatra Foundation (GNM Foundation)' on 18th May 2010, helping people of all walks of life, and those looking for solutions to complex problems in poor, underprivileged, and mentally challenged children, adults, etc.

Awards, Honors, and Accolades

Dr. Mohapatra was a towering personality in the state of Odisha and has been decorated with large numbers of awards, honors, and accolades during his lifetime. Some of them are:

1959	Cooper Memorial Gold Medal of the Institution of Chemists (India)

1964 & 1982	Odisha Sahitya Academy Award for the popularization of science for his book 'Best Discovery of this Era'
1968	Odisha Bigyan Academy Award for science popularization
1988	Samanta Chandrasekhar Award of Odisha Bigyan Academy
1989	'Sahakar Samman' by Sahakar Magazine, Cuttack
1994	'Sarala Puraskar' by Sarala Sahitya Sansad, Cuttack
1995	Prana Krushna Parija Bigyan Sahitya Samman of Utkal Sahitya Samaja
1996	Odisha Environmental Society Award for outstanding contribution to scientific research & popularization of science
1996	Bigyan Prachar Samiti Award for outstanding contribution to popularization of science spanning a period of 50 Years
2002	Odisha Bigyan Academy Award as a senior scientist of Odisha
2011	Honorary D.Sc Degree of Utkal University, Bhubaneswar
2011	Kalinga Samman for the popularization of science by Kalinga Foundation Trust
2012	Honorary D.Sc Degree of Ravenshaw University, Cuttack
2013	Life Time Achievement Award by Ravenshaw Chemistry Alumni Association

Personal Life

Dr. Mohapatra has two sons (Dr. Girija Nandan Mohapatra, Dr. Nanda Nandan Mohapatra) and three daughters (Dr. Jyotshna Mohapatra, Smt. Rashmi Mohapatra, Dr. Snigdharani Mohapatra), the third daughter, was a Senior Teacher in DAV Public School, Pokhriput, Bhubaneswar. His late wife Smt. Kumudini Mohapatra was the eldest daughter of Smt. Nishamani Devi and Sri Binod Bihari Ray, and was an accomplished writer on her own. Dr. Mahapatra passed away on 10th July 2013 at the age of 91 in Ahmadabad, Gujarat on the auspicious day of Ratha Yatra, while staying with his younger son Dr. Nanda Nandan Mahapatra. The H.G. Wells of Odisha is no more…

Acknowledgments

The author acknowledges with thanks the support and cooperation received from all quarters for the preparation of this article. Especially, the support and cooperation received from the family members of Dr. Gokulananda Mahapatra are gratefully acknowledged. The author is also grateful to all the Ph.D. students of Dr. Mahapatra for providing the necessary scientific inputs for incorporation in the article.

Bibliography

1. Prof. Gokulananda Mahapatra Birth Centenary Souvenir, 24th May, 2022.
2. Prof. Gokulananda Mahapatra Birth Centenary Smaranika, 24th May, 2022.
3. Ph.D. Thesis of Prof. Gokulananda Mahapatra.
4. All Research Papers Published by Prof. Gokulananda Mahapatra.
5. Chemistry textbooks and popular science books written by Prof. Gokulananda Mahapatra.
6. Biodata of Prof. Gokulananda Mahapatra.
7. Print & Electronic Media Interviews of Dr. Mahapatra.
8. Publishers who have published various books of Dr. Mahapatra.

AUTHOR PROFILE

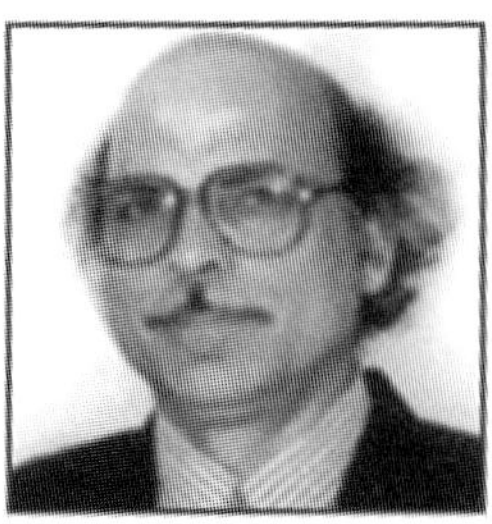

Dr. Chitta Ranjan Mishra is an eminent chemical scientist and technologist, columnist, television anchor, author, orator, popular science writer, and national science communicator. He obtained his M.Sc. degree in chemistry from Ravenshaw College, Cuttack; Ph.D. in Chemistry from the University of Calcutta; Post-Doctorate in chemistry from Indian

Institute of Science, Bangalore; D.Sc. in aluminum technology from the International University of Contemporary Studies, Washington D.C, USA; and D.Litt. in science communication (Honoris Causa) from Ashcroft University, UK. He served as a deputy general manager and Head (R&D) of National Aluminium Company Ltd. (NALCO), A Govt. of India Enterprise. He is a fellow of a host of professional bodies both in the country and abroad. He has published more than 100 research papers in International and national journals and has 12 national and international patents to his credit. He has published more than 1000 popular science articles, and 20 popular science books and uploaded more than 200 science and technology videos on YouTube. He has received more than 100 international, national, and state-level awards for his contributions to the field of scientific research and science popularization. He was President of the Odisha Chemical Society; chairman of the Indian Institute of Metals (Bhubaneswar Chapter); Vice-President, Indian Institute of Chemical Engineers (Bhubaneswar Chapter), and Governing Body Member of Odisha Bigyan Academy. Presently, he is working as a joint managing trustee of Kalinga Foundation Trust, Bhubaneswar; and President of Bigyan Prachar Samiti (Bhubaneswar Chapter).

Email: crmishra49@yahoo.in; URL: www.drcrmishra.com

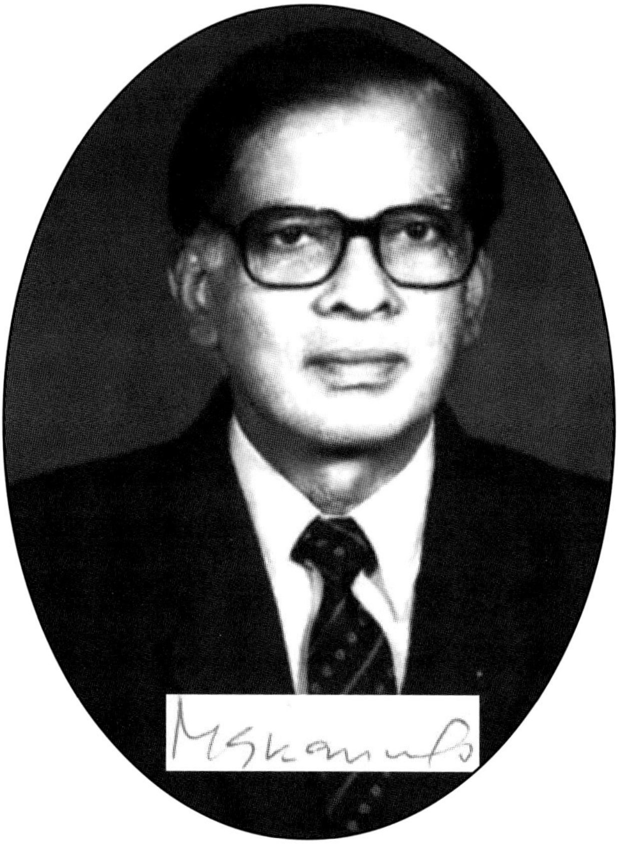

Madhu Sudan Kanungo

(1 April 1927 – 26 July 2011)

MADHU SUDAN KANUNGO: A VISIONARY WHO WAS AHEAD OF HIS TIME

Padmanabh Singh & Vijay Paramanik

Early Life and Education

Professor Madhu Sudan Kanungo was born on 1st April 1927 in Berhampur in the Orissa (now Odisha) state of India. He was second among five brothers and two sisters. His father late Krishna Chandra Mohanty was Headmaster of Ravenshaw Collegiate School at Cuttack, Sambalpur Zila School, and Angul High School. He retired as Inspector of Schools of the Orissa Government in 1949. Young Kanungo learned English and other disciplines from his father, who played a key role in shaping his academic career. His mother late Smt. Sundaramoni Devi was a housewife. Prof. Kanungo had an illustrious academic career. He passed the Matriculation examination with first division from the Angul High School in 1944. He completed his intermediate in science (I.Sc.) in 1946 and B. Sc. (Hons) in 1949 from Ravenshaw College, Cuttack. He was a good player and a fan of cricket, football, and tennis, and represented the college team. He was the first lawn tennis Champion in Orissa. During his college days, he got fascinated to see that Science laboratories remained open at night, and several researchers/teachers were doing research for their doctorate degrees. This inspired him to go for higher study and become a scientist of fame. Since there was no M.Sc. course in Zoology in Orissa at that time, he did M. Sc. from Lucknow University (1949-51). Inspired by his teacher Prof. KN Bahl, he joined him for Ph.D., with a UP Government scholarship. He found animal physiology very exciting. In the meantime, Prof. Bahl left Lucknow in 1952, So he had to join Dr. MB Lal who had limited knowledge of animal physiology. Therefore, he left research after one year and joined as a Lecturer in Zoology at Ravenshaw College (3rd September 1952). In September 1956, he went to the USA for doing Ph.D. (Sept. 1956 – Dec. 1958) and joined the Department of Physiology, University of Illinois (Urbana). His previous research helped him to get a research fellowship under Prof. C. Ladd Prosser, a legend of comparative physiology and the 42nd President of the American Physiological Society. There he received excellent training, which provided him with a strong foundation in Physiology and Biochemistry. He studied adaptations to cold and warm temperatures, oxygen consumption, and oxidative phosphorylation in goldfish.

Contributions to the Science

Prof. Kanungo started his research activity at Lucknow on the physiology of scorpions and reported the presence of invertase in their hepatopancreas. Subsequently, he worked independently and reported (i) the myogenic nature of the heartbeat, (ii) the excretion of nitrogen as several purines, (iii) high lactate and low malate dehydrogenase activity in the muscle and hepatopancreas, and (iv) a decrease in glycogen but increase in amino acids in the hepatopancreas during the first few days of starvation of the scorpion. One of his unique qualities as a scientist was his ability to take up unbeaten paths, adopt and apply emerging technologies to his research, and always thought ahead of his time. This is exemplified by his works on aging at a time when very few scientists thought about it. He joined the Department of Zoology, Banaras Hindu University (BHU) in February 1962. There he established a modern biochemistry and molecular biology laboratory for conducting research on the biology of aging.

Besides research, Prof. Kanungo's devotion to teaching and research in the field of physiology, biochemistry, molecular biology, and neurobiology was absolute. He was an inspiring example for younger generations at BHU, an active and popular teacher for more than 40 years. He always had a strong desire to update himself with current literature not only in his field of research but also in the broader field of biochemistry and molecular biology. Until the early 1960s, Zoology was taught in a classical manner. He introduced experimental courses like physiology and biochemistry that helped the department to be recognized as the Centre of Advanced Study by UGC. Later, other universities also adopted these courses.

The Biochemistry Laboratory and Aging Research

For Prof. Kanungo, his Biochemistry Laboratory was the 'place of worship'. His laboratory had its own library containing cataloged bound volumes of journals/papers mostly on aging, physiology, biochemistry, molecular cell biology, and techniques, most of which were collected by Prof. Kanungo himself. The biochemistry laboratory provided excellent exposure and training to students, which helped them in teaching and research in the later period of their careers. Some of his students continued their own research careers in the field of Aging.

His research on aging for which he received several awards including Padma Shri in 2005 had an interesting beginning. After joining BHU, he wanted to take up an interesting and challenging research problem that would be beneficial to humanity. He was living in a rented house at Dumrao Colony in Assi near the river Ganges. In the neighborhood, there were a few old-age homes where several elderly people were spending their last days. Varanasi (also known as Banaras or 'Kashi' from ancient times) is one of the oldest cities in the world located on the bank of the river Ganges and is believed to be the abode of Lord Shiva (Vishwanath). According to the Hindu religion, it is believed that if one dies at 'Kashi', one gets 'salvation (moksha)'.

Seeing elderly people often inspired Prof. Kanungo to conduct research on the 'biology of aging'- a discipline he introduced in India in the 1960s, and a scientific pursuit he continued for almost half a century until the end of his life. In recent times, the 'research on aging' has attracted considerable attention from the Indian Government, as by 2020, there would be more than 100 million people in India above the age of 65. Prof. Kanungo wanted to address a few fundamental questions about aging such as "What changes occur in the body during aging? Why and how do we age? How can the aging process be delayed or postponed, if not prevented?" He read several articles on the subject and found that little was known about the biochemical aspects of old age. So, he decided to work on the Biochemical and Molecular aspects of growing old to find out the answer to his queries. He believed that once these questions were answered, it would be possible to prolong the active adulthood period and provide a better quality of life to the elderly.

He pioneered a research group on 'Aging/Gerontology'. Traditional and rural India always believes in and practices the joint-family system with three-four generations living together in the same house, where the grandparents live with the family of their sons and the grandchildren. This allows the life of the elderly to be enriched by the young children, while the latter has exposure to the natural learning system from the knowledge and experience of the old. Prof. Kanungo's joint research laboratory was a living example of this age-old practice. Even his students, who became faculty and scientists in other universities and institutes in India and abroad, regularly visited their original laboratory at BHU.

During his research career of over 50 years, Prof. Kanungo and his co-workers used rats, mice, and birds as models to study the biochemical basis of aging, and made a significant contribution in areas ranging from enzymes to gene expression. The whole journey can be divided into three phases. The first phase (1962–1977) focused mostly on biochemical and physiological changes in metabolic pathways in tissues under *in vivo* conditions during the aging of the rat. This was an early reflection of the now-popular concept of 'metabolomics'. From 1977-88, his laboratory studied the changes in the structure and conformation of the chromatin as well as post-translational modifications of the chromosomal proteins in relation to the nuclear incorporation of bases into DNA and transcription in the tissues during the aging of the rat. This has become an emerging area of research these days and is popularly known as 'epigenetics'. The last phase of studies (1988-2011) focused on DNA methylation and expression of specific genes into mRNAs and proteins and binding of transcription factors into promoter/enhancer sequences of genes in the tissues of the rat and mice during aging. Below we highlight some of the important and original findings of his research:

(i) Activity of the enzyme, lactate dehydrogenase (LDH) and its isoenzymes, decreases in the heart and brain after adulthood, making the tissues more oxygen dependent in old age. Further, the ability of these tissues to tolerate anaerobic conditions decreases in old age (Singh and Kanungo 1968). Oxygen is essential for energy production and organ function. During breathing, oxygen is transported from the lungs to the organs by blood vessels, when this supply gets blocked by a clot in the blood vessel, it causes a heart attack or stroke in the brain as the cells beneath the clot die without oxygen. Hence, the frequency of heart attack and stroke increases after adulthood. Breathing exercises like *Pranayam* from adulthood onwards raise the level of LDH and reduce such danger.

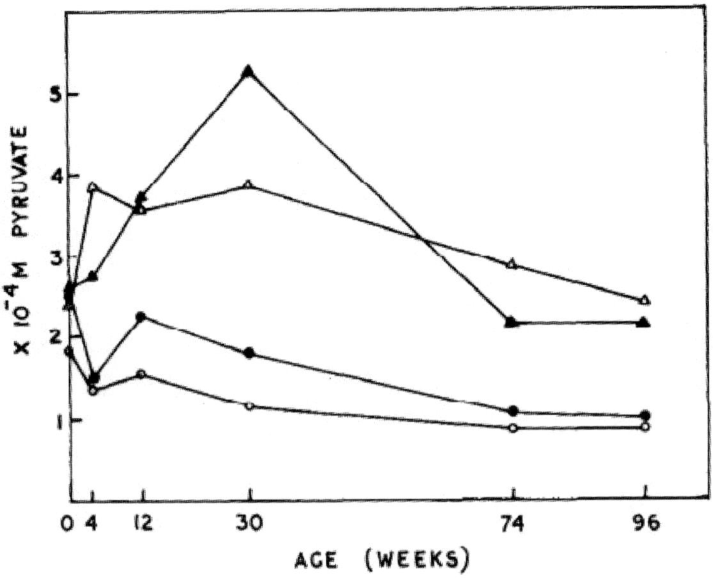

Figure 1: Effect of age on apparent *Km* for pyruvate of lactate dehydrogenase of the brain (●), heart (○), skeletal muscle (▲) and liver (△) of rat. Data were obtained from five or six animals. The enzyme was assayed in 0.033, 0.066, 0.11, 0.33, 0.66, and 1.3. The enzyme was assayed in 0.033, 0.066, 0.11, 0.33, 0.66, and 1.3mM of pyruvate (Diagram from Singh and Kanungo 1968).

(ii) The enzymes acetylcholinesterase and cholineacetyl transferase are essential for brain function. Their levels decrease after adulthood contributing to lower brain function in old age. However, the levels of these enzymes in the brain can be raised by administering appropriate doses of the steroid hormone estradiol (Moudgil and Kanungo 1973a, Moudgil and Kanungo 1973b). Acetylcholine (ACh) acts as a neurotransmitter for normal brain function. Its action is mediated by a protein receptor, AChR, whose level decreases after adulthood, causing lower brain function. Also, the expression of genes that code for dopamine and NMDA receptors, which are required for normal brain function decline after adulthood. This contributes to an increase in the frequency of neurodegenerative diseases such as Parkinson's and Huntington's in old age.

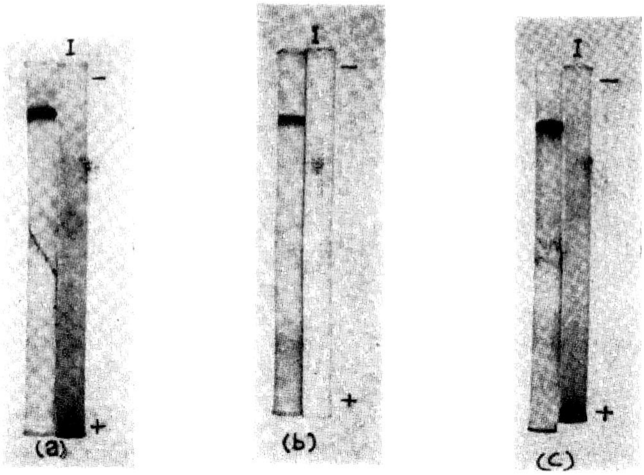

Figure 2: Polyacrylamide gel electrophoresis of acetylcholinesterase from 9-week- (a), 29-week- (b), and 65-week-old (c) rats. The band reacts with a specific stain for acetylcholinesterase. I, gels preincubated with eserine. (Diagram from Moudgil and Kanungo 1973).

(iii) The egg production by birds declines after adulthood as the expression of the genes for egg white protein, ovalbumin, and egg yolk protein, vitellogenin, decreases. However, if steroid hormones, progesterone and 17β-estradiol, are administered to the bird from 30 - 35 weeks of age, the egg-laying period would be extended (Upadhyay et al. 1996; Gupta et al. 1998).

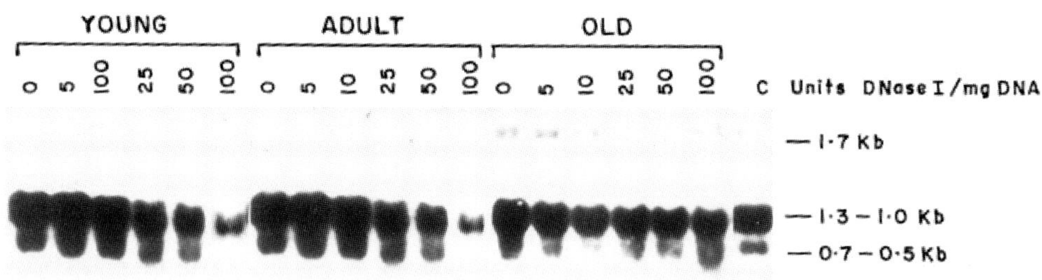

Figure 3: Nuclease hypersensitive sites of the 5* region of the *Ov* gene of the oviduct of Japanese quail. Nuclei from the oviduct of birds of different ages were digested with DNaseI at the concentrations indicated above each lane in the autoradiogram. DNA was further digested with EcoRI and PstI and electrophoresed on 1% agarose gel in TBE buffer, blotted to nytran membrane and hybridized to a ^{32}P-labelled *Ov* probe. C - high mol. wt. DNA digested by EcoRI/PstI. (Diagram from Upadhyay et al. 1996).

(iv) Epigenetic modifications such as DNA methylation and post-translational modifications (PTMs) of histone and non-histone chromosomal proteins (NHCP) regulate the expression of synaptic plasticity genes at the transcriptional level and thereby learning and memory also. Both DNA methylation and PTMs such as acetylation, methylation, and phosphorylation levels of histone and NHCP altered in the brain of old animals. Epigenetic modifications are reversible in nature and can be altered by calcium, small molecules such as butyrate, and steroid hormones such as epinephrine and estradiol. Administration of these molecules induced the gene transcription in the brain of young and adults but not in old animals (Kanungo and Thakur 1977, Thakur et al. 1978, Kanungo and Thakur 1979a, Kanungo and Thakur 1979b, Thakur and Kanungo 1981).

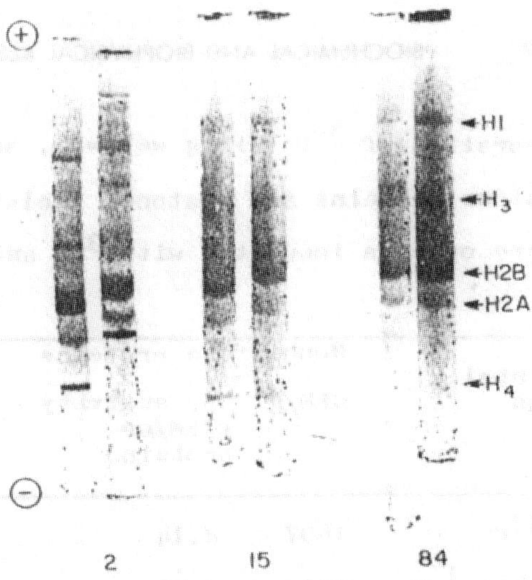

Figure 4: Polyacrylamide gel electrophoretic patterns of histones of normal (left) and calcium-treated (right) slices of cerebral hemisphere of 2-, 15- and 84-week-old female rats. (Diagram from Kanungo and Thakur 1977).

(v) Glial cells outnumber the neurons in the brain. They change with age and thus may contribute significantly to the maintenance of brain integrative ability and adaptation during postnatal development and aging. The calcium-binding protein S100b is released by glial cells and is associated with brain injury, apoptosis, and neurodegeneration. The expression of S100b is upregulated in the cerebral cortex and cerebellar cortex of old compared to young animals. This age-associated upregulation may be implicated in neurodegenerative disorders like Alzheimer's disease (Modi and Kanungo 2010).

(vi) Based on his experimental findings, Prof. Kanungo proposed the "Gene regulation" theory of aging, according to which sequential activation and repression of genes are responsible for the development of an organism up to adulthood (Kanungo 1975). Adulthood does not continue indefinitely; rather, it is subjected to various types of stress such as disease, malnutrition, reproduction, radiation, temperature, pollution, psychological stress, etc., that affect different organs differently and lead to aging and death. Different individuals inherit different sets of genes and are subject to different types of stress. Hence, we all do not age the same way. The "Gene regulation" theory was supported by experiments carried out by Kanungo's team and others.

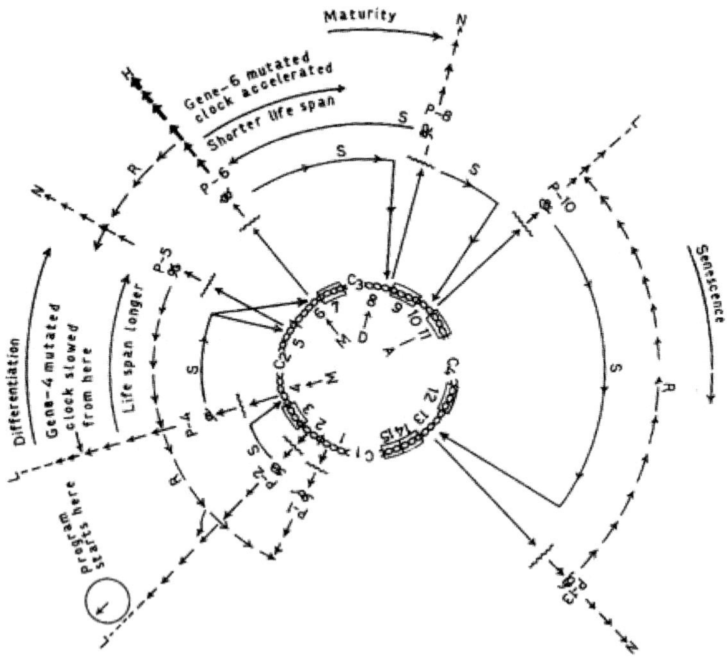

Figure 5: Model for aging - The number of chromosomes and genes has been kept at a minimum and the chromosomes are shown in a circle for clarity. Certain genes remain repressed throughout (shown in blocks). Two parameters of the program may be seen: (1) from the chromosome towards the periphery

which shows the phase of the lifespan at which various genes are activated or repressed, e.g. gene-i and -2 are activated at the earliest phase of the life span, that is, at the beginning of differentiation, gene-6 before maturity, and gene-13 during senescence; (2) clockwise direction beginning from gene-1 shows the sequence in which various genes are activated or repressed by gene products. Different gene products appear at different phases of the life span, e.g. product of gene-6 (p-6) appears before maturity which on reaching a particular level activates gene-10 to produce p-10 long after maturity. Certain gene products including enzymes begin to increase (I-Dor decrease (L) in level at different phases of the life span and with increasing age depending on when their activators or repressors reach threshold levels. Certain gene products including enzymes do not change in level (N) with increasing age. Gene-I is assumed to govern mitosis which is repressed by the product of gene-5 after differentiation is complete. Gene-4 and -5, on mutation (M), alter the speed of the program, and hence the life span. Gene-8 when deleted (D) from the sequence, gene-ll when added (A) to the sequence, accelerate and decelerate the program and hence shorten and lengthen the life span, respectively. C, chromosome; P, gene product; R, repression; S, stimulation; 1-15, gene numbers. (Diagram from Kanungo 1975).

Educator, Academic Legacy & Carrier Achievements

Academic Administrator

After completing his Ph D. (Sept. 1956-Dec. 1958), he returned to India and joined Ravenshaw College of Utkal University in January 1959 and became Reader in Zoology in February 1961. While teaching there, he found the atmosphere not very conducive to higher research and wanted to move. In the meantime, he was selected as a Reader in Zoology at Banaras Hindu University (BHU), one of the leading universities in India, founded by the great visionary, Mahamana Pandit Madan Mohan Malaviya. He joined BHU as a Reader on 14th February 1962, became Professor in January 1970, and retired from there on 31st March 1987. During his stay at BHU, he served as Head of the Department of Zoology (1974-76 and 1980-82), Coordinator of the Centre of Advanced Study in Zoology, and Dean of the Faculty of Science (1986). Prof. Kanungo received several awards and honors in recognition of his research, and BHU honored him by appointing the Lifetime Professor Emeritus in 1993. He was provided accommodation on the campus so that he could stay comfortably with his wife and continue his research and teaching unhindered.

Honors and Awards (including public recognition)

- SS Bhatnagar Prize (Biology) (1971)
- Fellow of the Indian National Science Academy (FNA), New Delhi (1975)
- Fellow of the Indian Academy of Sciences, Bangalore (FASc) (1975)
- National Fellow (1976-1977)
- National Lecturer of UGC (1982)
- Jawaharlal Nehru Fellowship (1987)
- Emeritus Scientist of CSIR, New Delhi (1989-1994)
- Third Age Award-14th International Congress of Gerontology, Mexico (1989)
- Fellowship of Indian Chambers of Commerce & Industry (FICCI) (1989)
- Fellow of the National Academy of Sciences in India (FNASc), Allahabad (1989)
- Golden Jubilee Commemoration Medal, INSA (1992)
- Senior Scientist INSA (1995-1999)
- Fellow of the National Academy of Medical Sciences, India (1996)
- Sir Sriram memorial Oration award, National Academy of Medical Sciences (1998)
- Padma Shri (2005)
- Fellow of the Indian Academy of Neuroscience (2008)
- Chancellor of Nagaland University (2009-2011)

Service to the Professional Bodies

1. Member of Steering Committee for Binational Conference on Biological Sciences, Bangalore, sponsored by UGC (India) and National Science Foundation (USA) for modernizing teaching and research in Biological Sciences (1971).
2. Member Secretary of a High-Level Committee to look into the working of the Indian Council of Agricultural Research (ICAR) (1971-1972).
3. Founder President, Association of Gerontology, India (AGI) (1982-1988).
4. Patron, Association of Gerontology, India (1989-2011).

5. Founder Director, Institute of Life Sciences, Bhubaneswar (1990-1996).
6. Member and Secretary of Animal Sciences Sectional Committee of INSA, and INSA nominee on the Council of Indian Statistical Institute, Kolkata.
7. President's nominee for selection of academic staff in Aligarh Muslim University (1991-1997).
8. Member of the National Council for Older Persons (NCOP) of the Government of India under the Ministry of Social Justice and Empowerment (1999-2004).
9. Chancellor, Nagaland University, Lumami, Nagaland (2009-2011).

Death

Prof. Kanungo passed away on July 26, 2011, at the age of 84 years at his residence at the Banaras Hindu University, Varanasi.

Personal Life

Prof. Kanungo married Sarat Kumari Das on 21st April 1954. They were an exemplary couple, and his wife encouraged him in all his academic endeavors. They have three sons (Manas, Rajesh, and Tapas), who all are engineers and settled in the USA. He had an ancestral house at Badamunda in Bhubaneswar, where he used to stay occasionally.

Acknowledgments

The authors acknowledge Prof. MK Thakur, who is one of the Ph.D. students of Prof. MS Kanungo for suggestions on this article.

Bibliography

1. https://fellows.ias.ac.in/profile/v/FL1975042, Indian Academy of Sciences
2. Padma Awards Directory (1954–2009) Ministry of Home Affairs
3. https://www.insaindia.res.in/detail.php?id=N75-0356, Indian National Science Academy Fellow INSA.
4. Singh, S.N., Kanungo, M.S. (1968) Alterations in lactate dehydrogenase of the brain, heart, skeletal muscle, and liver of rats of various ages. J Biol Chem 243, 4526-4529.

5. Moudgil, V.K., Kanungo, M.S. (1973) Effect of age of the rat on induction of acetylcholinesterase of the brain by 17β-estradiol. BBA - General Sub. 329, 211-220.
6. Moudgil, V.K., Kanungo, M.S. (1973) Induction of acetylcholinesterase by 17- estradiol in the brain of rats of various ages. Biochem Biophys Res Commun 52, 725-730.
7. Kanungo, M.S. (1975) A model for ageing. J Theor Biol 53, 253-261.
8. Kanungo, M.S., Thakur, M.K. (1977) Phosphorylation of chromosomal proteins as a function of age and its modulation by calcium. Biochem Biophys Res Commun 79, 1031-1036.
9. Thakur, M.K., Das, R., Kanungo, M.S. (1978) Modulation of acetylation of chromosomal proteins of the brain of rats of various ages by epinephrine and estradiol. Biochem Biophys Res Commun 81, 828-831.
10. Kanungo, M.S., Thakur, M.K. (1979) Modulation of acetylation of histones and transcription of chromatin by butyric acid and 17β-estradiol in the brain of rats of various ages. Biochem Biophys Res Commun 87, 266-271.
11. Kanungo, M.S., Thakur, M.K. (1979) Effects of oestradiol on covalent modifications of chromosomal proteins and transcription of chromatin of the brain of rats of various ages. J Steroid Biochem 11, 879-887.
12. Thakur, M.K., Kanungo, M.S. (1981) Methylation of chromosomal proteins and DNA of rat brain and its modulation by estradiol and calcium during aging. Exp Gerontol 16, 331-337.
13. Upadhyay, R., Gupta, S., Kanungo, M.S. (1996) Age-related changes in the ovalbumin gene of the Japanese quail. Biochem Biophys Res Commun 226, 356-361.
14. Gupta, S., Upadhyay, R., Kanungo, M.S. (1998) Activation of vitellogenin II gene expression by steroid hormones in the old Japanese quail. Mol Biol Rep 25, 245-251. Modi, P.K., Kanungo, M.S. (2010) Age-dependent expression of S100 beta in the brain of mice. Cell Mol Neurobiol 30, 709-716.
15. Koul, O, Aggarwal, B.B., Rath, P.C. (2012) Obituary: Madhu Sudan Kanungo, Ph.D. (1927 - 2011). J Gerontol A Biol Sci Med Sci 67, 1041-1042.

AUTHORS PROFILE

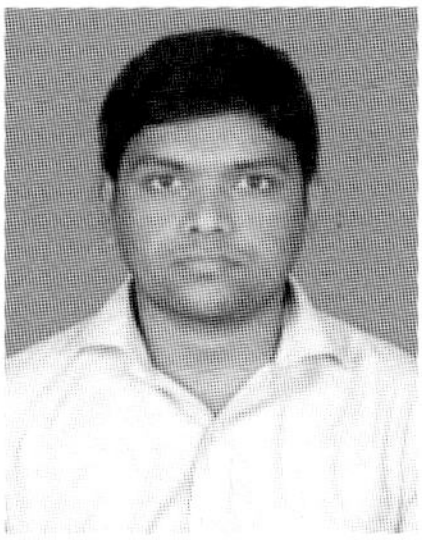

Padmanabh Singh earned his Master's in Biotechnology from Ravenshaw University, Cuttack, and his Ph.D. from the Department of Zoology, Banaras Hindu University, Varanasi, on the role of chromatin modification, particularly histone acetylation on learning and memory during aging. He joined the University of Freiburg, Germany as a Postdoctoral fellow, and is currently working aa s Research Associate at the Department of Zoology, Indira Gandhi National Tribal University, Amarkantak, on steroid hormone and chromatin modifications. He is a recipient of the DBT-BCIL BITP Fellowship (2010), CSIR Junior Research Fellowship (2010), and DBT-Research Associate Fellowship (2021). Apart from scientific research, he has an interest in Science Communications and shares research news through his social media page "The LifeScientist".

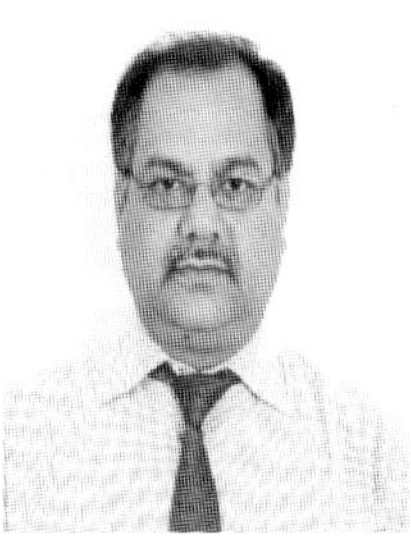

Vijay Paramanik is employed at the Department of Zoology, Indira Gandhi National Tribal University, Amarkantak (MP), India. He has an experience of over Ten years of teaching and 18 years of research. His research area is the neurobiology of learning and memory, aging, neuroprotection, and Indian Traditional medicine. He is a member of several scientific bodies in India and abroad namely NASI, IAN, AGI, SNCI, IBRO, JNS, etc. He is a recipient of several awards including the President Young Scientist Medal of IGNTU (UGC) 2018, IBRO Visiting research fellow to Monash University, Sunway Malaysia 2018, NASI Swarna Jayanti Puraskar 2012, etc. Dr. Paramanik has published several research papers, reviews, proceedings, letters, and reports; and has also authored one book He has guided Ph.D., postdoctoral, M.Sc. dissertations, handled several national and international research projects, and reviewed many research papers. He served as a resource person, chairperson, and coordinator of various national and international conference.

Email: vijayparamanik@gmail.com

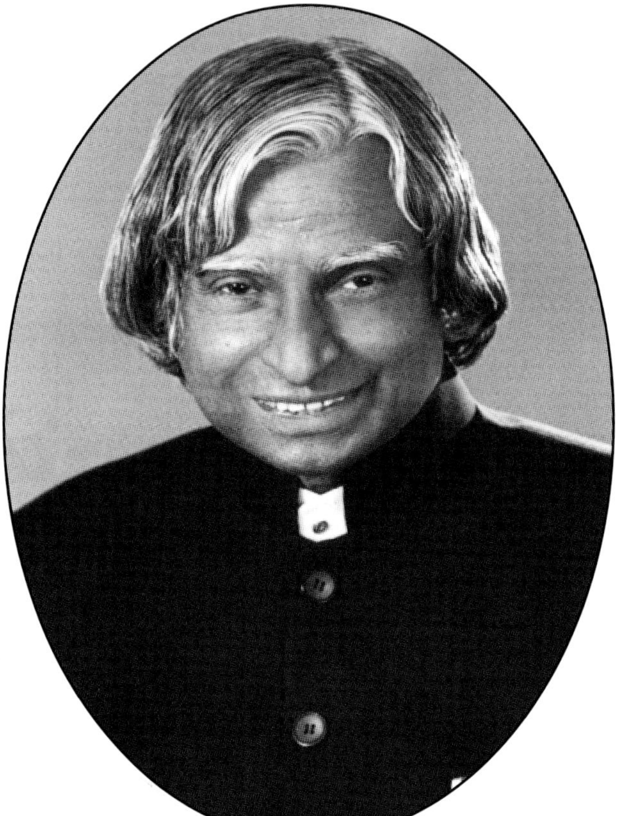

Avul Pakir Jainulabdeen Abdul Kalam

(15 October 1931 – 27 July 2015)

A. P. J. ABDUL KALAM: A NATIONALIST SCIENTIST

Arun Tiwari

A Long View

Science is inarguably the driving force of human civilization. As the 1000 years after the sacking of the Roman empire by the Germans led Europe into a dark age, lifted only by the Renaissance of science in the 15th century, the Indian dark age ended with the independence gained in 1947. With a nationalist fervor, riding on the crest of Dr. C. V. Raman's Nobel Prize in Physics and banking on the brilliance of nuclear physicist Dr. Homi J. Bhabha, India took the bold decision of pursuing the path of nuclear research. Another intense scholar, Dr. Vikram Sarabhai, pioneered space research. When food shortage undermined our sovereignty, Dr. M. S. Swaminathan led the Green Revolution, which saved the day for the nation. And when China cast its evil net upon Indian territory, colluding with Pakistan, Dr. APJ Abdul Kalm led the Missile Development Program and succeeded in India having a nuclear weapon on a long-range Agni missile that pushed China on the defensive. Even in these great stories of nationalist scientists, Dr. APJ Abdul Kalam stands out as rising to the august office of President of India. Dr. Kalam brought Indian science a new status in the world and appeal to its own people.

I worked with Dr. APJ Abdul Kalam for 33 years, staring in 1982 at the Defence Research & Development Laboratory (DRDL) in Hyderabad. He tasked me to develop India's first Titanium Air bottle used to power a missile control system and interact with the industry to make aeronautical grade aluminum alloys indigenously. In 1993, Dr. Kalam chose me to coordinate the development of civilian spinoffs of defense technology to make essential medical devices affordable for the vast Indian population. On becoming the President of India in 2002, he included me in his team, and I traveled extensively with him. I played a part in setting up telemedicine in India and started a Pan-African e-Network. After his Presidency, Dr. Kalam took up the mission of awakening the consciousness of school children.

Dr. APJ Abdul Kalam's autobiography – *Wings of Fire* – that I co-authored, turned out to be immensely popular and I was seen as Dr. Kalam's pupil. In 2013, we published *Squaring the Circle: Seven Steps to Indian Renaissance.*

In this book, Dr. Kalam predicted the commencement of a new era. He wrote, "It is time to scrap complex old laws and administrative procedures which are hindering a growth-oriented economy."[1] This eventually happened in 2014. A month before his departure, he published *Transcendence: My Spiritual Experiences with Pramukh Swamiji*, which foresees India leading the world in 2047, through its enlightened citizenry.

In this article, I attempt to put Dr. APJ Abdul Kalam's scientific achievements in a broader societal perspective, how he created an impetus for new generations of knowledge workers and set the ball rolling for self-reliance, and above all, for millions of children to pursue science. Like a tree bears fruit after years of growth and only in a season, Dr. Kalam's achievements must be seen in the matrix of how Indian economy has changed track from agriculture to IT, and now to automated manufacturing; and how the culture of interdisciplinary research fostered unleased innovation and transformation of the Indian MedTech industry. Dr. Kalam acted as a perfect integrator linking scientists across organizational boundaries to do what must be done to serve the Indian people. He brought Indian public sector units, private industries, and academic institutions together in a way that was as transformative as it was revolutionary.

Dr. Kalam's legacy can be analyzed as comprising five phases: project management, system integration, self-reliance in critical technology, innovation for affordability, and finally, navigating into the global economy. These phases have manifested as India's first Satellite Launch Vehicle (SLV-3) putting the Rohini Satellite into orbit in the 1970s, the Integrated Guided Missile Development Programme (IGMDP) in the 1980s, the development of the Indian Light Combat Aircraft in the 1990s and its induction into the Air Force in the 2010s, a 10-billion-dollar Indian MedTech industry exporting products, and Indian entry in the global defence and aerospace market in the 2020s.

Project Management

The general perception about science is of a genius scientist developing a new idea through imagination, observation, or experimentation. But the hidden hand of the larger body of science, and the conditions in the world, choose and guide people to pick up new ideas, and improve upon the old ones. Many people play their roles and immense resources are used to make progress happen. The story of Indian science indeed began with project management. Two prodigious scientists – Dr. Homi J. Bhabha and Dr. Vikram A. Sarabhai – envisioned the newly independent India to have the capability of harnessing nuclear energy and utilizing space for weather forecasting, imaging, and communication. They were wholeheartedly supported by Prime Minister Jawaharlal Nehru. The legacy of Dr. Kalam has its origin in the intersection of these two programs. Dr. Kalam's work on missiles had the establishment of the Indian Space Programme and the Indian Nuclear Programme as precursors.

In 1962, the Department of Atomic Energy, headed by Dr. Bhabha, established a new entity called the Indian National Committee for Space Research (INCOSPAR), with Dr. Sarabhai, the director of the Physical Research Laboratory (PRL) in Ahmedabad, at the lead. The group was tasked with developing India's space program. INCOSPAR started working as a division of the Prof. M. G. K. Menon-directed Tata Institute of Fundamental Research. Its initial job was to find the best young scientists in India who had experience in this field and train them to be capable of performing their new duties. Prof. Menon picked young Kalam working at the Aeronautical Development Establishment (ADE) in Bangalore.

The live broadcast of the Tokyo Olympic Games across the Pacific by the American satellite "Syncom-3" in 1964 was a stunning show of space science. India had to integrate itself into what was happening in the world. For the new group of scientists, the first task was to build a modest rocket launch station in Thumba in Kerala that could also be used for data collection for the world's scientific community. On November 21, 1963, the successful launch of the Nike Apache rocket carrying a vapour cloud payload served as the birth of India's space program. The French Centaure and Russian M-100 sounding rockets were launched after it.

In 1966, an agreement for the Satellite Instructional Television Experiment (SITE) was signed with NASA. The Indian government's quick realization of the crucial role that space communications would play in the development of the country led to the setting up of the Experimental Satellite Communication Earth Station (ESCES) in Ahmedabad in 1967. On August 15, 1969, the Department of Space was created, metamorphosing the INSCOPAR. Dr. Sarabhai headed the new organization.

Dr. Sarabhai personally chose Kalam over many senior scientists to lead the Satellite Launch Vehicle project (SLV) as he could see Project Management as a different art of doing science. This would be the first indigenous rocket development project to launch a satellite. A 40-kilogram satellite load was intended to be launched into a 400 km orbit. During the Bombay National Electronics Conference in 1970, Vikram Sarabhai, flanked by Kalam, announced proposals for an Indian National Satellite (INSAT). By launching its first satellite, the Aryabhata, from Kapustin Yar in Russia's Astrakhan Oblast on April 19, 1975, India officially entered the space age.

The Rohini satellite was successfully launched into orbit by the SLV-3 on July 18, 1980, making India the sixth member of a select group of spacefaring nations. The Augmented Satellite Launch Vehicle (ASLV), Polar Satellite Launch Vehicle (PSLV), and Geosynchronous Satellite Launch Vehicle (GSLV) projects would be made possible by the SLV-3 project's successful completion.

Dr. Kalam was conferred with the Padma Bhushan on Republic Day in 1981. A Doctor of Science honoris causa was awarded to Kalam by the Anna University of Madras. Nuclear physicist and creator of India's first nuclear reactor, Apsara, Dr. Raja Ramanna, then working as the chief of the Defence Research & Development Organization (DRDO), conferred the degree on him during the convocation. Dr. Ramanna invited Dr. Kalam to lead the Indian Missile Programme. On June 1, 1982, Dr. Kalam began serving as Director for DRDL, Hyderabad.

System Integration

While the creation of SLV-3 was a project management exercise – putting together the work of other scientists into a launch vehicle following a time schedule, the development of missiles was a different ball game altogether. Nothing indeed was available except some legacy Russian missile systems. Designing or building missiles with specific applications, integrating them with new or existing hardware, packaged and bespoke software, and implementing communications are all steps in the process of making a missile system. Most of the work relies on new knowledge and external vendors – the hallmark of system integration.

With many senior service officers holding key positions, the DRDO had a hierarchical culture. Dr. Kalam included middle-level scientists and engineers in the management of the laboratory and invoked the idea of management by participation. In 1984, Dr. Kalam inducted 280 young engineers, which was arguably the largest induction in a scientific institution in India. Dr. Kalam developed a matrix organization in which he added a task-driven work system while keeping the lab's typical hierarchical structure.

Technology division scientists were promoted to system managers and given exclusive charge of one project. Dr. Kalam would rely on the best technical and scientific minds he could muster, both inside and outside the government service. An external fabrication wing was established and private sector companies like L&T, Godrej, and Tata were invited to make missile components.

Dr. Kalam was now acting as India's Missile Man. He persuaded the political and bureaucratic establishment that missiles were superior to other types of weapons in specific military and strategic tasks. Dr. Kalam effectively communicated their virtues: It is possible to launch ballistic missiles at night or in inclement weather. Since they move at supersonic speeds, they can quickly reach strategic targets, such as enemy installations located far from the missile's place of deployment. They can be aimed at enemy air and naval targets as well as ground forces. In addition to being more efficient, they are also harder to detect and intercept than aircraft. They can also seriously dissuade aggressive powers due to their ability to deliver bombs deep into their territory.

The Integrated Guided Missile Development Programme (IGMDP) integrated IITs, Indian Institutes of Science (IISc), the Jadavpur University, the National Aerospace Laboratories (NAL), public sector companies like Hindustan Aeronautics Limited (HAL), Bharat Electronics Limited (BEL), Central Electronics Limited (CEL), Electronics Corporation of India Limited, and several private industries like L&T, Tatas, and Godrej. The creation of missile-specific facilities and laboratories was liberally funded, and hundreds of masters and doctoral students were assigned tasks that would otherwise be done in laboratories. Dr. Kalam indeed resurrected Indian science in the 1990s to be technology centric.

Dr. Kalam travelled to the US in 1985 as part of a group to purchase a supercomputer from Cray Inc. in Seattle, US, which was purportedly needed for weather forecasting but was necessary for computational fluid dynamics (CFD). Without a hypersonic wind tunnel, CFD was the only method to design the Agni re-entry payload. The Americans rudely informed Dr. Kalam that they would not be selling the machine to India., who adopted a *swadeshi* approach to technical advancement once more.

Dr. Kalam rallied together Indian computer specialists to build a homegrown supercomputer with the same performance as the Cray computer, which was then in the gigaflop range. He writes in *Wings of Fire*, "Now, the question was how to beat the system. Prof. SM Deshpande of the IISc found four young, bright scientists working in the field of fluid dynamics and, within six months, developed the software for Computational Fluid Dynamics for Hypersonic Regimes, which is one of its kind in the world."[2] Later, the Centre for Development of Advanced Computing (C-DAC), which was established in Pune in 1988 to lead India's national supercomputing program, produced the supercomputer PARAM.

The surface-to-surface Prithvi missile, capable of striking from 150 km, underwent a successful flight test on February 25, 1988. It was a turning point in India's military advancement because this test demonstrated the country's capacity to create the fundamental building blocks for the next guided missiles. The Prithvi could be converted into an air missile and was also capable of being launched from a ship. An accuracy of hitting within 100 meters was attained.

A coordinated technological embargo was placed on India by Canada, France, Germany, Italy, Japan, the United Kingdom, and the United States. Almost any product or substance that could be used in India's missile development was prohibited from being supplied, including computer processor chips, radio-frequency devices, electro-hydraulic components, maraging steel, magnesium alloy, gyroscopes, accelerometers, carbon fiber, and glass fiber.

Undeterred by the technology sanctions, under Dr. Kalam's direction, true *swadeshi* partnerships created magnesium alloy castings for missile frames, phase shifters for passive electronically scanned array radars, winding machines for composite materials, heat-resistant resins for the re-entry payload of the Agni missiles, and more. An impromptu consortium of the Mishra Dhatu Nigam Limited (MIDHANI), the Defence Metallurgical Research Laboratory (DMRL), and private enterprises created highly guarded maraging steel. This steel possesses superior strength and toughness without losing ductility and allows it to be formed into thinner rocket and missile skins, reducing weight for a given strength. The global effort to stop India's missile program was bravely thwarted.

On July 19, 1984, Prime Minister Indira Gandhi paid a visit to DRDL. Dr. Kalam and the Prime Minister had already met on multiple occasions, but this time he would be meeting her on behalf of his lab. Dr. Kalam could feel that while Smt. Gandhi maintained her father's admiration for science and respect for scientists, she could also appreciate "technology." She commended Dr. Kalam for making the difficult but ultimately more fruitful decision to pursue his objectives with Indian businesses and people rather than importing high-tech facilities.

Dr. Kalam was aware that system integration posed his biggest challenge in the IGMDP. Without a solid technological base, developing missiles would be impossible. Front-line research had to be done immediately in fields like embedded electronics, unique materials, and software. They would form the cornerstone on which a comprehensive missile program could be effectively built. Furthermore, testing and evaluation facilities for missile systems would be necessary.

In August 1985, Prime Minister Rajiv Gandhi laid the foundation stone for the new building. The Centre would be equipped with cutting-edge missile integration and checkout, environmental, and electronic warfare test facilities. Besides a composites production facility, a high enthalpy facility, and an inertial instrumentation laboratory was created.

Self-reliance in Critical Technology

IIT, Bombay, in 1991 conferred upon Dr. Kalam an honorary Doctor of Science degree. According to the citation, he served as "an inspiration for building a strong technological foundation from which India's future aerospace programmes might be launched to address the challenges of the twenty-first century." Dr. Kalam assumed his position as the Director General of DRDO's Scientific Adviser in July 1992.

The Indian government established a high-power committee headed by Dr. Kalam to build a roadmap for developing crucial vital technologies domestically as a defence against wealthy nations' rejections. The committee included representatives from the three services and defence industrial facilities. The complicated system of licenses, regulations and related red tape that was necessary to establish and operate a business in India between 1947 and 1990 was abolished by Prime Minister P. V. Narasimha Rao. He was certain that the nation would become more powerful only through technology and Dr. Kalam, with his experience and charisma, would be the ideal leader to accomplish it. Dr. Bhabha and Dr. Sarabhai had been gone for twenty years. It was about time someone of that caliber saw the larger picture. Dr. Kalam was now regarded as being on par with his former heroes and given his natural ability to see many different components as an integrated whole, was the man of the moment.

Dr. Kalam accessed and went through the 1963 reports of the Subramanian Committee, which had the powerful J. R. D. Tata as a member. The committee emphasized that the design knowledge base was insufficient to meet the demands of the rapidly evolving aircraft industry. In response, the committee recommended that cooperative development of aviation engines be explored with reputable engine producers like G.E., Rolls Royce, and Snecma Moteurs. India had a long way to go before its technological needs were met. Undoubtedly, a compromise would need to be made between the ambitious goal of producing all the nation's military and civilian technological requirements domestically, and what was practical.

Although both phrases have been used interchangeably in the Indian context, the Self-Reliance Committee distinguished between the ideas of "self-sufficiency" and "self-reliance" for this. It was decided that self-reliance meant arming the Armed Forces with a wide range of equipment that might draw from a variety of foreign and domestic sources, as opposed to self-sufficiency, which meant producing all the Armed Forces required locally. A very practical man, Dr. Kalam understood that an unbending commitment to "self-sufficiency" was not the best course for a nation like India because its industrial and R&D bases were not yet sufficiently developed. Also, Dr. Kalam was frank about the capacity gap that existed between India's defense production industry and its research and development facilities, and that of its international competitors. He believed that one method to deal with this would be through joint ventures for the co-production and development of defense technology with nations like France and Russia.

The Kalam Committee stressed the importance of raising India's self-reliance level from 30% in 1992 to 70% by 2005. The committee also recognized the essential technologies needed, including hypersonic propulsion, fiber optics, smart weapon subsystems, heavy particle beams, and gallium arsenide devices. It suggested setting up a Defence Technology Fund with a budget of Rs. 100 crore to concentrate on the "mother" and "core" technologies required to construct cutting-edge defense equipment, which might include, for instance, multimode radars, aero engines, carbon fibers, and the capacity of Light Combat Aircraft (LCA) to fly stealthily.

The Indian Navy acknowledged in 1996 the critical need for a quick-response air defense system to shield its warships from airplanes and anti-ship missiles while at sea. The American Harpoon and French Exocet sea-skimming missiles were now part of the Pakistani Navy. These missiles could strike our ships at close to supersonic speeds, during day or night, regardless of the weather. The anti-missile system had to not only "see" the incoming missile through the visual disturbance of the waves, but also fire its missile as soon as possible. The sea-skimming Trishul missile's development, which was planned for this purpose, was getting delayed.

Dr. Kalam acknowledged the situation facing the Navy. He didn't go into denial or make any justifications. He never allowed reason to be eclipsed by his ego. The Israeli Barak missile was chosen after the Navy considered numerous other options. Together with the installation of Barak missiles on Indian Navy ships, this initial procurement resulted in a 350-million-dollar joint venture between the DRDO and the Israeli military technology industry. Ten years later, this partnership would create the Barak Extended Range SAM, which could be used to attack targets more than 100 kilometers away from a launch point. This is the power of taking the right decisions at the tight time.

Dr. Kalam was seen by this time as a symbol of India's scientific might. To make a strong statement about the significance the government places on India's security, in November 1997, Dr. Kalam was given the country's highest honor, the Bharat Ratna. After Sir C. V. Raman, he was the second scientist to win the honor.

Pakistan had acquired North Korean "No-Dong" missiles in a nefarious trade that had given the covert regime tools for nuclear design and enrichment in exchange. To restore the delicate balance between the two countries, India was left with no choice but to build its nuclear capabilities in synchrony with Pakistan's. The Agni family of ballistic missiles had to be nuclear armed as soon as possible for this reason.

On May 11, 1998, at 3:43:44.2 IST, the three explosions' combined energy raised a region the size of a cricket field to a few meters above the surface, sending billowing clouds of sand and dust into the air. There was no consideration of claiming that they were "peaceful tests," unlike the explosion in 1974. The military aspect of the explosions was rapidly stressed by government officials. Two days later, on May 13, 1998, the two sub-kiloton devices were detonated underground. India declared itself a nuclear weapon power.

Dr. Kalam mocked the uproar in the Western media that followed the tests in May 1998. Why should Britain have a nuclear arsenal but not India, he asked. Why were there no protests while the French were testing nuclear weapons in the atmosphere in occupied Algiers? Are these inquiries not valid? The solution does not lie in asserting that France and Britain had a divine right to nuclear weapons, but rather in a truly moral example of unilateral nuclear disarmament, in which neither the West nor the Soviet Union or China were interested.

On January 4, 2001, at the HAL Airport in Bangalore, Wing Commander Rajiv Kothiyal took off with the LCA, designated as Technology Demonstration 1 (TD-I), marking the pinnacle of Dr. Kalam's career. Together with the LCA prototype, two support Mirage 2000 aircraft took to the skies. Chief of Air Staff Air Marshal A. Y. Tipnis flew one of them, leading from the front. The flight had no problems. Amazing work was done by the design, evaluation, flight-testing, and airworthiness teams. Prime Minister Atal Bihar Vajpayee named it *Tejas*, meaning splendor.

India joined the privileged group of nations with an indigenous fighter aircraft because of this feat. Our nation has acquired several technologies because of the LCA initiative, creating numerous spin-off advantages. Many businesses that produced technologies for the LCA exported them, making handsome profits. France would later gladly agree to set up local assembly lines for the Panther helicopters and Rafale jet fighters that it is providing to the Indian Armed Forces after losing out on the *Tejas* engine and avionics contracts.

Innovation for Affordability

India's Missile Man would not be limited to just aerospace engineering. He played a crucial role in developing several technologies for the least fortunate in society since he was incredibly adaptable and had a mind that went far beyond the boundaries of his own area. Inspired by him, and with his support, a Floor Reaction Orthosis (FRO) was created using cutting-edge composite material created by DRDL to assist children with polio in walking. The development of austenitic steel wires devoid of delta-ferrite, and with a surface free of wire-drawing-induced micro-channels led to the creation of a coronary stent as well.

Dr. Kalam was invited to speak at the Indian Science Congress' 81st Congress in 1994, which was held in Jaipur. He made a strong case for creating technology spin-offs to reduce the need for healthcare imports. He emphasized that using homegrown technologies and biological endeavors would help reduce the suffering brought on by the exorbitant expense of medical care. He said, "Let my brain take away your anguish." Dr. Kalam announced the formation of the Society for Biomedical Technology (SBMT) as an inter-ministerial working group with the aim of bringing together medical professionals, engineers, and public sector executives.

Under Dr. Kalam's stewardship, a compendium of 35 Technology Vision documents has been released by the Technology Information, Forecasting and Assessment Council (TIFAC). Along with Dr. Y. S. Rajan, Dr. Kalam published *India 2020: A Vision for the New Millennium*, exhorting the transformation of India in five areas, namely, agriculture and food processing; education and healthcare; information and communication technology; infrastructure development, which includes reliable and quality electric power, surface transport and infrastructure for all parts of the country; and self-reliance in critical technologies. Since that time, Dr. Kalam started taking interest in agriculture and healthcare.

Dr. Kalam visited Wipro-GE in August 2000. Working with BEL, Wipro-GE produced a low-cost CT scanner for the Indian market. The price reduction facilitated this essential diagnostic technology to reach towns across India. But the most revolutionary was the development of Logic 100, a low-cost ultrasound machine. It empowered doctors even in small towns in serving their patients by having the machines right in their clinics. D. A. Prasanna, the first CEO of Wipro-GE, later wrote, "Frugal innovation is fashionable to talk about in the current century, but we laid down its cornerstone. Total India development cost of Logiq 100 was US$1.5M. Compare that with the Logiq 700 development budget, which was US$80M in the USA. We could develop at not half or one-third but one-fifth of US or Japan cost. . . There is no going back now – we have hoisted our flag on the global MedTech turf."[3]

During his first Presidential visit to Tripura, Dr. Kalam got a telemedicine link established between Kalashar, a remote town there, with Hyderabad. The Bharat Sanchar Nigam Limited (BSNL) provided connectivity using a hybrid of telephone lines and microwave towers. A 14-year-old boy suffering from a leaking heart valve was diagnosed and treated in Hyderabad to live a normal life later. During his visit to Tanzania in 2004, Dr. Kalam, moved by the plight of children suffering from holes in their hearts, organized for 24 children to be airlifted to Hyderabad by Air India and operated on. Computer apps were developed to monitor these children, across the continent.

Harvesting the seeds sown by Dr. Kalam, when COVID-19 struck in 2019, the National Digital Health Mission, a nearly instantaneous adoption of telemedicine, and significant advancements in *Made in India*, together with the widespread use of smartphones and the internet, have altered how Indians view and access healthcare. The rollout of the COVID-19 vaccine in India was excellent in part due to the release of the COWIN app. Even during a period of vaccine shortage in a nation of 1.4 billion, the rollout prioritized those who faced the highest danger. There were no connections to make or levers to pull. Simply reserve your time, wait for your turn, and depart. The vaccination centers had no lines either. India has emerged in the world as an example of affordable healthcare. No wonder that the 11-billion-dollar Indian MedTech industry in 2022 exports 3 billion dollars' worth of products.

Dr. Kalam visited the International Crops Research Institute for the Semi-arid Tropics (ICRISAT), Hyderabad in December 2002 on its 30th anniversary celebrations. He was among the first Indian leaders to support the genetic modification of seeds to increase yield, resistance to diseases, and drought. In June 2013, Dr. Kalam inaugurated a new greenhouse containment facility for transgenic crops at the ICRISAT as a part of the Platform for Translational Research on Transgenic Crops. Of course, plant genetics remains controversial in India but when in 2022, the Indian government allowed gene editing in the same species, it was as if Dr. Kalam's dream came true.

Navigating into the Global Economy

Despite the success of the Light Combat Aircraft *Tejas* in 2001, it faced a long cascade of indecisiveness in the government, and adverse lobbying by the global aviation industry. It was a pity Dr. Kalam could not witness the 2016 Bahrain Air Show, when *Tejas* was flown in full view of a worldwide audience, forcing Pakistan to withdraw from the air show, the JF-17 Thunder fighter made with Chinese technology. The global industry was awed to see 60% indigenous content in *Tejas*, including the high technology-based composite material.

Under Prime Minister Narendra Modi, India has shifted its strategy in the Aerospace and Defence Sector (A&D) from being the largest importer of defense goods to being a global manufacturing hub. Major manufacturers are becoming more aware of India's geographic and technological possibilities as the home economy grows. To make India a regional hub, most manufacturers have indicated that Maintenance, Repair, and Overhaul (MRO) facilities for their aircraft will be localized.

In recent years, India has implemented several policy changes to strengthen its domestic defense equipment design, research, and production capabilities, and produce equipment of the highest quality. To support indigenous manufacture, two defense industrial corridors have been developed, one each in Tamil Nadu and Uttar Pradesh. Defense exports grew by over 300 percent in the last five years. India exports to over 75 countries due to collaborative efforts, including to the United States. By 2025, the Defence Ministry wants to produce Rs. 1.75 lakh crore of weapons, including Rs. 35,000 crores for export.

Great souls are said to transcend their mortal lives and Dr. APJ Abdul Kalam was indeed a great soul. From a B.Sc. in Physics to graduation in aeronautical engineering, his journey into the highest echelons of the scientific world is surreal. Caught up in doing projects of urgent national needs early into his career, Dr. Kalam could not do a formal Ph.D. but received 48 honorary doctorates from the best universities in India and abroad.

The legacy of science with a nationalist fervor must continue. As always, new problems have arrived with new times. I mention here five of them: cyber security, malnutrition, the second agricultural revolution based on organic fertilizers and genetically edited seeds, an equitable education system, and care of the elderly. Technology will play its own role, but it must be backed by corruption-free governance and assimilated by an enlightened citizenry. India needs people like Dr. Kalam, believing in their destiny to be useful to their country and people. I conclude with Dr. Kalam's words in *Wings of Fire*, "You can win only by retaining your birthright to be a person. And to retain this right, you will have to be willing to take the social or external risks involved in ignoring pressures to do things the way others say they should be done."[4] What better definition could there be than this for a scientific temper?

Bibliography

1. Abdul Kalam, A.P.J., Tiwari, A. (2013) *Squaring the Circle*, Hyderabad: University Press, p. 269
2. Abdul Kalam, A.P.J., Tiwari, A. (1999) *Wings of Fire*, Hyderabad: University Press, p. 84.
3. Prasanna, D. A., Tiwari, A. (2022) *Innovate Locally to Win Globally*, Pune: Sakal Media Pvt. Ltd.
4. Abdul Kalam, A.P.J., Tiwari, A. (1999) *Wings of Fire*, Hyderabad: University Press, p. 101.

AUTHOR PROFILE

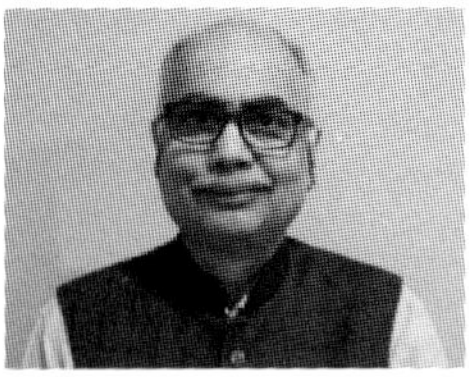

Arun Kumar Tiwari is an Indian missile scientist, author, and professor. He has written several books, of these, five co-authored with Dr. APJ Abdul Kalam, including his autobiography '*Wings of Fire*'.

Email: tiwariarun@gmail.com; webpage: http://aruntiwari.com/

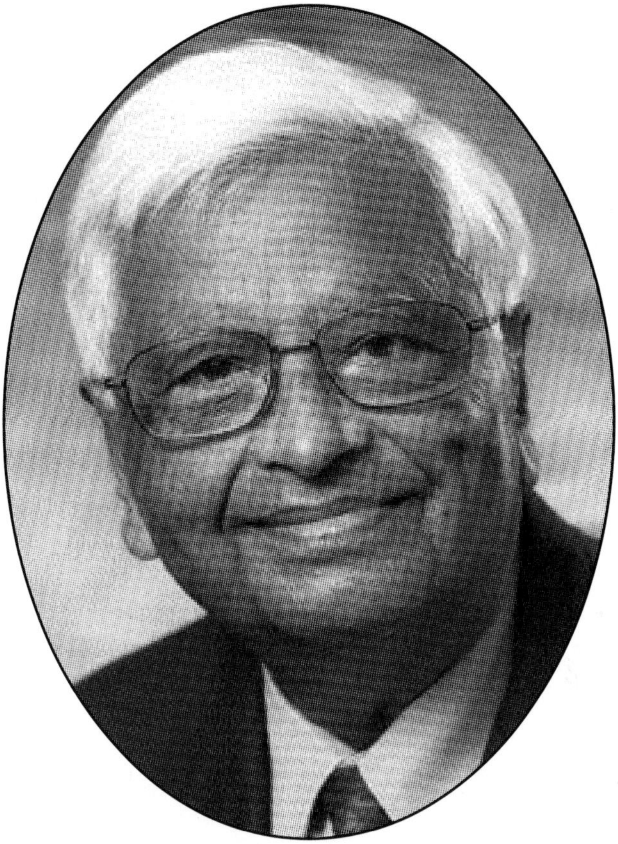

Govindjee Govindjee

(Born 24 October 1932)

GOVINDJEE GOVINDJEE: INDIA'S GIFT TO THE PHOTOSYNTHETIC COMMUNITY

Naveen Kumar Sharma

Govindjee and photosynthesis research are synonymous. In his long scientific career, he has made vital discoveries, written trendsetting publications, and been conferred numerous awards and honors. A researcher and educator *par excellence*, he has been an incredible and persuasive communicator on photosynthesis including its history for students, professional scientists, and the general public. He is one of the luminaries of photosynthesis, who learned from the great fathers, worked with masters, and trained many leading lights of the disciplines. A legend that we are immensely proud of.

Early Life and Education

Govindjee was born on October 24, 1932 to Mrs. Savitri Devi and Mr. Vishveshwar Prasad in Allahabad (now Prayagraj), India. His father was first a college teacher, who also served as the General Secretary of the U.P. (United Provinces) Teachers Association, and then as the representative of the Oxford University Press in Northern India. The couple had three sons and one daughter, namely – Krishnaji, Gopalji and Govindjee (sons), and Malati (daughter). Govindjee was the youngest of the siblings. Though by birth an "Asthana", which represents a specific caste. The family never used last name, as his father was an 'Arya Samajist' and did not believe in the caste system. Therefore, he always has been known by only one name 'Govindjee', which remained his legal name, but in 2019, he changed it to "Govindjee Govindjee". Because of citations and many other problems, intermittently, from 1956 to 2018, he has been known by many other names (see Eaton-Rye, 2007).

Like any ordinary student, Govindjee too was reluctant to learn. He started his formal schooling from the 4th class onwards. Govindjee completed his schooling (4th – 10th class) at Colonelganj High School (1943–1948), and Kayastha Pathshala (K.P.) Intermediate College (11 & 12th class) (1948–1950) at Allahabad, India. According to Govindjee, he studied all the subjects in High School, but Science! rather than Arts was his focus. Sadly, his father passed away in 1943, and his older brother Krishnaji, who was a Professor of Physics, at Allahabad University, took care of him. He was his role model (Krishnaji passed away in August 1997). He remembered Govindjee as an inquisitive child, wanting to know the why and how of everything he saw. Also, Govindjee's passion for discussions was to the extent that he disliked those who avoided discussion. The early life of Govindjee had a significant impact of ongoing India's Independence, still, he vividly recalls all those moments. His sister Malati took it upon herself to boycott West-made clothes, she used to spin her own yarn, and always wore "khadi" fabric. Govindjee was touched deeply by the powerful speeches of Gandhiji and Nehruji whom he listened to at Purushottam Das Tandon Park (see Block 2022 for further details). In fact, his family never owned a house in Allahabad; they always lived in rented homes and therefore kept on moving from one neighbourhood to another until they settled at 14 B Bank Road (now Lala Ram Narain Road). This allowed Govindjee to see the whole city of Allahabad.

In 1950, he took admission at Allahabad University (1950–1954) and completed his Bachelor of Science (B.Sc.) with Chemistry, Botany, and Zoology, in the first division, and Master of Science (M.Sc.) in Botany, (in the first division, and first position) in 1952, and 1954, respectively. He specialized in Plant Physiology under Shri Ranjan (a former student of Felix Frost Blackman). In his college days, Govindjee was influenced and helped by many good teachers, notably, the late Jalpa Prasad (Chemistry) and M.L. Gaur (Biology) who ignited his interest in both Chemistry and Biology, and were used to loan their personal books to him. Govindjee fondly remembers that he was good at learning from books, but was always unsure of himself in practical's. He found sectioning plants easier than dissecting animals. Maybe, this was the reason why he took up Botany as a subject.

Since Govindjee had secured the first position and first class, and someone was needed to teach "Plant Physiology", After completing his M.Sc. in the autumn of 1954, he was hired as a Lecturer in Botany at Allahabad University and worked there from 1954 to 1956. While teaching plant physiology, he got interested in the research of Richard Willstätter, Hans Fischer, and Robert Emerson. He applied for admission to the University of Illinois at Urbana-Champaign (UIUC), Illinois, USA, under its Fellowship Program (UIUC Graduate Fellowship) and was accepted into its doctoral program in 1955. He also received the prestigious Fulbright Foundation travel grant to go to the USA. In 1956, he reached UIUC to work for his Ph.D. in Physico-Chemical Biology (later changed to Biophysics) under Robert Emerson. However, after Emerson's untimely death in a plane crash in February 1959, he worked with Eugene Rabinowitch, and obtained his Ph.D. in Biophysics from UIUC (1960) on the topic '*Action Spectra of the Emerson Enhancement Effect in Algae.*' Meantime, on October 24, 1957, Govindjee married Rajni Varma in Urbana, Illinois. He had met Rajni in 1953 when both were M.Sc. students at Allahabad University. There, she was a year junior to him. At UIUC they were Ph.D. students of Robert Emerson.

From 1960 to 1961, Govindjee worked as a Postdoctoral Fellow at United States Public Health (USPH). And from 1961 to today, he has served the UIUC in various capacities: From 1961-1965 as an Assistant Professor of Botany (later renamed Plant Biology); from 1965 to 1969 an Associate Professor of Biophysics and Botany; from 1969 to 1999 a Professor of Biophysics and Plant Biology, and from 1998–1999, as a Professor of Plant Biology, Biochemistry and Biophysics. On August 1, 1999, he became Professor Emeritus of Plant Biology, Biochemistry and Biophysics, at UIUC.

Contribution to the Science[20,21,22,23,32,57,69]

A. Pre-Photosynthesis days' work on the effect of virus infection on plant metabolism and use of paper chromatography (1955-56)

While working as a lecturer at Allahabad University, Govindjee became interested in the viruses, organisms responsible for yellowed and sickly plants growing in his uncle's garden. At that time, he was working in the laboratory of Shri Ranjan with his schoolmate Manmohan Laloraya, who was a Ph.D. student of Shri Ranjan (Fig. 1). They reported that the tobacco-mosaic virus and tobacco-leaf curl virus causes an increase in asparagine and several amino acids, especially aspartic acid, supporting the idea that virus infection may cause the formation of new proteins in the infected plants (*Croton sparsiflorus*). They for the first time used a 16-sector radial-cut circular filter paper horizontal chromatography (suggested by T. Rajarao) to separate free amino acids (Laloraya, and Govindjee, 1955; Laloraya et al. 1955, 1956).

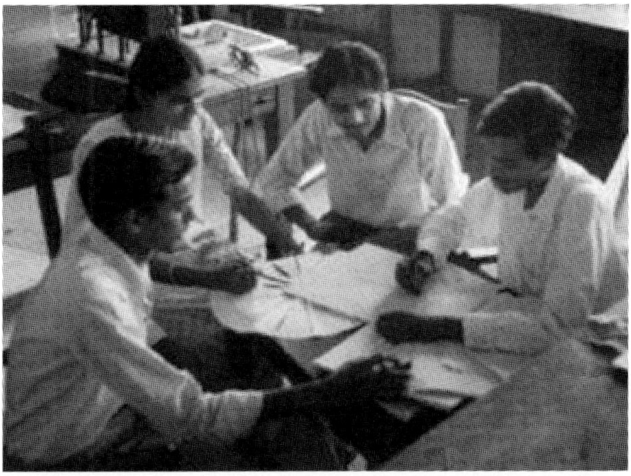

Figure 1: Left to right: T. Rajarao, Rajni Varma, Manmohan Laloraya, and Govindjee, graduate students of Professor Shri Ranjan at the University of Allahabad, India, in 1955 (Source: Govindjee's Archives).

B. Contribution to Photosynthesis Research (1960 - onwards)

Govindjee has made a seminal contribution to photosynthesis research, particularly on Photosystem II (PSII). This system oxidizes water to oxygen and reduces plastoquinone to plastoquinol. He has co-authored more than 400 research papers and reviews on many aspects of photosynthesis including PSII; the topics have ranged from the mechanism of excitation energy transfer, prompt and delayed fluorescence, thermoluminescence, primary charge separation, and the role of bicarbonate in PSII. Besides, Govindjee and colleagues worked on the primary photochemistry of both PSII and photosystem I (PSI) including those from cyanobacteria. He also pioneered and exploited the use of chlorophyll (Chl)*a* fluorescence measurements to study the phenomenon of photoprotection in plants and algae. Some of his notable contributions are mentioned below -

1. The two-light reaction and two-pigment system in oxygenic photosynthesis and minimum quantum requirement

The singular process of photosynthesis completes in two steps - the "light" and the "dark" reactions, the latter being carbon fixation. Govindjee was curious about the phenomenon of the "Red Drop" i.e., low photosynthesis yield when plants receive only far-red light. However, by the time he reached UIUC, Robert Emerson had discovered the "Enhancement Effect" in photosynthesis. Wherein two beams of different wavelengths of light (short and long) given simultaneously resulted in a higher photosynthetic rate than the sum of the rates when both beams were given separately. This phenomenon became known as Emerson Enhancement Effect; it suggested the existence of two light reactions and two pigment systems in photosynthesis (Emerson et al. 1957) (Fig. 2). However, the very conclusion of Emerson that one system was run by chlorophyll *a* and another by chlorophyll *b* (or other accessory pigments) was wrong, as Govindjee has told us personally. He knew that Duysens (1952) had already shown that 100% of the energy absorbed by chlorophyll *b* was transferred to chlorophyll *a*. The second issue was, as Govindjee told us, that Emerson had used manometry, which could not establish with surety whether the effect was on photosynthesis or respiration. First, Govindjee established that both the photosystems are run by chlorophyll *a* (Govindjee and Rabinovitch 1960); in addition, he showed a two-light effect in chlorophyll *a* fluorescence (Govindjee et al. 1960a) where no respiration was involved. In addition, his wife Rajni Govindjee used para-benzoquinone (pbQ) to inactivate respiration and discovered Emerson Effect in pbQ Hill reaction (Govindjee R et al., 1960b). Further work on NADP (nicotinamide adenine dinucleotide phosphate) reduction in spinach thylakoids (Govindjee R et al. 1964) and the use of mass spectroscopy with oxygen -18 water isotopes clearly established the involvement of photosynthesis, not respiration (Govindjee et al. 1963; also see Bedell and Govindjee 1966; Govindjee and Björn 2012 for further details. See Govindjee (2023) for the above in his own words.

Emerson had already shown that during photosynthesis a minimum of 8-10 quanta of light is required to release one molecule of oxygen, which had been disputed by Emerson's doctoral thesis advisor Otto Warburg, who had insisted the number is 3-4. Govindjee and Rajni Govindjee repeated the experiments under Warburg's conditions (using young synchronous *Chlorella* culture provided with 10% CO_2, and blue catalytic light) and proved their former mentor Emerson to be right and the Nobel laureate Warburg to be wrong (Govindjee R et al. 1968; Govindjee 1999 for further information; see Nickelson and Govindjee 2011).

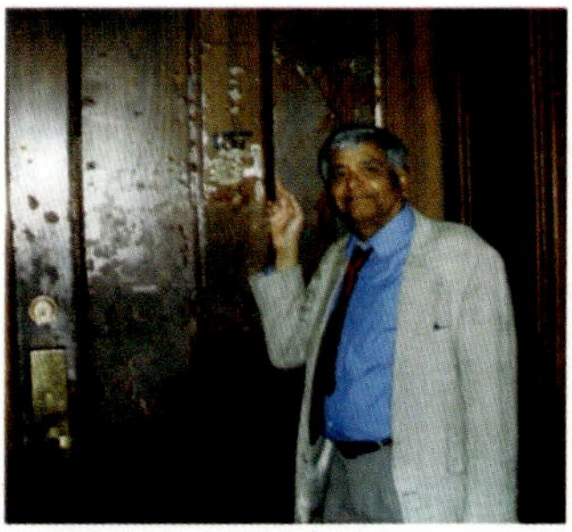

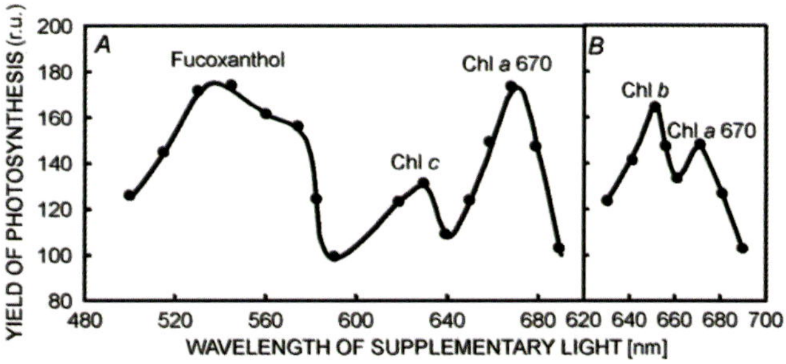

Figure 2: Govindjee in front of the historical door of 157 Natural History Building (NHB) through which Emerson and all his students would go through each day to do their experiments (left); the action spectra of the Emerson enhancement effect in the diatom *Navicula*, when a second light beam of different wavelengths was given on top of far-red light – showing the presence of peaks for fucoxanthol, chlorophyll *c*, and chlorophyll (Chl) *a* 670 (right A), and the same for the green alga *Chlorella* showing chlorophyll *b* and Chl *a* 670. (Right b) (after Govindjee 2023).

2. The discovery of new absorption and emission bands in photosynthetic organisms

In their pursuit to characterize the pigment systems, Govindjee, and his graduate students discovered many new absorption and emission bands - earlier, there was the discovery of P750 in the cyanobacterium *Anacystis nidulans* (now *Synechococcus elongates* strain PCCC 7942) (Govindjee et al. 1961), which is unfortunately not involved in photosynthesis. However, Govindjee's research group discovered a new fluorescence band at 696 nm (at 77K), labeled as F696; later found to be arising from the PSII core antenna protein CP47; further, his group discovered an emission band in the 693-700nm range when photosynthesis is saturated at high light, or inhibited by the DCMU (3-(3,4-dichlorophenyl)-1, 1-dimethylurea), which was a counterpart of the 77K F696 at room temperature (see Govindjee and Shevela 2011 for details and original references).

3. Thermoluminescence and delayed light emission in photosynthetic systems

William Arnold, a student of Emerson had discovered the phenomenon of delayed light emission (Strehler and Arnold 1951) as thermoluminescence (Arnold and Sherwood 1957). Arnold had proposed electron-hole recombination theory to explain the process. However, Mar and Govindjee (1971) found that when pre-illuminated spinach chloroplasts, and cells of *Chlorella pyrenoidosa*, were given a quick temperature jump of about 15°C, they emitted light both in normal and in DCMU-treated samples (where electron transport to PS I is blocked). However, the thermoluminescence was absent when hydroxylamine which blocks electron transport on the electron donor side of PS II was added into these samples, due to a back reaction of PS II of photosynthesis. Later on, Govindjee and coworkers reported that the temperature-dependent equilibria between two or more electron carriers in PS II act as traps for electrons or holes. Thus, he modified the existing theory of thermoluminescence and explained the abnormally large activation energies and the abnormal frequency factors involved in the process (see e.g., Tatake et al. 1981; DeVault et al. 1983; DeVault and Govindjee 1990).

Earlier, Govindjee had proposed an alternative triplet-triplet fusion hypothesis for delayed light emission in photosynthetic systems (Stacy et al. 1971), which did not survive. On the other hand, Govindjee proved his idea of a back reaction of PS II in various ways – by using DCMU to block the electron transport on the electron acceptor side of PS II (Jursinic and Govindjee 1972); by diverting electrons from PS II to silicomolybdate from $Q_{\bar{A}}$ (Zilinskas and Govindjee 1975); and by blocking electron donation on the water side of PS II by Tris-washing the samples (Jursinic and Govindjee 1977a). Jursinic and Govindjee (1977b) measured the temperature dependence of delayed light in a few to hundreds of microseconds and discovered that the former was independent of temperature in the 0 to 35°C range, whereas the latter was not. The short-term component was I^2 dependent, whereas the latter remained linear with light intensity. Further, Govindjee discovered that there was a major difference in the microsecond and the millisecond delayed light, the former was insensitive to membrane potential, whereas the latter was sensitive to it in the presence of ΔpH (Jursinic et al. 1978). Thus, although most delayed light is due to a back reaction of PS II, detailed mechanisms are different for the fast and slower components was his conclusion.

4. Measurement of Photosystem II reactions including primary charge separation

Govindjee started studies on the mechanism of excitation energy transfer as a function of temperature down to liquid helium temperature (Cho and Govindjee 1970a, b), and on oxygen evolution (Mar and Govindjee 1972).

For the first time his group applied Nuclear Magnetic Resonance (NMR) to monitor the oxygen clock (Wydrzynski et al. 1976; Baianu et al. 1984). Govindjee studied the nature of the very first intermediates involved, and the efficiency and speed of the primary charge separation in PSII, and showed that the charge separation occurred from chlorophyll to a pheophytin molecule, within a few picoseconds (Wasielewski et al. 1989). Also, his works on PS I primary photochemistry (Fenton et al. 1979; Wasielewski et al. 1987) were pivotal, and subsequent refinements to these findings have led to a clearer and more detailed picture.

5. Chlorophyll a fluorescence and its relationship to photosynthesis

Govindjee was the first one to introduce measurements of the lifetime of chlorophyll *a* fluorescence to understand photoprotection in plants. Steve Brody at the University of Illinois was the first to measure the lifetime of chlorophyll *a* fluorescence in a photosynthetic system. However, Govindjee and Henri Merkelo used mode-locked lasers to make such measurements (Merkelo et al. 1969). Followed by the use of the phase method (with Enrico Gratton's group) to measure the lifetime of chlorophyll *a* fluorescence (Govindjee et al., 1990), which was the first of its kind in understanding photoprotection by plants, under excess light, in terms of changes in rate constants of deactivation of the excited states of chlorophyll. Since fluorescence intensity changes alone could not distinguish between changes in chlorophyll concentration and changes in rate constants of de-excitation of excited states. Gilmore et al. (1995) used a *dimmer switch* to explain it. As more and more light was given to a photosynthetic system, a proportion of chlorophyll *a* that had a ~ 2 ns lifetime of chlorophyll fluorescence was converted into a component that had a 0.4 ns lifetime! A relationship with carotenoids (zeaxanthin and antheraxanthin) was also established (Gilmore et al. 1998). Subsequently, in collaboration with the late Robert Clegg, and Oliver Holub Fluorescence Lifetime Imaging Microscopy (FLIM) was introduced, to observe differences in lifetimes of chlorophyll fluorescence in single cells with fluorescence intensity remaining the same.

6. The role of bicarbonate (hydrogen carbonate) in electron (and proton) transport in Photosystem II (PSII)

Govindjee is one of many scientists who has stated that Otto Warburg was wrong in his conclusion that during photosynthesis oxygen comes from

CO_2. However, his suggestion on the requirement of 'bicarbonate' in the Hill reaction inspired Govindjee and his graduate students to study this 'bicarbonate effect' on the relaxation of the 'S-states' of the oxygen-evolving complex (Stemler et al. 1974). They studied the effects of 'bicarbonate' on the electron and proton flow on the intermediates in Z-scheme of photosynthesis. Govindjee's research group was the first to establish the effect of bicarbonate at the 'two-electron gate' of PS II (see Wydrzynski and Govindjee 1975; Govindjee et al. 1976; Eaton-Rye and Govindjee 1988a, b). They found that without bicarbonate, $Cytb_6f$ complex would not receive any electrons from PS II. There are two effects of bicarbonate: one is on the electron acceptor side of PS II, bicarbonate is bound to the non-heme iron located between Q_A and Q_B, and the other is on the electron donor side of PS II. The 'bicarbonate' effect on the electron acceptor side is essential at a site where several herbicides inhibit photosynthesis. Govindjee et al. (1991) showed that formate can be used to achieve a state deficient in bicarbonate that releases CO_2. The role of bicarbonate on the electron donor side clearly needs to be studied further. Govindjee is eager to learn about that aspect of the functioning.

C. Other contributions

Govindjee's current scientific interests include improving photosynthesis through genetic engineering, and understanding how slow chlorophyll *a* fluorescence changes can be used to monitor regulation mechanisms in plants, algae, and cyanobacteria. In the later part of his carrier, he started working on the *History of Photosynthesis Research*; in addition, he is actively involved in photosynthesis education, and in remembering and recognizing other scientists in the field. In 1994, he started the book series '*Advances in Photosynthesis and Respiration Including Bioenergy and Related Processes*' which shows his interest in the subject. He has documented the progress of research in photosynthesis, through interviews, obituaries, tributes, personal perspectives, and news of scientists around the world. He is the founder of the 'History & Biography' section of the journal 'Photosynthesis Research'. These publications, accompanied by photographs of key people and places, are unique contributions to the history of science, and photosynthesis, in particular. Apart from his research and educational activities, Govindjee encourages young students at conferences by giving them book awards. At UIUC, he and his wife have established the Govindjee and Rajni Govindjee Awards for Excellence in Biological Sciences.

He has authored/edited many books, including - "Photosynthesis" (John Wiley, 1969); with Rabinowitch; "Bioenergetics of Photosynthesis" (Academic Press, 1975); "Photosynthesis" (in 2 volumes, Academic Press, 1982, Russian translation, 1987); "Light Emission by Plants and Bacteria" (Academic Press, 1986); "Chlorophyll a Fluorescence: A Signature of Photosynthesis" (Kluwer/Springer, 2004); and "Discoveries in Photosynthesis" (Springer, 2006). He has edited special issues of journals dedicated to leading figures in the biophysics of photosynthesis: Eugene Rabinowitch (Biophysical Journal, 1972), Warren Butler (Photosynthesis Research, 1986), Bessel Kok (Photosynthesis Research, 1993), and William Arnold (Photosynthesis Research, 1996). He has always been an outstanding teacher, highly sought after by students. His collaborative spirit is unparallel. As on July 4, 2022, he has worked with 580 researchers including 238 from The USA, 63 from India, 55 from China, 24 from Russia, 22 from Germany, 18 each from France and the Czech Republic, 17 from The Netherlands, 13 from Japan, 11 from Canada, 11 each from Hungary, Mexico and The UK, 8 from Australia, 6 from Finland, 5 each from Azerbaijan, Sweden, Israel, Switzerland, 4 from Greece and Iran, 3 from Poland and Slovac Republic, 2 each from Belgium, Estonia and Egypt, and 1 each from New Zealand, Norway, Bulgaria, and South Korea.

Awards and Honors

- He is Fellow of the American Association for the Advancement of Science (AAAS) (1976);
- Fellow and Life Member of the National Academy of Sciences (NASI), India (1979);
- President of the American Society for Photobiology (1981);
- Fulbright Senior Lecturer to India (1996–1997);
- Honorary President of the 2004 International Photosynthesis Congress (Montreal, Canada);
- The first recipient of the Lifetime Achievement award from the Rebeiz Foundation for Basic Research (2006);
- Communication Award of the International Society of Photosynthesis Research (2007);
- Alumni Achievement Award from the University of Illinois at Urbana-Champaign (2008);

- In 2013, in honor of his 80th birthday, a tribute to Govindjee's life's work in photosynthesis appeared in the journal Photosynthesis Research [116(2), 111–144, doi: 10.1007/s11120-013-9921-3];
- Dr. B.M. Johri Memorial award of the Society for Plant Research, India (2016);
- Pravasi (Foreign) Fellow of the National Academy of Agricultural Sciences (NAAS), India (2018);
- In 2018, in honor of his 85th birthday, a special issue of Photosynthetica [56(4), 1235–1236; doi: 10.1007/s11099-018-0826-4] was released;
- In 2019, the University of Illinois at Urbana-Champaign published an article on his research in photosynthesis and dedicated a museum to him "Govindjee's Photosynthesis Museum";
- In 2020, Govindjee's innovative research and historical contributions (1999–2020) were highlighted, with messages from around the world (refer to Eaton-Rye et al. 2020; Stirbet et al. 2020);
- Lifetime Award of the ISPR (2022).
- Emeritus member of the American Society of Plant Biology (formerly Physiology).
- Member of the Biophysical Society of America;
- Member, Sigma Xi;
- Member of the International Society of Photosynthesis Research;

Personal Life

Govindjee is married to Rajni Varma nee Govindjee (Fig. 3). They have two children – a daughter, Anita, who is a software engineer for IBM, and she is married to Morten Christiansen, Professor of Psychology at Cornell University, Ithaca, NY; they have one daughter, Sunita. His son, Sanjay is a Distinguished Professor of Civil and Environmental Engineering and the Horace, Dorothy, and Katherine Johnson Endowed Professor at the University of California, Berkeley; and is married to Marilyn Hubbs, the couple have two sons: Arjun and Rajiv.

Rajni Govindjee played a major role in the life and early research of Govindjee. She is a leading authority in photosynthesis and photobiology. She completed her Ph.D. in Botany in 1961 under Eugene Rabinowitch at UIUC. Her works demonstrated that Emerson's two-light effect was due to photosynthesis and that the minimum quantum requirement be 8-10., Post-1974, she worked in photobiology with retinal proteins. Thomas Ebrey described her as *"Brighter than the sun: Rajni Govindjee at 80 and her fifty years in photobiology*" (Ebrey 2015).

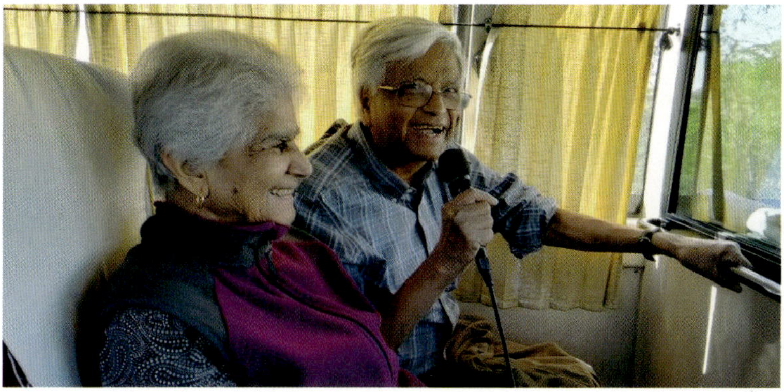

Figure 3: Govindjee in a bus with his wife Rajni (Source: Govindjee's Archives).

Epilogue

Govindjee is a Professor Emeritus of Plant Biology, Biochemistry and Biophysics at UIUC, USA. He made path-setting contributions to the mechanism of Photosystem II. He demonstrated that the first step of conversion of light into chemical energy occurs in a picosecond time scale, and bicarbonate ions are uniquely required in steps other than in carbon fixation. He established the participation of Chl*a* in both the light reactions I and II, and along with his wife Rajni, he showed the effect of the two-light reactions and two pigment systems in the reduction of NADP in chloroplasts, providing a fundamental background to the current Z- scheme of the "Light Reactions" of photosynthesis. He has also been an immensely effective and energetic advocate for photosynthesis research and has dedicated his entire life to educating students and researchers throughout the world. His advocacy and educational outreach have included numerous lectures around the world, delivered at various workshops, and conferences, in Universities and Colleges. He is a scientific gem, a gift from India to the global science communities. Though, he himself says "Scientists belong to the World, not just one country." May God bless him with a long and healthy life.

Bibliography

1. Arnold, W.A., Sherwood, H.K. (1957) Are chloroplasts semiconductors? Proc Natl Acad Sci USA 43,105-114.
2. Baianu, I.C., Critchley, C., Govindjee., Gutowsky, H.S. (1984) NMR study of chloride-ion interactions with thylakoid membranes. Proc Natl Acad Sci USA 81, 3713-3717.
3. Bedell, G., Govindjee. (1966) Quantum yield of oxygen evolution and the Emerson enhancement effect in deuterated Chlorella. Science 152, 1383–1385.
4. Bedell, G.W., Govindjee. (1973) Photophosphorylation in intact algae: effects of inhibitors, intensity of light, electron acceptors and donors. Plant Cell Physiol 14, 1081-1097.
5. Björn, L.O., Govindjee. (2009) The evolution of photosynthesis and chloroplasts. Curr Sci (India) 96, 1466-1474.
6. Blankenship, R. E. (2007) 2007 Awards of the International Society of Photosynthesis Research (ISPR). Photosynth Res, DOI 10.1007/s11120-007-9268-8.
7. Blankenship, R.E. (2007) 2007 Awards of the International Society of Photosynthesis Research (ISPR). Photosynth Res, DOI 10.1007/s11120-007-9268-8.
8. Block, J.E. (2022) Life of Govindjee, known as Mister Photosynthesis. Jour Pl Sci Res 38 (1), 1-22.
9. Brody, S.S. (2002) Fluorescence lifetime, yield, energy transfer and spectrum in photosynthesis, 1950–1960. Photosynth Res 73,127-132.
10. Cederstrand, C., Govindjee. (1961) Some properties of spinach chloroplast fractions obtained by digitonin solubilization. Biochim Biophys Acta 120,177-180.
11. Cederstrand, C., Rabinowitch, E., Govindjee. (1966a) Absorption and fluorescence spectra of spinach chloroplast fractions obtained by solvent extraction. Biochim Biophys Acta 120, 247-258.
12. Cederstrand, C., Rabinowitch. E., Govindjee. (1966b) Analysis of the red absorption band of chlorophyll a in vivo. Biochim Biophys Acta 126,1-12.
13. Cho, F., Govindjee. (1970a) Low-temperature (4–77 K) spectroscopy of *Chlorella*: temperature dependence of energy transfer efficiency. Biochim Biophys Acta 216,139-150.

14. Cho, F., Govindjee. (1970b) Low temperature (4–77 K) spectroscopy of *Anacystis*: temperature dependence of energy transfer efficiency. Biochim Biophys Acta 216,151-161.
15. Das, M., Govindjee. (1967) A long-wave absorbing form of chlorophyll a responsible for the red drop in fluorescence at 298 K and the F723 band at 77 K. Biochim Biophys Acta 143,570-576.
16. DeVault, D., Govindjee, Arnold, W. (1983) Energetics of photosynthetic glow peaks. Proc Natl Acad Sci USA 80,983-987.
17. DeVault, D., Govindjee. (1990) Photosynthetic glow peaks and their relationship with the free energy changes. Photosynth Res 24,175-181.
18. Duysens, L.N.M. (1952) Transfer of excitation energy in photosynthesis. Doctoral Thesis, State University Utrecht, The Netherlands.
19. Eaton-Rye, J,J,, Govindjee. (1988b) Electron transfer through the quinone acceptor complex of Photosystem II after one or two actinic flashes in bicarbonate-depleted spinach thylakoid membranes. Biochim Biophys Acta 935,248-257.
20. Eaton-Rye, J.J. (2007) Celebrating Govindjee's 50 years in photosynthesis research and his 75th birthday. Photosynth Res 93, 1-5.
21. Eaton-Rye, J.J. (2007) Govindjee at 80: more than 50 years of free energy for photosynthesis. Photosynth Res 116, 111-144.
22. Eaton-Rye, J.J. (2007) Snapshots of the Govindjee lab from the late 1960s to the late 1990s, and beyond. Photosynth Res 94, 153-178.
23. Eaton-Rye, J.J. (2018) Foreword. Photosynthetica 56 (1), 1-10.
24. Eaton-Rye, J.J., Guieysse, B., Packer, M. A., Summerfield, T.C., Wood S. A. (2020) Biology and biotechnological applications of microalgae and photosynthetic prokaryotes: part 2. New Zealand Journal of Botany 58 (4), 275-333.
25. Ebrey, T. (2015) Tribute Brighter than the sun: Rajni Govindjee at 80 and her fifty years in photobiology. Photosynth Res 124, 1-5.
26. Emerson, R., Chalmers, R., Cederstrand, C. (1957) Some factors influencing the long-wave limit of photosynthesis. P Natl Acad Sci USA 43, 133-143.
27. Emerson, R., Lewis, C.M (1943) The dependence of the quantum yield of *Chlorella* photosynthesis on wave length of light. Am J Bot 30, 165-178.
28. Fenton, J.M., Pellin, M.J., Kaufmann, K., Govindjee (1979) Primary photochemistry of the reaction center of Photosystem I. FEBS Lett, 100, 1-4.

29. Garab, G., Rozsa, Z., Govindjee. (1988) Carbon dioxide affects charge accumulation in leaves: measurements by thermoluminescence. Naturwiisenschaften 75,517-519.
30. Gilmore, A.M., Hazlett. T.L., Govindjee. (1995) Xanthophyll cycle-dependent quenching of Photosystem II chlorophyll a fluorescence: formation of a quenching complex with a short fluorescence lifetime. Proc Natl Acad Sci USA 92, 2273-2277.
31. Gilmore, A.M., Shinkarev, V.P., Hazlett, T.L., Govindjee. (1998) Quantitative analysis of the effects of intrathylakoid pH and the xanthophyll cycle pigments on chlorophyll a fluorescence lifetime distributions and intensity in thylakoids. Biochemistry 37, 13582-13593.
32. Govindjee (2018) A sixty-year tryst with photosynthesis and related processes: an informal personal perspective. Photosynth Res, DOI. org/10.1007/s11120-018-0590-0.
33. Govindjee, Briantais, J.M. (1972) Chlorophyll b fluorescence and an emission band at 700 nm at room temperature in green algae. FEBS Lett 19, 278-280.
34. Govindjee, Cederstrand, C., Rabinowitch, E. (1961) Existence of absorption bands at 730–740 and 750–760 millimicrons in algae of different divisions. Science 134, 391-392.
35. Govindjee, G. (2023). On the evolution of the concept of two light reactions and two photosystems for oxygenic photosynthesis: A personal perspective. Photosynthetica (in press).
36. Govindjee, Govindjee, R. (1974) Primary events in photosynthesis. Sci Am 231, 68-82.
37. Govindjee, Jursinic, P.A. (1979) Photosynthesis and fast changes in light emission by green plants. Photochem Photobiol Rev 4, 125-205.
38. Govindjee, Owens, OvH., Hoch, G. (1963) A mass spectroscopic study of the Emerson enhancement effect. Biochim Biophys Acta 75, 281-284.
39. Govindjee, R., Govindjee., Hoch, G. (1964) Emerson enhancement effect in chloroplast reactions. Plant Physiol 39,10-14.
40. Govindjee, R., Rabinowitch, E.I., Govindjee. (1968) Maximum quantum yield and action spectra of photosynthesis and fluorescence in *Chlorella*. Biochim Biophys Acta 162, 530-54.
41. Govindjee, R., Thomas, J.B., Rabinowitch, E. (1960b) Second Emerson effect in the Hill reaction of *Chlorella* cells with quinone as oxidant. Science 132, 421.

42. Govindjee, Rabinowitch, E. (1960) Two forms of chlorophyll a in vivo with distinct photochemical functions. Science 132, 355-356.
43. Govindjee, Rabinowitch, E. (1960) Two forms of chlorophyll a in vivo with distinct photochemical function. Science 132, 355-356.
44. Govindjee, Rabinowitch, E., Thomas, J.B. (1960a) Inhibition of photosynthesis in some algae by extreme red light. Biophys J 1, 91-97.
45. Govindjee, Shevela, D. (2011) Adventures with cyanobacteria: a personal perspective. Front Plant Sci 2, 28.
46. Govindjee. (1999) On the requirement of minimum number of four versus eight quanta of light for the evolution of one molecule of oxygen in photosynthesis: a historical note. Photosynth Res 59, 249–254.
47. Govindjee., Pulles, M.P.J., Govindjee, R., Van Gorkom, H.J., Duysens, L.N.M. (1976) Inhibition of the reoxidation of the secondary electron acceptor of Photosystem II by bicarbonate depletion. Biochim Biophys Acta 449, 602-605.
48. Govindjee., Van de Ven, M, Preston, C., Seibert, M., Gratton, E. (1990) Chlorophyll *a* fluorescence lifetime distributions in open and closed Photosystem II reaction center preparations: analysis by multifrequency phase fluorometry. Biochim Biophys Acta 1015, 173-179.
49. Jaiswal, S., Bansal, M., Roy, S., Bharati, A., Padhi, B. (2016) Electron flow from water to $NADP^+$ with students acting as molecules in the chain: A Z-scheme drama in a classroom. Photosynth Res, DOI 10.1007/s11120-016-0317-z.
50. Jursinic, P., Govindjee, (1977b) Temperature dependence of delayed light emission in the 6 to 340 microsecond range after a single flash in chloroplasts. Photochem Photobiol 26, 617-628.
51. Jursinic, P., Govindjee. (1972) Thermoluminescence and temperature effects on delayed light emission (corrected for changes in quantum yield of fluorescence) in DCMU-treated algae. Photochem Photobiol 15, 331-348.
52. Jursinic, P., Govindjee. (1977a) The rise in chlorophyll a fluorescence yield and decay in delayed light emission in tris-washed chloroplasts in the 6-100-microsecond time range after an excitation flash. Biochim Biophys Acta 461, 253-267.
53. Jursinic, P., Govindjee., Wraight, C.A. (1978) Membrane potential and microsecond to millisecond delayed light emission after a single excitation flash in isolated chloroplasts. Photochem Photobiol 27,61-71.

54. Khanna, Wagner, R., Junge, W., Govindjee. (1980) Effects of CO2-depletion on proton uptake and release in thylakoid membranes. FEBS Lett 121, 222-224.
55. Kramer, D.M., Roffey, R.A., Govindjee., Sayre, R.T. (1994) The At thermoluminescence band from *Chlamydomonas reinhardtii* and the effects of mutagenesis of histidine residues on the donor side of Photosystem II D1 polypeptide. Biochim Biophys Acta 1185, 228-237.
56. Krey, A., Govindjee. (1964) Fluorescence changes in *Porphyridium* exposed to green light of different intensity: a new emission band at 693 nm and its significance to photosynthesis. Proc Natl Acad Sci USA 52, 1568-1572.
57. Kumar, A., Block, J.E., Nonomura, A.M. (2021) Mister Photosynthesis of the 21st Century, Govindjee. LS- An International Journal of Life Science 10 (2), 61-80.
58. Laloraya, M.M., Govindjee, Rajarao, T. (1955) A chromatographic study of the amino acids (and sugars) of healthy and diseased leaves of *Acalypha indica*. Curr Sci (India) 24, 203.
59. Laloraya, M.M., Govindjee, Varma, R, Rajarao, T. (1956) Increased formation of asparagine in Carica-curl virus infected leaves. Experientia 12, 58-59.
60. Laloraya, M.M., Govindjee. (1955) Effect of tobacco leaf curl and tobacco mosaic virus on the amino acid and amide content of *Nicotiana* sp. Nature 175, 907.
61. Lichtenthaler, H.K. (2020) My contact and cooperation with Govindjee over the last five decades: Chlorophyll fluorescence and Rebeiz Foundation. Photosynthetica 58 (4), 976-983.
62. Mar, T., Govindjee. (1971) Thermoluminescence in spinach chloroplasts and in *Chlorella*. Biochim Biophys Acta 226, 200-203.
63. Mar, T., Govindjee. (1972) Kinetic models of oxygen evolution in photosynthesis. J Theor Biol 36, 427-446.
64. Merkelo, H., Hartman, S.R., Mar, T., Singhal, G.S., Govindjee. (1969) Mode-locked lasers: measurements of very fast radiative decay in fluorescent systems. Science 164, 301-302.
65. Mohapatra, P.K., Singh, N.R. (2014) Teaching the Z-Scheme of electron transport in photosynthesis: a perspective. Photosynth Res, DOI 10.1007/s11120-014-0034-4.

66. Papageorgiou, G.C., Govindjee. (1967) Changes in intensity and spectral distribution of fluorescence. Effect of light treatment on normal and DCMU-poisoned *Anacystis nidulans*. Biophys J 7, 375-390.
67. Papageorgiou, G.C., Govindjee. (1968a) Light-induced changes in the fluorescence yield of chlorophyll *a* in vivo I. *Anacystis nidulans*. Biophys J 8, 1299-1315.
68. Papageorgiou, G.C., Govindjee. (1968b) Light-induced changes in the fluorescence yield of chlorophyll *a* in vivo. II. *Chlorella pyrenoidosa*. Biophys J 8, 1316-1328
69. Prášil, O. (2014) Govindjee, an institution, at his 80th (really 81st) birthday in Třeboň in October 2013: A pictorial essay. Photosynth Res 122,113-119.
70. Rebeiz, C. A., Benning, C., Bohnert, H., Hoober, J. K., Portis, A. R. (2007) Govindjee was honored with the First Lifetime Achievement Award, and Britta Föo¨rster and coworkers, with the First Annual Paper Prize of the Rebeiz Foundation for Basic Research. Photosynth Res 94,147-151.
71. Rebeiz, C.A., Benning, C., Bohnert, H., Hoober, J.K., Portis, A.R. (2007) Govindjee was honored with the First Lifetime Achievement Award, and Britta Förster and coworkers, with the First Annual Paper Prize of the Rebeiz Foundation for Basic Research. Photosynth Res 94, 147-151.
72. Seibert, M., Picorel, R., Rubin, A.B., Connolly, J.S. (1988) Spectral, photophysical and stability properties of isolated Photosystem II reaction center. Plant Physiol 87, 303-306.
73. Shevela, D., Eaton-Rye, J.J., Shen, J-R., Govindjee. (2012) Photosystem II and unique role of bicarbonate: a historical perspective. Biochim Biophys Acta 1817, 1134-1151.
74. Stacy, W.T., Mar, T., Swenberg, C.E., Govindjee. (1971) An analysis of a triplet exciton model for the delayed light in *Chlorella*. Photochem Photobiol 14, 197-219.
75. Stemler, A., Babcock, G.T., Govindjee. (1974) The effect of bicarbonate on photosynthetic oxygen evolution in flashing light in chloroplast fragments. Proc Natl Acad Sci USA 71, 4679-4683.
76. Stirbet, A., Govindjee. (2011) On the relation between the Kautsky effect (chlorophyll a fluorescence induction) and Photosystem II: basics and applications of the OJIP transient. J Photochem Photobiol B 104, 236-257.

77. Stirbet, A., Govindjee. (2012) Chlorophyll a fluorescence induction: a personal perspective of the thermal phase, the J-I-P rise. Photosynth Res 113, 15-61.
78. Stirbet, A., Govindjee., Strasser, B.J. (1998) Chlorophyll a fluorescence induction in higher plants: modelling and numerical simulation. J Theor Biol 193, 131-151.
79. Tatake, V.G., Desai, T.S., Govindjee., Sane, P.V. (1981) Energy storage states of photosynthetic membranes: activation energies and lifetimes of electrons in the trap states by thermoluminescence method. Photochem Photobiol 33, 243-250.
80. Wasielewski, M.R., Fenton, J.M., Govindjee. (1987) The rate of formation of P700 [$^+$]–Ao [$^-$] in Photosystem I particles from spinach as measured by picosecond transient absorption spectroscopy. Photosynth Res 12, 181-190.
81. Wasielewski, M.R., Johnson, D.G., Seibert, M., Govindjee. (1989) Determination of the primary charge separation rate in isolated Photosystem II reaction centers with 500 femtosecond time resolution. Proc Natl Acad Sci USA 86, 524-548.
82. Wydrzynski, T., Govindjee. (1975) A new site of bicarbonate effect in Photosystem II of photosynthesis: evidence from chlorophyll fluorescence transients in spinach chloroplasts. Biochim Biophys Acta 387, 403-408.
83. Wydrzynski, T., Zumbulyadis, N., Schmidt, P.G., Gutowsky, H.S., Govindjee. (1976) Proton relaxation and charge accumulation during oxygen evolution in photosynthesis. Proc Natl Acad Sci USA 73, 1196-1198.

Acknowledgments

It is a personal honor to write about Govindjee, I express my sincere gratitude to him for providing the necessary resources, and doing the necessary check despite being unwell.

AUTHOR PROFILE

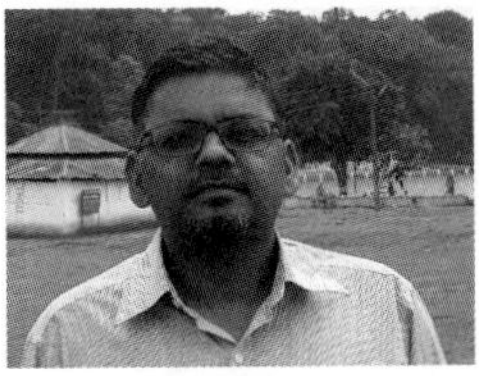

The author is a professor in Botany at Indira Gandhi National Tribal University, Amarkantak, India. His research interest includes ecophysiology of cyanobacteria and plant related-traditional knowledge of the Central Indian Tribes.

Email: naveen.sharma@igntu.ac.in

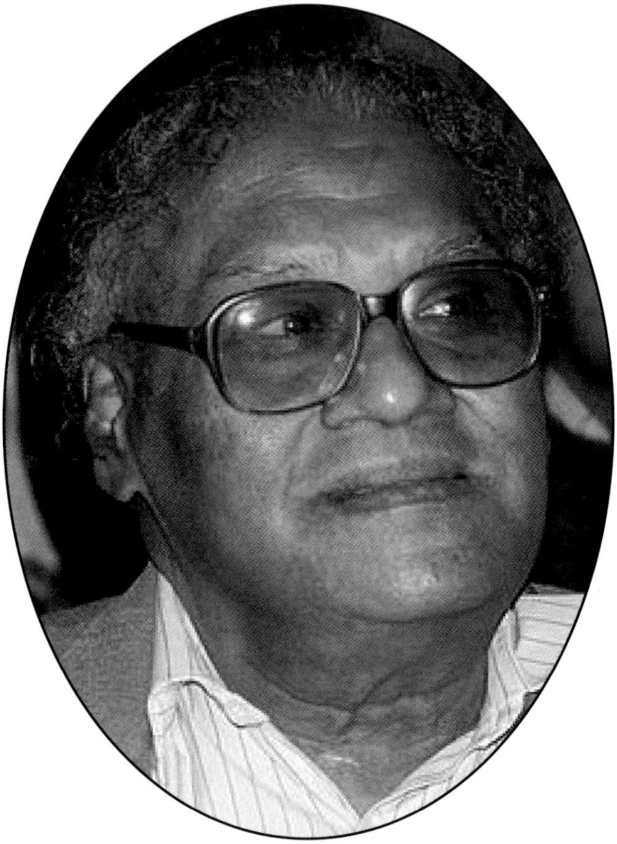

Chintamani Nagesa Ramachandra Rao

CHINTAMANI NAGESA RAMACHANDRA RAO: A LIVING LEGEND IN INDIAN SCIENCE

Khemchand Dewangan

Professor Chintamani Nagesa Ramachandra Rao (popularly known as C.N.R. Rao) is a distinguished chemist who mainly works in the field of solid-state and material chemistry. For his outstanding contributions to science and technology, the President of India bestowed upon him the 'Bharat Ratna' in 2014, India's highest civilian honor (Fig. 1). He is an inspiration to students, teachers, and researchers over the past many decades. He is also a great institution builder and a joyous communicator of science in India and abroad.

Early Life and Education

Prof. Rao was born on 30th June 1934 to Hanumanth Nagesa Rao and Nagamma in Basavanagudi, a locality in Bangalore in the Indian state of Karnataka. He was the only child of his parents. He did not go to primary school and studied at home under his mother's guidance, who mainly taught him arithmetic and used to tell stories from Mahabharata, Ramayana, and Bhagwat Geeta. At the age of six, his father enrolled him in middle school at the local village school. Although he was the youngest in his class, he used to tutor his classmates in mathematics and English. At the same time, he use to spend his time accompanying his father to interior areas, especially hills and jungles, encountering wild animals in their natural habitat. This early experience developed his lifelong love of climbing and home-grown produce. He completed the lower secondary examination with a first class. At the age of eleven, he got excited about doing science for the first time by looking at C. V. Raman in his school. He did his schooling in Bangalore and nearby towns in Mysore. He developed his communication skills in Kannada and English and learned Sanskrit.

Prof. Rao entered Central College, Bangalore, and completed his bachelor's degree (B.Sc.) at the age of seventeenth. He completed his master's in physical chemistry from Banaras Hindu University (BHU), with a thesis on electrical discharges under the supervision of Prof. S. S. Joshi. He undertook a Ph.D. at Purdue University, USA, with Prof. R. L. Livingston and completed his work within three years at the age of twenty-four. Afterward, he continued postdoctoral research at the University of California and Berkeley. He returned to India and joined the Indian Institute of Science (IISc), Bangalore (now Bengaluru), as a faculty. He was awarded a D.Sc. degree for his thesis in 1961.

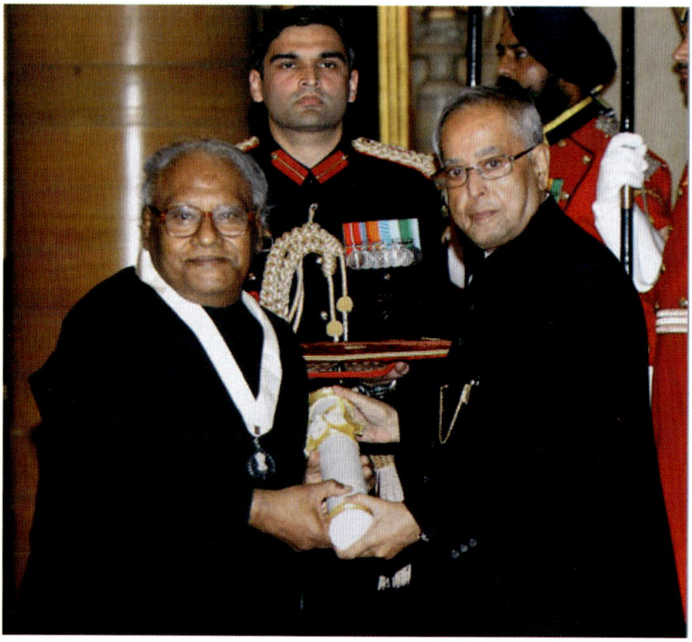

Figure 1: Prof. Rao receiving Bharat Ratna from Hon'ble President of India, Pranab Mukherjee.

Professional Life

After four years in IISc, he moved to the newly established Indian Institute of Technology (IIT) Kanpur in 1963. He became a professor, the first head of the Department of Chemistry, and later the Dean of Research. He returned to IISc in 1976 and set up the Solid State and Structural Chemistry Unit (SSCU) and the Materials Research Center (MRC) and headed them until 1984. He was appointed the Director of IISc and continued until 1994. In 1989 on the birth centenary year of Pandit Jawaharlal Nehru, he pursued the Government of India to establish the Jawaharlal Nehru Center for Advanced Scientific Research (JNCASR) at Bengaluru, Karnataka.

He has received *honoris causa* doctorate degrees from 84 universities, including Purdue, Bordeaux, BHU, Calcutta, Delhi, Northwestern, Notre

Dame, Novosibirsk, Oxford, Stellenbosch, Temple, Université Joseph Fourier, Grenoble, Uppsala, Wales, Wroclaw, Caen, Liverpool, St. Andrews, Canberra, Taiwan, and Visva-Bharati; IITs (Bombay, Kharagpur, Kanpur, New Delhi, Guwahati); Indian Institute of Science Education and Research (IISERs) (Bhopal, Kolkata, Mohali, Pune). He is a lifetime Honorary Professor at IISc.

Teacher, Researcher, and Mentor

Prof. Rao has an unparalleled love for teaching, research, and interaction with students at all stages of his carriers. During his time at IIT Kanpur, he started teaching and research work with a small group of students that developed great apprentices in science–technology graduate curricula for the first time in India. He was the first to offer integrated M.Sc. and coursework for a Ph.D. in India (Sathyamurthy and Rao 2019). Research by Prof. Rao and his group in chemical science made the subject and co-related areas (physical and material chemistry) more exciting. Many of his lab's alumni rose to national and international eminence. The importance of his revolutionary research work in the field of solid-state chemistry was recognized when he was just thirty. He was awarded the Marlow Medal of the Faraday Society, UK, in 1967. He received the Bhatnagar Award (1968) (Fig. 2) and the Fellowship of the Indian Academy of Sciences (1965).

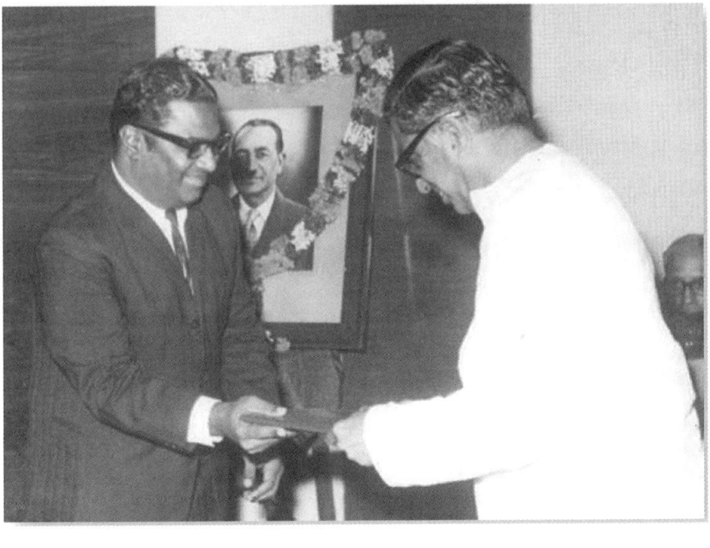

Figure 2: Prof. Rao receiving Bhatnagar Award in Chemical Science (1968).

His encouragement, guidance, and constructive criticism have developed a large number of accomplished scientists worldwide. For his students, he is the best mentor and an enjoyable person who provides extensive training and enabled them to be a freethinker and independent scientists. More than 150 students have received their Ph.D. degrees working with him. He and his team collaborate extensively with experts and scientists in Europe and USA. He developed textbooks and multimedia content on General Chemistry for school children (National Council of Educational Research and Training (NCERT) syllabus) and is still continuing to bring out science education materials for school and college students (Sathyamurthy and Rao 2019). He interacts with children directly through lectures/talks across the country through Winter Schools, Conferences, and Discussion Meetings. He encourages and motivates students from schools and colleges by replying to every letter. His deep insights about the future of higher education and science in India are reflected in his book, conversation, and editorial notes (Editorial 2009; Jayaraman 2010b; Ganguli and Ramakrishnan 2016; Rao, 2009a; Rao 2009b; Weiss 2009).

Prof Rao as Institution Builder

Prof. Rao is an irreplaceable planner and architect of scientific and research institutions in India. In the early-1960s, he started his carrier with the Department of Chemistry at the nascent IIT Kanpur. He helped to build up this department and its ethos. In the mid-1970s, he moved back to IISc Bangalore to set up the SSCU along with a relatively small professional group. Within a short period, his hard work made this unit flourish with an adequate number of people working with him.

During his directorship in IISc, he served as a transformative Director. His management and guidance have developed many highly creative and wide-ranging science and technology research centers in the institute. In 1989, he started to build the JNCASR at Jakkur, Bangalore (Fig. 3). In his leadership, the Science Advisory Council to Prime Minister (SAC to PM), five IISERs were started at Kolkata, Pune, Bhopal, Thiruvananthapuram, and Mohali. The quality of these institutions has been remarkable. They are providing collegiate education in basic science and research at the undergraduate level.

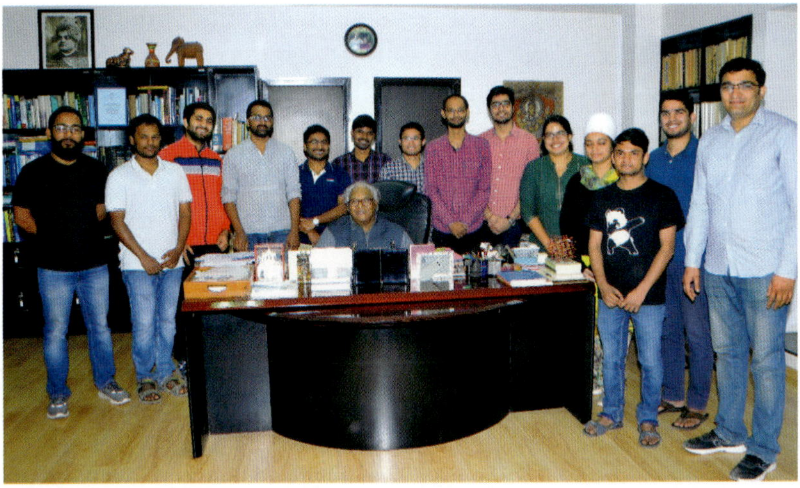

Figure 3: Prof. Rao and his students at JNCASR.

Science Frontrunner

In 1971, Prof. Rao was appointed to the National Committee on Science and Technology (NCST), formed by the Minister of Science, C. Subramanian, another Bharat Ratna. He was the youngest member of the committee. One of the committee's first recommendations was to create the Department of Science & Technology (DST) to integrate S & T into socio-economic platforms. This committee has tried to improve women's participation in science and improve workplace and employment conditions for women scientists. He was the Chairman of the SAC during the prime ministership of Rajiv Gandhi and Manmohan Singh. He initiated the creation of the Chemical Research Society and the Materials Research Society of India.

He became a member of the International Union of Pure and Applied Chemistry (IUPAC) in 1971 and continued till 1990 in various capacities. As President of the IUPAC (1985–1987), he played a central role in restructuring the organization to reflect modern trends in chemistry. As President of the Third World Academy of Sciences (TWAS, now known as the Academy of Sciences for the Developing World) (2000-2007), he visited several least-developed countries (LDCs) and found meager scientific facilities in the schools. This was one of the critical phases in his life and worked hard to improve the conditions in LCDs.

He is on the Editorial Board of several international/national scientific journals. He has been a reviewer and adviser to many departments of chemistry. Several governments seek his advice for restructuring and reinvigorating science activities in their countries.

Notable Contributions to the Science

Prof. Rao is the author of over 1774 research papers and 54 books. His primary research works are in solid state and materials chemistry – a field he initiated and nurtured for over six decades in India. Besides, he has made immense contributions to chemical spectroscopy, molecular structure, phase transitions, high-temperature superconductivity, fullerenes, graphene, and nanomaterials. He has been working on transition metal oxides (especially perovskite), nonstoichiometric defects, metal-insulator transitions, crystal and electronic structures of various solids, superconducting cuprates, magnetoresistive manganites, multiferroic metal oxides, etc. He contributed to the development of novel chemical synthesis strategies for different kinds of solids, including nanomaterials and framework solids in different dimensionalities. In his autobiography, he quoted that "science is not about getting awards or writing papers; it is a way of life. It involves climbing the limitless ladder of excellence" (Jayaraman 2010a; Rao 2010).

Spectroscopy and Solid-State Structural Chemistry

Prof. Rao's started his carrier with two Ph.D. students in IISc and began working on the molecular structure using spectroscopic methods. He used Ultraviolet-Visible (UV-Vis) and infrared (IR) spectroscopy methods to solve chemically important problems like spectra-structural co-relationship, charge-transfer interaction, environmental effects, and other related phenomena (Livingston et al. 1960; Rao and Venkataraghavan 1961). According to him (Rao, 2010), two themes have had long-lasting impacts on several works he published during this period. The first one was the investigation of brookite-rutile-anatase structural transformations in TiO_2 (Rao, 1961; Rao et al., 1961). The second was the structural examination of unusual composition (nonstoichiometric) in rare earth metal oxides, Pr_6O_{11} and Tb_4O_7 (Rao et al. 1970; Sastry et al. 1966). How to confirm the composition of the compound was a big mystery for Prof. Rao at that period. These systematic investigations have led to a better understanding of the structural relation between nonstoichiometric and stoichiometric (PrO_2 and TbO_2) compounds.

Prof. Rao joined the new IIT Kanpur as an associate professor. There, he focused his research activities on solid-state chemistry and different kinds of complex structural models, *viz.,* binary and ternary metal oxides, and explored their electrical and magnetic properties, phase transitions, defects, etc. A range of perovskite structure (ABO_3) based compounds exhibiting metallic ($LaTiO_3$, $LaNiO_3$), semiconducting ($LaVO_3$, $LaCrO_3$), and phase transition ($LaCoO_3$) phenomena were synthesized and their associated properties were investigated (Bhide et al. 1972; Rao 1974; Subba Rao et al. 1971). The group observed that $LaCoO_3$ shows novel phase transitions resulting from low-spin and high-spin Co(III) and electron transfer between them as a function of temperature. The defect in solids (alkali–halides and silver–halides) was another aspect that attracted his attention (Ramdas et al. 1972; Shukla et al. 1973a; Shukla et al. 1973b). He pursued works on the theory, interaction, and migration of point defects in ionic solids, and employed theoretical models and computer simulations to investigate the mechanism. The findings helped in understanding the important structure–property relationship in complex solids and point defects that do not exist in real solids.

They (Rao and his group) continued their research on more complex nonstoichiometric perovskite oxides (e.g., $LaNi_xM_{1-x}O_3$, $LaCoO_{3-x}$, $Ca_2(Fe/Mn)O_5$) and layered type of cuprates (Ganguly et al. 1984; Rao et al. 1984; Singh et al. 1982). Previous works on the crystal structure of a cuprate La_2CuO_4 showed that this could be the mother oxide for high-temperature superconductivity. They prepared the well-known and famous 123 superconductor $YBa_2Cu_3O_7$ with a transition temperature around liquid nitrogen, and investigated in detail the crystal structure and deviation from the stoichiometry of $YBa_2Cu_3O_7$ and revealed the role of oxygen vacancies in crystal lattice for high-temperature superconductivity (Subbanna et al. 1987). They independently synthesized many other series of interesting superconducting oxides and studied their structure-property relationship with superconducting cuprates (Rao et al. 1987; Rao and Ganguli 1995). Based on these works, many unusual compounds of iron and cobalt have been prepared by researchers that exhibit superconducting properties.

His interest in the phase transition of solids took him to a new emerging direction of physical chemistry. The group uncovered metal-insulator transition for a broad range of binary transition metal oxides (TiO, VO, VO_2, RuO_2, V_2O_3, etc.) and ReO_3/perovskite-related structures ($La_{1-x}Sr_xCoO_3$ and La $Co_{1-x}Ni_xO_3$) (Edwards et al. 1995; Rao 1996). Concurrently, he made numerous contributions to the field of colossal magnetoresistance manganites family ($Ln_{1-x}A_xMnO_3$) by characterizing the properties of metallic state versus charge ordered (insulating) state (Rao et al. 1996; Rao and Raveau 1998). His group probably was among the first to discuss phase separation in these manganites. They also worked on multiferroic – A material that simultaneously possesses magnetic and ferroelectric properties. They reported the unusual coexistence of both ferromagnetism and ferroelectricity in $BiMnO_3$ (Moreira dos Santos et al., 2002). Moreover, Prof. Rao and his group have made noteworthy contributions to this field, which include synthesis, characterization, and determination of the composition of several other multiferroic materials such as $LnFe_2O_3$, $YCrO_3$, $Pb(Zr_{0.5}Ti_{0.5})O_3$ (PZT), etc., (Aiyer et al., 1997; Sahu et al., 2008; Serrao et al., 2008). He also worked on microporous solids (silicates and zeolites) and open frameworks of metal phosphate, etc.

Nanoscience and Nanotechnology

The lecture of American physicist Richard Feynman "*There's Plenty of Room at the Bottom*," at an American Physical Society meeting at Caltech on 29th December 1959, opened a new field of nanoscience and nanotechnology (Feynman, 1960). The invention of the electron microscope in 1981, and the discovery of fullerenes (1985) revolutionized the subject of nanoscience and nanotechnology. Fullerene was prepared in the laboratory in 1990. Its extension a carbon nanotube (CNT) was discovered in the same year and attracted scientists and researchers toward nanomaterials applications.

Prof. Rao shifted his interest to this fascinating and evolving area and made tremendous contributions to the novel synthesis, characterization, functionalization, investigation of properties, etc. He worked on the interaction of nickel clusters with Buckminsterfullerene C_{60} (Vijayakrishnan et al. 1992) and extended this work to other nano carbons (CNT, graphene, and carbon dots) (Rao et al. 2013; Voggu et al. 2010). He and his group worked extensively on nanoscale metal oxides and nitrides that show magnetism at room temperature due to surface effects. In his laboratory, a large variety of various dimensionalities (0D, 1D, 2D, and 3D) based nanomaterials (Fig. 4) have been synthesized and characterized, and new phenomena have been explored (Table 1). A comprehensive account of Prof. Rao's research work in nanoscience can be found in numerous publications and monographs (Rao et al. 2007).

Prof. Rao has been working on producing green hydrogen energy for the greater benefit of humanity (Sathyamurthy and Rao 2019). Notably, hydrogen storage, photochemical and electrochemical production of hydrogen, solar production of hydrogen, and non-metallic catalysis are the highlights of his work. The Energy Frontiers Eni (2020) award has been conferred on him for his work on metal oxides, CNTs, and other two-dimensional nanosystems, including graphene, boron-nitrogen-carbon hybrid materials, and molybdenum sulfide (MoS_2) for energy applications and green hydrogen production.

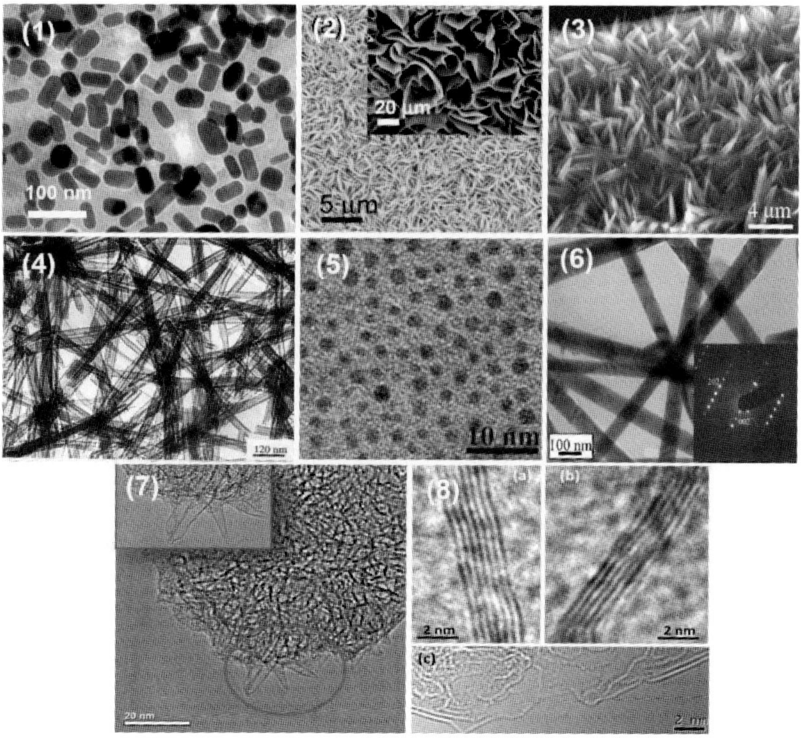

Figure 4: Electron microscopy images: (1) Au nanorods (Varghese et al. 2008), (2) 1D nanostructure of diphenylalanine (Biswas and Rao 2009), (3) GaSe nanoflowers (Gautam et al. 2005), (4) CdSe nanotubes (Rao et al. 2001), (5) GaN nanocrystals (Sardar and Rao 2004), (6) Te nanorods (Gautam and Rao 2004), (7) carbon nanohorns (Kadambi et al. 2015), and (8) BN nanosheets (Nag et al. 2010).

Table: Nanomaterials of various dimensionalities investigated by C. N. R. Rao and his group.

Type	Dimensional	Description	Examples
Nano-objects	–	Material with one, two, or three external dimensions in the nanoscale (1–100 nm)	1 nm = 10^{-9} m
Quantum Dots	0D	Nano-object with all three external dimensions in the nanoscale, but electron movement is restricted in all three directions: QDs, nanodots, and fullerenes.	C-dots, ZnO, CuO, CuS, CdS, GaN, InN
Nanoparticles	3D	Nano-object with all three external dimensions in the nanoscale, but electron movement is allowed in all directions – for example, nano-powder, nanodiamond.	Ag, Au, Pt, Pd, ZnO, Cu_2O
Nanotemplate	2D	Nano-object with one external dimension in the nanoscale and the other two external dimensions significantly larger – for example, nanofilms, nanocoatings, graphenes	Graphene, BN, MoS_2 V_2O_5, MoO_3
Nanofiber/ Nanowires (Electronic conducting)	1D	Nano-object (flexible or rigid) with two external dimensions in the nanoscale and a third dimension significantly larger	V_2O_5, MoO_3, WS_2, GaS
Nanotube	1D	Hollow nanofiber	CNTs, GaN, BN, TiO_2, ZnO, InN
Nanorod	1D	Solid nanofiber	TiO_2, Ga_2O_3, ZnO, ZnSe, Ag, Au
Nanocomposites	–	Mixing of more than one material at a nanoscale level	Au@Ag, FePt, Au-Graphene, BN-Graphene

Personal and Social Life

Prof. Rao was married to Indumati (Indu) Rao on 15th May 1960. The couple has two children, Sanjay and Suchitra. Suchitra is married to Krishna N. Ganesh, former Director of the IISER, Pune, Maharashtra. Sanjay works as a science popularizer in schools around Bangalore. Prof. Rao is technophobic and even refrains from using a mobile phone and has said, "I do not use my mobile phone except to speak to my wife." He always says that he takes a personal interest in the well-being of anybody who comes across his life, even for a short period of time. He believes in spirituality and science has many common features. He said his faith in God had helped him in all his endeavors.

Honors and Awards

Fellowships of Academic Societies

- Fellow of the Indian Academy of Science (FASc) (1965)
- Fellow of the Indian National Science Academy (FNA) (1974)
- Founding Fellow of the World Academy of Science (FTWAS) (1983)
- Honorary Fellow of the Royal Society of Chemistry (Hon. FRSC) (1989)
- Foreign Member of the Academy Europaea (MAE) (1997)
- Honorary Fellow of the Institute of Physics (Hon. FInstP) London (2006)
- Honorary doctorates from several universities in India and abroad.
- He is a member of many science academies across the world, including - the Royal Society, London, the National Academy of Sciences, U.S.A., the Russian, French, and Japanese Academies, and the American Philosophical Society. He is a Member of the Pontifical Academy of Sciences and a Foreign Fellow of Academia Europaea, the Royal Society of Canada, and the Chinese Academy of Sciences. He is a distinguished visiting professor at the University of California.

Major Scientific Awards and Medals

- Marlow Medal of the Faraday Society (1967)
- Bhatnagar Prize (1981)
- Royal Society of Chemistry (London) Medal (1981)
- Blackett Lectureship of the Royal Society (1991)
- Einstein Gold Medal of UNESCO (1996)
- Linnett Professorship of the University of Cambridge (1998)
- Centenary Medal of the Royal Society of Chemistry (2000)
- Hughes Medal of the Royal Society for original discovery in physical sciences (2000)
- Order of Scientific Merit (Grand-Cross) from the President of Brazil (2002)
- Somiya Award of the International Union of Materials Research (2004)
- Dan David Prize for science in the future dimension for his research in Materials Science (2005)
- Nikkei Asia Prize for Science, Technology and Innovation (2008)
- Royal Medal by the Royal Society (2009)
- August-Wilhelm-von-Hoffmann Medal by the German Chemical Society (2010)
- Ernesto Illy Trieste Science Prize for materials research (2011)
- Albert Einstein Professor of the Chinese Academy of Sciences (2012)
- Rising Sun, Gold and Silver Star award by the Emperor of Japan (2015)
- von Hippel award by the Materials Research Society (2017)
- First Sheikh Saud International Prize for Materials Research (2019)
- Karnataka Science and Technology Academy Lifetime Achievement Award in STEAM (2020)
- Eni Award (Edition of the Energy Frontiers Prize) (2020)

Indian Governmental Honors

- Padma Shri (1974)
- Padma Vibhushan (1985)
- Karnataka Ratna (2001)
- Bharat Ratna (2014)

Service to Professional Bodies

- Chairman, Science Advisory Council to the Prime Minister of India (2004-2009)
- Chairman, Science Advisory Council to the Prime Minister of India (1985-1989)
- President, Indian National Science Academy (1986-1986)
- President, Indian Academy of Sciences (1989-1991)
- President, International Union of Pure and Applied Chemistry (1985-1987)
- Director, IISc, Bengaluru (1984–1994)
- Chairman, Scientific Advisory Committee to the Union Cabinet (1997-1998)
- Chairman, Scientific Advisory Committee to the Albert Einstein Research Professor (1995-1999)
- Founder-President of both the Chemical Research Society and the Materials Research Society of India

Acknowledgments

The portrait photograph was taken from his autobiography "Claiming the Limitless Ladder: A life in Chemistry" and website https://www.jncasr.ac.in/faculty/cnrrao. The author gratefully acknowledges the works of Angell et al. (1994), Natarajan, (2009), Rao, (2009a), Rao, (2010), Jayaraman (2010a), Prasad (2014), Gopalakrishnan (2014), Chamoli (2015), Ganguli and Ramakrishnan (2016), conversations and interviews (Brasted, 1982; Kamat, 2016; Malhotra, 2011; Sathyamurthy and Rao, 2019; Weiss, 2009), monographs (Rao, 1991; Rao, 2000; Rao and Raveau, 1998), and research and review articles of Prof Rao (Editorial, 2017), as a valuable source of information for the article.

Bibliography

1. Aiyer, H.N., Raju, A.R., Subbanna, G.N., Rao, C.N.R. (1997) Epitaxial nature of the films of $LaNiO_3$, $Pb(Zr_{0.5}Ti_{0.5})O_3$, and $La_{0.95}Mn_{0.95}O_3$ obtained by nebulized spray pyrolysis. Chemistry of Materials 9, 755-760.

2. Angell, C., Bagchi, B., Buckingham, A., Thomas, S.J., Rao, C.N.R. (1994) C. N. R. Rao Festschrift. The Journal of Physical Chemistry 98, 9083-9096.
3. Bhide, V.G., Rajoria, D.S., Rao, G.R., Rao, C.N.R. (1972) Mössbauer studies of the high-spin-low-spin equilibria and the localized-collective electron transition in $LaCoO_3$. Physical Review B 6, 1021-1032.
4. Biswas, K., Rao, C.N.R. (2009) Nanostructured peptide fibrils formed at the organic–aqueous interface and their use as templates to prepare inorganic nanostructures. ACS Applied Materials & Interfaces 1, 811-815.
5. Brasted, R.C. (1982) Interview with R. C. Mehrotra and C. N. R. Rao. Journal of Chemical Education 59, 113.
6. Chamoli, R.P. (2015) Prof. C.N.R. Rao: A life dedicated to science. International Journal of Humanities Social Sciences and Education 2, 95-99.
7. Editorial, (2009) Challenges for science in India. Nature Materials 8, 361-361.
8. Editorial, (2017) Physical Chemistry in India. The Journal of Physical Chemistry B 121, 6287-6293.
9. Edwards, P.P., Ramakrishnan, T.V., Rao, C.N.R. (1995) The metal-nonmetal transition: A global perspective. The Journal of Physical Chemistry 99, 5228-5239.
10. Feynman, R.P. (1960) There's plenty of room at the bottom. Engineering and Science 23, 22-36.
11. Ganguli, A.K., Ramakrishnan, T.V. (2016) Living legends in Indian science: C. N. R. Rao. Current Science 111, 926-931.
12. Ganguly, P., Vasanthacharya, N.Y., Rao, C.N.R., Edwards, P.P. (1984) Composition-controlled metal-insulator transitions and minimum metallic conductivity in the oxide systems $LaNi_{1-x}M_xO_3$ (M = Cr, Mn, Fe, or Co). Journal of Solid State Chemistry 54, 400-406.
13. Gautam, U.K., Rao, C.N.R. (2004) Controlled synthesis of crystalline tellurium nanorods, nanowires, nanobelts and related structures by a self-seeding solution process. Journal of Materials Chemistry 14, 2530-2535.
14. Gautam, U.K., Vivekchand, S.R.C., Govindaraj, A., Kulkarni, G.U., Selvi, N.R., Rao, C.N.R. (2005) Generation of onions and nanotubes of GaS and GaSe through laser and thermally induced exfoliation. Journal of the American Chemical Society 127, 3658-3659.

15. Gopalakrishnan, J. (2014) C. N. R. Rao and the growth of solid state and materials chemistry as a central domain of research. Zeitschrift für anorganische und allgemeine Chemie 640, 1031-1041.
16. Jayaraman, K.S. (2010a) Autobiography of an unusual chemist. Nature India doi: https://doi.org/10.1038/nindia.2010.184.
17. Jayaraman, K.S. (2010b) Need young scientists to lead: C N R Rao. Nature India doi: https://doi.org/10.1038/nindia.2009.365.
18. Kadambi, S.B., Pramoda, K., Ramamurty, U., Rao, C.N.R. (2015) Carbon-nanohorn-reinforced polymer matrix composites: Synergetic benefits in mechanical properties. ACS Applied Materials & Interfaces 7, 17016-17022.
19. Kamat, P.V. (2016) A conversation with C. N. R. Rao. ACS Energy Letters 1, 1189-1191.
20. Livingston, R.L., Lurie, C., Rao, C.N.R. (1960) Molecular structure of neopentane. Nature 185, 458-459.
21. Malhotra, R. (2011) In conversation: Making of a leading scientist – C. N. R. Rao. Current Science 100, 1466-1471.
22. Moreira dos Santos, A., Parashar, S., Raju, A.R., Zhao, Y.S., Cheetham, A.K., Rao, C.N.R. (2002) Evidence for the likely occurrence of magnetoferroelectricity in the simple perovskite, $BiMnO_3$. Solid State Communications 122, 49-52.
23. Nag, A., Raidongia, K., Hembram, K.P.S.S., Datta, R., Waghmare, U.V., Rao, C.N.R. (2010) Graphene analogues of BN: Novel synthesis and properties. ACS Nano 4, 1539-1544.
24. Natarajan, S. (2009) In Celebration of the 75th Birthday of Professor C.N.R. Rao. Chemistry – An Asian Journal 4, 780-781.
25. Prasad, B.L.V. (2014) Chemistry of Materials Celebrates the 80th Birthday of One of the Premier "Chemists of Materials". Chemistry of Materials 26, 3593-3594.
26. Ramdas, S., Shukla, A.K., Rao, C.N.R. (1972) Association energies of intrinsic and extrinsic defect pairs in KCl. Chemical Physics Letters 16, 14-17.
27. Rao, C.N.R. (1961) Kinetics and thermodynamics of the crystal structure transformation of spectroscopically pure anatase to rutile. Canadian Journal of Chemistry 39, 498-500.
28. Rao, C.N.R. (1974) Localized versus collective behavior of d-electrons in transition-metal oxide systems of perovskite structure. Journal of the Indian Chemical Society 51, 979-987.

29. Rao, C.N.R. (1991) Chemistry of high temperature superconductors. World Scientific.
30. Rao, C.N.R. (1996) Virtues of marginally metallic oxides. Chemical Communications 10.1039/CC9960002217 2217-2222.
31. Rao, C.N.R. (2000) Understanding Chemistry. Universities Press
32. Rao, C.N.R. (2009a) Chemistry of Materials - A Letter to a Young Friend. Resonance 14, 508-517.
33. Rao, C.N.R. (2009b) Science in the future of India. Science 325, 126-126.
34. Rao, C.N.R. (2010) Climbing the Limitless Ladder: A Life in Chemistry. Chennai: IISc Press, World Scientific Publishing Co. P. Ltd.
35. Rao, C.N.R., Cheetham, A.K., Mahesh, R. (1996) Giant magnetoresistance and related properties of rare-earth manganates and other oxide systems. Chemistry of Materials 8, 2421-2432.
36. Rao, C.N.R., Ganguli, A.K. (1995) Structure–property relationship in superconducting cuprates. Chemical Society Reviews 24, 1-7.
37. Rao, C.N.R., Ganguly, P., Raychaudhuri, A.K., Ram, R.A.M., Sreedhar, K. (1987) Identification of the phase responsible for high-temperature superconductivity in Y–Ba–Cu oxides. Nature 326, 856-857.
38. Rao, C.N.R., Gopalakrishnan, J., Vidyasagar, K. (1984) Superstructures, ordered defects and nonstoichiometry in metal-oxides of perovskite and related structures. Indian Journal of Chemistry Section A 23, 265-284.
39. Rao, C.N.R., Govindaraj, A., Deepak, L.F., Gunari, N.A., Nath, M. (2001) Surfactant-assisted synthesis of semiconductor nanotubes and nanowires. Applied Physics Letters 78, 1853-1855.
40. Rao, C.N.R., Matte, H.S.S.R., Subrahmanyam, K.S. (2013) Synthesis and selected properties of graphene and graphene mimics. Accounts of Chemical Research 46, 149-159.
41. Rao, C.N.R., Raveau, B. (1998) Colossal magnetoresistance, charge-ordering and related aspects of manganese oxides. World-Scientific.
42. Rao, C.N.R., Thomas, P.J., Kulkarni, G.U. (2007) Nanocrystals: Synthesis Properties and Applications. Springer.
43. Rao, C.N.R., Venkataraghavan, R. (1961) Correlations of infrared group frequencies and band intensities in organic molecules with substituent constants: A statistical evaluation. Canadian Journal of Chemistry 39, 1757-1764.

44. Rao, C.N.R., Yoganarasimhan, S.R., Faeth, P.A. (1961) Studies on the brookite-rutile transformation. Transactions of the Faraday Society 57, 504-510.
45. Rao, G.V.S., Ramdas, S., Mehrotra, P.N., Rao, C.N.R. (1970) Electrical transport in rare-earth oxides. Journal of Solid State Chemistry 2, 377-384.
46. Sahu, J.R., Serrao, C.R., Rao, C.N.R. (2008) Modification of the multiferroic properties of $YCrO_3$ and LuCrO3 by Mn substitution. Solid State Communications 145, 52-55.
47. Sardar, K., Rao, C.N.R. (2004) New solvothermal routes for GaN nanocrystals. Advanced Materials 16, 425-429.
48. Sastry, R.L.N., Mehrotra, P.N., Rao, C.N.R. (1966) Solvolytic disproportionation of non-stoichiometric oxides of praseodymium and terbium. Journal of Inorganic and Nuclear Chemistry 28, 2167-2173.
49. Sathyamurthy, N., Rao, C.N.R. (2019) Face to face with Professor C N R Rao. Resonance 24, 775-791.
50. Serrao, C.R., Sahu, J.R., Ramesha, K., Rao, C.N.R. (2008) Magnetoelectric effect in rare earth ferrites, $LnFe_2O_4$. Journal of Applied Physics 104, 016102.
51. Shukla, A.K., Ramdas, S., Rao, C.N.R. (1973a) Intrinsic and extrinsic defect pairs in caesium halides. Journal of the Chemical Society, Faraday Transactions 2: Molecular and Chemical Physics 69, 207-216.
52. Shukla, A.K., Ramdas, S., Rao, C.N.R. (1973b) Mechanism of ion movement in AgCl and AgBr. Journal of Solid State Chemistry 8, 120-125.
53. Singh, K.K., Ganguly, P., Rao, C.N.R. (1982) Structural transitions in $(La,Ln)_2CuO_4$ and $La_2(Cu,Ni)O_4$ systems. Materials Research Bulletin 17, 493-500.
54. Subba Rao, G.V., Wanklyn, B.M., Rao, C.N.R. (1971) Electrical transport in rare earth ortho-chromites, -manganites and -ferrites. Journal of Physics and Chemistry of Solids 32, 345-358.
55. Subbanna, G.N., Ganguly, P., Rao, C.N.R. (1987) The $YBa_2Cu_3O_{7-\delta}$ system: Structure, stoichiometry and orbital ordering and their role in superconductivity. Modern Physics Letters B 01, 155-165.
56. Varghese, N., Vivekchand, S.R.C., Govindaraj, A., Rao, C.N.R. (2008) A calorimetric investigation of the assembly of gold nanorods to form necklaces. Chemical Physics Letters 450, 340-344.

57. Vijayakrishnan, V., Santra, A.K., Seshadri, R., Nagarajan, R., Pradeep, T., Rao, C.N.R. (1992) A comparative study of the interaction of nickel clusters with buckminsterfullerene, C60, and graphite. Surface Science 262, L87-L90.
58. Voggu, R., Rao, K.V., George, S.J., Rao, C.N.R. (2010) A simple method of separating metallic and semiconducting single-walled carbon nanotubes based on molecular charge transfer. Journal of the American Chemical Society 132, 5560-5561.
59. Weiss, P.S. (2009) A Conversation with Prof. C. N. R. Rao: The Future of Science in India and the Developing World. ACS Nano 3, 2056-2061.

AUTHOR PROFILE

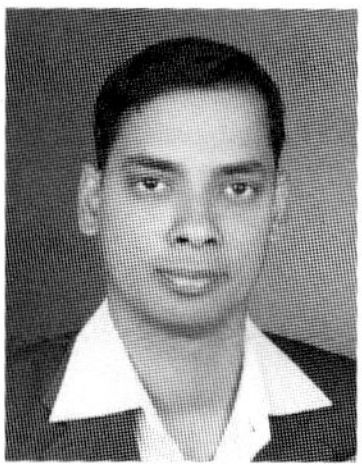

Dr. Khemchand Dewangan is a Senior Assistant Professor at the Department of Chemistry, Indira Gandhi National Tribal University (IGNTU), Amarkantak, INDIA. He received his Ph.D. in Chemistry from the Indian Institute of Technology, Kanpur, India. After that, he joined IGNTU as an Assistant Professor in 2012. His current research centers on physical chemistry, with an emphasis on nanoscience and nanotechnology, particularly the development of specific pure/hybrid functional nanomaterials for various applications in the fields of energy storage, environmental remediation, nanocatalyst, etc.

E-mail: khemchand.dewangan@igntu.ac.in

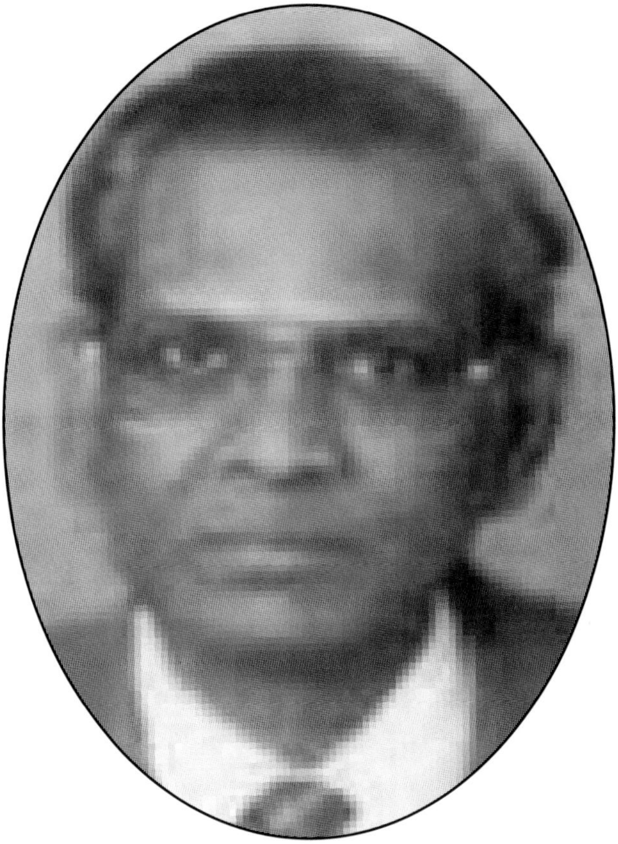

Ebrahimali Abubacker Siddiq

(b. 1937)

EBRAHIMALI ABUBACKER SIDDIQ: FATHER OF HYBRID RICE IN INDIA

Kalambur Muralidharan

Dr. Ebrahim Ali Siddiq was born in 1938 in Ilayangudi, present-day Sivaganga district, in Tamil Nadu. He grew to despise poverty. Dr. EA Siddiq is the epitome of hard work, and anyone who learns about the life of Dr. Siddiq will be awestruck by his competitive drive. He aspired for greatness and worked intensely throughout his career on the realization that talent needs to be coupled with hard work, and demanded excellence from everyone around him. He lived frugally into his mid-thirties. His identity is integrally tied to producing food for all. The search started with his early childhood and ended with finding a role model in Prof. M. S. Swaminathan, who dramatically changed his life. His life is inspirational, but even more magnificent is the intense unity created among his teammates as they pursued increased rice and food production. After two decades of tenacious pursuit, he succeeded in developing the world's first semidwarf and high-yielding Pusa Basmati 1 that brought in bountiful harvest to farmers and abundant foreign exchange to the country This is an incredible story of a creative, complex, innovative, and enigmatic man who sought to put a dent and free world from hunger. He bent reality and convinced others that they could do the impossible. As a doyen of Basmati varieties and agricultural production, Dr. EA Siddiq provided consistent leadership and played a critical role in the process of reaching self-sufficiency in rice and food in India. Dr. Siddiq persuasively preached to all those involved in agricultural research and development that all of us are motivated not by pleasure or happiness but by the significance of the task to aid the nation-building process. His accomplishments can give a person the insight, inspiration, and perspective a budding scientist or an executive need to overcome obstacles and take his or her career to the next level.

Poverty and Struggle in Early Life and Education

Ebrahim Ali Siddiq was born on 11th July 1938 as the second child to Ebrahim Ali and Pathimaal at Ilayangudi, Tamil Nadu. A remote village in India's southernmost district of the then composite Ramanathapuram, and now present-day's Sivaganga district. His great-grandmother widely known as Katchipillai Ammal was one of the three famous 'sufi' poets of Tamil Nadu. With the passing away of his two brothers in their childhood, Siddiq remained the only living child of his parents. With his father confined to Burma (Myanmar) until the end of World War II, it was his mother, who brought him up and also shaped him with many a human virtue, which guided him all through his life's journey. Over the years Siddiq could realize that it was his mother's dream despite poverty stalking them to see him successful and help her find an end to suffering. Siddiq's hobbies used to be reading books and encouraging reading habits amongst boys of his age group, writing plays and acting, and extending help to illiterate families residing in the neighborhood by reading letters and writing replies to their overseas bread-earners. On holidays, Siddiq used to spend time at the Library in Tanjavur. He also had an opportunity to go through the work of Mahakavi Subrahmanya Bharathi and the Revolutionary poet Bharadhidasan (Kanakasabai Subburathinam). Bharathi's potent patriotic poems composed in simple Tamil had created a political awakening amongst the people of Tamil Nadu (then known as Madras Province) during the days of India's Freedom Movement. Barathidasan's grammatically superb yet written in simple Tamil works were largely devoted to social awakening. Their works in essence were reflections of their dreams and aspirations of how India should emerge as a country politically and economically. Siddiq started the 'Students' Reading Club' at school for boys of his age. The scheme was to run the club for the benefit of boys by enrolling those interested in magazine reading as members and meeting the expenses from the nominal membership subscription of $1/4^{th}$ 'Anna' collected every month. Beyond two years, the club could not meet the expectations of the members due to increased financial constraints limiting the procurement of magazines. He later launched a hand-written single-copy children's magazine '*Roja*'. It made Siddiq think at one stage that there was something in him that should be brought out as well. He was the writer, artist, and handwritten copy producer. Young Siddiq's efforts as a writer were rewarded when his short story "*Police Ponnambalam*" was accepted and published in a widely read Sunday Issue of the magazine *Tamilnadu.*

Certain thoughts about his mother and grandmother were etched permanently on Siddiq and they had a profound effect on his life. Despite poverty, the affectionate mother on demand gave four Annas to spend at *Jatra*. Young

Siddiq succumbed to the temptation of quick money in gambling. Although he doubled in the first round, then last everything in the next two rounds. He learned a bitter lesson that greed will dull the mind and lead to losses. Mother sold her jewelry to buy a three-acre land in the hamlet at the cost of one thousand rupees. On two acres, mother cultivated corn, pearl millet, etc., working along with others in the field. This experience gave assurance to Siddiq that he can also work hard just like his mother in agricultural work. Alas, Siddiq's mother left for the heavenly abode just three months prior to his school final (Board) examinations due to a Cholera attack. It was a tragic end as she gave away her "*tali or mangal surta*" to sell and pay his examination fee.

With none to support, Siddiq joined his elder uncle Janab Sickandar Batcha to assist in a small grocery shop at Mannadi in Madras. With his father's assurances to meet the college expenses (Rs. 30 per month), his uncle Ebrahim Ali helped him to college life at Raja Doraisingham Memorial Arts and Science College at Sivaganga. Mr. Subbaiah, the single teacher with whom Siddiq joined, and then Mr. Shanmugam, taught him with loving care how to confidently meet with new situations. Soon, his father's promised support abruptly ended because of losses suffered in business in Burma. Siddiq had to abandon pursuing 2nd year because he was moneyless to pay for food and fees. He appeared for the position of primary teacher at a monthly salary of Rs. 61. Mr. Dandapani, who was then the principal listened to the financial crisis and encouraged with an assurance to admit Siddiq in the second year if he could return by the next academic session. All Siddiq had saved was Rs.300/- (Rs.61/- as salary per month minus Rs 18 for boarding and Rs.2/- as pocket money). The people in the village did not fail to read his troubled state of mind. Mrs. Chellamma, the house owner offered her gold chain to sell to pay his initial College admission-related expenses. It was the people's goodwill that enabled him to sustain himself. Later with the help of Mr. Sivarama Iyer, the resident owner, Siddiq boldly met the German Fr. Earhart, Principal of the College, and argued to elect a course in Botany. He thanked the Almighty for what all he was blessed with at a crucial period of his life recounting for a moment under what kind of financial and health problems he studied and appeared and achieved success in the examination. During Siddiq's school and college days and service period, his good friends were Hindus, Christians, and several castes, and he saw them as Indians.

On acquiring a degree, Siddiq joined as a Demonstrator at Madhurai College for six months. Later on, he was selected and joined service in the State Agriculture Department at Agricultural College and Research Institute, Coimbatore, to assist in breeding research on grapes. On May 23, 1962, Siddiq married his uncle's eldest daughter Fathimuthu who was in the school final. It was then that the provident provided an unexpected meeting with the visiting Professor M.S. Swaminathan (fondly called MSS) of the Indian Agricultural Research Institute (IARI), New Delhi. Siddiq used this divine opportunity to explain his research efforts on grapes. Impressed with his enthusiasm, MSS suggested that he should apply for admission to PG at IARI. Siddiq applied and was fortunately selected to work with MSS himself! He then succeeded in the interview to obtain a Rockefeller Foundation scholarship. For this, MSS awarded Siddiq with a book on Mendel's breeding work with peas. The RF fellowship was Rs. 200/- per month, which was no less than the salary he was getting at Coimbatore. With the highest-grade point average (GPA) and timely submission of the thesis, Siddiq was awarded the Golden Jubilee Medal of the Indian Council of Agricultural Research. His father-in-law wrote, recounting Siddiq's responsibility of supporting his wife and baby during the first two-year study period in Delhi. Siddiq set up his family in Delhi despite the meager student fellowship of Rs. 400/- a month in addition to Rs. 100/- support from his father-in-law. Two young brothers-in-law Sheikh Abdul Khaddar and Nanina Mohammed also joined him following the sudden demise of his father-in-law. In spite of financial hardships, his wife helped to speed up his thesis research. MSS further advised him to take up research for his Ph.D. (1964-68) on rice with the advent of high-yielding dwarf Taichung Native1.

Opportunities for research and achievements

For his PG thesis, Siddiq received the Golden Jubilee Medal from the then Prime Minister of India. He was also awarded the Assam Government Gold Medal for his contributions to the development of high-yielding rice varieties. On his return from Egypt in 1986 after serving for three years as a Rice breeder under IRRI's outreach program, he joined back IARI, Delhi. After a brief stint as a Professor of Genetics there, he was appointed as Director, ICAR-Indian Institute of Rice Research (Formerly Directorate of Rice Research and All-India Coordinated Rice Improvement Project), Rajendranagar, Hyderabad. With single-minded devotion, he pursued research for more than 20 years to develop a semidwarf and high-yielding Basmati variety. These persistent efforts led him to produce Pusa Basmati 1, the world's first high-yielding semidwarf Basmati variety. Later, understanding the special need for the rice-wheat rotation system in the Indo-Gangetic region, he developed Pusa 44, which proved its suitability as farmers widely adopted it by growing over a large area. Several other rice varieties were also released by him for cultivating in farmers' fields (**Table 1**). To reduce the time taken for preparing the workshop reports and the postal charges incurred for dispatching so heavy reports, Dr. Siddiq with the help of some senior scientists worked out the likely cost. Dr. Sidddiq contributed over 150 research publications that appeared in reputed international scientific journals.

Table 1: List of high-yielding dwarf varieties developed and released by Dr. E. A. Siddiq.

Variety name, year of release, recommended areas, and remarks
• **Jamuna**, 1971, Basmati growing areas. Combines many features of traditional basmati rice but yields moderately
• **Sabarmati**, 1971, Basmati growing areas. Combines many features of traditional basmati rice but yields moderately (A higher yielding sister line designated as improved Sabarmati replaced it in the very next season)
• **Pusa 2-21 (Kannagi)**, 1975, All over India. Quick maturing (<100 d) and ideally suited to varied cropping systems and short seasons
• **Pusa 4-11**, 1975, Tamil Nadu. Very early maturing first fine grain variety
• **Pusa 33**, 1975, All over India. Aromatic, high yielding, and quick maturing but not comparable to basmati rices; highly suited to multiple cropping
• **Himalaya2**, 1982, Himachal Pradesh. Aromatic long slender grain type, tolerant to low temperature and ideally suited to hill ecology
• **Pusa169**, 1986, Punjab, Western UP, Bihar, and West Bengal. Long slender grain type, ideal for rice-wheat rotation
• **Pusa 205**, 1986, Orissa, West Bengal, Punjab, and Madhya Pradesh. Long slender grain variety of medium maturity, resistant to fungal diseases and suited to rice-wheat system

- **Pusa Basmati 1**, 1989, Punjab, Haryana, and Western Uttar Pradesh. World's first high-yielding semidwarf basmati variety
- **Pusa 44-33**, 1993, Punjab, Haryana, Western Uttar Pradesh, Bihar, Karnataka, Tamil Nadu, and many other states. Most popular high-yielding fine grain variety and the only one amenable to combine harvest in the Northwestern Indo-Gangetic plains
- **Pusa 834**, 1994, Andhra Pradesh, Karnataka & Eastern Uttar Pradesh. Early maturing fine grain variety suitable for multiple cropping
- **DRRH-1**, 1995, Southern states. First hybrid to be released in India with about 15% yield advantage over the best-inbred varieties
- **Pusa 677**, 1997, Tamil Nadu, Karnataka, A.P. and M.P. Early maturing, fine grain type suitable for multiple cropping

Dr. Siddiq's contributions as Research Manager

The new position as Director, AICRIP, and DRR required him to primarily coordinate the countrywide conduct of multi-location testing of improved rice genotypes developed and nominated by cooperating rice research institutes/centers over appropriate rice ecologies for a minimum period of three years. The unique advantage of the multilocation evaluation of test entries in three-tier test nurseries is that it generates in a short period of 2-3 years sufficient database to compute genotype X environment interaction comparable to that of one or two locations over many years of testing as practiced earlier, enabling thereby rapid identification of entries of promise to targeted rice ecology or location. But for such a rapid evaluation system conceived and practiced by the AICRIP, the country would not have catered to the requirement of varied rice growing conditions with a wide choice of over a thousand high-yielding varieties. It was the extensive adoption of high-yielding varieties suiting primarily to irrigated ecology identified under the AICRIP system of evaluation that made the chronic food grain and rice-deficit country become self-sufficient by the early eighties and achieve a sizeable surplus thereafter to enable India to join the rice exporting countries in 1990s.

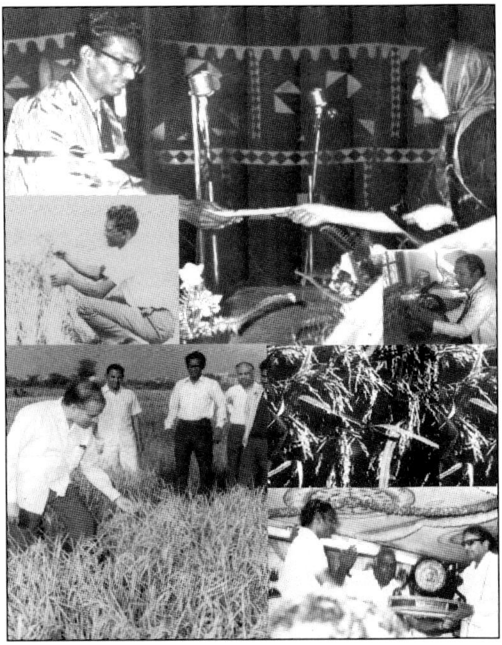

Figure 1: Dr. Siddiq as a research student in rice breeding; Cytogeneticist, IARI; receiving a Doctoral degree and Assam Government Award from Mrs. Indira Gandhi, the then Prime Minister of India; Siddiq's mentor and role model Professor M.S. Swaminathan inspecting experimental field; and Mr. M. Karunanidhi, Honorable Chief Minister of Tamil Nadu honoring him for evolving the high-yielding variety Pusa 2-21 named *Kannagi*.

The real status of rice production in varied ecologies of Eastern Indian states was clearly defined in a document prepared for the Planning Commission of India before Dr. Siddiq joined DRR and published in *Oryza* by DRR scientists, Muralidharan K, Shinde JE, Pasalu IC, Venkataraman S, Prasad ASR, Kalode MB, Rao AV, and Reddy APK. They had brought out the lack of access to seeds of high-yielding varieties and appropriate production technologies as serious constraints to extensive adoption. Realizing these constraints in rice production, the scientists conceived a novel on-farm demonstration named as '*Frontline Demonstration*' (FLD) to exhibit technology to overcome the limitations to yield in farmers' fields. The package practices included the right choice of improved varieties appropriate to the water regime, the use of quality seeds, and crop management tips to motivate farmers to adopt them. The FLD packages designed exclusively for different water regimes viz, shallow lowland (<50 cm) and semi-deep water

(50 cm to 1m) ecologies were planned and launched in five eastern states viz, Assam Bihar, Orissa, Uttar Pradesh, and West Bengal as an activity to commemorate the 25th Anniversary of the Directorate of Rice Research. The FLD was designed in such a way that the improved varietal-cum-production technology was demonstrated in as large as 5-to-10-acre plots surrounded by farmers' fields (planted to farmers customarily preferred old varieties) as control plots in an area representing typically the targeted handicapped rainfed lowland ecology. As no individual farmer would own and make available above 2-3-acre fields, to demonstrate the technology over a 5–10-acre size plot, they had to include 4-5 farmers' lands to lay out FLDs. Such demonstrations were laid out in the initial years at around 25-50 locations per stress ecology per state covering overall 1000-1500 acres with generous financial assistance from the Department of Agriculture, Union Ministry of Agriculture.

In planning and laying out the FLDs, the scientists had actively involved the participation of the state Department of Agriculture, State Agricultural University, and concerned rice research institutes of the ICAR such as CRRI in Orissa, jointly with DRR. Right from crop establishment to every critical phase of crop management, farmers of the region were apprised by the pre-trained master trainer designated for the region on the appropriateness of stress-specific varietal choice, the need to use quality seed and adoption of the recommended packages of cultivation practices with an emphasis on nutrient and weed management, timely harvest and safe post-harvest processing and storage of the produce. On the day of harvest, a farmers' gathering of the location was organized so as to demonstrate the superior yield performance of the demonstration plot as compared to that of farmers' control plots planted to traditional varieties and managed to adopt farmers' cultivation practices. This extension strategy convinced farmers of the superiority of improved varieties over the age-old traditional varieties and motivated them to adopt extensively the new varieties and recommended the package of cultivation practices. The impact of the extension strategy was seen in the incremental per-hectare rice yield increase and overall rice production in such handicapped ecologies. Convinced of the effectiveness of the novel extension strategy, ICAR had recommended this FLD developed by us at DRR to other crop institutes to reach out to farmers with new varietal and production technologies; it is to the credit of Dr. Siddiq as Director, who conceived the strategy with DRR staff.

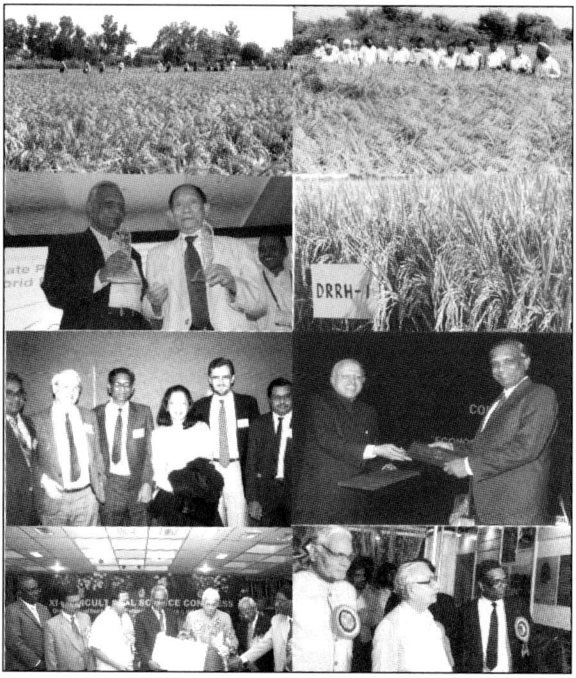

Figure 2: The world's first short-stature and high-yielding Basmati, Pusa Basmati 1; breeding for the productive rice-wheat cropping system Pusa 44 variety; planning with Prof. Long Ping Yuan, China to develop hybrid rice; DRRH 1 - India's first hybrid rice variety; with Dr. Ralph Reliegh, Professor of Genetics, and Coordinator Dr. John O'Tool and others from Rockefeller Foundation; Norman Borlaug Award from Professor M.S. Swaminathan; B.P. Pal Medal of the National Agricultural Science Academy; inaguration of Silver Jubilee Celebration of AICRIP-DRR, by His Excellency Mr. Krishan Kant, Governor of Andhra Pradesh, and His Excellency Mr. Bhanu Prasad Singh, Governor of Karnataka.

Effective publication strategy to disseminate new technologies

The agricultural research institutions in India have made enviable contributions over the past seventy years, but for which the country would not have achieved the kind of production levels we are all proud of today. Yet, avoidable delay and lack of effective means to reach out the same to the targeted beneficiaries are the major reasons for the shortfall of the envisaged pace of growth in agricultural production rather than the lack of technology. Scientists world over engaged in basic research find scientific journals and platforms such as international and national symposia and seminars to present and share research findings with their fraternity. But such avenues are hardly available for researchers engaged in applied research. Their research accomplishments often do not reach beyond finding a brief mention in bulky annual reports periodically brought out by research centers often in a casual way. Despite containing findings of value, they are hardly gone through seriously by the concerned higher-ups for planning and executing needed follow-up action so as to timely reach out to the technology for the benefit of the targeted farmers and other end users. Ineffective periodical inter-phases between scientists from research centers and extension personnel from departments of agriculture on new research developments that would benefit farmers were the avoidable constraints that slowed down the pace of adoption of such technologies of value by farmers in targeted ecologies. On assuming charge as Project Director, DRR, Dr. Siddiq was surprised to notice that this center was as well no exception to experiencing such a gap between the development of a technology of value and its pace of adoption. He then initiated a series of corrective measures, which included (a) urging and encouraging scientists at the Directorate to publish their research findings of both basic and applied value in appropriate high-impact scientific journals, (b) organizing international and national symposia and seminars on themes relevant to rice improvement, (c) bringing out state-wise publications on ecology specific package of rice production technologies, (d) continue to publish periodically the research highlights of the Directorate and (e) holding exhibitions highlighting research and developmental advances in India. Dr. Siddiq had chosen the exceptionally talented Dr. K. Muralidharan, Principal Scientist, Rice Pathology Division in the Directorate, for this assignment, who despite working earlier alone at CRRI-Uint at Nellore had made a significant contribution to the dreaded rice blast and published several articles on its epidemiology and control in Indian and foreign journals. From 1984, along with Dr. G.S.V. Prasad and Dr. I.C. Pasalu, he edited and elegantly designed to bring out colorfully printed 'Research Highlights' of the Directorate, not exceeding 50 pages giving comprehensive ideas on rice research activities of the country.

With Dr. Siddiq joining DRR, the first innovation attempted and found success in reaching farmers was through state or region-wise booklets on *Technology for Rice Production* covering Andhra Pradesh, Assam, Bihar, Gujarat, Haryana, Himachal Pradesh, Jammu & Kashmir, Karnataka, Kerala, Madhya Pradesh, Maharashtra, Odissa, Punjab, Tamil Nadu, Uttar Pradesh, and West Bengal. The bulletins were published (~100,000 copies) in English and state languages (Tamil, Telugu, Kannada, Bengali, Odiya, Hindi, Assamese, Marathi, etc.). They provided extension personnel and farmers with the needed information on varietal choice, source of quality seed, the package of cultivation practices with an emphasis on timely planting and ensuring optimum population, water, and fertilizer management, timely management of weeds, insect pests and diseases, timely harvest and post-harvest processing and storage, etc. Copies of the bulletin colorfully printed in thousands of copies were freely distributed among extension personnel, village-level master farmer trainers, and progressive farmers in the targeted major rice-growing states. Its impact, especially in the irrigated ecology was seen in rapidly narrowing down the gap that existed between the attainable and farmer-achieved average yield and thereby rising rice production. This extension strategy through crop commodity-specific production technology bulletins had successfully induced many commodity research centers under the Council to follow suit and bring out such publications for all crops. Such innovations conceived and introduced in the publication domain by the Directorate would not have been possible but for Dr. K. Muralidharan, who was instrumental in bringing out many such publications of extension value.

Holding international symposia on rice research

Symposia and seminars provide an excellent forum for global scientists to share their recent research achievements and research underway in their laboratories. To commemorate the Silver Jubilee of the Directorate of Rice Research in 1990, besides the launch of FLDs, an International Symposium on 'Rice Research: New Frontiers' and an exhibition on 'Rice Research and Development in India' were organized on a grand scale to highlight advances in rice research at global level and to give an idea of the historical perspective of rice research in India and accomplishments. What DRR experienced and succeeded in bringing out the proceedings of the symposium in print within 15 months after the event, when CGIAR institutes like IRRI and CIMMYT used to take those days for several years, is Dr. Siddiq's outstanding achievement. Another impact of the proceedings was in the founding of the DRR Silver Jubilee Endowment Trust with a sizeable amount saved from the sale proceeds of "*New Frontiers in Rice Research*". The trust was established with the objective of recognizing annually an outstanding rice scientist with a cash prize of Rs. 20,000, a Citation, and a Medal.

Exhibition on rice at silver jubilee celebrations of AICIRP

To befittingly commemorate the Silver Jubilee of AICRIP, an exhibition entitled 'Rice and Rice Science in India' was organized. It was designed with the idea of reaching out to the stakeholders of rice with our status before and after the introduction of high-yielding dwarf varieties. Primarily, to impress upon the policymakers the relevance of rice to India's food security, the exhibition was so designed to narrate as well to highlight the challenges in sustaining self-sufficiency in India's food and rice need, strategic research and developmental efforts underway and those being contemplated and favorable policy environment needed to meet the future demand projections. The manners in which researchers, research managers, and policymakers chronologically narrated through charts, photographs, and specimens describing the long story of rice and rice science, attracted the attention of thousands of school and college students and the general public. Particularly, the origin and differentiation into *indica, japonica,* and *javanica* ecotypes and the antiquity of rice depicted through carbonized seed samples and pieces of pottery with impressions of rice husk excavated from 3000-year-old settlements in India proved a major attraction to students and others from Hyderabad and adjoining townships districts. Besides the cooperating scientists of AICRIP from across the country, due to an unending surge of visitors, the exhibition had to be extended for a week beyond the period of the symposium.

Generating indigenous hybrid rice to raise yield levels on farms

International Rice Research Institute (IIRR) was charged with rising per-hectare yields of rice in the mid-1980s. A wild abortive (WA) cytoplasm was located in Hainan, China as a natural mutation of wild rice (*Oryza sativa* f.sp. *spontanea*), which led to the sterility of pollens. This mutant was developed into a cytoplasmic male sterile (CMS) genotype. The exploitation of hybrid heterosis (10 to 20% higher yield) in commercial rice production started when the essential genetic resources of the three-line system were successfully developed by Prof Yuvan Long Ping in China. The commercial hybrid seed is produced by pollinating the CMS line with its corresponding maintainer line to generate more CMS seeds, and by hybridizing with the restorer line to produce commercial F_1 hybrid seeds. But the grain quality of these hybrids was unacceptable to Indian consumers and so lacked marketability in India. Therefore, with the approval of ICAR, Dr. Siddiq initiated a national network program involving several state agricultural universities for the development of suitable hybrids in December 1987. It was further strengthened with technical support from the IRRI, Philippines, and financial support from the Food and Agriculture Organization (FAO), the United Nations Development Fund (UNDP), Maharashtra Hybrid Seeds Company (MAHAYCO) Private Limited, the World Bank, and the IRRI and Asian Development Bank (ADB) consortium. Dr. Siddiq also made sure to include privately funded commercial research units across the country. Mr. Badrinath Barvale of MAHAYCO came forward to provide an additional Rs. 3 crores for this initiative. Several hybrids were developed and released for commercial cultivation in farmers' fields.

Professor M.S.S: Siddiq's mentor and role model

Professor Monkombu Sambasivan Swaminathan fondly referred to as 'MSS' by all those who had been associated with him, is an outstanding agricultural scientist of the 20th century. Widely known as the chief architect of India's 'Green Revolution', he is a visionary and astute policy maker, given his contribution that transformed the chronic food grain deficit in India into a self-sufficient and surplus nation. Siddiq's association with him had begun since joining as a post-graduate student in 1962 at the IARI, Delhi. The association of over 60 years has given Siddiq the rare opportunity and privilege of knowing him quite closely as a researcher and research manager, visionary planner, and developer as well as a person with admirable human virtues. In every role, he had played and made achievements one could see his foresight, patriotism, and human face. Siddiq believed that nature provide him an opportunity to be a PG student and later a lucky research associate. Siddiq is ever grateful for what he learned from MSS guidance to raise questions on issues concerning basic science without any hesitation or fear, express in clear terms to enable others to understand opinions, and communicate with self-confidence and boldness while maintaining human dignity.

In recognition of Dr. Siddiq's contribution to basic and applied research and development, he was honored with many research and academic awards (**Table 2**). Among them, election to the Fellowship of the country's all three academies of science (INSA, NASI, NAS) and their prestigious medals (BP Pal Medal and Sundarlal Hora Medal, etc), appointment as National Professor and the national honor of 'Padmasri - 2011' as the most valuable rewards. When he was asked by media friends how he felt on such occasions, Dr. Siddiq responded by saying that the country had truly recognized the fraternity of agricultural scientists and reminded him that he still owed many contributions to the nation. It was this mindset that stimulated him to contribute his humble little to the country's agricultural growth and development to date!

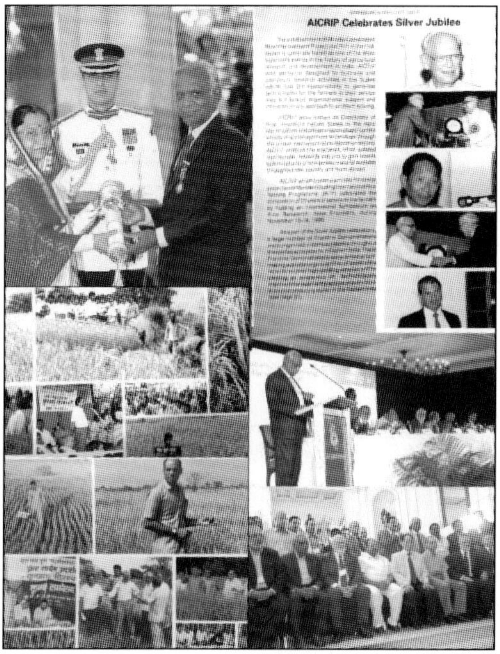

Figure 3: The coveted national award *Padmasri* conferred by Honorable Mrs. Pratiba Patil, the President of India; excerpts from *Research Highlights* published at AICRIP's Silver Jubilee; *Frontline Demonstration* in farmers' fields; and at the 6th International Conference on Hybrid Rice, Hyderabad, India.

Table 2: Awards and Honors bestowed on Dr. Siddiq.

- Hari Om Ahsram Trust National Award (1975)
- VASVIK Foundation National Award (1981)
- Amrik Singh Cheema Award (1987-88)
- Om Prakash Bhasin Award (1994)
- Rafi Ahmed Kidwai Prize (1995)
- Norman Borlaug Award (1995)
- INSA Silver Jubilee Medal (1997)

- GP Chatterjee Memorial Lecture Award, ISCA, (2001)
- Research Leadership Award of Agriculture Today (2008)
- Professor Sundar Lal Hora Medal, (2011) INSA
- Dr. B.P. Pal Memorial Award (2011-12), NAAS.
- Elected Fellow of the National Academy of Sciences (India), Allahabad, National Academy of Agricultural Sciences, (NAAS) New Delhi, and Indian National Science Academy (INSA), New Delhi.
- The Government of India conferred *Padmasri* in 2011
- Adjunct Professor, Indian Agricultural Research Institute, 2012-2016
- NASI Platinum Jubilee Senior Scientist Fellowship 2012-2016
- INSA Senior Scientist Fellowship 2017-2019
- Green Revolution Golden Jubilee Award, ICAR-IARI, 2015
- Centenary Lions Leadership Award (Research), 2018
- Lifetime Achievement Agriculture Award, Mahindra & Mahindra, 2019

Organizing several international and national symposia

Dr. Siddiq organized as many as five international and national symposia on topics of contemporary relevance focusing mainly on prospects of raising rice yield and stability on a sustainable basis (**Table 3**). The proceeding including recommendations of deliberations was published and made freely available to all rice researchers in the country and the world over.

Table 3: International and national symposia and dialogue on rice organized between 1990 and 2018 by Dr. Siddiq.

- New Frontiers in Rice Research, 1990
- Advances in Hybrid Rice Technology, 1996
- Genomics and Crop Improvement: Relevance and Reservations, 2011
- Designer Rice Perception and Prospects, 2013
- Modern Breeding strategies for Crop Improvement, 2017

Proceedings/extended summary of the symposia published are:

- New Frontiers in Rice Research, 1993. Directorate of Rice Research, Hyderabad India. 400p.
- Extended Summary, 1990. Proc. Intl. Symposium on Rice Research: New Frontiers, 1990, DRR, Hyderabad-500030, India. Directorate of Rice Research, Hyderabad 500030, India.
- The 2nd International Conference on Hybrid Technology, Crop improvement through genomics and Management of Change in All India Coordinated Crop Improvement Projects. 1992.

- Group Discussion. February 24-26, 1992. Directorate of Rice Research Hyderabad. Indian Council of Agricultural Research. ISBN 81-7232-003-5
- Advances in Hybrid Rice Technology. 1996. S.S. Virmani, E.A. Siddiq, and K. Muralidharan. Proceedings of the 3rd International Symposium on Hybrid Rice, 14-16 November 1996 Hyderabad, India, 443p. Published by International Rice Research Institute, Los Banos, Philippines. ISBN 971-22-011-55
- Genomics and Crop Improvement: Relevance and Reservations. 2011. Institute of Biotechnology, Acharya NG Ranga Agricultural University, Hyderabad 500 030, Indian Council of Agricultural Research (ICAR), and Department of Biotechnology (DBT). 438p.
- International Dialogue on Perception and Prospects of Designer Rice. 2013. Society for Advancement of Rice Research, Directorate of Rice Research, Hyderabad 500030, India. 386 p. ISBN 978-81-926809-0-3
- Integrated Farming Systems for Sustainable Agriculture and Enhancement of Rural Livelihoods. 2017. Muralidharan K, Prasad MVR, and Siddiq EA, editors. 280 p. ISBN 978-81-933823-0-1
- Modern Breeding Strategies for Crop Improvement. 2018. Proceedings of One-day Dialogue on July 10, 2017, Professor Jayashankar Telangana State Agricultural University (PJTSAU), Rajendranagar, Hyderabad 500 030, India, 250p. ISBN 978-81-936934-0-7

Master of exhibitions to educate and inform agricultural progress

ICAR organized an exhibition to illustrate on the developments in Indian agriculture to worldwide researchers on the occasion of the Second International Crop Science Congress held in Delhi. The organizing committee of the symposium with Prof. M.S. Swaminathan as Chairman and Dr. R.S. Paroda, DG, ICAR as the Secretary, identified Dr. Siddiq then Deputy Director General (Crop Science), as the Convener-Exhibition Committee. The challenging task was to arrange an exhibition that would showcase the growth and development of Indian agriculture since prehistoric days. With experts drawn from the National Museum, Delhi, and the Department of Archaeology, as members of the committee, relying on the knowledge and experience of colleagues Dr. K. Muralidharan of IIRR and senior Technical Officer Mr. Ravi Viswanathan of ICAR, Dr. Siddiq accepted the challenging assignment of designing and structuring the exhibition befitting the International Crop Science Congress in the quite large and spacious annex of the Vigyan Bhavan, the venue of the symposium. His colleagues and Dr. Siddiq had spent quite some time drafting chronologically the storyline and what and how to showcase the landmark developments during the long history of Indian agriculture with relevant exhibits. The story began right from the prehistoric (Mohenjo-Daro–Harappa Civilization period) to the Green Revolution era and its socio-economic impact. The highlight of the exhibition was the prehistoric agriculture displayed with 3000-year-old carbonized seed samples of rice, wheat, etc., and farm implements excavated at the sites of the prehistoric era in the Indian subcontinent.

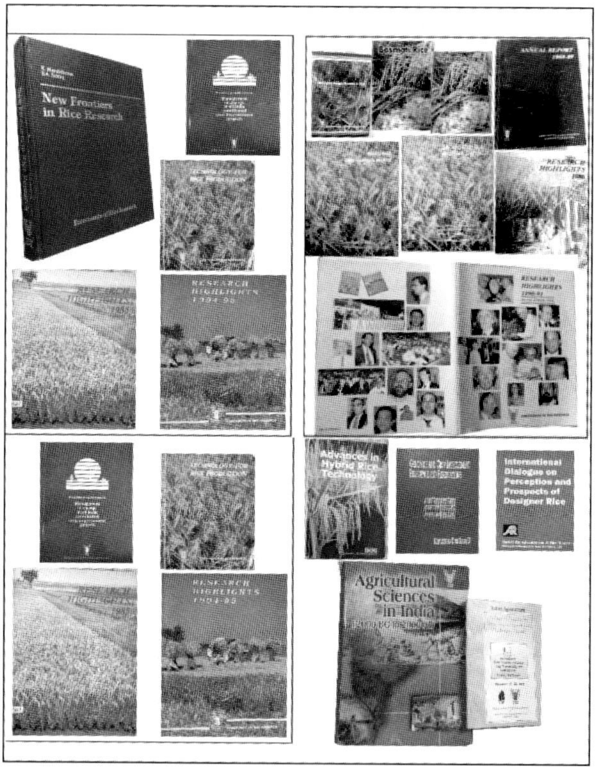

Figure 4: Some publications on Group Discussion on All-India Coordinated Crop Research Projects of ICAR, and on rice research and rice production technology; Review of All-India Coordinated Crop Improvement Projects, the 2nd International Conference on Hybrid Rice Technology, IIRR, and Crop improvement through genomics, ANGRAU, Hyderabad; and background document for National Agricultural Museum, NAAS, and Hand Book released at the 2nd International Crop Science Congress, New Delhi.

Recognitions received for research and research-related accomplishments

Dr. Siddiq was fortunate to remain a rice researcher all throughout his academic and professional life for over six decades. Starting as a post-graduate student in the mid-1960s, his rice research journey included IARI Delhi as a Rice geneticist and breeder, as Project Director, Directorate of Rice Research (now known by IIRR), and later as National Professor, ICAR, and CDFD, as Chair Distinguished Professor and ANGRAU or PJTSAU, as Honorary Professor and Science Academies (INSA, NAS India), and honorary scientist and adjunct professor at IARI and HCU. Dr. Siddiq employed in total close to 40 Ph.D. and several research associates under different externally funded projects and engaged in mission-oriented basic research, and had published over 150 research papers in reputed international and national scientific journals. With junior research colleagues, more than 14 high-yielding rice varieties were developed by him. It included inbred Pusa 2-21, Pusa Basmati 1, Pusa 44-33, and hybrid rice variety DRRH-1 released and notified by the Government of India (Table 1). Dr. Siddiq held many positions (**Table 4**) and research/research-related responsibilities assigned and undertaken during his period as chairman/ president/ member (**Table 5**).

Table 4: Positions held by Dr. E. A. Siddiq.

1.	1968-1976: Cytogeneticist, Indian Agricultural Research Institute, New Delhi
2.	1976-1983: Senior Scientist (Breeding), Indian Agricultural Research Institute, New Delhi
3.	1983-1986: Rice Expert in Egypt, International Rice Research Institute, The Philippines
4.	1986-1987: Professor of Genetics, Indian Agricultural Research Institute, New Delhi
5.	1987 Nov -June 1994: Project Director, Directorate of Rice Research, Hyderabad
6.	1994 June - Mar 1997: Deputy Director General, Indian Council of Agricultural Research, (Crop Science),
7.	1997 Apr –June 2002: National Professor, ICAR, Directorate of Rice Research, Hyderabad

8. 2002 July-June 2007: Hon. Chair Distinguished, Centre for DNA Fingerprinting & Diagnostics, Department of Biotechnology, Hyderabad

9. 2008-2011: Adjunct Professor, Life Sciences, University of Hyderabad, Hyderabad

10. 2008-2011: Adjunct Professor, Indian Agricultural Research Institute, New Delhi

11. 2011-2016: Honorary Scientist, National Science Academy (India), Allahabad

12. 2011-2019: Honorary Scientist, Indian National Science Academy, New Delhi

13. 2002 Nov Onwards: Honorary Director/Honorary Scientist, Institute of Biotechnology, ANGRAU/PJTSAU, Hyderabad

Responsibilities reposed on Dr. Siddiq by the Government of India

Many important national and international assignments were entrusted to Dr. Siddiq that included consultancy in Vietnam and Egypt, Trustee on the Governing Board of the International Rice Research Institute, Philippines, Member of the International Genetic Evaluation Research in Rice, Chairman of the Biotech Task Force, Rice Genome Sequence Project, and Genome Sequencing of Tomato.

Table 5: Additional Positions/Responsibilities held by Dr. E. A. Siddiq.

1980: Rice Expert, Vietnam, Planning & Development of Rice Research and Establishment of National Rice Research Institute.

1983 – 1986: Rice Breeder, International Rice Research & Training Institute for Strengthening Rice Research and Establishment of National Rice Research Institute of Egypt

1987-1994: National Project Coordinator - Hybrid Rice Research

1987-1994: National Research Coordinator - Basmati Rice Research

1990: Member, International Network on Genetic Evaluation of Rice, IRRI

1990-2000: President of the Association of Rice Research Workers of India.

1990-1993: President, Association of Indian Oilseeds researchers, India

1990-1996: International Rice Expert (FAO, UNDP, DFID, World Bank) for Planning Agricultural Development (Srilanka, Assam); Hybrid Rice Research / Integrated Crop Management (Indonesia, Bangladesh, Egypt)

1990-2002: Member, International Network on Genetic Evaluation of Rice, IRRI

1990-2002: National Convener & Coordinator for Rice Biotechnology Research Network, India

1994-2002: Chairman, Technical Committee / Member, Inter-Ministerial Committee, Re-examination of Basmati Patent Rights Dispute with Rice Tec., American Seed Company

1995-2017: President, Six International Conferences, and Symposia on Rice Research

1995-1996: Coordinator, 'Frontline Demonstration' of Rice Varieties & Production Technology for Increasing Rice Production in Rainfed Ecologies of Eastern India

1995-2016: Member Chairman, Academic Advisory Committee, DOFCO (NDDB) - Delhi University, Biotechnology Project on Mustard Improvement

1997-2002: Chairman, Crop Biotechnology Task Force, Department of Biotechnology

1997-2002: Member, Biotechnology Research and Promotion Committee, Department of Biotechnology, Government of India

1998-2008: Member, Academic Advisory Committee, National Centre for Plant Genome Research

1999-2001; 2002-2005: Member, Board of Trustees of the International Rice Research Institute, The Philippines

2000-2002: Chairman, Monitoring & Evaluation Committee for Genetically Modified Plants, Department of Biotechnology,

2001-2014: Chairman, Research Advisory Committee, National Bureau of Plant Genetic Resources, Central Rice Research Institute, Central Oilseed Research Institute, and other ICAR Crop Research Institutes

2002 onwards: Vice President, Society for Advancement of Breeding Research in Asia and Oceania

2002-2011: Chairman/Member, Quinquennial Review Team (QRT), Indian Agricultural Research Institute; Central Rice Research Institute; Central Agricultural Research Institute, Andaman, etc.

2013-2021: Member, University Board of Management, Acharya N.G. Ranga, Agricultural University (2013-2015) and Professor Jayashankar Telangana State Agricultural University- 1st term 2016-Dec 2018 and 2nd term 2019-2021

Chairman (India Specific Rice Genome Research Network), International Network on Rice Genome Sequence (Phase I) & Functional & Application Genomics (Phase II), Department of Biotechnology.

Member Executive/Academic/Research Advisory Committees of SAUs and other institutions

Member, External Research / Research Management Review Committee, International Centre of Genetic Engineering and Biotechnology (ICGEB), New Delhi

Member, Scientific Advisory Council to the Prime Minister of India (2004-2009)

Experience With Media Friends

Dr. Siddiq was of the opinion that, it had been the media that motivated largely illiterate but enterprising farmers to adopt the new varietal and production technologies extensively leading to widely acclaimed India's 'Green Revolution'. He professed that if the media is not briefed properly even on scientific breakthroughs and details on them by scientists, it would lead to undesirable controversies that are counter-productive.

Reforms made to provide appropriate benefits to staff for services made

The foremost effort Dr. Siddiq made was to obtain CGHS facilities not only for IIRR staff but also extend to other ICAR institutes in Hyderabad. Seeing the plight of daily labor engaged in rice research work, he discussed with ICAR to recognize their service rendered for many years. These efforts enabled Dr. Siddiq to systematically study their attendance records and award semi-permanent status to many seniors along with monetary benefits appropriate to their service. Another arrangement made was to financially support staff on their untimely or accidental death while in service.

Memorable stalwart who inspired him with their visionary achievements

Although we come across many great achievers in our lifetime, only a few remain forever in our memory. In Dr. Siddiq's own journey, many had come and gone but he remembered and recalled with nostalgic feelings only a few, who were inspired through one or the other of their noble qualities, disciplined lifestyle, patriotic mindset, and admirable knowledge and administrative skill. They included broadly his teachers, colleagues, research managers, friends, and other acquaintances. Dr. A.B. Joshi was an exceptional teacher and boss for Dr. Siddiq. He also considered Mr. Chaturanan Mishra, a down-to-earth union minister, with a great sense of humor. During his service at the ICAR as DDG (CS), Dr. Siddiq learned much from observing Mr. Mishra's style of administration, concern for the downtrodden, courage to speak out mind with facts and figures, uncompromising and true to conviction and socialistic ideology, and patriotic fervor. Dr. Siddiq also enjoyed an association with Sri B.R. Barwale, who established the world's fourth-largest seed industry to enable India to become a food grain-sufficient and surplus nation. Today, if the country is in the global seed market by virtue of its production, supplying capacity, and confidence to ensure the seed quality matches the European standards it was all because of the level of advance India had made in seed science and technology.

Dr. Siddiq experienced a 60-year friendly association with Dr. Raj Paroda, as a classmate at IARI and a colleague when he was Director, NBPGR, and boss him and later as Secretary, DARE & Director General, ICAR. He had seen Dr. Paroda as a visionary researcher cum research manager, an institution builder, and a human being with temperamental and lovable qualities. He trusted and rewarded people who impressed him most whenever he discussed the launch of any research or governance-related programs he was contemplating for implementation with all senior officials. He would dissect the proposal pointing out its flaws and deficiencies along with suggestions for improvement before its formal launch.

Dr. Siddiq often recalls stalwarts Dr. R. Mashelkar, former Director General of the Council of Scientific and Industrial Research (CSIR), Dr. Manju Sharma, Former Secretary of the Department of Biotechnology (DBT), Ministry of Science and Technology and Dr. Amrita Patel, Ex-Chairman, National Dairy Development Board, who impressed with their unique governance style. Important among others associated with Dr. Siddiq were Dr. Alapati Appa Rao, the then Vice-chancellor of Acharya NG Ranga Agricultural University, and Dr. Attavar, the Founder Chairman and Managing Director, Indo-American Hybrid Seed Company Ltd. Dr. K.V. Raman as a successful research management expert was always helpful with advice when needed on certain administrative problems of Dr. Siddiq especially after joining DRR as Director. Dr. I.V. Subba Rao was a rare workaholic Vice-Chancellor of ANGRAU and soon after Dr. Siddiq ceased to be the National Professor (ICAR) in 2002, Dr. Subba Rao appointed him as Honorary Professor, ANGRAU to set up a biotechnology unit at the University College of Agriculture. Dr. Syed E. Hasnain, Founder Director, CDFD was one of the researcher-cum-research managers in the new bioscience field, with admirable leadership qualities who appointed Dr. Siddiq as Distinguished Chair and Honorary Professor at the Centre for DNA Fingerprinting & Diagnostics (CDFD), Department of Biotechnology (DBT). It was basmati rice and the participation of Rashmi Thakrar, a well-wisher from the rice industry in the AICRIP's Silver Jubilee symposium that marked actually the beginning of a close relationship. His closeness reached the level of respect when he learned that Dr. Siddiq was the developer of the world's first high-yielding dwarf basmati variety Pusa Basmati 1, which was then Tilda's preferred basmati quality variety for export to middle-east countries. At the age of 70, Dr. Siddiq organized a one-day strategic dialogue on 'Rice Research: The Way Forward' with the help of Prof. Deepak Pental, then Vice-chancellor of Delhi University, and Mr. Rashmi of Tilda Rice. Among many acquaintances, Dr. Siddiq fondly recalls Dr. K. Palanisamy a fellow researcher, Sri. K.S. Parmar, a Gandhian scholar had stirred him by the simple living. Dr. Siddiq felt that it was 'humanism' experienced with Dr. Chawla a senior physician of Indian origin working at the Mussouri Medical Institute that made the human race unique and still alive across caste, religion, and radical walls.

Dr. Siddiq's family

Siddiq's two brothers-in-law, Naina Mohammad and Sheikh Abdul Khader retired as professors; and passed away two years after their superannuation. His wife Fathimuthu Siddiq published the collection of her poetry '*Letter from Egypt*', and has written several other books. His son Ahamed Ali joined the Nuclear Power Corporation of India Ltd (NPCIL) as a Process Design Engineer (Scientific Officer-C). He has a son Salim, a daughter Shirin Fathima and a daughter-in-law Saniya and lives in Mumbai with his wife Bushra after retirement. Dr. Jauhar Ali, the second son, leads the hybrid rice program at the International Rice Research Institute (IRRI), Philippines and resides there with his wife Naseema Banu, and sons Sameer Ali Siddiq and Sajid Ali Siddiq. Dr. Siddiq's third son Dr. Zakir

Ali Siddiq, MBBS, DNB, is heading the Nuclear Medicine Department at Basavatarakam Indo-American Cancer Hospital and Research Institute at Hyderabad. Dr. Zakir Ali and his wife Aneesa have been blessed with two sons, Salman Ali Siddiq and Syed Ali Siddiq, and a daughter Simin Fathima.

ESFT: A humble expression of social commitment

Among the enviable achievements of post-independent India, advancement in literacy level is one Dr. Siddiq was proud of. Sadly, however, he felt that the achievement was not inclusive enough, given the lopsided surge in favor of the urban and affluent. The malady is traceable to widely prevailing poverty and compulsion for rural families to engage even their young children in bread-earning activities. It was this background that made Dr. Siddiq and his wife founded the ESFT Trust on August 20, 2006, with their small lifetime savings as the corpus, and formally registered under the Registration Act, 1908 (No.99/V/06) on August 28, 2006, at Hyderabad. ESFT Trust's mission is to support '*Deserving Needy*' students for meeting their educational aspirations at school and college levels, keeping economic condition as the sole criterion for those hailing from socio-economically backward regions of the country irrespective of caste, religion, and gender. The ESFT has constituted selection committees at college and school levels to identify outstanding professors/teachers and awarded Medals and Certificates of Appreciation for Meritorious Service. Toppers in university, college, or Secondary/Higher Secondary Board examinations are subject-wise recognized every year with a cash prize and certificate. The Trust. Funds are donated for various other connected activities like providing safe drinking water, essential developing infrastructure, erecting statues of Great Sons of India at schools, establishing a science laboratory, computer training centers, etc. Dr. Siddiq has penned down the hard-learned experience in his life with the hope that it would help the future generation to shape their life. In the autobiography "*Journey of my life without dreams*" published by ESFT Trust, he has expressed that if anyone derived benefit, he would feel satisfied that the purpose, for which this book is written, has achieved its goal!

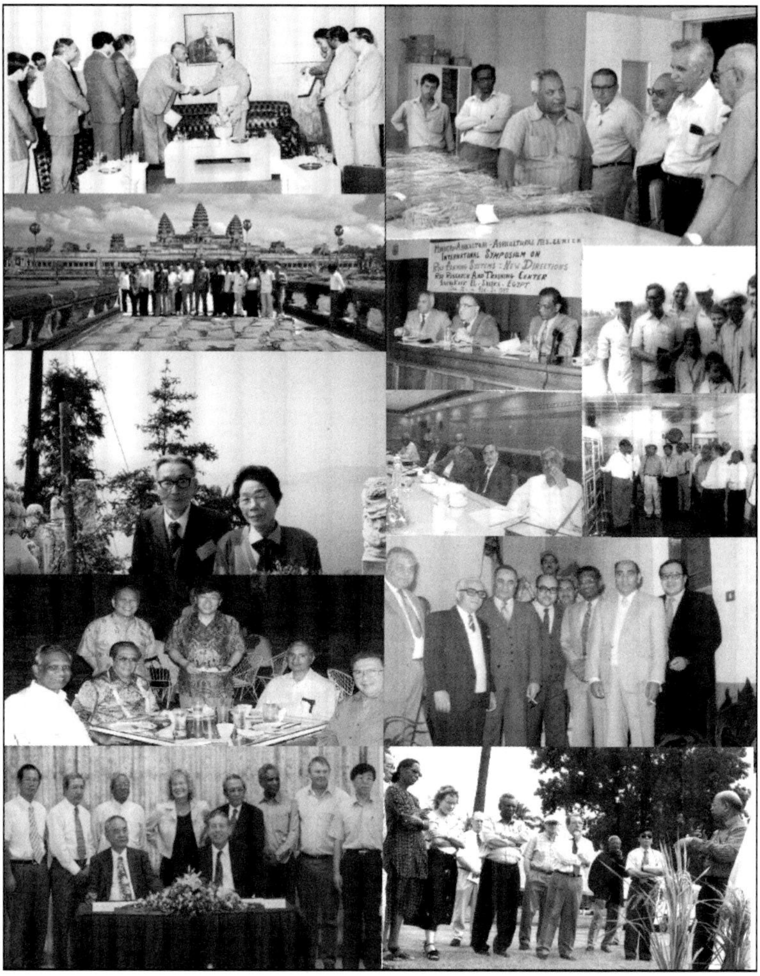

Figure 5: Members of the Indian Government's Indo-China Mission meeting with the President of Laos under the leadership of Union Cabinet Secretary Dr. G.V.K. Rao, members and officials of Kampuchea at Angkor Wat, the World Heritage Centre of 13thcentury Hindu Temple; Egyptian Agricultural Scientists along with American US AID Scientists engaged in rice research and training; meeting Dr. H,I. Oka with his wife at National Institute of Genetics, Japan; With the renowned rice geneticist and plant Breeder, Dr. Gurudev S. Khush, IRRI, Philippines; Board of Trustees and Dr. Ronald Cantrel, Director General of IRRI, Philippines; and Board of Trustees interacting with Dr. S. S. Virmani, Hybrid rice breeder.

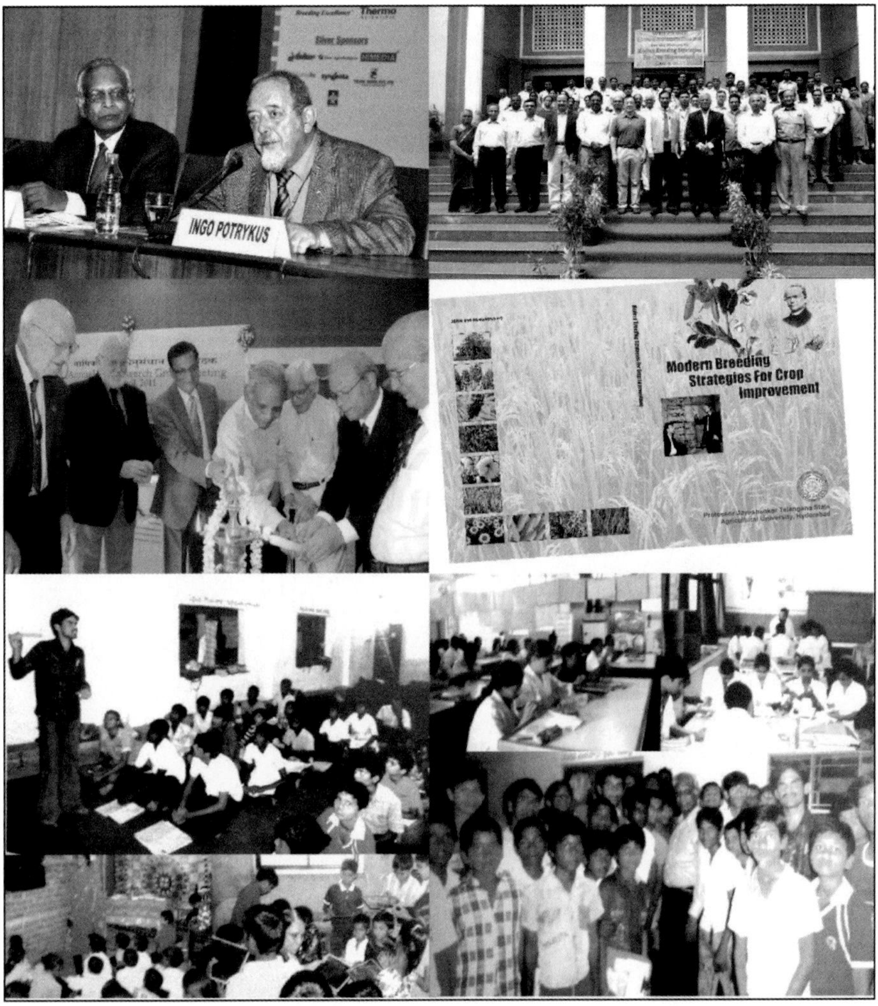

Figure 6: With Professor Dr. Ingo Potrykus who produced beta carotene (vitamin A) enriched rice golden rice through genetic engineering; Dr. Robert Zeigler, Director General IRRI, Dr. W.H. Freeman, with scientists Dr. S.V.S. Shastri and Dr. Swapan Datta at the International Dialogue on Designer Rice.; One-day Dialogue on Modern Breeding Strategies for Crop Improvement at Prof. Jaishankar Telangana State Agricultural University; and ESFT financially supporting *deserving needy* students.

AUTHOR PROFILE

Dr. Kalambur Muralidharan received his master's from the University of Poona and a Ph.D. from the University of Madras. He was an associate Principal Scientist with Dr. Siddiq from 1988 and produced many publications. During 1993-98 led NARP-World Bank project on IPM. He was an FAO Visiting Scientist at North Carolina State University, USA. He visited The Netherlands, Germany, France, the UK, Denmark, and The Philippines to present research results on yield modeling in rice. In 1995, he authored with Dr. S. Nagarajan, a textbook on *Dynamics of Plant Diseases,* and with Dr. Shastry *Production and Marketing of Seed and Seed Material.* He guided several students for Ph. D. degrees. He is the leading author of over 120 publications and editor of 89 books and extension bulletins. After retirement from ARS of ICAR, he was the Technical Consultant at Sowbhagya Biotech, Krishi Rasayan Exports, and, Gayathri Biotech; now a Hon. Technical consultant to Vice-Chancellor, PJTSAU.

Email: muralidharan_km@yahoo.com

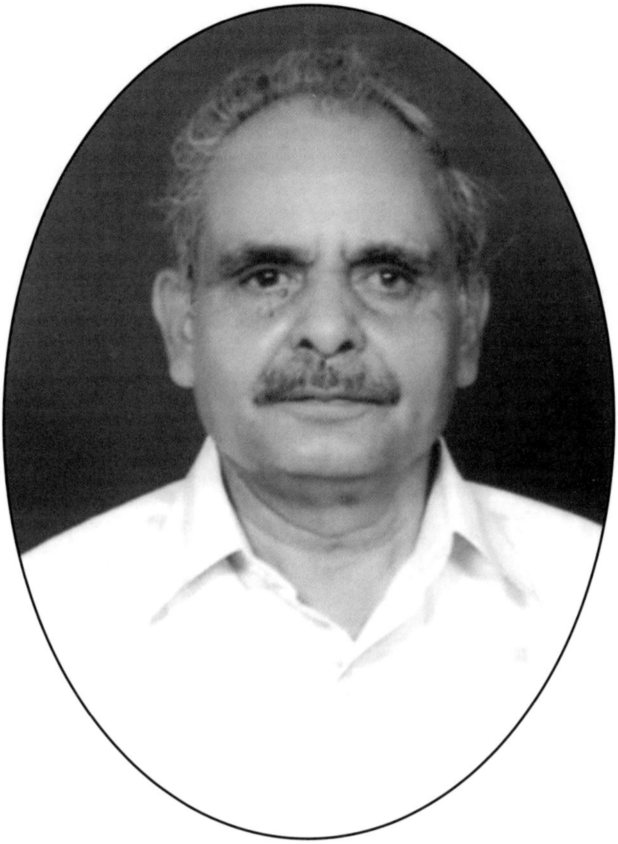

Jamuna Sharan Singh

(b. 26 December 1941)

JAMUNA SHARAN SINGH: A LIFE DEDICATED TO ECOLOGY

Gyan Prakash Sharma

Prof. Jamuna Sharan Singh (Fig. 1) has completed 82 years of his life. I, with all humility salute to one of the leading ecologists of the century. His passion for nature drove him into the fascinating journey of deep ecology. His works deciphered the key mechanisms, and how various ecological sub-components are interconnecting to attain the tacit balance for a sustainable future, which still continues as INSA Honorary Scientist and Professor Emeritus at Banaras Hindu University. He inspired many young researchers to follow and imbibe the culture of ecological research in the country.

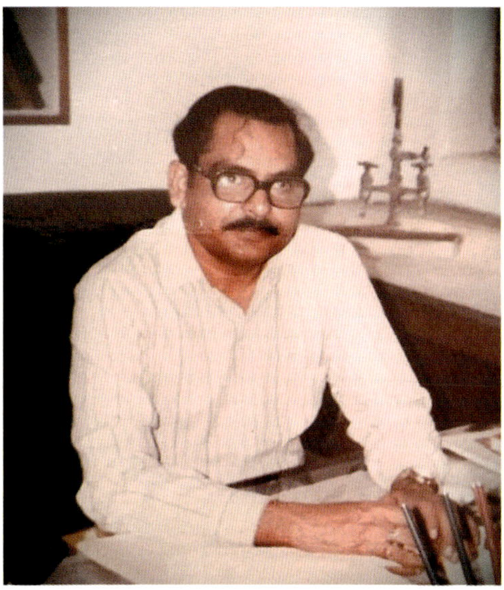

Figure 1: Professor Jamuna Sharan Singh during the 1980s (Courtesy Prof. Hema Singh).

Early Life and Education

Jamuna Sharan Singh (JS Singh) was born on 26 December 1941 to Shri Vishwambher Sharan Singh and Smt Chandrakali Devi in Allahabad (now Prayagraj). He obtained his Bachelor of Science (B.Sc.) degree from the University of Allahabad in 1957; and completed his post-graduation in

Botany from the same university in the year 1959. He stood first in both examinations. In 1960 he moved to Banaras Hindu University to pursue his doctorate (PhD) in Botany under the guidance of professors Ramdeo Misra and Kailash C. Misra and completed the degree in 1967.

Professional Life

After completing his PhD, in 1968, he joined Kurukshetra University as a Lecturer in Botany to start his academic career. After a small stint there, he moved to the Natural Resource Ecology Laboratory, at Colorado State University (1971-1974) as a Visiting Scientist (under the US/IBP Grassland Biome program). He worked as a Reader at the Department of Landscape Architecture, School of Planning and Architecture for a year. In 1976, he relocated to Kumaun University as Reader. He revisited the Natural Resource Ecology Laboratory, at Colorado State University (1981-1982). Subsequently, he joined the Department of Botany at Banaras Hindu University (BHU) as Professor in 1984 and served as head of the department from 1991 to 1993. And, also as Coordinator, Centre for Advanced Studies in Botany, BHU, Varanasi (1997-2003). He joined the Department of Rangeland Ecosystem Science, Colorado State University as a Visiting Professor (1993-1994). He was INSA Honorary Scientist (2007-08) and is currently working as Professor Emeritus at BHU (2004 - onwards) and NASI Senior Scientist (2009- onwards). To honour his contributions BHU has appointed him as a lifetime professor (Fig. 2).

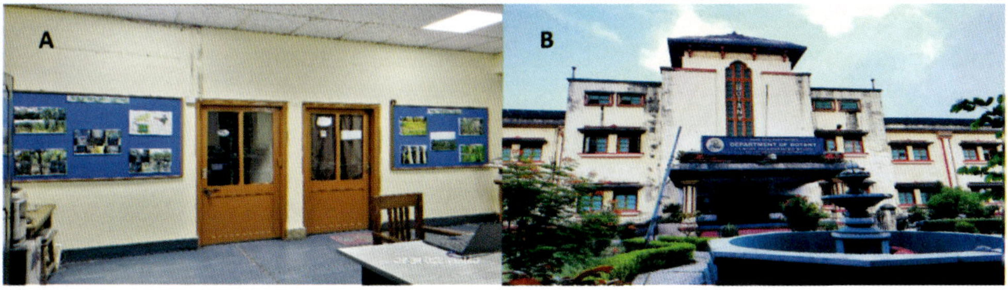

Figure 2: The Ecosystems Analysis Lab (EAL) (A) of Prof. J. S. Singh at the Department of Botany (B), Banaras Hindu University, Varanasi, India (Courtesy Prof. Hema Singh).

During his long career which spanned more than four decades, Prof. JS Singh mentored 43 PhDs and has published more than 400 articles. He is a highly cited ecologist (BHU 2019; CSIR 2014; IAS 2019). He has written five books - *Tropical Ecosystems: Ecology and Management* (1), *Grassland Vegetation: Its Structure, Function, Utilization and Management* (2), *Forests of Himalaya: Structure, Functioning, and Impact of Man* (3), *Research Methods in Plant Ecology, and Science and Rural Development in Mountains* (4), and *Ecology, Environmental Science and Conservation* (with co-authors SP Singh and SR Gupta). The book "*Ecology, Environmental Science and Conservation*" is one of the influential books on ecology in India.

Contributions to the Science

Prof. JS Singh has made significant contributions towards understanding the development, dynamics and disruption of natural ecosystems to provide a scientific basis for environmental protection, management and conservation. His works on tropical dry deciduous forests are praiseworthy. Particularly, to the causative factors resulting in their degradation, and the management of these forests. He pioneered the idea of the "*microbial hypothesis*" that helped in understanding how above-ground eco-physiological changes in plants are linked to the below-ground functions of soil microbes, which subsequently affect the dynamics of soil nitrogen.

Besides dry tropical forests, his contribution to the ecology of grassland ecosystems includes studies on tropical, temperate and alpine grasslands, oak and pine forests, restoration ecology and biodiversity. These works highlighted the interrelations among biomass, energy, ecophysiology, and biodiversity. He is credited to generate comprehensive data on these ecosystems that augmented the eco-management strategies and conservation. He studied almost all the facets of the tropical dry deciduous forest of India, namely, biodiversity, bio-geological cycle, invasive species, eco-physiology, restoration of coal mines, phenology of tree species, carbon sequestration, plant functional traits of species, seed biology, socio-ecological factors: grazing, habitat destruction, etc. The Scopus search with author name "Jamuna Sharan Singh" and/or "Jamuna S Singh" and/or "JS Singh" yielded almost 99 key ecological niches of his research (Fig. 3).

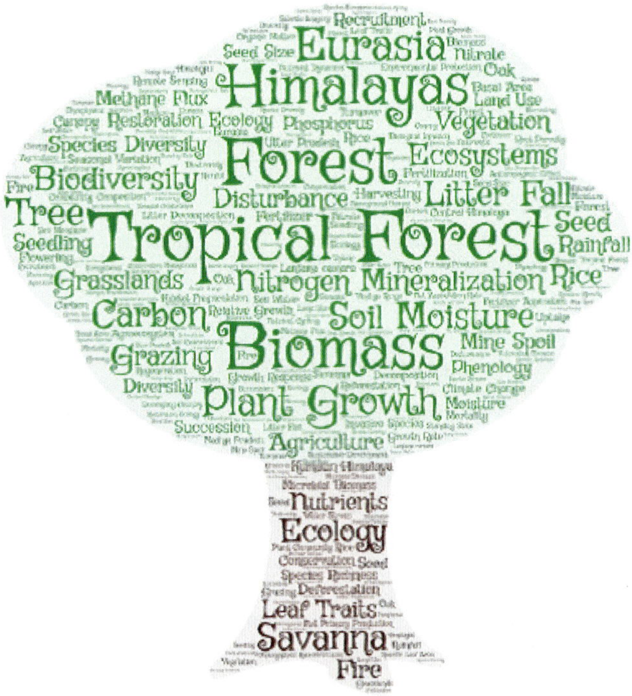

Figure 3: The extent of the work done by "Jamuna Sharan Singh" and/or "Jamuna S Singh" and/or "JS Singh" in various arena of ecology is illustrated using the word cloud (https://wordart.com).

Awards, Honours and Contribution to Professional Bodies

Prof JS Singh has been bestowed with various awards and honours highlighting his research acumenship and dedication. To name a few - Shanti Swarup Bhatnagar Prize of the Council of Science and Industrial Research, India (1980); Pitamber Pant National Environment Fellowship of the Ministry of Environment, Government of India (1984) - Pranavanand Saraswati Award of the University Grants Commission (1985); Dr. Birbal Sahni Gold Medal of Indian Botanical Society (1999); Prof. S.B. Saksena Memorial Medal of Indian National Science Academy (INSA), New Delhi (1999); Honour of Distinction from the Society for Protection of Environment and Sustainable Development (2003); Vidwan Bhushan by Akhil Bhartiya Viddwat Parishad (2005); Lifetime Achievement Award by AWA (2005); Biodiversity Lecture Award by the National Academy of Sciences in India (NASI), Allahabad (2009); Bishambher Nath Chopra Lecture award by INSA (2010). He is a fellow of almost all three science academies in India. Table 1 lists the award, honours and contributions to various professional and government bodies rendered by Prof JS Singh.

Table 1: Accolades and contribution of Prof. JS Singh in academia, administration and other professional bodies.

Fellow/Member	Institution
Fellow	• Third World Academy of Sciences • Indian National Science Academy • Indian Academy of Sciences • National Academy of Sciences, India • International Society for Tropical Ecology • National Institute of Ecology, India • Indian Range Management Society • Central Himalayan Environment Association.
Member	• The Ecological Society of America • International Association for Vegetation Science • Society for Scientific Values • Current Science Association • Indian Science Congress Association • Indian Botanical Society
Member, Board of Editors	• Journal of Bombay Natural History Society (1993 Onwards) • Ecologia Montana (Czechoslovakia) (1991 onwards) • Journal of Vegetation Science (Sweden) (1990-2002). • Applied Vegetation Science (Sweden) (1998-2002). • Advisory Board, Himalayan Journal of Environment and Zoology (1990 onwards) • Proceedings of the Indian Academy of Sciences (Plant Sciences), (1986-1991). • Proceedings of the Indian National Science Academy (1986-1990). • Proceedings of the National Academy of Sciences, India (1997-2000). • Chief Editor, Tropical Ecology (1984-1990). • Reclamation and Revegetation Research (Elsevier) (1984-87). • Journal of Plant Biology (1999 onwards). • Editor, The Palaeobotanist (2000 onwards).

Fellow/Member	Institution
Membership of Professional International Committees	• Secretary, International Society for Tropical Ecology (2002 onwards) • Executive Council, International Association for Vegetation Science, Sweden (2002-2005). • Board of Governors, International Centre for Integrated Mountain Development (2002-2006). • Board of Directors, International Centre for Integrated Mountain Development Trust (2002-2006). • Programme Advisory Committee, International Centre for Integrated Mountain Development (2002-2006). • Interdisciplinary Committee of the World Cultural Council, Mexico (2000 onwards). • Special Committee for International Geosphere-Biosphere Programme, ICSU (1987-1990). • Advisory Board of Ecological Society for SAARC Countries (1992 onwards). • Indian National Executive Committee for the International Society for Tropical Ecology (1976-1990). • Grassland Biome Working Group for International Biological Programme, PT Section of India (1967-71). • Committee formed for drafting the Constitution of the International Society for Tropical Ecology (1964).
Advisory Committees for National Institutes	• Chairman, Governing Body, Birbal Institute of Palaeobotany, Lucknow (2003-2006) • Member, Governing Body, Birbal Sahni Institute of Palaeobotany, Lucknow (2000-2003) • Chairman, Research Advisory Council, Birbal Sahni Institute of Palaeobotany (2000-2003) • Member, Research Council, National Botanical Research Institute, Lucknow (1999-2000). • Member, Research Advisory Council, Birbal Sahni Institute of Palaeobotany, Lucknow (1997-2000). • Chairman, Science Advisory Committee, G.B. Pant Institute of Himalayan Environment & Development, Almora (1996-2002). • Member, Indian Council of Forestry Research & Education Society, Dehra Dun (1997-1999).

Fellow/Member	Institution
	• Member, Scientific Advisory Committee, G.B. Pant Institute of Himalayan Environment and Development (Ministry of Environment and Forests) (1991-93). • Member, Governing Body, G.B. Pant Institute of Himalayan Environment and Development (Ministry of Environment and Forests) (1995-1997, 2006-) • Member, Research Advisory Committee, Wildlife Institute of India (1992-1995). • Member, Advisory Committee to implement the UGC's Special Assistance Programme, Botany Department, NEHU, Shillong (1993). • Member, Academic Council, Central Institute of Fisheries Education, Bombay (1991-92). • Member, Academic Council, University of Allahabad (1998). • Member, Governing Body, Birbal Sahni Institute of Palaeobotany (INSA representative) (1989-1991). • Member, Technical Advisory Committee for Biological Sciences Division, Indian Statistical Institute, Calcutta (1989-1991) • Joint Secretary, National Institute of Ecology (1983-87). • President, National Institute of Ecology (1997-1999).
National Committees of Academies and Societies	• President of the Section of Environmental Sciences, The Indian Science Congress Association (2003-2004). • Chairman, Joint National Committee of IGBP, WCRP and SCOPE (2004). • Chairman, Indian National Committee for SCOPE (1994-1997). • Member, Council, Indian National Science Academy (1989-91). • Member, National Committee for the Geosphere-Biosphere Programme, Indian National Science Academy (1987-1991). • Secretary-Member, Indian National Committee for SCOPE, Indian National Science Academy (1988-1990).

<table>
<tr><th>Fellow/Member</th><th>Institution</th></tr>
<tr><td></td><td>• Member, Sectional Committee (Plant Sciences), Indian National Science Academy (1986-1988).
• Member, Sectional Committee (Animal/Plant Sciences), Indian Academy of Sciences (1986-1988).
• Member, Indian National Committee for SCOPE, Indian National Science Academy (1982-85).
• Member, Nomenclature Committee, Indian Science Congress Association (1985-86).
• Secretary, International Society for Tropical Ecology (1995-2000; 2001 onwards).
• President, Eco-transformation - Centre for Environment and Rural Upliftment (1996-1997).
• Joint Secretary, Central Himalayan Environment Association (1983-85).
• Member, Steering Committee for Organizing Ecology Symposium during 57th Session of the Indian Science Congress Association held at Kharagpur (1970).
• Member, Publication Committee for Indian Science Congress Association held at Kharagpur (1968).</td></tr>
<tr><td>Membership of Government Committees</td><td>• Member, National Forest Commission, Ministry of Environment & Forests, New Delhi (2003-2005).
• Member, Forest Advisory Committee, Gov. Of India (2007)
• Chairman, Research Committee, Wetlands, MoEF (2004)
• Member, National Wetlands Development Board, MoEF (2004)
• Member, Task Force on Forests and Environment, Planning Commission, New Delhi (2004).
• Member, Expert Group on Botany and Ecology, UGC (2004)
• Member, Ecosystem Study Committee, MoEF (2003)
• Chairman, Programme Advisory Committee on Plant Sciences, Ministry of Science and Technology, New Delhi (2001-2004).
• Member, Science and Engineering Research Council, Ministry of Science & Technology, New Delhi (2001-2004).</td></tr>
</table>

Fellow/Member	Institution
	• Member, Plant Sciences Research Committee, CSIR, New Delhi (2001-2004). • Member, Expert Group on Landuse and Forestry, Ministry of Environment and Forests, New Delhi (1999-2000). • Member, Expert Group on Greenhouse Gas Emission Inventories, Scenarios and national Communications, Ministry of Environment and Forests, New Delhi (1999). • Coordinator, Thematic Working Group on Natural Terrestrial Ecosystems, Ministry of Environment and Forests, New Delhi (2000). • Member, Standing Committee on Biodiversity Conservation, Madhya Pradesh Biodiversity Board, M.P. • Member, Task Force on Sal Borer Attack in M.P. Forests, Ministry of Environment & Forests, New Delhi (1998-1999). • Chairman, Programme Advisory Committee on Plant Sciences, Ministry of Science and Technology, New Delhi (1998-2001). • Member, Programme Advisory Committee for Botanical and Zoological Survey of India, Ministry of Environment & Forests, New Delhi (1997-1999). • Member, Advisory Committee, Council of Science & Technology, U.P. (1997). • Member, Programme Advisory Committee on Animal Behaviour, Ecology and Evolution, Ministry of Science and Technology, New Delhi (1991-97). • Member, Task Force on Environmental Biotechnology, Department of Biotechnology, New Delhi (1990-93). • Member, Task Force on Environment and Conservation Biotechnology, Department of Biotechnology, New Delhi (1993-96). • Member, Plant, Agriculture and Forestry Research Committee, CSIR, New Delhi (1989-92). • Chairman, Expert Working Group for Integrated Action Oriented Ecodevelopment Research Programme in Himalayan Region, Ministry of Environment and Forests, New Delhi (1988-1991).

Fellow/Member	Institution
	• Member, Planning Team for Upper Gangetic Plains, Planning Commission (1988-89). • Member, Steering Group of Planning Commission on Environment, Forests and Wastelands Development for the formulation of Eighth Five Year Plan (1988-89). • Member, Working Group for the formulation of the Ninth Five Year Plan for the Department of Biotechnology, Planning Commission, New Delhi (1996). • Member, Steering Committee on Environment, Forests & Wildlife and Wastelands Development for the formulation of Ninth Five Year Plan, Planning Commission, New Delhi (1996). • Member, Task Force on Biodiversity, Planning Commission, New Delhi (1996-1997). • Member, Study Group on Fuel and Fodder, Planning Commission, Govt. of India (1987-88). • Member, Working Group for Coordinated Ecodevelopment Project in the Himalayan Region, Ministry of Environment and Forests, New Delhi (1984-88). • Member, Working Group on Management of Renewable Resources, Science Advisory Council to the Prime Minister (1984-87). • Member, Working Group to Study the Impact of the Hydroelectric Projects on the Ecology of the Himalayan Region, Govt. of India, Planning Commission, New Delhi (1984-86). • Member, Expert Committee for Finalizing Areas for Environmental Mapping, Ministry of Environment and Forests (1985-86). • Member, MAB Committee, Ministry of Environment and Forests (1984-87). • Member, Committee on Environmental Sciences, University Grants Commission (1985-86). • Member, Science Advisory Committee to the cabinet on Forestry Research, Department of Science and Technology (1985-86).

Personal Life

Prof. JS Singh is married to Smt. Tripura and the couple have two daughters (Prof. Hema Singh and Dr Anupa Singh) and two sons (Dr Anuj Kumar Singh and Mr Atul Kumar Singh). The work of Prof. JS Singh in all the facets of ecology revolves around the Vedic philosophy -

आ नो भद्राःक्रतवो यन्तु वश्वितः "Aano bhadra krtavo yantu vishwatah"

(i.e., Let noble thoughts come to me from all directions)

Acknowledgement

The author is indebted to his Guru (Prof. JS Singh) for constant encouragement, igniting and inculcating in him the idea of being curious about ecological processes and synergism with nature. The author is grateful to Prof. Hema Singh for her key insights/inputs on the content of the article.

Bibliography

1. BHU (2019) Faculty content of Banaras Hindu University Retrieved 9 October 2022 (https://bhu.ac.in/Content/FacultyCV/jssingh@bhu.ac.in.pdf).
2. CSIR (2014) Shanti Swarup Bhatnagar Prize. Brief Profile of the Awardee. Retrieved 9 October 2022 (http://ssbprize.gov.in/Content/Detail.aspx?AID=58).
3. IAS (2019) Fellow profile - J. S. Singh, Indian Academy of Sciences. Retrieved 9 October 2022 (https://fellows.ias.ac.in/listing/a?profile.name.display=Jamuna+&contact.city=&fellowship.section=&profile.specialization=&fellowship.yearelected=&id=%40FL)
4. INSA (2016) Indian Fellow - J. S. Singh Indian National Science Academy. Retrieved 9 October 2022 (http://insaindia.res.in/detail.php?id=N84-0770).
5. TWAS (2018) TWAS fellow - Jamuna Sharan Singh, The World Academy of Sciences. 2016. Retrieved 9 October 2022. (http://twas.org/member/singh-jamuna-sharan).

AUTHOR PROFILE

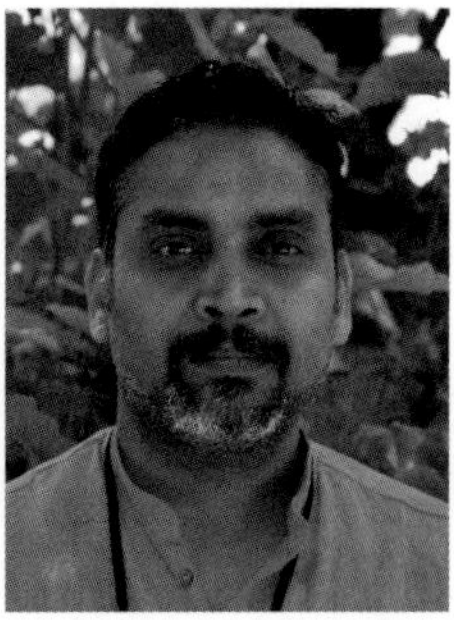

Gyan Prakash Sharma is an Associate Professor of Environmental Studies at the University of Delhi, India. He did his doctorate at the Ecosystems Analysis Lab (EAL), Department of Botany, Banaras Hindu University (2007), and worked as a Post-Doctoral Fellow at the Centre for Invasion Biology, Stellenbosch University, South Africa. He is awarded with International CLAUDE LEON FELLOWSHIP – 2010, Claude Leon Foundation, London and FONDECYT- CONICYT-2010, Institute of Ecology and Biodiversity, University of Chile, Chile. Dr Sharma is a plant ecologist, inspired by the Eltonian-based roots of invasion ecology. His research intends to augment the primary operating paradigm of plant invaders and mainly focuses on providing adequate scientific proof that could assist in reducing the impact of biological invasions. He is interested in fundamental ecological questions pertinent to plant invasions *viz.* phenotypic plasticity in plants, habitat fragmentation, plant functional traits, ecosystem structure and function in invaded systems, evolutionary perspectives in plant invasions, flow cytometry of plant cells, plant diversity, invasive plant-native insect interactions, ecosystem services in agro-ecosystems, etc. He is trying to understand the evolutionary perspective of plant invasions that can give a bigger picture of rapid plant evolution with invasive species as a novel system to observe real-time evolution.

Email: gyanprakashsharma@gmail.com

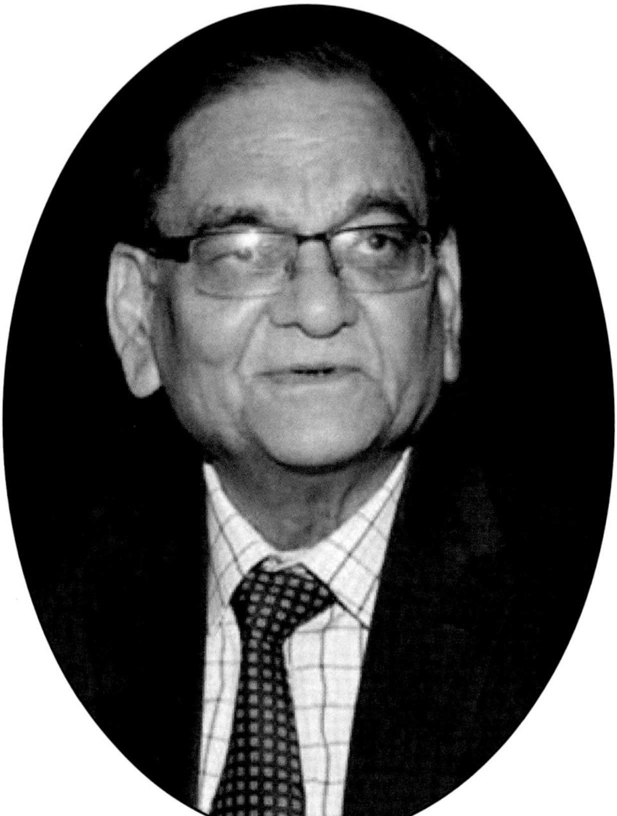

Onkar Nath Srivastava

(31 December 1942 – 24 April 2021)

ONKAR NATH SRIVASTAVA: A PIONEER IN HYDROGEN ENERGY RESEARCH

Thakur Prasad Yadav

Prof. Onkar Nath Srivastava was an Indian material physicist known for his outstanding contributions to the disciplines of Hydrogen Energy, nanomaterials, carbon nanotubes, carbon nanofibres, high-power superconductors, and quasi-crystals.

Early Life and Education

Prof. Srivastava was born on December 31, 1942, in the village of Mohammadabad of the district Ghazipur (Uttar Pradesh, India). His father was an employee of the state Government. Since the job was transferable, young Onkar Nath did his early schooling at Government schools in Lucknow, Sitapur, and Gorakhpur, depending on his father's posting. He did his Bachelor of Science (B.Sc.) in 1959, his Master's degree in Physics (M.Sc.) in 1961 from Banaras Hindu University (BHU), and his Ph.D. in 1966 on "Studies on Layered Structures" from BHU under the guidance of Prof. Ajit Ram Verma. Thereafter, he went to Cornell University, USA for his postdoctoral research on the 'Study of rare earth metals and compounds superconductors' (1966-1969).

Upon his return to India, he joined the Department of Physics, BHU as a Lecturer; and served the University in different capacities as a Reader, Professor, Head of the Department, and Coordinator to the Centre of Advance Studies, Hydrogen Energy Centre, and Nanoscience Centre. After his superannuation, he continued as a Professor Emeritus and an associate faculty member of the Condensed Matter Experiment Research Program of the University.

Contributions to the Science

Prof. Srivastava was an institution and a team-builder, a visionary, and a dreamer, who aspired to make India strong and self-sufficient especially, in the field of renewable hydrogen energy. He believed that investment in science, technology, and innovation is essential for the economic development and social progress of the country. He described the investment as vital for the creation of a bank of knowledge, which is needed for sustainable development and human well-being. He was a source of inspiration as a researcher, teacher, and scientist, and above all was a wonderful human being. He enthused a passion in his students, colleagues, and collaborators for research in science and technology. He was helpful and supportive to everyone around him, but never compromised on his work ethic; always emphasized dedication, devotion, and determination in the work ethic. He was an awesome perfectionist and always encouraged to strive for excellence with his down-to-earth attitude. He had never said 'NO' to any type of work and challenges thrown at him, even at the age of 78 years. He never left BHU and his lab after joining BHU as Lecturer (1969) besides getting many lucrative offers from other Indian Institutions/ Universities. He had a unique style of picking students interested in research amongst the M.Sc. students from BHU and other institutions in India. His popular statement was "*Research is like finding a needle in the darkroom*". He worked in diverse areas of physics - Hydrogen *Energy*, *Hydrogen Storage Materials*, *Nanomaterials*, *Quasicrystalline Materials*, *High-Temperature Superconductors*, *Colossal Magnetoresistance Materials*, *Carbon Nanotubes*, *Carbon Nanofibres, Graphene, Polytypism, Layered Semiconductors* (Fig. 1a). He mainly published research articles (86.4%), however, he also published in conference proceedings (Fig. 1b). He did groundbreaking work in Hydrogen Energy.

We know that hydrogen can be produced from water through solar energy, and it can be burnt back to the water after use in internal combustion (IC) engines or Fuel cells. Besides addressing various issues of hydrogen production, he also addressed the challenges in hydrogen storage. He developed and demonstrated hydrogen fuel devices using a solid-state hydrogen storage tank for the first time in India as shown in Figure 2. The solid-state hydrogen storage is the safest and most efficient storage mode of hydrogen storage typified by $LaNi_5$, $MmNi_5$, FeTi, $ZrFe_2$, $NaAlH_4$, $Mg(NH_4)_2$/LiH and their derivatives[2-4]. He had tested and developed nearly 24 different hydrides[5-9]. Since India has one of the largest deposits of mischmetal (Mm), he used $MmNi_{4.5}Fe_{0.5}$ hydride as a storage material for application in hydrogen-fueled two-wheelers (Fig. 2a). His team at BHU converted the gasoline-fueled two-wheelers into hydrogen-fueled vehicles by incorporating two major changes. First, the development of a variable injection system for inducting hydrogen in the 100 cc, 1 HP internal combustion (IC) engine of the two-wheeler that enables direct injection of

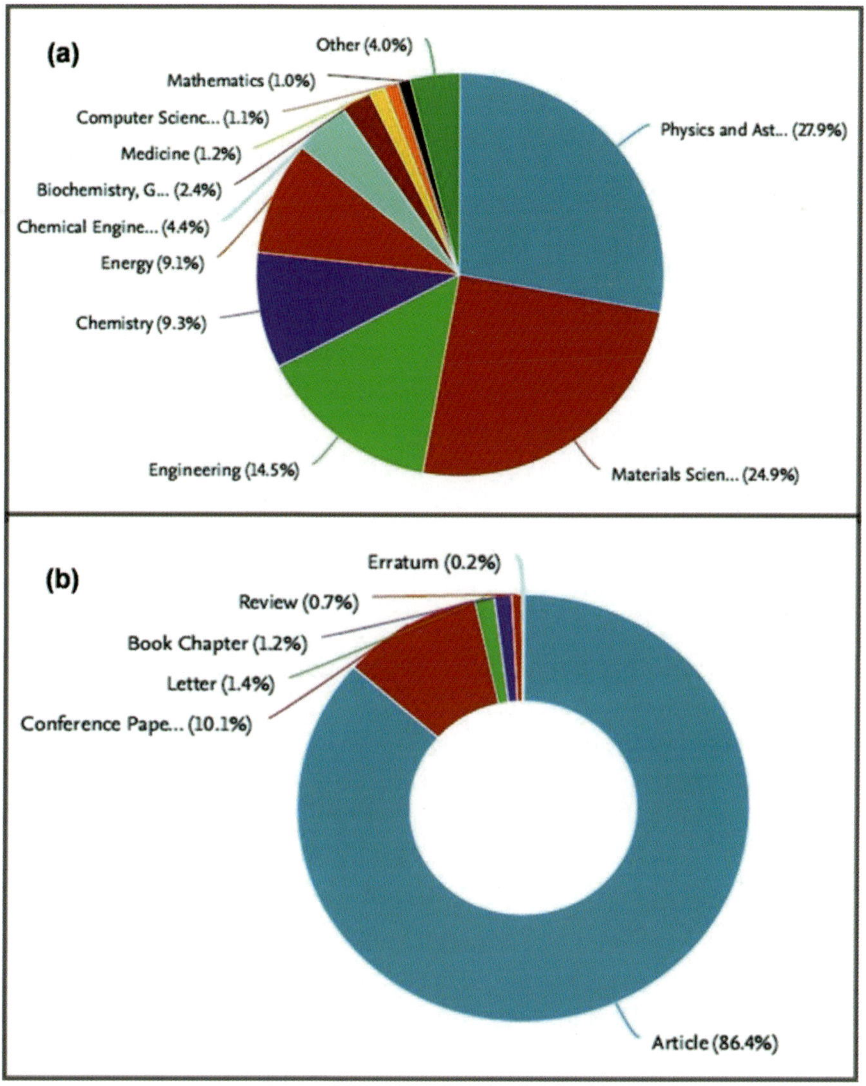

Figure 1: Publication details of Prof. O. N. Srivastava drawn shown by Scopus - subject area (a) and types of publications (b).

hydrogen into the engine combustion cylinder. The unique design of the variable injector takes care of the varying flows of hydrogen during the running of the vehicle on the road. Secondly, the interfacing of a hydrogen storage hydride tank in the conventional gasoline-fueled two-wheelers (Fig. 2a). In earlier hydrogen-fueled two-wheelers, the hydride tank was located near the silencer. To make a two-wheeler more user-friendly, the conventional seat was removed and interfaced with the hydride tank. The hydride material of about 20 kg (the vehicle can take an extra weight of 80 kg) stores about 350-400 g of hydrogen. The vehicle's range is about 72km, complying with the average distance travelled per day in most Indian cities, which is about 40 km[10]. This range is now being increased by using front-running hydride MgH_2 as storage material and also by other modifications in the hydride tank design. The development of a hydrogen-fueled two-wheeler was the first attempt of its type in the world[10]. The University Grants Commission (UGC), India during its Golden Jubilee Celebration considered this work as the best research done in Indian Universities. He continued his hydrogen research further and developed hydrogen-fueled three-wheelers (Fig. 3b). The upscaling of hydrogen-fueled vehicle production was done in collaboration with the Kinetic Honda, and International Cars and Motors Limited (ICML).

The Hydrogen fueled three-wheeler developed by his team was put to a public demonstration by ICML. For the first time, Prof. Srivastava and his team modified the conventional car and converted it into a hydrogen-fueled car [Fig. 2d). The incredible work started by Prof. O.N. Srivastava is ever-progressing. His group sets a milestone by having general people ride on hydrogen-fueled vehicles and realized a paradigm shift from gasoline-fueled to hydrogen-fueled vehicles. Prof. O.N. Srivastava to his credit has patents on hydrogen storage materials and publication (Fig. 3).

The work done by the hydrogen energy group under the leadership of Prof. O.N. Srivastava has been recognized and supported by several funding agencies (Fig. 3c). The existing Hydrogen Energy Center (HEC) at BHU was recommended for upgradation as the Center of Excellence in the National Hydrogen Energy Road Map Report of the National Hydrogen Energy Board, Ministry of New and Renewable Energy, Government of India 2006. Because of his extensive work on all aspects of "Hydrogen" Ex-President of India, Late A.P.J. Abdul Kalam, and Ex-President of the International Association of Hydrogen Energy (IAHE), USA, Prof. T. N. Veziroglu opined that Varanasi (also known as Kashi) be turned into "Hydrogen City of India".

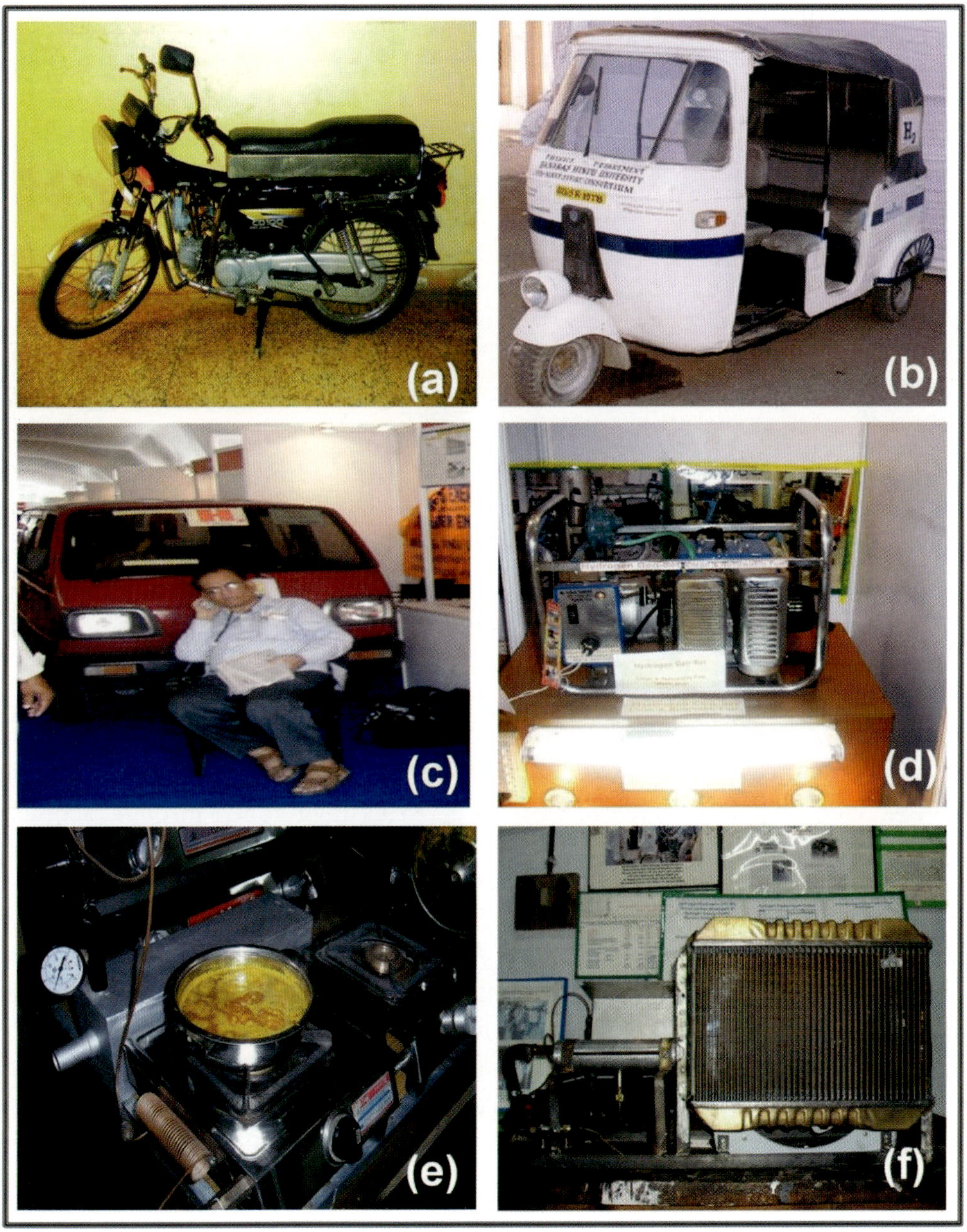

Figure 2: Hydrogen fuel devices developed at Hydrogen Energy Centre, BHU (a) hydrogen-fueled two-wheeler, (b) hydrogen-fueled three-wheeler, (c) hydrogen-fueled Car, (d) hydrogen-fueled electric Genset, (e) hydrogen fueled home cooker, (f) hydrogen fueled heat radiator.

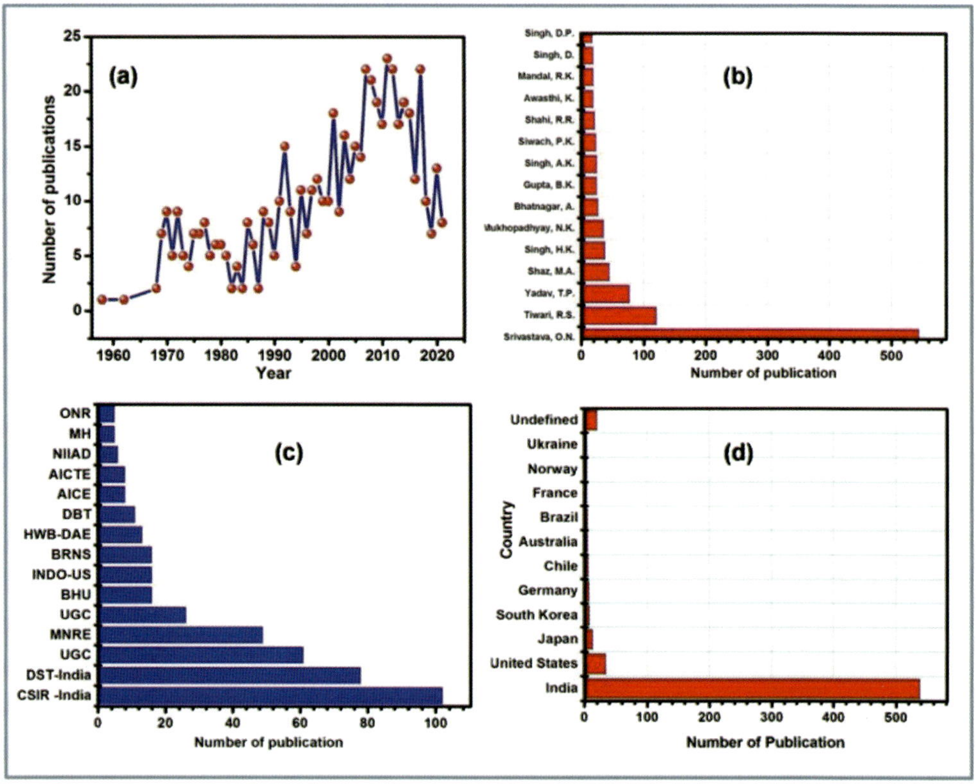

Figure 3: Publication details of Prof. O.N. Srivastava mined through Scopus; yearly publications (a), publications with collaborators (b), publications under different funding agencies (c), publications with other countries (d).

Besides hydrogen Energy, Prof. O.N. Srivastava did innovative and unparalleled R&D in the area of Nano-Science and Technology, with due support of the Nano-Science Mission of DST. Particularly, on synthesis and application of carbon Nano Structures [carbon nanotubes (CNT) and Graphene] (Fig. 3d). The work on radially aligned CNT forming carbon hollow cylinder and their applications in filtration of water and heavy oils was published in *Nature Materials*[11], and was mentioned by the then president A.P.J. Kalam in his Science Day lecture on February 28, 2005, as one of the six top research work done in India; and BHU as one of the nanotechnology initiators in India. He visited Prof. O.N. Srivastava's laboratory in 2013 (Fig. 4). The superior flirters made up of CNTs have the capacity to remove all kinds of impurities from water, including minerals, salt, inorganic and organic compounds, and bacteria. CNTs also offer antibacterial capabilities. The antibacterial capabilities of CNTs are greatly influenced by their diameter, length, structure, and number of walls. Further, his group demonstrated that CNTs are capable of effectively filtering *E. coli* out of water. These inventions would help in producing safe drinking water.

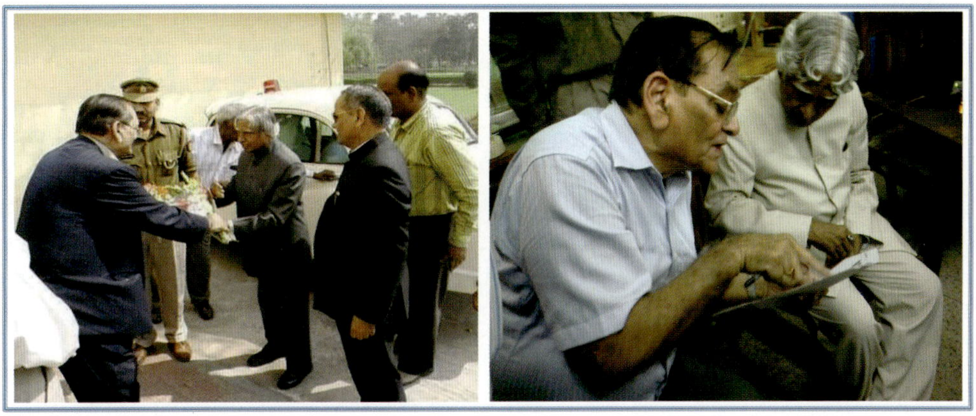

Figure 4: the visit of the then President of India, A.P.J. Kalam to Prof. O.N. Srivastava's laboratory at Hydrogen Energy Centre, BHU.

He brought in several high-end facilities under one roof at the Department of Physics BHU, which include Transmission Electron Microscope (TEM), Scanning Electron Microscope (SEM), X-ray Diffraction (XRD), Atomic Force Microscope (AFM), Raman Spectrometer, Fourier Transform Infrared Spectroscopy (FTIR), Differential Scanning Calorimetry (DSC) and Thermo Gravimetric Analyser (TGA). His team designed and got fabricated the rapid solidification system in his laboratory for the synthesis of quasicrystals and metallic glasses, as well as developed a High-Temperature Superconducting (HTSC) materials synthesis laboratory at BHU[13]. During the latter part of his life, he worked rigorously on the state-of-art technique of using nanotechnology for increasing the efficiency of hydrogen-fueled devices. He tried to collaborate with the industrial sector like Hydrogen Energy Uddyog Nepal to enhance the reach of for his innovations to society.

Educator and Institution Builder

Prof. Srivastava was deeply concerned about the teaching standards in the country. He worked tirelessly to garner the status of the Centre for Advanced Studies (CAS) and get the UGC Networking Programme for the Department of Physics, BHU. He played important role in establishing the Nanoscience

Centre of the University. He played his part in getting BHU the status of the Institute of Eminence (IOE). His tea club meetings were an important fixture for discussion with research scholars and staff.

Prof. Srivastava was a member of the Board of Directors of 'The World Academy of Sciences', and the Vice-President (India & South Asia) of the International Association of Hydrogen Energy. Under his guidance, the Hydrogen Energy Centre of BHU was involved in advanced research on the practical applications of hydrogen fuel, in association with the 'Ministry of New and Renewable Energy' and the Department of Science and Technology (DST), Government of India. He successfully executed several projects for various government agencies such as - Nanoscience and Technology of the Department of Science and Technology (2005–2010), Support to Hydrogen Energy Centre (2007–2012), Development & Demonstration of Hydrogen Catalytic Combustion Cookers (2007–2010), Development & Demonstration of Hydrogen Fueled three wheelers (2009–2012), Mission Mode Project on Hydrogen Storage Materials (Hydride) (2009–2014). All by the Ministry of New and Renewable Energy. He also pursued the project of DRDO on 'Synthesis Characterization and Properties of Single-Walled Carbon Nanotubes' (2009–2012). He mentored 74 students for their doctoral thesis.

Honour and Awards

- Shanti Swaroop Bhatnagar Award in Physical Sciences by CSIR, New Delhi (1988)
- Fellow of the National Academy of Sciences (FNASc), Allahabad (1989)
- Goyal Award in Physical Sciences, Goyal Foundation, India (1993)
- Fellow of Indian National Science Academy (FNA), New Delhi (1994)
- K.S. Rao Memorial Award on Renewable Energy, Solar Energy Society of India (by KS Rao Trust) (1995)
- Bharat Excellence Award by the Friendship Society of India (1997)
- Homi J. Bhabha Award for Applied Sciences, UGC, New Delhi (2002)

- MRSI-ICSC Award by the Materials Research Society of India (2009)
- Lifetime Achievement Award in the field of Electron Microscope-EMSI (2014)
- IPA Award by the BARC for Excellence in Applied Physics (2014)
- Padma Shri by the Government of India (2016)
- The International Association of Hydrogen Energy has established the IJHE Onkar N. Srivastava Award to be presented at the WHEC Conference Gala Dinner to the authors of the most cited Fuel Cells related paper during the previous odd year (2018).
- NASI-Senior Scientist by the National Academy of Sciences, India (2019)
- National Research Award (Nano Science & Technology) by the Department of Science & Technology, Government of India (2019)
- Top 2% scientists of in the world (2020), Stanford University

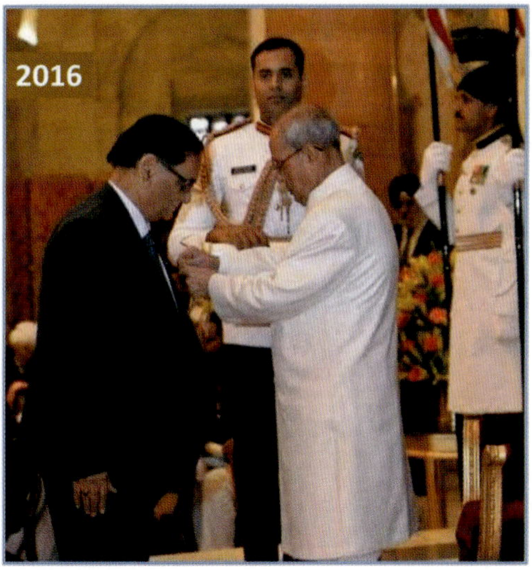

Figure 5: The then President of India Shri Pranab Mukherjee conferring 'Padma Shri' to Prof. O.N. Srivastava on 28th March 2016.

Death

On April 24, 2021, the scientific community lost one of the greatest advocates of hydrogen energy. He succumbed to the COVID 19 related complications.

Acknowledgement

The author expresses his sincere gratitude to Prof. S. Ranganathan, Prof. K. Chattopadhyay, Prof. S. Lele, Prof. N.K. Mukhopadhyay, Prof. R.S. Tiwari, Prof. G.V.S. Sastry, Prof. R.K. Mandal, Prof. B.S. Murty, and Prof. M.A. Shaz, for their valuable help.

Bibliography

1. Verma, R., Srivastava, O.N. (1991) Crystallography Applied to Solid State Physics. New Age International. pp. 466.
2. Bhatnagar, A., Vashistha, S., Veziroglu, A., Gupta, B. K. (2021) Brief memory of Prof. O.N. Srivastava and his major contribution for hydrogen energy technologies. International Journal of Hydrogen Energy 46, 28367- 28369.
3. Singh, S.K., Singh, A.K., Ramakrishna, K., Srivastava, O.N. (1985) Investigations on the structural and hydrogenation characteristics of $LaNi_5$, $HoNi_5$, $GdNi_5$, $SmNi_5$, $MmNi_5$, and $CFMmNi_4$. $5Al_{0.5}$ thin films. International Journal of Hydrogen Energy 10(7-8), 523-529.
4. Yadav, T.P. Shahi, R.R., Srivastava, O.N. (2012) Synthesis, characterization and hydrogen storage behaviour of AB_2 ($ZrFe_2$, Zr $(Fe_{0.75}V_{0\cdot25})_2$, $Zr(Fe_{0\cdot5}V_{0\cdot5})_2$ type materials. International Journal of Hydrogen Energy 37 (4) 3689-3696
5. Srivastava, O.N., Yadav, T.P., Shahi, R.R., Pandey, S.K., Shaz, M.A., Bhatnagar, A. (2015) Hydrogen energy in India: storage to application. Proc Indian Natn Sci Acad 81(4), 915-937.
6. Shahi, R.R., Yadav, T.P., Shaz, M.A., Srivastava, O.N., van Smaalen, S. (2011) Effect of processing parameter on hydrogen storage characteristics of as quenched Ti45Zr38Ni17 quasicrystalline alloys. International Journal of Hydrogen Energy 36 (1), 592-599.
7. Pandey, S.K., Bhatnagar, A., Mishra, S.S., Yadav, T.P., Shaz, M.A., Srivastava, O.N. (2017) Curious Catalytic Characteristics of Al–Cu–Fe Quasicrystal for De/Rehydrogenation of MgH. The Journal of Physical Chemistry C 121(45), 24936-24944.
8. Dixit, V., Bhatnagar, A., Pandey, S., Yadav, T.P., Shaz, M.A., Sinha, A.S.K., Srivastava, O.N. (2017) Carbon Derived from Solid Kernel of Coconut: Its Structural, Microstructural Characteristics and Use as New Hydrogen Storage Material. Materials Focus 6(5), 502-507.

9. Verma, S.K., Bhatnagar, A., Shukla, V., Soni, P.K., Pandey, A.P., Yadav, T.P., Srivastava, O.N. (2020) Multiple improvements of hydrogen sorption and their mechanism for MgH_2 catalyzed through TiH2@ Gr. International Journal of Hydrogen Energy 45(38), 19516-19530.
10. Srivastava, O.N. (2004) Hydrogen fueled two wheelers on the Indian roads. International Journal of Hydrogen Energy 29(4) 437-440.
11. Srivastava, A., Srivastava, O.N., Talapatra, S., Vajtai, R., Ajayan, P.M. (2004) Carbon nanotube filters. Nature Materials 3(9), 610-614

AUTHOR PROFILE

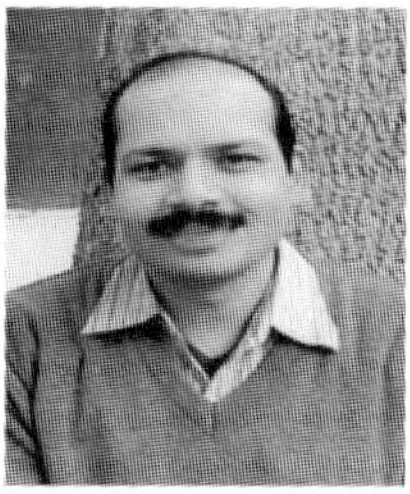

Dr Thakur Prasad Yadav is an Associate Professor at The University of Allahabad, Prayagraj. Previously, he was a Scientist/Senior Scientist at the Hydrogen Energy Centre, Department of Physics, Institute of Science, Banaras Hindu University, Varanasi. He did his PhD in Physics in 2009 from Banaras Hindu University under the supervision of Prof. O.N. Srivastava. His research interests include the physics of materials, structure-property correlations in various advanced materials for structural and functional applications, nanocrystalline materials, quasicrystals, 2D materials, amorphous (bulk metallic glasses), materials for energy harvesting, energy storage (hydrogen storage), high entropy alloys, non-equilibrium processing of materials (high energy ball milling and rapid solidification processing), etc. He has been a Visiting Scholar at The University of Liverpool, (United Kingdom) as a BOYSCAST Fellow (2011-2012) and at Rice University, Houston, Texas (USA) under Raman Research Fellowship (2016-2017).

Email: thakurp.yadav@bhu.ac.in

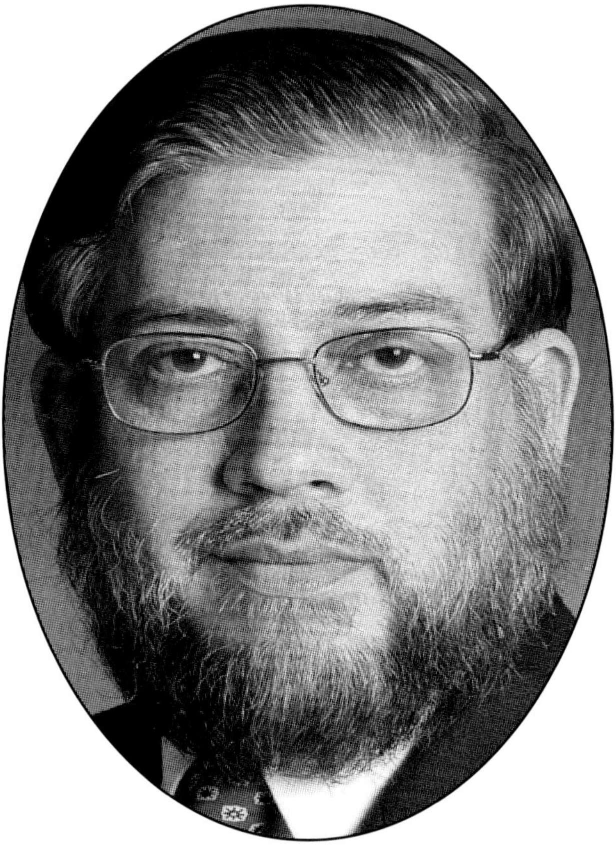

Raghavendra Gadagkar

(b. 28 June 1953)

RAGHAVENDRA GADAGKAR AND THE WASP STORY

Anindita Bhadra

Prof. Gadagkar has made important contributions to the origin and evolution of cooperation in animals, especially, in social insects, such as ants, bees, and wasps. He identified and utilized crucial elements in India's biodiversity, and has added a special Indian touch to his research.

Early life and Education

Born in Kanpur, on 28th June 1953, Raghavendra Gadagkar spent his early years travelling across India, as his father was in the Indian Air Force. He started his schooling in Madras (now Chennai), in fact, he first stepped into school in the second standard, when he was at an age eligible for the third standard. He was allowed to start at the second standard, with the threat of being demoted if he did not do well in class. This was presented to young Raghavendra as a challenge by his father, which he must have taken up quite seriously, as he eventually got a double promotion at the end of the academic year. Thus began a career that epitomized brilliance over the next six decades or so. He finally, at the age of ten, settled with his family in Bangalore (now Bengaluru). Here, he started his journey in science as a pre-university student at St. Joseph's College, studying the Oestrus Cycle of laboratory mice, which he reared at home. His research took him to the J.R.D. Tata library at the Indian Institute of Science (IISc), Bangalore, where a fifteen-year-old did not gain entry. Not one to give up easily, he insisted on being let in, to consult the Journal of Endocrinology. The librarian, perhaps intrigued by his zeal, did allow him to access the journal, though eventually, the young boy hardly managed to make sense of the high level of science that he read. However, his research project did succeed, as this was in preparation for National Talent Scholarship, which he won. Needless to say, he was an excellent student, and thereby, a favourite of his teachers. In his own recollections, he has often said that his Hindi teacher was convinced that he should study Hindi literature, while his Biology teacher wanted him to study Biology. He enjoyed both, in addition to other subjects, and did not really want to choose.

Interestingly, his journey has been one where he has chosen a path at junctions, following his heart, but also taking rational decisions. During his

Bachelor's years [B.Sc (Hons) in 1972] at the Central College, Bangalore, he was totally in love with two branches of Biology that appeared to be highly divergent – molecular biology and animal behaviour. His fascination with molecular biology started with the reading of 'The Double Helix', and his love for animal behaviour originated from the reading of 'King Solomon's Ring', both books written by Nobel laureates. He spent hours in the library of his college, pouring over journals and books, and it was here that he read about the discovery of the bacteriophage I3 by a research group at IISc. He promptly visited IISc and met the first author, who introduced him to the most cutting-edge research of the time, which would eventually be a theme for his Ph.D. He obtained his MSc (1974) in Zoology from Bangalore University.

He joined the Ph.D. program in molecular biology at the Microbiology and Cell Biology Laboratory of IISc at the age of 21, and never left (Fig 1). Having obtained a Ph.D. (1979), his teachers and friends expected him to take the usual trajectory of going abroad for postdoctoral research. However, he decided to take an alternative path, away from the happening field of molecular biology and the ever-alluring West, to study the societies of a paper wasp that he had fallen in love with, having spent hours observing their colonies in the corridors of Central College. This wasp, *Ropalidia marginata*, became the focus of his life's work, and eventually earned him the distinction of being one of the most accomplished ethologists in the World. Currently, he is an honorary professor and DST Year of Science Chair Professor, at the Centre for Ecological Sciences, IISc in Bangalore, where he has built his entire scientific career.

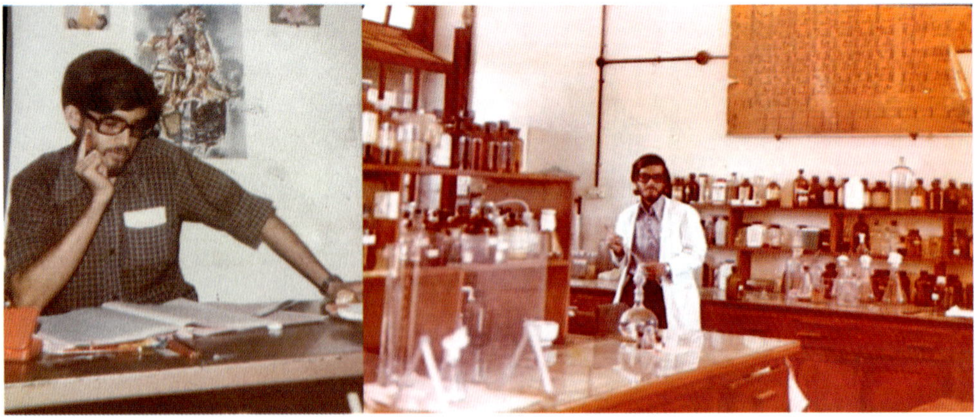

Figure 1: Raghavendra Gadagkar during his PhD days.

Notable Contribution to the Science

R. marginata is a species of paper wasps, that is quite common in peninsular India. These orangish-brown wasps make open nests out of paper, literally, using pulp from plants or other easily available sources. The young Raghavendra noticed these colonies in the corridors of his college and was fascinated by their active, buzzing lives. He spent hours watching these wasps, noting their various activities, but he did not know how to study them scientifically. During his Ph.D., he read an article on these wasps, written by Prof. Madhav Gadgil, a young professor at the Centre for Theoretical Studies. Gadagkar met Gadgil, quizzing him about these wasps, and thereby began a relationship of many years. What began as a hobby for Gadagkar, became his lifetime passion and research.

Prof. Gadagkar and his students have spent about half a century studying the social biology of the wasp, an intriguing species, displaying features typical of both primitive and highly eusocial (truly social) societies. This "trishanku" nature of the species makes it an ideal model organism for studying the evolution of insect societies, a question to which Prof. Gadagkar has dedicated his life. Their work, which is typically based on patient observations of the wasp societies and clever experiments, has provided insights into varied behaviours of the wasps, from a division of labour to work regulation, foraging and navigation to population genetics, natural history to politics, within the wasp society.

In this species, unlike highly eusocial species like honeybees, hornets and most ants, queens are not morphologically distinguishable from workers, and the queen can only be identified when she lays eggs. There is only one queen in the colony, but if she dies or is lost in some other way, one of the existing workers takes over as a potential queen, showing extreme aggression towards all others, and eventually, in a week, she gradually decreases her aggression level and starts laying eggs, thereby becoming the new queen. In a stable colony, workers use low levels of aggression towards each other to maintain work organization within the colony, in a rather democratic manner. It is interesting that aggressive behaviours serve very different functions in the workers and in the PQ, which needs to show aggression to develop her ovaries, a rather counter-intuitive finding that nevertheless is true. Perhaps the most surprising insight into the social dynamics of these wasps was that though we cannot identify the would-be successor of the queen in her presence, there is indeed an "heir designate" within the colony, who is just an average worker in the normal colony but is known to all as the next in line of succession. If the queen is removed, she becomes the PQ, and there is actually a veritable queue for succession, that can be identified using well-designed experiments. The queen produces a pheromone from a gland in her abdomen, and this signals her presence (and health) to her workers. As a PQ transforms into a queen, her pheromonal profile changes, from being worker-like on the first day to becoming queen-like when she starts to lay eggs. Age and nutrition seem to play important roles in the process of queen determination.

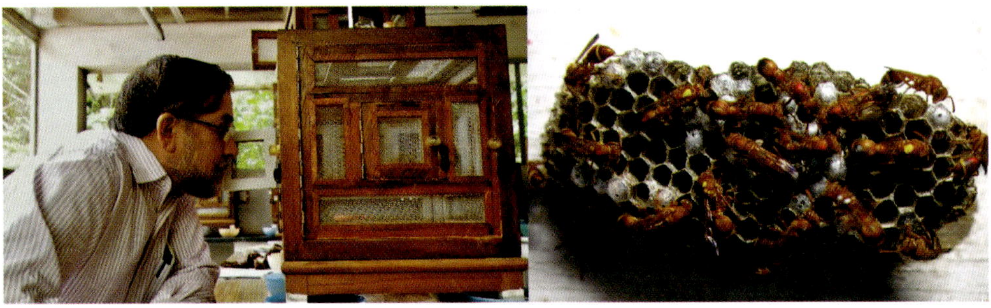

Figure 2: Prof. Gadadkar observing his favourite wasps in their cage, designed by him during the early days of setting up his research group (left); a colony of *Ropalidia marginata* (right).

While Prof. Gadagkar's research has consistently probed deeper into the proximate questions of how a colony of *R. marginata* functions on a day-to-day basis, he has pondered over the evolutionary question of sociality in these wasps. Perhaps his most significant contribution to the field of sociobiology, and definitely the one closest to his heart is the theoretical framework that he and some of his early students envisaged and ratified using field data, to show how being social is an evolutionarily stable strategy for the species. He proposed Assured Fitness Returns as the key to sociality. The idea is that being social gives individuals the advantage of sharing responsibilities of brood rearing, and if one individual dies, she does not lose the benefit of having reared her offspring for some time, as others ensure their survival. This becomes all the more interesting when the co-habiting individuals are closely related to each other, thereby helping to pass on their genes to the next generation through cooperative brood care. His colleague and friend, the reputed evolutionary biologist and author, Lee Dugatkin once said that his work, "spans the gamut from the empirical and theoretical to the conceptual, and touch on virtually every aspect of animal behaviour". One couldn't have summed up Prof. Gadagkar's contribution to science more succinctly.

Educator, Academic Legacy & Carrier Achievements

While much can be written about his renown in academia, his best contribution to society has been through his mentorship. He is a teacher *par excellence*, and someone who loves to interact with students at all levels. He spends a lot of time travelling and delivering lectures to college students, schoolchildren, the general public and accomplished academicians. He is the happiest when he is invited to speak to young children and has the rare capability to establish a connection with his young audience. He has been a role model to at least two generations of scientists, some of whom are school and college teachers. Several of his past students are well-established scientists in institutions across the country as well as in other countries and training more students in animal behaviour. He has published over 300 research articles and a large number of general articles, reviews and commentaries. His three books are examples of his prowess in communicating to both a general audience as well as to a more learned one.

His first book, "*Survival Strategies - Cooperation and Conflict in Animal Societies*" is a delight to read and one that has enthused a large number of students to enter the field of animal behaviour research in India. I have been one such student, who was motivated to delve into the curiosities of animal societies after reading this book as an undergraduate student. In fact, my career in animal behaviour would perhaps not have started if I hadn't been part of a group that visited the Centre for Ecological Sciences during a college excursion and happened to hear an excellent lecture by Prof. Gadagkar. I still remember the excitement I felt and the thrill of being allowed to ask numerous questions during the talk. The book, "*The Social Biology of Ropalidia marginata: Toward Understanding the Evolution of Eusociality*" is an extremely well-written one, meant for researchers interested in animal behaviour and evolution in general and sociobiology in particular. This book is highly rated in the sociobiology community. His third book, *"Experiments in Animal Behaviour : Cutting-Edge Research at Trifling Cost"* is a collection of essays on animal behaviour research, on diverse model systems, ranging from ants to mammals, published by the Indian Academy of Sciences, Bangalore. This book is a must-read for every student and teacher interested in animal behaviour. The book is written in lucid language and shows how world-class research can be carried out with little money and a lot of passion.

He inculcates the spirit of questioning in his students. All his research begins with a question and opens up more questions along with the answers. He insists that a student should not accept that their teacher knows all, and should not trust anything without proof. His classes are a delightful experience, which focuses on planting the seed of curiosity in the minds of students, taking them on a quest, rather than giving them facts. He always focuses on a student who does not know, rather than praising students who claim to have the answer to a question. He is a true teacher, who engages in dialogue and debate with his students and draws out their ability to reason, instead of throwing knowledge at them. During the pandemic, when we all were struggling for stability and normalcy, he took up the challenge of being stranded by converting his home into his office and started writing a column titled "*More fun than fun*" for The Wire Science. This column is written for a general audience full of informative, lucid, engaging, high literary value scientific content.

Academic Administrator

Prof. Gadagkar is an excellent administrator. He was Chairman of the Centre for Ecological Sciences for about 10 years and being a student in the department, I have first-hand knowledge of how the department was run impeccably during his chairmanship. He has headed numerous committees, both nationally and internationally. He has been, a member of the Scientific Advisory Committee to the Cabinet, Government of India.

1. Secretary (1995 – 2000) and Vice President (2007 – 2010) of the Indian Academy of Sciences, Bangalore.
2. President of the Indian National Science Academy (INSA) (2014-2017)
3. Instrumental in founding the Indian National Young Academy of Science during his tenure as president of INSA. This allowed India to gain recognition from the Global Young Academy and put young Indian Scientists at the forefront of global scientific interactions.
4. Vice Secretary General, International Council of Ethologists (2015-19);

5. Founder President, Fellow and Life Member of the Indian Society of Evolutionary Biologists (ISEB), established in 2019;
6. He is a fellow of all Three Science Academies of India (FNA, FASc, FNASc);
7. Fellow of The World Academy of Sciences (FTWAS);
8. Fellow of the National Academy of Sciences, USA, the Leopoldina, Germany, and the American Association for the Advancement of Science, USA.

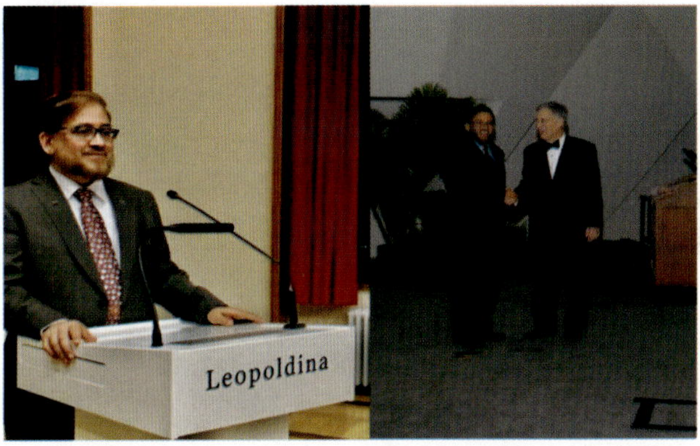

Figure 3: Prof. Gadagkar at Leopoldina (left) and National Academy of Sciences, USA (right).

He founded and led the Centre for Contemporary Studies (CCS) at IISc in 2005. This centre was a melting pot for all disciplines, bringing together natural and social scientists to discuss various ways of knowledge production. The centre hosts researchers and practitioners from varied disciplines outside (historians, economists, musicians, authors, dancers, artists, thespians, lawyers, civil servants, political theorists, journalists, social activists, archaeologists, filmmakers) the sphere of the natural sciences, leading to interesting discourses, which are also open to the general public. Much before the NEP was conceived, the centre was providing inter-disciplinary experience to the members of IISc.

Honours, Awards and Services

Prof. Gadagkar's list of academic honours and awards is rather long, starting. It started with the National Science Talent Scholarship in 1969, to the much-coveted Distinguished Animal Behaviorist Award for Outstanding Lifetime Achievement in Animal Behavior by the Animal Behavior Society,

USA, in 2021. Some other notable awards include - INSA Medal for Young Scientists (1985), Jawaharlal Nehru Birth Centenary Visiting Fellowship (2007), S.N.Bose Professorship (2010-14), and Etienne Wolf - Ramanujan Lecture (2015). He is one of the very few researchers in Ecology, and the only ethologist to have been bestowed with the Shanti Swarup Bhatnagar Award in Biological Sciences (1993). The Federal Republic of Germany conferred upon him the Cross of the Order of Merit, the highest civilian award of Germany, in 2015. He is a fellow of several academies, both national and international and has served on a large number of committees of importance and held positions of responsibility. The alumni association of IISc honoured him with the Distinguished Alumnus award in 2019.

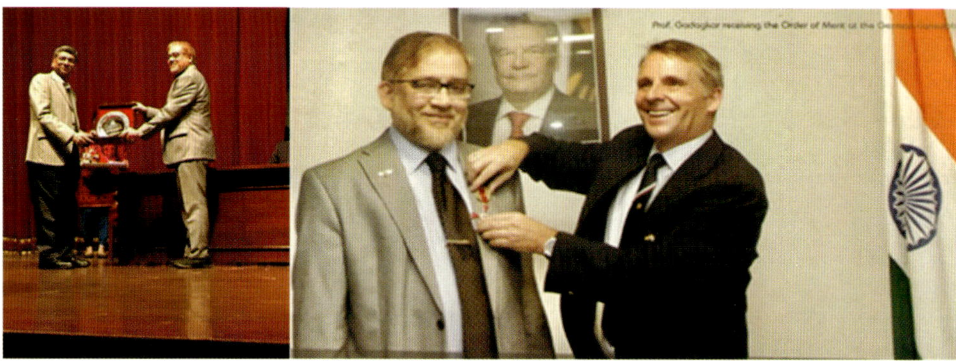

Figure 4: Prof. Gadagkar receiving IISc Distinguished alumnus award (left) and the Cross of the Order of Merit, Germany (Right).

Prof. Gadagkar has been actively engaged in various activities of the IISc. He has served as the President of the Gymkhana and as the chairman of the Hindi cell of IISc. He has mentored numerous students outside his research group. He has been an Honorary Professor at the Jawaharlal Nehru Centre for Advanced Scientific Research, Indian Institute of Science Education and Research Kolkata and Mohali and IISc, adjunct professor at IISER Kolkata and visiting faculty member at Manipal Academy of Higher Education and the Central University of Punjab. During his tenure as the President of INSA, he was instrumental in the founding of the Indian National Young Academy of Science (INYAS), an organization that is nationally and internationally recognized as the voice of young scientists of India.

He played a prominent role in the initiation of the Women Scientist Fellowships of the Department of Science and Technology, New Delhi. He has been vocal about the need for more research on biodiversity, ecology and animal behaviour in India, and has mentored a large number of early-career researchers to establish their careers in these areas of research. He was involved in designing the curricula for IISERs during their founding stage, due to which, the IISERs have a healthy proportion of ecology, animal behaviour and evolution covered in their syllabi. He has organized a number of workshops, symposia, and meetings to engage young researchers with senior ones and create an ambience for ecological research in India. He has been involved in the brainstorming sessions that led to the New Education Policy of India. He insists that a country like India needs more people to engage in research that is inexpensive, yet world-class. In his latest book, he has dedicated a chapter to discussing how brilliant research can be carried out on a small budget, using a mix of curiosity, intelligent experiment design and passion. He has extensively spoken on these issues on various platforms and has inspired many to aspire for a career in research even when they had no funds, especially in colleges and schools. His passion for research is infectious, and his worldview is practical but can create a dream that one can hope to achieve.

Personal life

Raghavendra Gadagkar met Geetha during their first year as undergraduate students when he was elected as the class president. Their friendship continues till date, from being young students to a young couple, to parents, and now grandparents. He has spent most of his life on the campus of IISc, where their son, Vikram grew up in an environment rich in knowledge and natural diversity. Vikram went on to do a PhD at Cornell University, where he carried on as a postdoctoral researcher and is now a faculty member, having shifted from Physics to neurobiology – a journey that recapitulates his father's in many ways.

Prof. Gadagkar has a very amicable personality and is easy to approach. His is an ever-welcoming space for his students, who became part of the family soon after joining the research group. On his 60th birthday, organized the "Being Social" conference at IISc. Many of his students, staff and colleagues contributed to a collection of essays on him, titled "*But to Reason Why: Celebrating a Life in Science*", edited by Ruchira Sen and Alok Bang, and was released during the conference. The essays in the book are testimony to the great intellectual, perfect mentor and wonderful person that is Raghavendra Gadagkar.

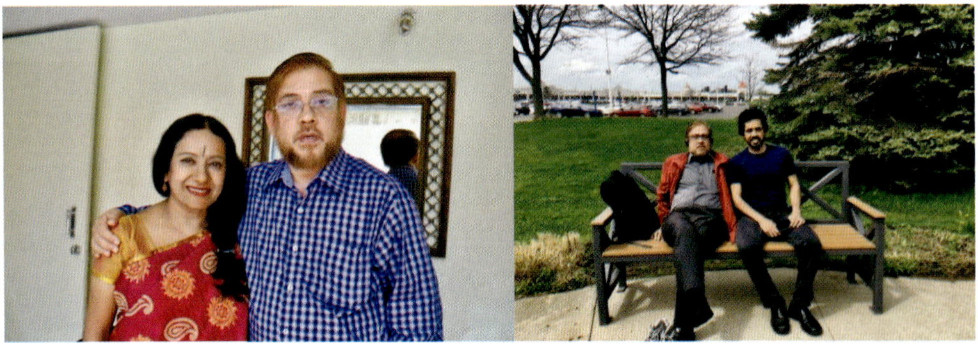

Figure 5: Prof. Gadagkar with wife Geetha Gadagkar (left) and son Vikram Gadagkar (Right).

Acknowledgements

I would like to thank Geetha Gadagkar for providing the sources of information that helped me to write this article.

Bibliography

1. Gadagkar, R. (1997). *Survival Strategies - Cooperation and Conflict in Animal Societies*. Harvard University Press, Cambridge, Massachusetts, USA and Universities Press, Hyderabad, India.
2. Gadagkar, R. (2001) *The Social Biology of Ropalidia marginata: Toward Understanding the Evolution of Eusociality.* Harvard University Press, Cambridge, Massachusetts, USA.
3. Gadagkar, R. (2009) Interrogating an Insect Society. *Proceedings of the National Academy of Sciences, USA,* 106, 10407-10414. doi: 10.1073/pnas.0904317106.
4. Gadagkar, R. (2011) War and Peace - Conflict & Cooperation in an Insect Society. *Science Reporter*, January, 8-12.
5. Gadagkar, R. (2011) Science as a hobby: How and why I came to study the social life of an Indian Primitively eusocial wasp. *Current Science*, 100, 845-858.
6. Gadagkar, R. (2017) Choosing a New Queen: Consensus without Conflict in a Social Wasp Colony. In: *Landscapes of Collectivity in the Life Sciences*. (Eds.) S.B. Gissis, E. Lamm and A. Shavit, The MIT Press, Cambridge, Massachusetts, pp.67-75.

7. Gadagkar, R. (2019) Half a Century of Worship at "Tata's Temple of Science". *Connect – Indian Institute of Science*, 6(4), 16-19. https://connect.iisc.ac.in/2019/12/half-a-century-of- workship-at-tatas-temple-of-science/
8. Gadagkar, R. (2020) More Fun Than Fun: A Story of Stephen Fry, Honey Bees, Greek Myths - and Science. *The Wire Science*. 16 September. https://science.thewire.in/the- sciences/more-fun-than-fun-science-stories-raghavendra-gadagkar/
9. Gadagkar, R. (2021) *Experiments in Animal Behaviour : Cutting-Edge Research at Trifling Cost.* e-Books of the Indian Academy of Sciences. Indian Academy of Sciences, Bangalore. https://www.ias.ac.in/Publications/e-Books/Experiments_in_Animal_Behaviour
10. Prof. Gadagkar's website: Raghavendra Gadagkar (google.com)

AUTHOR PROFILE

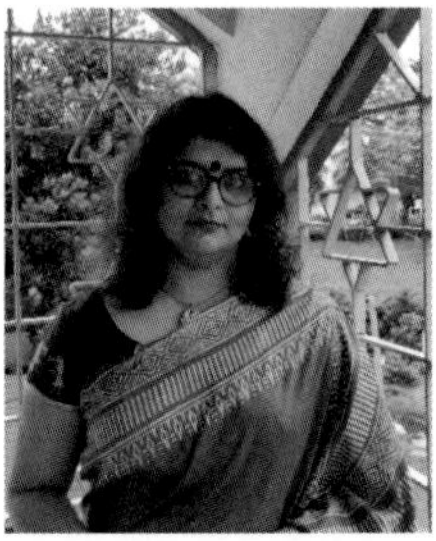

Anindita Bhadra did her PhD on wasp politics under the supervision of Prof. Gadagkar. She is currently an Associate Professor at the Department of Biological Sciences, IISER Kolkata. She works on the behavioural ecology of free-ranging/stray dogs in India. She serves as the Associate Dean of International Relations and Outreach at IISER Kolkata. She was the founding Chair of INYAS, and has been a member of the Global Young Academy, where she was a member of the Executive Council and then a Co-Chair. She serves on the editorial boards of several journals and is a member of the editorial board of Frontiers Policy Labs. She is a recipient of the INSA medal for Young Scientists, SERB Women Excellence Award, IAP Young Scientist Award and Janaki Ammal National Bioscientist Award (young). She is a mother of two and an active thespian.

Email: abhadra@iiserkol.ac.in

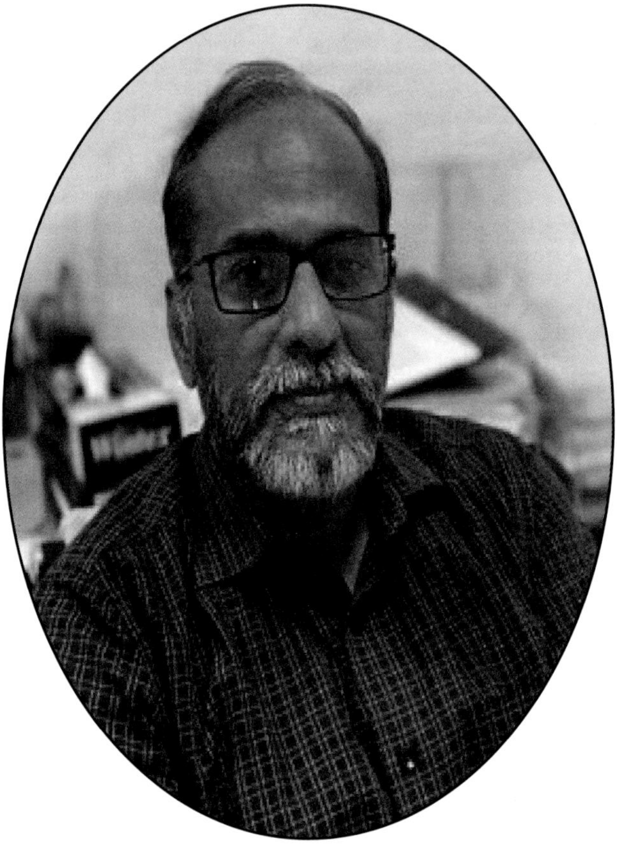

Vilayanoor Venkataraman Ramamurthy

(Born 27.06.1952)

VILAYANOOR VENKATARAMAN RAMAMURTHY: A BIOLOGIST WITH FASCINATION FOR INSECTS

Sandeep Kaushik and Desh Deepak Chaudhary

Dr. V. V. Ramamurthy is a noted biologist who has devoted his entire academic career to entomology. He is a leader in insect taxonomy, and in a carrier of more than four decades, he has discovered more than 160 new species/ genera of insects and mites and developed a rich insect repository. A perfectionist who created a pool of second-generation entomologists working in diverse fields of insect biology.

Early Life, Education, and Carrier

Dr. Vilayanoor Venkataraman Ramamurthy was born on 27th June 1952 in Palakkad, Kerala, India. He did his schooling at Municipal High school, Coimbatore. He obtained his B.Sc. (Agriculture) degree in 1973, and M.Sc. (Agriculture) degree in 1975 from the Tamil Nadu Agricultural University, Coimbatore, Tamil Nadu. He received the Indian Council of Agricultural Research (ICAR) Junior Fellowship during his master's. Subsequently, he was awarded the ICAR- IARI Senior Fellowship for his Ph.D. studies in Entomology. He earned his doctorate in entomology from Indian Agriculture Research Institute (IARI), New Delhi in 1986. As a Darwin fellow, he did his post-doctoral training at the Natural History Museum/ CAB International Institute of Entomology, London (1995-1996) on insect biosystematics. He is married to Kalyani Ramamurthy.

For a brief period, he taught at his alma mater (1975-1976), which he re-joined as an Adjunct faculty/Liaison officer in 2014, which he continues to date. He joined IARI, New Delhi as Scientist S-1 at the division of Entomology in 1976 (1976-1982), and worked as Scientist (S-2 and SG) up to 1986. In 1986, he became a Senior Scientist/Associate Professor, thereafter, served as Professor/Principal Scientist for nearly 16 years. In teaching his interest lies in insect taxonomy, insect biodiversity, insect morphology, principles of biosystematics, etc. He has been actively involved in the formulation and introduction of new academic programs such as Biosystematics in Pest Management and Recent Advances in Entomology at the postgraduate level at IARI. He has developed E-Learning and Distance learning materials on Hymenoptera and Coleopteran biodiversity in rice; Diagnostics of

Lepidoptera in rice, published by the IARI; and has played a pivotal role in developing the teacher training curriculum by DST-SERB in Insect Biology.

Contributions to the Science[1-12]

Dr. Ramamurthy worked extensively on the biosystematics of Coleoptera and Lepidoptera, and the ecology of insects and mites. He has focussed his studies on the taxa namely *Myllocerus*, *Tanymecus*, *Derelomorphus*, *Dereodus*, *Lepropus, Episomus, Indomias,* and published their respective monographs. He has discovered more than 50 new species, five (5) new genera, 10 new combinations, and eight (8) new subspecies of insects. His textbook on Economic Entomology is well-received by entomologists. He worked on faunistic, ecological, biogeographical, and phylogenetic aspects of Coleoptera and other plant gall inducers in the Orient and eastern Palearctic is highly appreciated. This includes - revision of the genus *Indomias* Marshall (Coleoptera, Curculionidae, Entiminae, Tanymecini), *Blosyrus* Schoenherr (Coleoptera: Curculionidae: Entiminae), *Atmetonychus* (Coleoptera: Curculionidae: Entiminae), *Geotragus* Schoenherr, 1845 (Coleoptera: Curculionidae), *Tanymecus* (Coleoptera: Curculionidae) from the Indian sub-continent; diagnostics of Lepidoptera in rice; cuticular hydrocarbons and biosystematics of entimine weevil genera *Lepropus* Schoenherr and *Brachyaspistes* Fahraeus (Curculionidae: Coleoptera); *Unocryptorhynchus*, a new cryptorhynchine weevil genus infesting ginger from India. (Insecta: Coleoptera: Curculionidae); taxonomic studies on *Myllocerus* with synonymy of *Hyperstylus* (Coleoptera: Curculionidae) and studies on *Derelomorphus* with a description of new species (Coleoptera: Curculionidae); study on the genus *Myllocerus* (Coleoptera: Curculionidae); occurrence of *Cryptocephalus* spp. *Cryptocephalinae*: Chrysomelidae) on mango leaves in India. He documented insect fauna in various landscapes. His research works involve classical taxonomy to biosystematics using advanced microscopy, and the use of molecular biology for phylogenetic analysis.

He has prepared several checklists such as those of the Long-horned Beetles (Coleoptera: Cerambycidae) of Arunachal Pradesh, lepidopterous pests of vegetables in India, insects associated with Jamun (*Syzygium cuminii* Skeels) in India, Genus *Blosyrus* Schoenherr (Coleoptera: Curculionidae: Entiminae) of the world, genus *Eublemma* Hubner, 1821 (Lepidoptera: Noctuidae: Eublemminae), annotated checklist of *Xanthopimpla* Saussure

(Hymenoptera: Ichneumonidae), weevils of the tribe Mecysolobini (Coleoptera: Curculionidae: Molytinae), *Otopheidomenidae* (Acari: Mesostigmata), genus *Leptomias* Faust (Coleoptera: Curculionidae: Entiminae) of the world, annotated checklist of genus *Phytoscaphus* Schoenherr (Coleoptera: Curculionidae: Cyphicerini). He also worked on biology, morphology, and molecular characterization of *Sitophilus oryzae* and *S. zeamais* (Coleoptera: Curculionidae) and reconstructed the macroevolutionary patterns of aphids (Hemiptera: Aphididae). He investigated the morphological diversity of the labial sensilla of phytophagous and predatory *Pentatomidae* (Hemiptera: Heteroptera), and *Kerria lacca* (Hemiptera: Heteroptera). His works on sexual dimorphism in the puparium of four whiteflies, viz., *Aleyrodes* sp. on *Oxalis corniculata* (Oxalidaceae) and mouthparts of *Kerria lacca* have been well cited. His other notable contributions are - RNAi-mediated management of Diamond Back Moth (Lepidoptera: Plutellidae); in silico prediction and characterization of microRNAs from large milkweed bug (Hemiptera: Lygaeidae) genome; elucidation of collagen playing a supportive role in virus transmission by *Bemisia tabaci* (Gennadius); on *Phenacoccus solenopsis* of cotton and distribution of *Bemisia tabaci* genetic groups in India are widely acclaimed.

He contributed immensely to the building and upkeeping of over 118 years old National Pusa Collection (NPC), the national biodiversity wealth, with more than 22000 species, and over 0.5 million specimens. He helped in creating state-of-the-art infrastructure for the development of the insect repository. For the last four decades, he has been providing a national insect identification service that has helped in identifying more than 25000 specimens to date. As an academic administrator, he has been instrumental in designing and augmentation of the infrastructural network and human resource/capacity at IARI, State Agricultural Institutes, and other institutions (Zoological Survey of India, Silk Board, Coffee Board, MoEF&CC, DST SERB, NAIP, NFBSFARA, NASF, ICFRE, CSIR, etc.), for enhancing entomological research and teaching. He served as Head of the Department and National Coordinator, Nodal Officer, NAIP Projects, IARI, New Delhi. He is highly involved in providing training to young entomologists through various outreach programs. He has been chief editor of the Indian Journal of Entomology; and Editor of various research journals notably - Oriental Insects, Current Science, Journal of Biological Control, and Entomon, to name a few. He has published nearly 250 research articles in journals, abstracts, book reviews, proceedings, as book chapters and CDROM, etc.

Awards, Honors, and Recognitions

- Darwin Fellow in Biosystematics, CAB International Institute of Entomology, London (1995-96);
- Ex-Member, Genetic Engineering Appraisal Committee of the Ministry of Environment, Forest & Climate Change, New Delhi;
- Ex-Member, EcoR Expert Committee & AICOPTAX, MoEE&CC, New Delhi
- Ex-Member, Sub Committee on beekeeping, Economic Advisory Council to prime Minister, NITI Ayog, New Delhi;
- Member, DST Program Advisory Committee in Animal Science (1998-2004 & 2015-2028 (coopted member) and 2019 onwards (special expert);
- Member, DoE National Committee on National Repositories of Animal Collection (1998);
- Invited to present his views on the Biological Diversity Bill, 2000 to the Parliamentary Standing Committee on Science, Technology, Environment and Forests, on 18th October 2000;
- Best Teacher Award by the IARI, New Delhi (2001);
- Foundation Fellow of the Entomology Academy of India, Chennai (Hexapoda), and the Entomological Society of India, New Delhi;
- Vice President of the Entomology Academy of India, Chennai (Hexapoda);
- Section Advisor to Young Entomologist's Society Quarterly, USA;
- President of the Entomological Society of India;
- General Secretary, Society of Plant Protection;
- Member of the Coleopterists' Society, USA;
- Member, Asociacion Europea de Coleopterologia, Spain;
- Member, Entomological Society of America, USA.

Bibliography

1. https://www.researchgate.net/profile/V-Ramamurthy-3
2. https://scholar.google.co.in/citations?user=BqTHQ2QAAAAJ&hl=en&oi=sra
3. http://npc.iari.res.in/index.php/about-us/history-of-npc
4. http://www.informaticsjournals.com/public/site/images/Dr_V_V_Ramamurthy_CV.pdf
5. https://entosocindia.org/Put 5-6 important publications

6. Vennila, S., Deshmukh, A.J., Pinjarkar, D., Agarwal, M., Ramamurthy, V.V., Joshi, S., Kranthi, K.R., Bambawale, O.M. (2010) Biology of the mealybug, *Phenacoccus solenopsis* on cotton in the laboratory. J Insect Sci 10:115, doi: 10.1673/031.010.11501.
7. Ellango, R., Singh, S.T., Rana, V.S., Gayatri Priya, N., Raina, H., Chaubey, R., Naveen, N.C., Mahmood, R., Ramamurthy, V.V., Asokan, R., Rajagopal, R. (2015) Distribution of *Bemisia tabaci* genetic groups in India. Environ Entomol 44(4), 1258-1264.
8. Devi, S.R., Thomas, A., Rebijith, K.B., Ramamurthy, V.V. (2017) Biology, morphology and molecular characterization of *Sitophilus oryzae* and *S. zeamais* (Coleoptera: Curculionidae), Journal of Stored Products Research 73, 135-141.
9. Gnaneswaran, M.R., Gnaneswaran, R., Ramamurthy, V.V. (2018) Review of the genus *Blosyrus* Schoenherr (Coleoptera: Curculionidae: Entiminae) from India and adjacent countries. Oriental Insects 52(3), 286-312.
10. Mahendiran, G., Ramamurthy, V.V. (2013) The weevil genus *Pachynotus* Redtenbacher (Coleoptera: Curculionidae: Entiminae) from India. Oriental Insects 47(1), 76-85.
11. Ramesha, B., Ramamurthy, V.V. (2011) A study on the *Baris* from India (Coleoptera: Curculionidae). Oriental Insects 45(4), 304-392.
12. Ramamurthy, V.V., Nathan, B.P., Anand, R.K. (1992) Further taxonomic studies on *Myllocerus* with new synonymy of *Hyperstylus* (Coleoptera: Curculionidae). Oriental Insects 26(1), 119-152.

Acknowledgments

The authors are thankful to Dr. VV Ramamurthy for sharing his professional experiences.

AUTHORS PROFILE

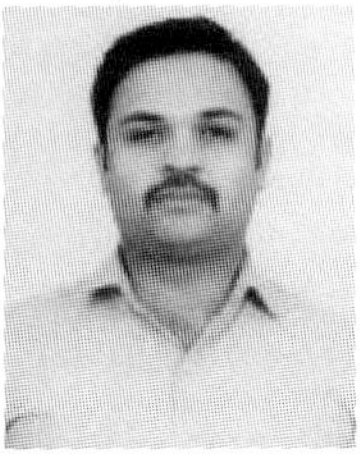

Dr. Sandeep Kaushik is an Assistant Professor at the Department of Environmental Science at Indira Gandhi National Tribal University, Amarkantak, Madhya Pradesh. Dr. Kaushik has obtained his M.Sc. and Ph.D. from the Department of Botany, Delhi University, India. He has been awarded the P.S. Ganpathy Gold Medal at the University level. His research interest includes Plant-Insect interactions and endosymbionts associated with insects.

Email: sskaushik2002@igntu.ac.in

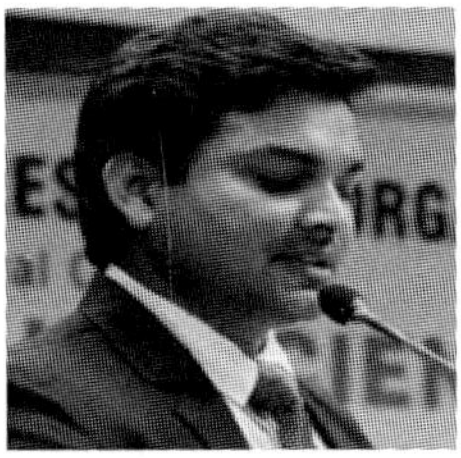

Dr. Desh Deepak Chaudhary is an Assistant professor at the Department of Zoology, Indira Gandhi National Tribal University, Amarkantak, Madhya Pradesh. He obtained his M.Sc. and Ph.D. from the Department of Zoology, University of Lucknow, Uttar Pradesh, India. He received the DST-ISNPIRE Fellowship. His area of research is the behavioral and molecular ecology of Insects.